RASA

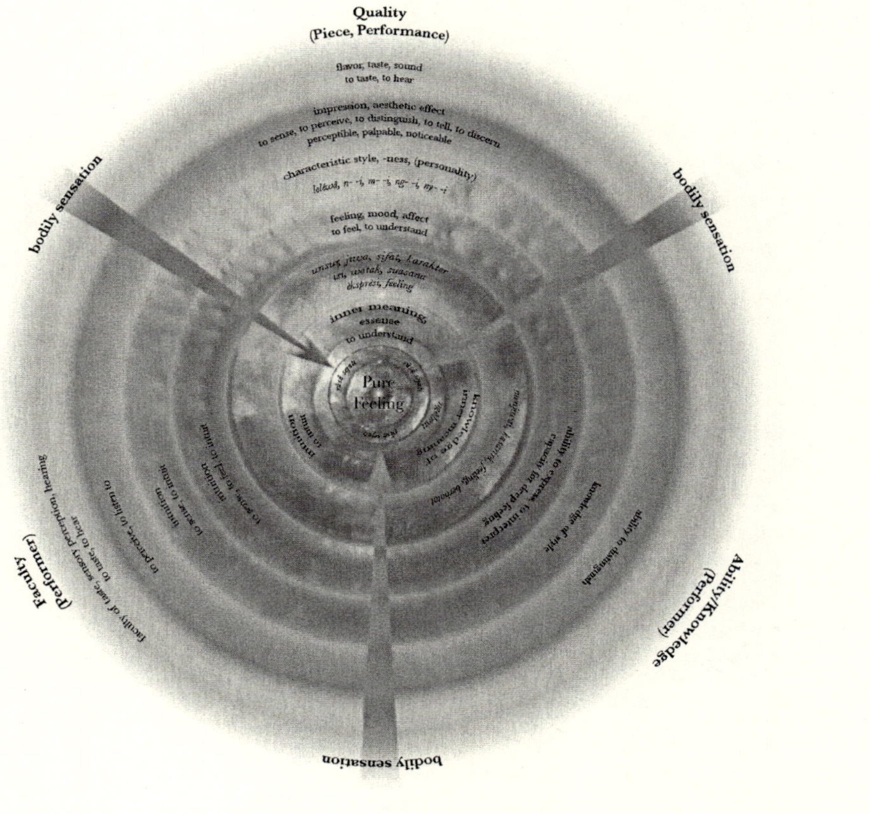

Quality
(Piece, Performance)
flavor, taste, sound
to taste, to hear
impression, aesthetic effect
to sense, to perceive, to distinguish, to tell, to discern
perceptible, palpable, noticeable
characteristic style, -ness, (personality)
feeling, mood, affect
to feel, to understand
inner meaning,
essense
to understand
Pure
Feeling
bodily sensation
bodily sensation
bodily sensation
Ability/Knowledge
(Performer)
ability to distinguish
knowledge of style
ability to express, to interpret
capacity for deep feeling
knowledge of
inner meaning
Faculty
(Performer)
faculty of taste, sensory perception, hearing
to taste, to hear
to perceive, to listen to
intuition
to sense, to intuit
intuition
to sense, to feel, to intuit
intuition
to intuit

AMS Studies in Music

Conceptualizing Music:
Cognitive Structure, Theory, and Analysis
Lawrence Zbikowski

Inventing the Business of Opera:
The Impresario and His World in Seventeenth-Century Venice
Beth L. Glixon and Jonathan Glixon

Lateness and Brahms:
Music and Culture in the Twilight of Viennese Liberalism
Margaret Notley

The Critical Nexus:
Tone-System, Mode, and Notation in Early Medieval Music
Charles M. Atkinson

Music, Criticism, and the Challenge of History:
Shaping Modern Musical Thought in Late Nineteenth-Century Vienna
Kevin C. Karnes

Jewish Music and Modernity
Philip V. Bohlman

Changing the Score:
Arias, Prima Donnas, and the Authority of Performance
Hilary Poriss

Rasa:
Affect and Intuition in Javanese Musical Aesthetics
Marc Benamou

RASA

Affect and Intuition in Javanese Musical Aesthetics

Marc Benamou

OXFORD
UNIVERSITY PRESS
2010

OXFORD
UNIVERSITY PRESS

Oxford University Press, Inc., publishes works that further
Oxford University's objective of excellence
in research, scholarship, and education.

Oxford New York
Auckland Cape Town Dar es Salaam Hong Kong Karachi
Kuala Lumpur Madrid Melbourne Mexico City Nairobi
New Delhi Shanghai Taipei Toronto

With offices in
Argentina Austria Brazil Chile Czech Republic France Greece
Guatemala Hungary Italy Japan Poland Portugal Singapore
South Korea Switzerland Thailand Turkey Ukraine Vietnam

Published by Oxford University Press, Inc.
198 Madison Avenue, New York, New York 10016

www.oup.com

Library of Congress Cataloging-in-Publication Data
Benamou, Marc.
Rasa : affect and intuition in Javanese
musical aesthetics / Marc Benamou.
p. cm. — (AMS studies in music)
ISBN 978-0-19-518943-8
1. Music—Indonesia—Java—History and criticism.
2. Music—Philosophy and aesthetics. 3. Rasas.
I. Title.
ML3758.I53B46 2009
780.9598'2—dc22 2009009903

Recorded audio tracks (marked in text with 🔊) are available online at www.oup.com/us/rasa
Access with username Music4 and password Book2497
For more information on Oxford Web Music, visit www.oxfordwebmusic.com

3 5 7 9 8 6 4 2

Printed in the United States of America
on acid-free paper

To Pak Panggah, Pak Harta, Bu Judith, and my many other guides, both intellectual and musical, who have shared with me their treasures, this work is humbly and affectionately dedicated.

Et à la mémoire de mon père, Michel Benamou (1929-1978), et de ma mère, Gerane Weinreich (1930-2009).

Language is the frail bridge which we fling across the chasm of the inexpressible and the incommunicable.

—James A. Matisoff,
Blessings, Curses, Hopes, and Fears

ACKNOWLEDGMENTS

There would never be sufficient room to thank properly all of the people who have helped me along the way in producing this book, from start to finish. I will therefore mention in detail only a few who stand out as particularly vital to the current enterprise, and beg forgiveness of those whom I mention too briefly, or whom, through a shameful oversight, I have left out altogether.

Perhaps my greatest debt goes to two of my friends and teachers in Java, Rahayu Supanggah and Suhartå. Pak Panggah has not only taken me in as part of the family through the many years we have known each other, but he has also been a constant source of advice and clarification whenever I have needed him most. It was he, in fact, who initially steered me towards Pak Hartå, who turned out to be an exacting, brutally honest teacher, for which I am eternally grateful. Most of what I know about Javanese vocal music I learned from him: he is as articulate as he is knowledgeable, as generous as he is perceptive. From both of these men I have learned not only about music, but also about life.

My longtime mentor and friend, Judith Becker, deserves special mention as well. She had much to do with my choosing ethnomusicology—and Javanese music in particular—as a lifelong pursuit. Her patience and wisdom in guiding me through early stages of this research with a light but sure hand are not forgotten.

Several institutions were invaluable in helping me reach my goals. Fulbright funding made possible two extended stays in Java through a dissertation grant (nominally for 1989 to 1990, but in fact for a total of three years), and a teaching/research grant for six months in 2006. Aminef in Jakarta (and especially Nelly Paliama) helped out in countless ways in administering these grants. Equally important was STSI (now ISI) Surakarta, which sponsored both trips as well, generously extending campus privileges and administrative help beyond expectations, as well as providing a stimulating environment in which to try out my ideas. LIPI in Jakarta was equally important in helping to secure the necessary visas. RRI Solo, RRI Semarang, and TVRI Yogya all allowed me to observe and record gamelan and singing competitions they sponsored. Bp. Suripto and Ibu Hilya of the Mangkunegaran kindly allowed me to frequent the many musical activities there, and Gusti Koes Murtiyah and Bendårå Prabu Winoto allowed me to attend rehearsals and performances at the Kraton. I am indebted to Earlham College for a Professional Development Grant, which enabled me to spend the summer of 2003 in Solo reconnecting with the musical scene there and recording the tracks that would subsequently be released on a CD set of examples mentioned in this book, published by the Maison des Cultures du Monde in Paris. Finally, the American Musicological Society has been most generous in offering subventions for the AMS Studies in Music series, for which I am most grateful.

I feel a great debt to Mary Hunter for her patient and careful readings and for inviting me to contribute to the series in the first place. Thanks are due, as well, to the anonymous reader, whose excellent suggestions I'm afraid I have responded to only unevenly at best (out of sheer expediency). At Oxford University Press, I wish to thank Suzanne Ryan, Christine Dahlin, Norm Hirschy, Kim Robinson, Madelyn Sutton, and others there who have been exceedingly patient and helpful. Any weaknesses that remain after so much expert advice are entirely of my own making.

Many colleagues and friends at Earlham College have been most kind in their support, but most especially Connie Haselby, Deb Jackson, Bill Culverhouse, Yvette Issar, Micah Sommer, Randy Kouns, Wes Miller, and Walt Bistline, who have contributed directly to the book in various ways. Also nearby, Carvin Rinehart showed much insight in his brilliant cover art.

Friends, teachers, and colleagues in Java not already mentioned who have been of enormous help in recent years include Pak Suradji, the late Pak Waridi, Bu Sundari, Ray Weisling, Bu Mieke and the entire ISI library staff, Pak Harsono and Pak Anung of the Program Pasca Sarjana at ISI, Pak Dalimin, Mas Sartono, Pak Kamso, Kitsie Emerson, Pak Wakidi, and Pak Siswosumarto.

In the United States, the following people have contributed greatly to the making of the book, in one way or another: Pak Hardjito, Pak Sumarsam, Andy Sutton, Marc Perlman, Barry Drummond, Sarah Weiss, Lisa Sommers, Mike Izzo, and Jeff Hammond, among many others.

Those in France I wish to thank include, inter alia, Laurence Fayet, Kati Basset, Christine Guillebault, and Bernard Lortat-Jacob, for their friendship, dialogue, and support. Pierre Bois has been even more integral to this project, for without him *Gamelan de Solo* would very likely never have seen the light of day.

My entire family has been an unfailing source of support, both material and moral, and deserves praise for exceptional forbearance. My deepest gratitude goes to Gabi and Gerane Weinreich, Catherine Benamou, and Raúl Ianes, who have been most directly invested in the book.

Among the countless people not already mentioned who helped me in the first decade of research, I wish to thank—with some trepidation of the inevitable glaring omissions—the following: Pak AL Suwardi, Karen Ahlquist, Pak Amrih Widodo, Bu Anggit Mustikaningrum, Randy Baier, Robin Bates, Amy Beal, Pete Becker, Tom Bodie, Jim Borders, Kenneth Chen, Nancy Cooper, Alan Couldrey, Mike Cullinane, Pak Dar (Kentingan), Bu Darsiti Soeratman, Pak Darsono (STSI/ISI), Mas Druseno, Sune Fernando, Nancy Florida, David Foll, Iris Ford, Beth Genné, Susan Go, David Gramit, Pak Hadi Subagyo, Peter Hadley, Andrea Hammer, Pak Hardi (Yogya), Pak Hardjonegoro, Pak Hirdjan, Jo Hoskins, Pak Edijanto Joesoef and family, Joko Purwanto, Pak Kanto, Henry Klumpenhouwer, Bu Koestini, Tim Kortschak, Adam Krims, Bu Kurniati, Terell Lasane, Anne Leblans, Jennifer Lindsay, Rene Lysloff, Bill Malm, John McGlynn, Pak Minarno, Pak Mloyowidodo, Pak Mulyadi, Pak Ngaliman, Regula Qureshi, Pak Rasito, Bill Roberts, Pak Sastrotugiyo, Susan Schneider, Patrick Smith, the St. Mary's College library staff, Anne Stebinger, Pak Surip (RRI), Joan Suyenaga, Bu Tamènggito, Pak Tarman, Pak Tentrem Sarwanto, Jennifer Thom, Pak Tikno, Pak Wakidjo, Susan Walton, Pak Wignyosaputro, Deborah Wong, Bu Yayuk, and Yohannes Sumarjo.

PREFACE

This is a study about language about music. It describes the way in which Javanese musicians use words to characterize the meaning of their music. That is, it seeks to understand, through linguistic clues, what Javanese musicians hear—and above all, what they feel—when they listen to their music.

Although I use the word "Javanese" in the title and throughout the book, it should be obvious that this shorthand does not stand for the thoughts, attitudes, beliefs, values, idiolects, and practices of every one of Java's 130 million inhabitants, nor even of the approximately 80 million speakers of Javanese. My research was centered in the city of Solo (also called Surakarta), in the province of Central Java, and nearly all of the musicians I talked to hailed from within a 30-kilometer radius of the city. Even within that area, I limited my study to what may be loosely termed traditional music, and within that domain I focused on gamelan music and the vocal music that belongs to the same cultural sphere. Further limitations have to do with time. I first went to Java in 1986 and last returned in 2006, and so my firsthand observations are specific to that time span. But, upon reflection, the musical period that the commentary I recorded pertains to most directly is the height of the cassette era, which can be placed roughly between 1970 and 1990. A more accurate title, then, would have been *My Understanding of What the Small Sampling of Traditional Musicians I Observed and Spoke with between 1986 and 2006 in and around Solo, Central Java, Told Me about What Their Music Meant to Them*. The reader will perhaps forgive the poetic license of the title I chose in its place.

During my first trip to Java I came up against a breakdown in communication that was to puzzle and intrigue me for years to come and eventually to lie at the heart of my field research. The problem, I am convinced, did not lie with the somewhat restricted scope of my Indonesian at the time, but rather with the nature of the question. I had noticed that my singing teacher, Darsono,[1] in

1. The Darsono in question is not the one referred to throughout the rest of the book. The one I refer to here is usually called "Darsono Dagelan" ("Darsono the Clown"—he is known to be very

demonstrating certain examples, used a deeper, more "covered" voice quality than in other examples. I tried to ask whether different vocal genres required different timbres. He said that, yes, some genres were "light" (*ringan* [I]), while others were "heavy" (*berat* [I]). So far so good. It wasn't until a few days later, upon hearing these same terms applied to *gendèr* (double-mallet metallophone) players—or, more precisely, to their respective characteristic playing styles—that I began to wonder if he had understood me and I him. For as they applied to *gendèr* playing, *ringan* and *berat* seemed to mean something like "lighthearted" and "serious." When I returned to my singing teacher and asked him for a fuller explanation, he described differences in melodic variation and ornamentation. Try as I might, I could not get him to talk about vocal timbre per se.

Several important realizations came from this otherwise frustrating encounter. The first was that Javanese voice types do not consist only in timbral differences. The second was that certain categories of pieces called for certain voice types. Third, at least some of the terms used to describe voices could also be used to describe instrumentalists' playing styles. And finally, there seemed to be a twofold division, or at least a continuum between two poles, to which performers, pieces, and voices could be related.

When I returned to Java in 1989 to do my doctoral research, I arrived with an open-ended program, and no real topic to speak of—no hypothesis to be tested, no large theoretical questions to be answered. I knew I was interested in aesthetics, and I had always felt the problem of aesthetic evaluation to be the most fascinating, intractable, and urgent question of all. The object of my study was thus the way local musicians evaluated other performers (particularly singers)—what their criteria were, and what the terms were that they used to make their evaluations known.

My hope was to learn enough Javanese (as opposed to Indonesian, the national language) to be able to understand what musicians said amongst themselves. The idea was that casual comments overheard in actual musical interaction would be far more revealing of what was important to the musicians than the answers to

---

funny, and to have a naturally comedic voice), "Darsono STSI" (since he teaches at STSI, now ISI, the College/Institute of the Arts in Solo), or "Darsono Vokal" (since he teaches singing). (See the section on names in "Technical Notes.") The other Darsono is usually called "Darsono Kentingan" (which is where he lives; confusingly, this is also where the ISI campus is located). He is also called "Darsono Jepang" (because his wife is Japanese) or "Darsono Edan" ("Crazy" Darsono—this is meant affectionately). I shall distinguish the two by using their full names: Darsono "Kentingan" sometimes uses the prefix *Su-* (Sudarsono) and Darsono "STSI" does not (his full name is Darsono). At the risk of invoking Ionesco's Bobby Watson, I feel I must mention that there are two other Darsonos whose names come up in discussions of Javanese music. One is a dancer and dance historian who lives in Yogyakarta. Fortunately he uses the Dutch spelling of his full name, Soedarsono. The other is often referred to as "Darsono cilik" (the little Darsono), so called because he is considerably younger than the other Darsonos. He is considered one of the most talented among recent graduates of STSI/ISI and has recently taught at Wesleyan University in Middletown, Connecticut.

any questions I might formulate. Eventually I was, in fact, able to understand much of what was being said at rehearsals and performances. The problem with this method—language difficulties aside—was that there was no predicting when someone would say something interesting, and I simply could not, for practical reasons, have a tape recorder running constantly. So, in the long run, listening in context became primarily a way of confirming things learned by other means.

I had also planned to focus on gamelan and singing competitions (*lomba*s) as a way of honing in on specific criteria. Partly because of the great tension and secrecy arising from the cutthroat atmosphere of these government-sponsored competitions, this, too, proved to be somewhat impractical. Not only was it difficult to record under the circumstances, but judges were sometimes reluctant to speak freely about their decisions, lest one of the winners' rivals protest (a common occurrence, to be sure). In addition, because contest judging calls for impartiality and standardization, not all of the criteria used were weighted the same as they would have been outside that environment (for example, flexibility in performance counts for very little in a competition). Nevertheless, I did glean some valuable information from these lively events.

Another method I used was to elicit reactions to cassette recordings (commercial and otherwise) of male and female singers. This led to some interesting results. But it was time-consuming. And, at least for the commercial recordings, it yielded mostly general comments that were based on previous experience of hearing the singers.

By far the most productive approach in the beginning stages of my research (roughly the first two years) was to take singing lessons and to pursue conversations on topics that my teacher brought up during my lessons. I was fortunate in that my principal teacher, Suhartå, a lecturer at the Indonesian School for the Arts (STSI) in Solo, was as talkative, critical, and articulate as he was knowledgeable. During this initial period I also attended gamelan rehearsals in different sectors of the town and participated in concerts in a variety of venues. Not only did this help to hone my musical ability, it allowed me to get to know singers and musicians personally and to get a sense of the overall context of traditional Javanese music making. This dimension of my research should not be underestimated. Without a fairly extensive *practical* knowledge of repertoire and vocal techniques, I would not have been able to communicate with musicians theoretically, using their own terms. Moreover, my demonstrating a certain level of competence as a singer made me somehow more serious, more approachable, more "real." I found a huge difference, for instance, in the way musicians treated me before and after they had heard me sing.[2]

2. I am reminded of Marina Roseman's account, which she presented in a talk at the University of Michigan, of how she was able finally to make headway in her research with the Temiar people of highland Malaysia, after many months of living in a village. She had been trying to get information

After two years of listening to Javanese musicians talk in various contexts about their music, my topic finally came to me, and I realized that it had been staring me in the face ever since that early encounter in 1986. It became clear that at the heart of their talk about aesthetic evaluation, about performance, about listening, was *rasa*: "affect," "mood," "feeling," "intuition." Furthermore, this fundamental concept had been touched upon only in passing in the literature. It seems that, from Groneman (1890) on, writing by foreign researchers about Javanese music was focused primarily on how it was produced rather than on how it was listened to.

Having identified my topic, in the final stages of my research I was more aggressive about guiding conversations. It appeared that I had indeed hit upon issues of great concern to musicians: they showed obvious pleasure and excitement when I asked them about *rasa*. Moreover, their answers matched my questions very closely—a sign that what I was asking was deemed coherent and relevant. (There were two notable exceptions to this: one, the oldest living gamelan expert in Solo, who, I learned later, despised vocal music; the other, an older singer at the main palace, who, as far as I could determine, did not think abstractly about music—or about most things, for that matter.)

In conducting my interviews I avoided using questionnaires, feeling that they would have forced the musicians' thoughts too much into my own mold.[3] Perhaps at the end of my research I could have devised questionnaires that would have fit with their ways of thinking, but I didn't. Instead, I chose to have ongoing conversations with a few acknowledged experts. Some breadth was achieved by talking to a great many singers and musicians that I never formally interviewed—my field notes contain statements by 118 people. This provided me with a basis for judging the relative quirkiness of those with whom I did speak more extensively.

But my account of Javanese aesthetics does not attempt to represent the broadest possible consensus: experts' opinions, while often influential and usually respected, are notoriously quirky. Nevertheless, I decided to focus on them for the simple reason that experts have something others lack: expertise. This focus on a limited number of people allowed me to achieve, I hope, a richness and depth otherwise unobtainable. As Karl Heider put it (1991:63), ethnography—as opposed to psychology or sociology—favors "data that are

complex rather than simple
inclusive rather than exclusive
concrete rather than abstracted.

---

on the process by which songs were given to singers by spirits in dreams, but with little success. Then she had one of those dreams herself, and everything changed.

3. An additional problem with questionnaires is that the genre itself is relatively foreign to the world of Javanese musicians, some of whom are nonliterate. Nevertheless, Santosa seems to have had some success in surveying musicians in Solo (1990).

By choosing aesthetics as my topic, I am in essence arguing for a reaesthetization of the field. Not that I believe every ethnomusicologist must be an aesthetician. Rather, I endorse the more modest belief that aesthetics deserves to have a central place in our discipline. For many years—as a backlash against Hanslickian absolutism, against the supposed autonomy of the musical work; but also, perhaps, out of a genuine engagement with traditions in which the aesthetic is clearly subsumed by the social—we ethnographers of music have written as if musical meaning inheres almost entirely in the social or symbolic aspects of music: in its uses; in its functions; in its ability to define group identity, ritual space, ritual time, and other factors. This approach may ring more true for some traditions than for others. In our search for difference, we have fallen into the pattern Geertz (2000:64) describes for anthropologists: "we hawk the anomalous, peddle the strange." Our otherwise healthy effort to show the non-universality of Western music has led us to de-aestheticize even those non-Western traditions with a strong aesthetic sense.

One of the things I do in this book is to show how the meaning of musical sounds is dependent on the musical context.[4] That is, I try to bridge the notorious divide between music and context, between the aesthetic and the historical, between the musical and the social, between musicological and anthropological ethnomusicology—however you want to put it.

As Dahlhaus has stated in a provocative essay entitled "The Significance of Art: Historical or Aesthetic?" (1989 [1978]), the more one focuses on the circumstances in which music is produced, the more one moves away from music as an aesthetic object. That is, he sees history and aesthetics as mutually exclusive. This tension between sound and context has always been at the heart of the discipline of ethnomusicology. We might declare that music is an activity and not an object; that the "music itself" is necessarily what people do for people, not just the sounds they make; that sound and context are indissociable. And yet, as any good ethnographer knows, what people say they do and what they actually do are often two different things. Sometimes we describe the whatness of the musical object (its sound); and sometimes we describe its whoness, whereness, whenness, howness, or whyness (its context). Rarely do we do both. By attending to musical affect and how musicians talk about it, we are led to both musical object and musical activity at the same time. This is because affect is at the heart of the aesthetic experience, and yet it cannot be understood outside of a larger context. This context may be taken for granted when one is a cultural insider, but it becomes much less transparent in a cross-cultural setting. My first chapter, accordingly, sets the stage geographically and sociologically for what follows.

4. As a model of how this principle may be put into practice, I can think of no better example than Lortat-Jacob's exemplary study (1998) of sacred singing among a Sardinian brotherhood.

In the foregoing discussion I have spoken as if, according to Javanese musicians, music's content is its affect. The situation is in fact a bit more complicated than that. What makes music meaningful for them is *rasa*. This word may indeed be translated as "affect," and for much of the book this will do reasonably well. Yet *rasa* is much more than that. In chapter 2 I explore the meaning of this all-important word, basing my analysis largely on oral citations from musicians I have spoken to. Though what concerns me most is how the word is used in a musical context, we cannot answer the question "What is this thing called *rasa*?" without adventuring into Javanese psychological and philosophical theories, which have a strong foundation in Buddhism and Sufism. Readers who are not drawn to detailed lexicographic explorations should at least read the final paragraph of the chapter in order to follow the rest of the book.

In chapter 3 I whittle the meaning of *rasa* down to just "musical affect," leaving aside its other dimensions, and investigate the range of *rasa*s that may be expressed musically. To understand this panoply more fully, we must in turn ask how the various musical affects are related to each other—in other words, how the *rasa* lexicon is structured. An important point that emerges as *rasa*s are mapped into shifting constellations of relatedness, is just how paramount connotative meaning is. Chapters 2 and 3, then, are mainly semantic in nature.

It is in chapter 4 that I try to make good on my promise to weave together musical affect and musical context, or aesthetics and sociology. For in assessing who or what has *rasa*, we are led back to the Javanese categories of geography, gender, and social status first described in chapter 1. That is, in this chapter I look for patterns in just which performances—and, more particularly, which performers—are said to have more or less *rasa* than others. The question of what makes music "*rasa*ful" is continued in chapter 5, but with more of a focus on the moment of performance.

Chapter 6 consists mostly of lengthy excerpts from conversations with two noted musical experts. Following their lead, it takes a philosophical turn. The two main questions they tackle are "What is the relationship between what people say they feel when listening to music and what they actually feel?" and "How much of musical *rasa* is in the piece, how much in the performance, and how much in the perception of the performance?"

From philosophy thence to music theory: chapter 7 continues the question raised in chapters 4 and 5 about factors contributing to the creation of *rasa*. But here, instead of music and *rasa* as a quality of the performer, the focus is on the variety of *rasa*s catalogued in chapter 3 and on specific musical traits. That is, I seek to identify, other factors being equal, what effect various musical procedures have on any particular *rasa* as it is perceived by an experienced listener.

Finally, in my last chapter I raise some larger issues, though I offer little in the way of definitive answers and allow myself to be more speculative than in the rest of the book. Some of my conclusions I will save for the end. But, by way of further illustrating what it is I am setting out to do—why, that is, I think it is important, and why I think it is possible—I would like, here, to show what can happen when what I've learned from this research is put into practice.

Over the past few years, in teaching courses to undergraduates (mainly introductions to musics of the world, but also, inter alia, seminars in ethnomusicological theory), I have often conducted an informal experiment, in which I play recorded examples of Javanese music for which I have insiders' descriptions of affective meaning. If I have time, I also play a few examples of music more obviously familiar to those present. I ask students to write down adjectives that describe the respective moods of the various selections. Despite a certain looseness in the way I have conducted these experiments, several things have become clear. First, affect is of utmost importance in getting students to understand music; furthermore, it is interesting to them and something they feel comfortable talking about. Second, there is a difference in their reactions to familiar and unfamiliar music: there is almost always more consensus about the familiar pieces than about the unfamiliar ones. Third, they are sometimes spectacularly wrong about the intended affects of the Javanese pieces. Fourth, they are sometimes spectacularly right about these same pieces. (Interestingly, there does not seem to be a clear pattern as to which they get "right" and which "wrong.")

From points two through four, I draw several general conclusions. First of all, musical meaning is learned, just as linguistic meaning is. Hanslick's principal argument against associative meaning in music is that the same piece can elicit differing interpretations. But this is to misunderstand the nature of associations. I would posit, following Wittgenstein (1958), that linguistic meaning is also largely associative. No one would argue that language has no referential meaning simply because one needs to know a language to understand an utterance in it. Similarly, just because one has to be clued into the meaning of musical patterns—insofar as these have shared associations—in order to "get" it, does not mean that the patterns have no meaning beyond Hanslick's *tönend-bewegte Formen* (sounding forms in motion). For both language and music, then, meaning accrues through use—which is precisely why I try to avoid separating musical object and musical context.

My second general conclusion is that the more familiar the piece—that is, the more context one has for it (the more "prior text," in A. L. Becker's terminology) the more one will be led to certain associative affects over others. Again, this points up the interconnectedness of musical context and perception of musical affect. And if one's goal is to learn certain idiomatic affective responses, there is no way around paying a good deal of attention to musical context (who is composing or performing where, why, when, for whom, and in conjunction with what other activities) in an effort to make up for missing prior texts.

My third conclusion is that some aspects of affective meaning can cross cultural boundaries. This is not logically inconsistent with musical affect being learned; but it might also be explained by putative universal psychological dispositions (on the order of "quicker rhythms are perceived as being more exciting," "low pitches are perceived as more serious").[5] I am not prepared to try to settle this here. In either case, the important thing is that musical affect sometimes is, if not universal, at least cross-culturally accessible. Indeed, without this, there would be little point in my writing this book: if music cultures were mutually unintelligible in an absolute sense, there would be little hope of outsiders ever learning to hear like insiders—which is one of my main goals—or little motivation to even try to understand any musics but one's own.

A preliminary comment about who my teachers were is in order here. With one exception, all of the people whom I taped in conversation were respected music or dance teachers, all male, and all over the age of forty-five. One might legitimately ask why, if so many of the performers I was studying were female, I didn't talk more with female experts. This is, in fact, something I would like to have done, and the reasons I did not are instructive. First of all, I found activities and the demarcation of space to be considerably more segregated by gender in Javanese society than in the middle-class French and American milieux I was brought up in. This meant not only that I turned to Javanese males for advice on whom to ask about musical aesthetics, but also that it was more natural for me to spend time with male than with female musicians. Second, Javanese traditional music—and more especially, discourse about music—is very much dominated by males. To the general public, female singers are the best-known and most highly visible musicians. But because, with few exceptions, they don't "use mallets" (i.e., play instruments), they are thought to have at best an incomplete knowledge of the tradition: to a certain extent, "female musical expert" is an oxymoron in the Javanese context. When women study singing formally, it is usually with a male teacher. And, because women are not thought of as sources of musical knowledge, they are rarely called upon to teach or to theorize. They may therefore be less adept than men at verbalizing the musical techniques that they are so skilled at. Whatever the reasons, my gender bias is something I am aware of, and something I lament. Those seeking more information on the attitudes of women singers in the same community I studied may find it in Susan Walton's work (1996),[6] the fieldwork for which was conducted just after mine. Interestingly enough, it would seem that the female perspectives on *rasa* that she presents (chapters 5 and 6), are quite similar, in fact, to ways of talking about *rasa* I had encountered among male musicians.

5. Significantly, both of these examples were suggested to me by Rahayu Supanggah.

6. Other related research on women performers in central Java has been conducted by Nancy Cooper (1994) and Sarah Weiss (1998 and 2006). Suraji's study of female singers (2005) is notable in that it is the first monograph by a male Javanese musician to treat women as sources of information and not simply as producers of musical patterns to be analyzed by the researcher.

I have chosen to refer to most of my interviewees as "my teachers," whether I actually studied performance with them or not. Some of them I may have only spoken with two or three times; but they were experts and I ignorant, and they taught me much. I am uncomfortable with the outmoded notion that only the anthropologist can know the true import of what his or her "informants" say. This does not mean that I have avoided adding my perspective—such shaping and reshaping of the material is inevitable—but I want to emphasize that my role in the field was that of a learner.

In gathering information I sought, to the extent that this is possible, to remain true to the musicians' perspectives. In listening to my tapes, back in the United States, I realized just how much I had actively influenced the direction of the dialogue, especially towards the end of my stay, when I had absorbed much of the musicians' vocabulary, and time seemed short. But a great many of their comments were unsolicited by me. And, when occasionally two musicians were present during one of the taping sessions, and the conversation would switch from Indonesian to Javanese (a sign that I was not being addressed), there was not a sudden shift in emphasis. So I do think that in the end, by listening very carefully to what was being said, I was able to get some idea of what was important to my teachers.

The goal of being true to the insiders' perspectives is even more elusive, however, in the *presenting* of the material gathered, and it may not be entirely desirable. I do not mean by this that in constructing my narrative I should have been free to choose any interpretation that came to mind; rather, that another force besides the musicians' perspective was at work in shaping the material. As Goethe put it in his *Wilhelm Meister's Years of Travel*: "You do not need to have seen or experienced everything yourself; but if you wish to trust the other man and his descriptions, consider that you now have to deal with three factors, the object and two subjects." It would be disingenuous to pretend that these two subjects, the reader and I, did not exist. For practical and statistical reasons, I recognize that my primary (but, I hope, not exclusive) readership will be members of the musical and academic communities of the Western world, for want of a better word, most of whom will never have been to Java, and some of whom, sadly, will never have heard a live gamelan ensemble, let alone a highly accomplished one in its original setting. As any author must, I had to consider the needs of my readership, so that one of my roles in all of this was to sift through, organize, and make meaningful the texts that originated as exchanges between Javanese musicians and myself, and that have been inscribed on paper, on audio tape, and in my memory. The task was largely one of translation, in the broad sense of supplying missing "prior texts" (A. L. Becker 1995).

To be sure, the notion of cultural translation has been criticized as perpetuating colonialist attitudes (Crapanzano 1986, Asad 1986). But this is more a problem with the way it has been carried out within a colonialist (or neocolonialist) framework than with the notion itself—no better alternative has been proposed. Simply put, I was once in Java, I am now in a very different place, and I would like to tell the people where I now find myself what I learned while I was there. Clearly, it would not do simply to repeat verbatim what my teachers told me or to address myself primarily to Javanese musicians.[7]

One of the ways I have tried to bridge the gap between these two conceptual worlds is to include a large number of Javanese and Indonesian words. This is, after all, about how Javanese musicians talk about music. I expect my readership to include people with only a passing familiarity with gamelan music, and no knowledge of the Javanese and Indonesian languages, but who want to know more about what this music means. For these people, certain passages may seem needlessly detailed and eminently skippable. But the book is also meant as a manual, a sort of multidimensional glossary, for the increasing numbers of non-Javanese who are learning to perform this music, either in Java or from a Javanese musician living abroad. For them, it is intended to be both a guide to figuring out what their teachers are saying and to performing the music with deeper understanding.

Because I deal simultaneously with aesthetics, language about music, culturally constructed emotion concepts, and Javanese culture in general, I am hoping that the study will be of interest not only to ethnomusicologists, but also to music aestheticians, cognitive anthropologists, psychologists, linguists, Southeast Asianists, and to musicologists who focus on musical affect.

Yet another small but all-important readership must be mentioned. Returning to Goethe's comment, the ethnographer's object is also a subject, of course—a living, thinking being (in my case, a musician)—so that there are not two, but rather three subjects. The distinctions between these three subjects, while not irrelevant, are far from absolute. I am to some extent also part of the objective subject: I was among the participants creating the "texts" to be translated; and I am also at least a partial insider (or so I am told by my Javanese musician-friends; I am certainly no longer the same person I was before I went to Java). In a sense, then, I am continuing these dialogues here, addressing myself to the growing number of Javanese musicologists who read English (an Indonesian translation is in the works, for those who do not). I welcome them to compare my representation of their words, their music, and their world to their perceptions of these, and to point out the discrepancies that are sure to arise.

7. I once attended a demonstration of gamelan music for a U.S. audience, presented by a Javanese musician who spoke almost no English and had very little idea of what musical or cultural concepts his listeners already had. The audience came away with the distinct impression that here was a tradition they would never understand—even the bits of English they were able to catch made no sense to them. In a way this is good. Too often, people assume that music is the universal language; a little culture shock never hurt anybody. Yet I cannot but hope, in a work such as this, for a different result.

CONTENTS

BRIEF GLOSSARY

This glossary of commonly used terms has been laid out in such a way so that its four pages can be photocopied in landscape format, front and back, onto a single sheet of paper for easier reference. A complete glossary is provided at the back of the book. References to photos refer to the glossy insert.

ådå-ådå: a kind of *suluk* often used for tense situations

alus: refined, smooth, calm, controlled

anteb: solid, weighty

ASKI: Akademi Seni Karawitan Indonesia (Indonesian Academy of Gamelan-Related Arts), subsequently STSI, now ISI

balungan: outline or reference melody; notated melody in a collection of *gendhings* (analogous to fake-book notation); the melody played on the *sarons* and *slenthem*

båwå: extended, unmetered, solo vocal introduction to a gamelan piece, usually sung by a male singer

bedhåyå: genre of sacred, choreographed court dances accompanied by unison choral singing and gamelan music

bedhayan: in the style of *bedhåyå* accompaniment

bérag: exuberant

berwibawa: to have *wibawa* (*wibåwå*), be commanding, imposing

bonang: two-octave gong-chime played with padded mallets (photo 4)

bonangan: performed with no vocals and none of the softer-sounding instruments of the gamelan; what the *bonang* plays

branyak: brash, spirited, plucky

Bu: mother; Mrs.; Ma'am

campursari: Javanese songs accompanied by a mixture of Western and Javanese instruments

céngkok: melodic pattern; distinctive melodic contour; melodic phrase

ciblon: medium-sized drum often used for dance accompaniment (photo 3, foreground)

cocog: suitable, appropriate; to fit, to match

demung: the largest of the *sarons* (photo 5, foreground)

dhalang: puppeteer (for the shadow theater and related performing arts)

ènthèng: light, lightweight, easy

gagah: manly, strong

gambang: xylophone with trough resonator played with a pair of soft mallets (partially visible in photo 6, extreme left)

gamelan: an ensemble of Javanese or Balinese traditional instruments, made as a set, consisting mostly of tuned percussion made of bronze or other metal, and played by a handful up to thirty or so musicians (photos 1 through 7)

garap: interpretation, working out, musical treatment, performance practice, arrangement, improvisation (see also *nggarap*)

gecul: jocular, waggish, comical

gendèr: metallophone with tube resonators; *gendèr barung* (photo 7, foreground)

gendèr barung: an instrument of the *gendèr* family, with a medium-high range and played polyphonically with two padded mallets (photo 7, foreground)

gendhing: gamelan piece; a gamelan piece with a medium to long gong cycle

gendhing bonang: a long, stately *gendhing* using only the louder instruments of the gamelan (or, more loosely, a shorter piece in that style)

gendhing kréasi (baru): "newly created" gamelan pieces in a semi-popular idiom

gérong: unison male chorus that is an integral part of the overall gamelan texture (when it is present); *gérongan* (photo 2, right middle ground)

gérongan: unison male choral part to a gamelan piece

halus: see *alus*

imbal: a playing technique that involves rapid alternation of two musicians using the same kind of instrument to create a single melodic line

inggah: see *minggah*

iråmå: tempo ratio or level; degree of expansion or contraction of a *gendhing*

isi: contents, substance, content (sometimes related to a *gendhing*'s title)

ISI: Institut Seni Indonesia (Indonesian Institute for the Arts), formerly STSI

jiwa: soul, spirit

karawitan: traditional gamelan music

kasar: coarse, crude, rough, unrefined

kempul: a largish, medium-pitched gong with a rounded but penetrating sound, used as a time-marking instrument (photo 2, center-left background)

kendhang: double-headed, barrel-shaped hand drum (photo 3)

kendhangan: what the *kendhang* plays; a particular working out of the drum part to a piece

kenong: set of large, resonant, time-marking pot-gongs with a medium-high pitch (photo 5, right middle ground)

ketawang: a small *gendhing* form with 16 beats per gong cycle

kethuk: a small, dull-sounding pot-gong with a medium-low pitch (photo 5, left middle ground)

khidmat: devotional, reverential, calm

klenéngan: "concert" (an extended, formal or informal music-making session featuring gamelan music); concert repertoire or performance style

kråmå: high (respectful) Javanese

kråmå inggil: extra-respectful Javanese

Kraton: the palace of the senior royal line of Solo (cf. Mangkunegaran); (lowercase:) king's palace

kroncong: pan-Indonesian genre of popular music with Portuguese roots

ladrang (or **ladrangan**): a small *gendhing* structure with a 32-beat gong cycle

langgam: genre of Javanese popular song, related to *kroncong*, that may be performed with gamelan accompaniment

laras: tuning (high or low); tuning system (*sléndro* or *pélog*)

luruh: humble, with a downcast gaze; refined; calm

måcåpat: unaccompanied, unmetered sung recitation of poetry in indigenous poetic meters

Mangkunegaran: palace of the Solonese junior royal line

manteb: see *anteb*

Mas: older brother (used as a term of address)

mérong: the first, calm section of a medium-to-large *gendhing*

minggah: "to get higher"; the second, livelier major section of a medium-to-large *gendhing*

nggarap: to work out, interpret, arrange

ngoko: low Javanese

Pak: father; Mr.; Sir

palaran: a vocal genre based on *mâcâpat* in which a solo singer is accompanied by a reduced gamelan ensemble

pathet: melodic mode

pathetan: a kind of *suluk* for calm moods (may be performed in a concert setting as an unmetered, heterophonic modal prelude or postlude played by a small ensemble with or without a male voice)

pélog: seven-tone tuning system with markedly unequal intervals in its pentatonic modes

pélog limå: the *pélog pathet* with the lowest tessitura, and the greatest preponderance of long, serious pieces

pendhåpå: open-sided pavilion with high-pitched roof, often used for performances

pengrawit: gamelan musician

pesindhèn: (usually solo) female vocalist in a gamelan ensemble (photo 2, foreground)

prenès: coquettish, flirtatious, lighthearted

rangkep: "doubled"; usually refers to the fourth *irâmå* level

raos [K]: *krâmå* for *råså*

råså [Ng]: *rasa*, but often with strong mystical or specifically Javanese connotations

rasa [I]: taste, feeling, affect, mood, inner meaning, faculty of taste, intuition, deep understanding

rebab: bowed, two-stringed spike fiddle (photo 1, foreground)

rebaban: *rebab* part; a particular way of working out the *rebab* part to a gamelan piece

regu: stately

RRI: Radio Republik Indonesia

saron: one-octave metallophone with trough resonator played with a wooden mallet, of which there are three sizes, each an octave apart (from smallest to largest: *panerus, barung, demung*) (photo 4, background; photo 5, foreground)

sedhih: sad

sèlèh: finalis (the final pitch of a melodic phrase)

sendhon: a kind of *suluk* often used for sad moods

sereng: tense

sindhèn: *pesindhèn*; *sindhénan*

sindhénan: the part sung by the female solo vocalist in a gamelan ensemble; a particular way of working out the *sindhèn* part to a piece

sléndro: five-tone, nearly equidistant tuning

slenthem: the lowest of the instruments in the *gendèr* family, played with a single, padded mallet (photo 2, left middle ground)

Solo(adj., **Solonese**): a city in Central Java (a mercantile, artistic, and cultural center)

STSI: Sekolah Tinggi Seni Indonesia (Advanced Indonesian School for the Arts), now ISI, formerly ASKI

suling: end-blown bamboo fipple flute (photo 6, left middle ground)

suluk: *dhalang*'s mood song (*pathetan, sendhon, ådå-ådå*)

sunan: the king of Solo (the head of the senior royal line)

Surakarta: another name for Solo

TBS: Taman Budaya Surakarta, a municipal arts complex with a large *pendhåpå* where public performances are often held

trègèl: vivacious, impetuous, agile

watak: disposition, nature, character

wayang: shadow theater with perforated, painted, raw-hide puppets; any of various theater forms closely related to the shadow theater; shadow-play performance

wayang kulit: "leather" *wayang*, shadow theater

wayang orang [I] **wayang wong** [Ng]: dance drama about characters from the Mahabharatha (literally, "human *wayang*")

wibåwå: masculine authority, commanding presence

wiled: the third *irâmâ* level; *inggah*; *wiledan*

wiledan: a specific variant of a melodic pattern (*céngkok*)

Yogyakarta (**Yogya**): a city near Solo, with its own royal courts (a center of culture and tourism)

TECHNICAL NOTES

Indonesian, which until the 1920s was called Malay, is the national language of Indonesia. In central Java it is learned mostly in school and through television. It is used primarily in certain public situations, for communicating with people from a different region, and by any of the mass media aimed at a national audience. Across Indonesia hundreds of regional languages are used in the home, between friends, and in many local transactions and ceremonies. Except in areas where a variety of Malay is the local language, most Indonesians are thus at least bilingual.

In central Java the local language is Javanese. As an outgrowth of the feudal societies that were centered around powerful kingdoms for over a thousand years, the Javanese language was—and still is—stratified into usage levels. This is especially true in and around the two most recent court centers, Solo (= Surakarta) and Yogyakarta (= Yogya). The linguistic levels consist of a number of vocabulary sets and two sets of affixes, all of which are combined in various ways to show varying amounts of respect. Some Javanese grammarians name nine such levels, the details of which are complex and difficult to explain. For our purposes we need only point out (1) that the base vocabulary is *ngoko* (low Javanese); (2) that the general vocabulary of respect is *kråmå* or *båså* (high Javanese), which consists of several hundred lexical items that are substituted for the equivalent *ngoko* words where appropriate; and (3) that there are several dozen vocabulary items that are used to elevate or lower the addressee, the speaker, or the person or thing being talked about, with respect to oneself or someone else being talked to or about (generally these words are used to lower oneself and elevate others).

For example, the base (*ngoko*) word for "arrive" or "come" is *tekå*. If you were speaking high Javanese (*kråmå*) you would say *dhateng* or *dumugi*. If you were speaking either low or high Javanese, and wanted to show extra respect to the person arriving, you would say *rawuh* [*kråmå inggil*], and if the person in question were going to see someone of higher status, you would use *sowan* [*krâmâ andhap*] to describe his or her action. There is yet another word, *dugi*, which belongs to a small set of midlevel words (*krâmâ madyâ*).[1]

Throughout the book I have used a mixture of levels when giving a term in Javanese. Other things being equal, I would normally prefer the high Javanese (*krâmâ*) word for a text such as this, since that is the usual practice in written discourse (except for some poetry, for the popular press, and for didactic texts). But this book includes many foreign terms, and I have tried not to confuse the reader by using the *krâmâ* for a word previously introduced—say, in a quote—in *ngoko*. Sometimes the *ngoko* word is morphologically closer to Indonesian than the *krâmâ*, and so is less confusing for that reason as well.

SPELLING

Indonesian has long been written with the Latin alphabet. The older spelling, left over from colonial times, was strongly influenced by Dutch usage. Since the early 1970s a simplified system has been in effect. I have used the current system for both Indonesian and Javanese, except for some proper names and quotes from older sources. The old equivalents of the new standardized spelling may

TABLE T.1. Orthography.

New	Old	Pronunciation
a		as in *father*
c	tj	*ch*
e		as in *gate* (I have indicated this with the symbol é)
e		as in *let* (=è)
e		as in the *e* of *apple* (=*e*)
f (rare)		*f* or *p*
i		as in *feet*
j	dj	*j*
kh		*k*,*h*, or Spanish *j*
ng		as in *singing* (not as in *anger*)
o		as in *rose*
r		rolled, as in Spanish *r*
u	oe	as in *too*
v (rare)		*f* or *p*
y	j	as in *yes*
z (rare)		*z* or *j*

1. For more information on Javanese language levels see Soepomo 1968 and 1969; Keeler 1975, 1984:xvii–xx, and 1987:25–38; Errington 1985 and 1988; Uhlenbeck 1978:278–99; Robson 1992; and Anderson 1990:194–237. Geertz 1976 and Siegel 1986, to my mind, are not very reliable on this particular topic.

TABLE T.2. Pronunciation.

Javanese Romanization	How Pronounced
å	in final, open syllable,[2] *a* is rounded—somewhere between *gnaw* and *know*; this also applies in the penultimate syllable, if the last two syllables both have the vowel *a* and both are open[3] (there are some exceptions to these rules)
b	voiced (as in English *b*) but aspirated (as in English *p*)
c	tongue slightly further forward than in English (between *ts* and *ch*)
d	voiced, aspirated, dental
dh	voiced, aspirated, slightly retroflex
g	voiced (as in English *g*), aspirated (as in English *k*)
h	between two vowels, turns into semivowel *y* or disappears; otherwise, as in English
i	in closed syllables, as in *sit*
j	tongue slightly further forward than in English (between *dz* and *j*)
k	unvoiced (as in English *k*), unaspirated (as in English *g*)
l	slightly retroflex
n	slightly retroflex
o	in closed syllables, between *pun* and *pawn* (cf. French *tonne*)
p	unvoiced (as in English *p*), unaspirated (as in English *b*)
s	between *s* and *sh*
t	dental and unaspirated
th	retroflex and unaspirated
u	in closed syllables, as in *book*
w	not rounded (bottom lip comes up at onset, as in English *v*—but unvoiced and not fricative—bottom lip is pulled back down before air passes through)

2. An open syllable is one that ends in a vowel.

3. Syllable division in Javanese differs from that in English mainly with respect to the nasal consonants (*m, n, ng*). If a nasal consonant follows a vowel but does not close the word, it invariably belongs to the next syllable. Thus, the word *gangsa* [J] ("bronze") would be divided *ga-ngsa*, and hence is pronounced *gångså*. Other examples are *lå-mbå* [J] ("single"), *kå-ndhå* [Ng] ("to tell"), and *så-ngå* [J] ("nine").

be found in table T.1, along with American-English phonetic approximations wherever the pronunciation is problematic.

Until well into this century, Javanese was primarily handwritten in Javanese script (which was originally based on Devanagari—the script used for Sanskrit). Because of this, a wide variety of Latin spellings are deemed acceptable. I have tried to use the one I consider to be most common in current practice. As a guide to sounding out the Javanese words used in this study, I have provided in table T.2 some fairly detailed information about Javanese pronunciation (this is meant as a supplement to the notes on Indonesian pronunciation found in table T.1, which also apply to Javanese).

Note that aspiration is reversed between English and Javanese: in English the unvoiced consonants (*p, ch, t, k*) are aspirated, and the voiced ones (*b, j, d, g*) are largely unaspirated; in Javanese the unvoiced consonants are unaspirated, and the voiced ones are aspirated.[4]

Word stress is lighter than in English and almost always falls on the last syllable. (In many non-Javanese dialects of Indonesian, on the other hand, stress falls on the penultimate syllable.)

LANGUAGE IDENTIFICATION

Because this book discusses how Javanese musicians talk about their music, I felt it necessary to include a large number of non-English terms. In order to identify the language or vocabulary set each term was drawn from, I have used the following symbols, enclosed in brackets and directly following the term:

A	Arabic
I	Indonesian
J	Javanese
JI	Javanese Indonesian (not used in most other dialects of Indonesian)
Ng	*ngoko* (low Javanese)
K	*kråmå* (high Javanese)
KI	*kråmå inggil* (term of highest respect)
KA	*kråmå andhap* (term of self-deprecation)
KM	*kråmå madyå* (midlevel Javanese)
D	Dutch
E	English

JAVANESE LOAN WORDS IN ENGLISH

At least two Javanese words have made it into the standard English lexicon. Indeed, both *gong* and *gamelan* figure in any college-sized dictionary of American English. It will therefore come as no surprise if I normally refrain from setting these words in italics. For all other Javanese and Indonesian words that occur in English sentences I have italicized such terms throughout but have

4. For more extensive notes on Javanese pronunciation, see Keeler 1984:xxv–xxxvi and Ras 1985:3–16.

adopted the policy of adding unitalicized English suffixes to italicized foreign terms. I have broken this policy, however, in pluralizing compound nouns. Given that noun modifiers in Javanese and Indonesian *follow* the noun, adding a plural marker to the end of the unit is just as awkward as adding it to the noun itself. I have sought to avoid the inelegance found in plurals like *courts-martial* by simply leaving italicized compounds uninflected.

The glossary at the end of the book is designed to help the uninitiated with frequently used foreign words. In addition, short definitions for frequent foreign terms are given within the brief glossary in the front section.

NAMES OF PIECES AND SONGS

The titles of Javanese gamelan pieces have several parts: (1) form, (2) proper name, (3) additional information about form (for pieces with large gong cycles), (4) *laras*, and (5) *pathet*.[5] An example is *gendhing Babar Layar kethuk 4 kerep, minggah kethuk 8, laras pélog pathet limå*, which may be broken down as follows (see the specialized glossary that immediately follows this section for additional translations):

gendhing (large piece)

Babar Layar (Unfurling Sails)

kethuk 4 kerep (four "frequent" *kethuks* per *kenong* in the *mérong* section)

minggah 8 (eight *kethuks* per *kenong*, thus coming twice as often, in the *minggah* section)

laras pélog (*pélog* tuning)

pathet limå (*limå* mode).

The names for Javanese vocal pieces may have the following elements: (1) category of poetic meter; (2) name of specific poetic meter within the larger category; (3) number of feet in a line, and placement of caesura (for *sekar ageng* meters only); (4) the specific tune associated with the poetic meter (for some versions of songs in *måcåpat* meters); (5) *laras*; (6) *pathet* (often not specified for unaccompanied songs in *sléndro*, whose *pathet* may be ambiguous). An example of a *måcåpat* song title is *sekar måcåpat Pangkur Dhudhåkasmaran, laras sléndro*, which may be broken down thus:

sekar (classical sung poetry)

måcåpat (a category of verse using indigenous meters)

5. *Laras* may be translated as "tuning system," of which there are two standard ones (*sléndro* and *pélog*) in traditional Javanese music. *Pathet* is roughly equivalent to "melodic mode."

Pangkur (a category of *mâcâpat* meter)

Dhudhâkasmaran (a specific *lelagon* [tune] associated with *Pangkur*)

laras sléndro (*sléndro* tuning).

An example of a *sekar ageng* title is *bâwâ sekar Ageng Banjaransari, lampah 19 pedhotan 6; 6; 7, laras pélog pathet barang*, which may be broken down as follows:

bâwâ (unaccompanied vocal introduction to a *gendhing*)

sekar ageng (a category of sung poetry)

Banjaransari (one of over a hundred *sekar ageng* meters)

lampah 19 (nineteen syllables to the line)

pedhotan 6; 6; 7 (caesura after the sixth syllable, and again after the twelfth)

laras pélog (*pélog* tuning)

pathet barang (*barang* mode).

In naming pieces I capitalize only the proper names. For sung verse forms, which often do not have proper names per se, the capitalized word may be a specific poetic meter.

Glossary for the Naming of Pieces and Songs

awis [K], **arang** [Ng]—"infrequent," as defined by the number of *kethuk* strokes per *kenong* stroke

gendhing—(1) any gamelan piece (or, in archaic parlance, instrumental music, as opposed to *gendhèng*, vocal music); (2) a piece with a "large" *gongan*, defined as having a *kenong* phrase of at least sixteen beats

gong—short for one of several large, deep-sounding gongs (specifically the *gong ageng, gong siyem*, and *gong suwukan*)

gong ageng—the largest, lowest-pitched, and most final-sounding gong in a gamelan (usually tuned to an extremely low pitch 3 or 5)

gong siyem—the second-largest size of gong in a large gamelan ensemble (usually tuned to a very low pitch 6)

gong suwukan—the third-largest size of gong in a large gamelan ensemble, usually tuned to a low 7, 1, or 2

gongan—the largest analytical unit in gamelan music, a rhythmic cycle marked off at the end by a large gong

kenong—large kettle gong that marks time at the ends of phrases (of which there are usually two or four per gong cycle)

kerep—"frequent," as defined by the number of *kethuk* strokes per *kenong* stroke; the opposite (infrequent) is called *arang* [Ng] or *awis* [K]

kethuk—small, low-pitched kettle gong that subdivides the *kenong* phrases

lampah—"step"; number of syllables in a line of poetry

laras—tuning system, of which there are two: *sléndro* and *pélog*

lelagon—one of several tunes associated with a poetic meter (derived from *lagu*, melody)

måcåpat—sung poetry that employs Javanese (possibly pre-Hindu) poetic meters and literary but relatively modern language (also called *sekar alit* [K], "small" *sekar*)

mérong—the first, calm section of a *gendhing* in sense 2

minggah (also *inggah*)—the second, livelier section of a *gendhing* in sense 2

pathet—melodic mode, of which there are three in *sléndro* (*nem, sångå, manyurå*), and three basic ones in pélog (*limå, nem, barang*)

pedhotan—caesura

pélog—a tuning with seven unequal intervals in the octave

sekar [K] **tembang** [Ng]—classical sung poetry

sekar ageng—"great flower"; sung poetry using archaic language and Sanskrit meters of four lines, each of equal length

sléndro—a tuning with five nearly equidistant intervals to the octave

JAVANESE PERSONAL NAMES

In Java, most people have no surnames, only given names (they may have one or several). To distinguish between the many people named Joko, one adds a second given name, if available. If not, one either adds an epithet or a place name—usually the place of residence (see note 1 of the Preface for examples). Someone who has more than one given name may go by any one of them for short. Moreover, his or her principal name may be shortened in various ways. In conversation the common prefix *Su-* is usually dropped. A name may be further abbreviated by eliminating a syllable or more. Many people change their names or add on to them as they get older. This may happen at marriage, or, for instance, if one changes religions or is employed at one of the courts and receives a promotion. One further complication is that of spelling. I have tried to use the spellings used by the people themselves, if I knew that these did not follow the standard modern Romanization for Javanese words.

When using someone's name in conversation, either in the second or third person, one usually precedes it with an honorific that indicates the person's relationship to oneself (or sometimes to the listener). In Indonesian, for adult men whom one is not particularly close to, one usually uses *Pak* (Father, Mr.) or, more formally or respectfully, *Bapak*. In Javanese the even more respectful term is *Råmå* (usually reserved for nobility or Catholic priests). The female equivalents of *Pak* and *Bapak* are *Bu* and *Ibu* (Mother, Mrs.) in both Indonesian and Javanese. Javanese also has a more intimate, less respectful term, *Mbok*. Current convention in much academic writing in Indonesian is to drop these honorifics, and to use a relatively full version of the person's name. This is the policy I have adopted, even though it feels disrespectful. I hope I have not offended anyone as a result. Additional terms of address that may come up in quotations are *Mbak* and *Mas*. *Mbak*—literally, "older sister"—in addition to being employed in addressing or referring to actual older sisters, is used sometimes for young girls and often for young women as well as for adult women one is expressing a longstanding or informal relationship with—exact usage depends mostly on the age of the person in question and sometimes that of her siblings (is she an older sister to them?), the age of the speaker and its relation to that of the person in question, the respective social classes of those involved, how close these same people feel to each other, and the formality of the situation. *Mas*, literally "older brother," is the male equivalent of *Mbak*.

My principal teachers' names are given below, along with the dates of the first and last documented conversation with them during my original period of research. For those with two names, I have underlined the one used in the citations. I have also provided shortened forms in parentheses, the way they might appear in conversations.

Sudarsono (Dar)	(January 24, 1990, to June 18, 1992)
Suhartå (Hartå, Harto)	(November 17, 1989, to June 27, 1992)
Sukanto Sastrodarsono (Kanto)	(November 4, 1989, to June 24, 1992)
Mloyowidodo (Mloyo, Mlåyå)	(March 11, 1992, to May 2, 1992)
Rahayu Supanggah (Panggah)	(April 24, 1990, to November 6, 1993)
Sastro Tugiyo (Sastro)	(April 29, 1992, to May 6, 1992)
Sutarman (Tarman)	(August 21, 1991, to June 24, 1992)
Sudarsono Wignyosaputro (Wig)	(June 19, 1992, to June 24, 1992)

MUSICAL NOTATION

Musical notation has been in use in Java for just over a hundred years. Before that time the repertoire was transmitted orally. The transition to a written tradition has been slow and far from complete: even now, gamelan music still has a strong oral emphasis. Largely as a result of Dutch influence, various forms of writing musical notations were tried out in Java in the latter nineteenth century (J. Becker 1980, Sumarsam 1995). The one that was finally adopted by Solonese musicians is known as Kepatihan or cipher (or number) notation, and this is what I shall be using throughout this book.

The idea of using Arabic numerals to stand for steps of a scale goes back at least to sixteenth-century Spain. It was revived by a French monk in the seventeenth century, and then again by Rousseau in the eighteenth century.[6] In 1818, Pierre Galin, of the Galin-Paris-Chevé music school, published a revised version of Rousseau's system. Because this notation is so easy to learn and so adaptable to different musics—particularly those that are monophonic or heterophonic—what became known as the Galin-Paris-Chevé system spread throughout much of the world. It is still used in China and Japan as well as in Java.

The basic idea, again, is that each step of the scale is assigned a number, with higher numbers representing higher pitches. The seven notes of the *pélog* tuning are represented by the numbers 1 through 7. The five notes of the *sléndro* tuning are represented by the numbers 1, 2, 3, 5, and 6. Javanese vocal and instrumental melodies generally span about two octaves, divided into three registers. The highest register is indicated by dots placed above the numbers, the lowest register has dots below them. The melodic range is thus usually from about $\underset{\cdot}{3}$ to $\dot{3}$. One obvious advantage of Kepatihan notation, for our purposes, is that numbers do not imply exact pitches or intervals as strongly as do notes on a staff. And this is important for two reasons. First, for someone trained to read staff notation, it takes considerable effort to read lines and spaces on a staff as representing something other than pitches of the diatonic scale—that is, staff notation tends to make it even harder than it already is for a Western-trained listener to hear the intervals accurately. And second, gamelan pitches are not standardized, so that using staff notation implies a fixity of pitch that is misleading.

Another realm in which cipher notation is superior to staff notation in representing Javanese music is rhythm. It is, however, a somewhat mixed bag, as the standard way of showing rhythm in Kepatihan notation incorporates two opposing conceptions of meter, one of which sometimes runs counter to how the music is perceived by gamelan musicians. It is worth going into in some detail here, since it will help neophytes interpret the notes on the page.

6. Rousseau, in the *Confessions* (1959 [1770]:271–72) writes as if he had come up with the idea on his own, even though the seventeenth-century system had been reproduced in Brossard's famous dictionary of music published in 1703. When Rousseau presented his "Projet concernant de nouveaux signes pour la musique" before the Académie des Sciences in 1742, it was criticized for lacking originality (even though it differed in important respects from Souhaitty's seventeenth-century system). For a detailed history of this notation see Kleinman 1995 and Noll 1960. For a general history of gamelan notation, see J. Becker 1980 and Perlman 1991a. It should be said that some Javanese accounts of the invention of Kepatihan notation leave out Europeans entirely, although, according to Sindoesawarno (n.d./1987:338), R. M. T. Wreksadiningrat, who is credited with first coming up with the idea, was indeed familiar with the Galin-Paris-Chevé system. It was not such a large leap, though, from notes to numbers, since two of the traditional names for the notes of the scale were numbers and they retained the same names when the transfer was made to an all-cipher naming system (see Sastrapustaka 1953/1984 for an astonishing, mystical look at the symbolism of the traditional names, including why two of them were numbers).

The basic dominant conception of meter in Java places the strong beat at the end of a unit.[7] For those encountering this for the first time, counting backwards gives a very good approximation of what it feels like. In a four-beat unit, for example, the strongest beat is beat four, the second-strongest is beat two (counting backwards it would be one and three, respectively). As a result, in gamelan music the gong, which marks off the end of a large unit, is now virtually always placed at the end of a line. Likewise for the *kenong*, which also marks off a relatively large unit. The gong is shown by a circle around the number, or by double parentheses; the *kenong* is often shown by a "frown" above the number, or a closing parenthesis afterwards. Rests are indicated by dots (i.e., periods). Most of the time, though, these dots mean that the previous note is sustained rather than terminated. Occasionally in vocal music a *0* will be used to show where a sustained note is released.

On the next page is an example of one gong cycle of a short gamelan piece as it would be notated in a collection of such melodic outlines that a musician might use to derive his or her part or to remember how the piece goes. In actual performance there would be many other musical layers that are not normally notated. I have transcribed the excerpt into staff notation as well.

In lieu of a key signature, I have provided, at the beginning of the transcription into staff notation, a key to where the pitches lie.[8] A sharp symbol above a note thus indicates that its pitch class should be sharped throughout. An upward arrow attached to an accidental means that the pitch is microtonally higher than the pitch indicated; the reverse is true with the use of a downward arrow. A plus or a minus sign above the accidental means that that microtonal deviation is substantial—on the order of a quarter tone.

Note that the pitch equivalents given in these keys are only approximate. Notice, as well, that if one pitch of a Javanese tuning matches a pitch in a standard Western tuning, most of the time none of the others will. I have tried to use my Western-trained ear rather than an exact measuring tool in coming up with these equivalents because the ear can play tricks, and I would like not only to impart the impression the music gives to someone accustomed primarily to the diatonic scale, but also to show just how misleading that impression is. For example, pitch 2, notated here as E♭, is actually closer to E in the tuning I have used as my model, but I have chosen E♭ for pitch 2 because the resulting contour

7. By "strong" I mean that it is conceptually more weighted. This is not generally audible through accentuation in the same manner that strong beats usually are in Western music. In fact, in a given melodic or rhythmic part, the strong beat may be empty, even where there is no feeling of syncopation.

8. I have based these on the particular gamelan set used in recording *Gamelan de Solo* (see the Companion Recordings). As pointed out in chapter 7 (in the section titled "Pitch Relations"), one would very likely come up with a different approximation if basing the transcription on a different gamelan, or on singing or *rebab* playing by different people.

is what Western ears trick themselves into hearing. This has to do with the overall gestalt of the scale. Westerners usually hear the interval from 3 to 2 as a whole step, and from 2 to 1 as a half step, even though both of them are actually closer to three quarters of a step (from 3 to 1 is quite close to a minor third, with pitch 2 being more or less equidistant from both 1 and 3). In other words, if you ask someone with a Western-oriented ear (including many Indonesians) to sing back a melody played to them in the *pélog nem* mode, those are the Western intervals they are likely to sing (the original *pélog* melody will sound highly out of tune to them, rather than the other way around).

Note, as well, the discrepancy in how metric units are shown. Whereas in the cipher notation, the end-stressed metric units of four beats (called *gåtrås*) are grouped together, in the staff notation the strong note of each *gåtrå* is placed with notes belonging to another unit. In my view, this is even more of a distortion, and much harder to compensate for, than is the pitch problem.

As already mentioned, there is an opposing conception of meter to this basic principle of end stress, which shows up at the level of beat division and subdivision. It is always present in Kepatihan notation (unless, of course, there are no beat subdivisions), but is only sometimes conceptually present in the music. That is, sometimes the notation in this regard distorts Javanese rhythmic perception, and sometimes it reflects it. The equivalent of an eighth- or sixteenth-note (where a quarter-note gets one beat) is shown in Kepatihan notation by a single or double beam connecting the relevant notes into a single beat, as in staff notation. This practice had already been adopted by Rousseau and was retained when the system spread to Asia. It goes against the fundamental organization of Javanese meter, where divisions of the beat belong to the *next* beat rather than the preceding one. Where it coincides with Javanese musical practice is in singing, where the division of the beat is often tied to the preceding beat through melisma (as in European

FIGURE T.1. Kepatihan and staff notation for *ladrang Sri Sinubå, laras pélog pathet nem.*

music). A similar phenomenon occurs in the *rebab* (spike fiddle) and *suling* (flute) parts with respect to bowing and tonguing.[9] A basic rhythmic contrast can be made, then, between percussive instruments, which die out after being struck, and those vocal and voice-like parts in which a sustained tone is possible.

In *gérong* (unison male chorus) parts and, exceptionally, in *balungan* (outline melody) notation, the first subdivision of the beat into half-beats is shown without beams. This practice demonstrates the extent to which beams can go against the prevailing rhythmic organizing principle. Consider, for instance, an excerpt from *gendhing Elå-Elå Kalibeber* (see figure 3.18 for the rest of the piece) in figure T.2, as notated in two different Javanese collections of gamelan music notation. In the first set in the figure, taken from Gitosaprodjo (1997:26–27), beams are avoided and the notes are grouped as they would be metrically felt. In the second set in the figure, more usual way (Mloyowidodo 1976:90–91), beams are used for half beats, as is more usual, with the awkward

1̇ 1̇ . .   1̇ 2̇ 1̇ 6   3 3 . . 3 3 . .   3 3 5 2 . 3 . ⑤
6 3 . 2 2 3 6 5

1̇ 1̇ . .   1̇ 2̇ 1̇ 63   3 .3 3 .3   35 2 3 ⑤6
3 22 36 5

FIGURE T.2. Two ways of notating an excerpt from *gendhing Elå-Elå Kalibeber* using Kepatihan notation and staff notation for the same passage.

T/1

3 5 . 6 2 . 1 6̣ . 1223 1 . 12165̣
su- ma- wur gam- bir me- la- thi

FIGURE T.3. Kepatihan and staff notation for excerpt from *gérong* part to *ladrang Sri Sinubå.*

9. For a fuller discussion of Javanese meter, see Benamou 1989.

result that a pitch 6, which belongs metrically to the next gong unit, is left hanging by itself after the previous gong.[10] Note how much more similar the second one is to the transcription into staff notation that follows.

Melismas are shown by ties under the notes, or in typed notation by underscoring. The excerpt in figure T.2 is an example of *gérong* (male choral) singing in *pélog* that is taken, like our last example, from *ladrang Sri Sinubå* (note that the words are not specific to the piece, and can be replaced with others at will).

This passage would normally be sung with melodic ornaments not usually shown in Kepatihan notation, since an experienced singer would know instinctively where to add them and there is often variation from singer to singer (even the written notes are not always adhered to in performance, and there may be different written versions as well). But since my musical examples throughout the book are descriptive rather than prescriptive, I have included symbols for ornaments where appropriate. The symbols I use are similar to and inspired by those used in eighteenth-century European music to graphically represent the shapes of the melodic elements that are added. These are as follows (note that the intervals within ornaments are usually smaller than those between the indicated scale steps—in other words, they are microtonal; they are also internally quite rapid):

5 ^ 6 = 5 $^{6\,5}$ 6 — T/2

$\hat{5}$ 6 = 5 $^{6\,5}$ 6 — T/3

6 ~ 5 = 6 $^{7\,6\,5\,6}$ 5 — T/4

$\tilde{6}$ 5 = ^{7}6 $^{5\,6}$ 5 — T/5

6 ˅ 5 = 6 $^{5\,6}$ 5 — T/6

2 ~˅ 1 = 2 ^ ˅ ˅ 1 = 2 $^{3\,2\,1\,2\,1\,2}$ 1 — T/7

5 ˋ6 = 5 ^{7}6 — T/8

Finally, in vocal and *rebab* parts in the *sléndro* tuning it is fairly common to sing or play notes that are outside of *sléndro* proper and that evoke *pélog*. This is variously called *minor, minir, madenda, penangis, barang miring*, or just plain *miring* ("slanted"). This last term seems to refer to the practice of putting a slash through the altered *sléndro* note to indicate that it has been either lowered or raised. Sometimes these are differentiated by the direction of the slant, but more

10. The only alteration I've made is to place more space between four-beat units in the first example, so that it would match up better with the second one.

commonly there is nothing in the notation to indicate which of these is meant. I shall differentiate between the two, with a rising slant indicating a raised tone and a falling slant representing a lowered tone.

T/9 *plain sléndro:* 3 6 5

T/10 *miring:* 3 6̸ 5 = 3 ♭6 5

COMPANION RECORDINGS

Throughout the book, two different sets of recordings are indicated in the margins. The first of these is taken partly from lessons and interviews with my teachers and consists mostly of short snippets of singing that are transcribed in the text. The symbol ◉ indicates these. Those interested may listen to these recordings at www.oup.com/us/rasa.

Below is a listing of the online examples. All examples were performed by me in October 2008, except where noted.

Track T/1. Excerpt from the *gérong* part to *ladrang Sri Sinubå.*

Track T/2. Upward *gregel*: 5 ^ 6

Track T/3. Upward *gregel* on the beat: 5̂ 6

Track T/4. Turn-like figure: 6 ~ 5

Track T/5. Turn-like figure on the beat: 6̃ 5

Track T/6. Downward *gregel*: 6 ˇ 5

Track T/7. Turn-like figure followed by a downward *gregel*: 2 ~ˇ 1

Track T/8. *Kawilan*, in *rebab* terminology (upper-neighbor grace note): 5 `6

Track T/9. Three-note motive in plain *sléndro* tuning, played on the *gendèr.*

Track T/10. Three-note motive using *miring*, with the *gendèr* playing the first and third notes of the motive.

Track 3/1. A short motive occurring in a large number of vocal pieces, in two versions: one "listless," the other *gagah* (manly) or *prenès* (coquettish). Suhartå, in Jakarta, June 19, 1991.

Track 4/1. *Sekar måcåpat Dhandhanggulå, lelagon Buminatan.* Sutarman, in Solo, June 6, 1992.

Track 4/2. *Sekar måcåpat Dhandhanggulå Tlutur.* Sutarman, in Solo, June 6, 1992.

Track 5/1. Excerpt from *båwå sekar tengahan Kenyå Kedhiri, laras sléndro pathet sångå,* performed with four different variants (and a fifth that is only slightly different from the fourth). Suhartå, in Solo, March 11, 1990.

Track 6/1. *Ladrang Dhengklung, laras pélog pathet limå.* An example of a *gendhing soran* (loud-style piece, in which no voices and none of the softer instruments are used) or *gendhing bonangan* (piece in which the *bonang* is the melodic leader). Source: *Roning Tawang: Gendhing-gendhing Instrumental.* Ira Record cassette number WD 584. Recorded in the 1980s (?) by an ad hoc group from PKJT ASKI (Surakarta).

Track 6/2. The *balungan* to *ladrang Gégot, laras pélog pathet nem,* as sung by Wignyåsaputrå in Solo, June 19, 1992.

Track 6/3. The influence of vocal *garap* on the *rasa* of a *gendhing.* Wignyåsaputrå, in Solo, June 19, 1992.

Track 6/4. Example of *rujak-rujakan* (couplet nominally about spicy fruit salad sung by the *peshindhèn*) Wignyåsaputrå in Solo, June 19, 1992.

Track 6/5. An example of a sad *balungan* and how its sadness relates to the vocal part. Wignyåsaputrå, in Solo, June 19, 1992.

Track 7/1. An example of *balungan kadhalan* (an excerpt from *gendhing bonang Babar Layar, kethuk* 4 *kerep, laras pélog pathet limå*) as sung by Wignyåsaputrå in Solo, June 19, 1992.

Track 7/2. *Gendéran kembang tibå.*

Track 7/3. *Gendéran ukel pancaran.*

Track 7/4. *Pipilan* with the strong beats filled in. Marc Benamou, *bonang barung;* Micah Sommers, *slenthem.* Richmond, Indiana, October 11, 2008.

Track 7/5. *Pipilan* with rests on the strong beats. Marc Benamou, *bonang barung;* Micah Sommers, *slenthem.* Richmond, Indiana, October 11, 2008.

Track B/1. Excerpt from *ladrang Dhengklung* (Track 6/1), *irâmå tanggung.*

Track B/2. Excerpt from *ladrang Dhengklung* (Track 6/1), *irâmå dados.*

Track B/3. Excerpt from *ladrang Dhengklung* (Track 6/1), transition from *irâmå tanggung* to *irâmå dados.*

The second set of recordings consists of the four-CD box set *Indonésie, Java Centre: Gamelan de Solo: Le jeu des sentiments (Indonesia, Central Java: Solonese Gamelan: A Garland of Moods)* (Inédit W 260125) put out by La Maison des Cultures du Monde in 2006; I have shortened its title to *Gamelan de Solo.* It was recorded with this book in mind in 2003, at my instigation, with much help from Rahayu Supanggah and sound engineers from STSI. I have used the symbol ◉ to refer the reader to a corresponding passage. For instance, ◉ IV:2, 00:35–2:10 would mean CD 4, track 2, starting at thirty-five seconds and going up to two minutes, ten seconds. Options for acquiring the CD set or MP3 versions of the tracks as well as a link to download the liner notes are provided on the Web site of La Maison des Cultures du Monde at www.mcm.asso.fr, the direct link being www.mcm.asso.fr/site02/inedit/cd260125.htm.

The complete contents of the four CDs of *Gamelan de Solo* are given below. Note that greater detail is provided here than is usually given in such listings, and a few important omissions from the liner notes have been rectified. The capitalized words are proper names of specific pieces, whereas lowercase words indicate genres, tuning, melodic modes, gong-cycle structures, and the like. In view of the great concentration of technical terms, please refer to the glossary at the end of the book, or to the section "Names of Pieces and Songs" on pages xxxi–xxiii.

CD I

Track 1: *senggréngan—ådångiyah—bukå rebab—gendhing Kombang Mårå, kethuk 2 kerep minggah 4—pathetan Limå Wantah; laras pélog pathet limå*

Track 2: *senggréngan—bukå rebab—gendhing Elå-Elå Kalibeber, kethuk 2 kerep minggah 4—pathetan Sångå Jugag; laras sléndro pathet sångå*

Track 3: *bukå rebab—ketawang Sinom Wénigonjing; laras pélog pathet nem*

CD II

Track 1: *senggréngan—pathetan Nem Ageng—bukå rebab—gendhing Glondhong Pring, kethuk 2 kerep minggah ladrang Gudasih—ketawang Sumedhang—pathetan Nem Jugag; laras pélog pathet nem* (this version emulates the way it would be performed in the Kraton—the palace of the senior line of the Solonese royal family)

Track 2: *senggréngan—pathetan Sångå Wantah—båwå sekar ageng Rårâbéntrok—gendhing Gambir Sawit, kethuk 2 kerep minggah 4—pathet sendhon Abimanyu—srepeg—palaran Pangkur—srepeg—pathetan Sångå Jugag; laras sléndro pathet sångå*

Track 3: *bukå kendhang—srepeg—palaran Dhandhanggulå Pengantèn Anyar—palaran Sinom—palaran Durmå—srepeg*

CD III

Track 1: *bukå rebab—gendhing Laler Mengeng, kethuk 2 awis/kerep minggah ladrang Tlutur—pathetan Sångå Ngelik; laras sléndro pathet sångå*

Track 2: *bukå celuk—ketawang Subåkaståwå; laras pélog pathet nem* (Nartosabdho's choral arrangement)

Track 3: *bukå bonang—ladrang Gégot* (with *kébar*); *laras pélog pathet nem*

Track 4: *senggréngan—pathetan Barang Jugag—båwå sekar ageng Banjaransari—ladrang Pangkur* (with *kébar* and *jengglèng*); *laras pélog pathet barang*

CD IV

Track 1: *bukå kendhang—Ayak-Ayak* (as it might be played at the beginning of a shadow play); *laras sléndro pathet manyurå*

Track 2: *sendhon Pananggalan; laras sléndro pathet nem*

Track 3: *senggréngan—bukå rebab—gendhing Titipati kethuk kerep 2 minggah 4—pathetan Nem Jugag* (concert version); *laras sléndro pathet nem*

Track 4: *senggréngan—bukå rebab—gendhing Glondhong Pring, kethuk 2 kerep minggah ladrang Gudasih* (Nartosabdho's choral arrangement)*—pathetan Lasem; laras pélog pathet nem*

Track 5: *ådå-ådå Greget Saut Mataram; laras sléndro pathet nem*

Track 6: *bukå kendhang—srepeg—lagu dolanan Ménthog-Ménthog—lagu dolanan Kupu Kuwi—lagu dolanan Koning-Koning—srepeg*

Track 7: *bukå celuk—jineman Uler kambang; laras sléndro pathet sångå*

Track 8: *bukå celuk—jineman Gathik Glindhing; laras sléndro pathet sångå*

Track 9: *ådå-ådå Haståkuswålå; laras sléndro pathet sångå*

Track 10: *pathet sendhon Abimanyu; laras sléndro pathet sångå*

Track 11: *bukå kendhang—Ayak-Ayak* (as it might be performed towards the end of a shadow play); *laras sléndro pathet manyurå*

RASA

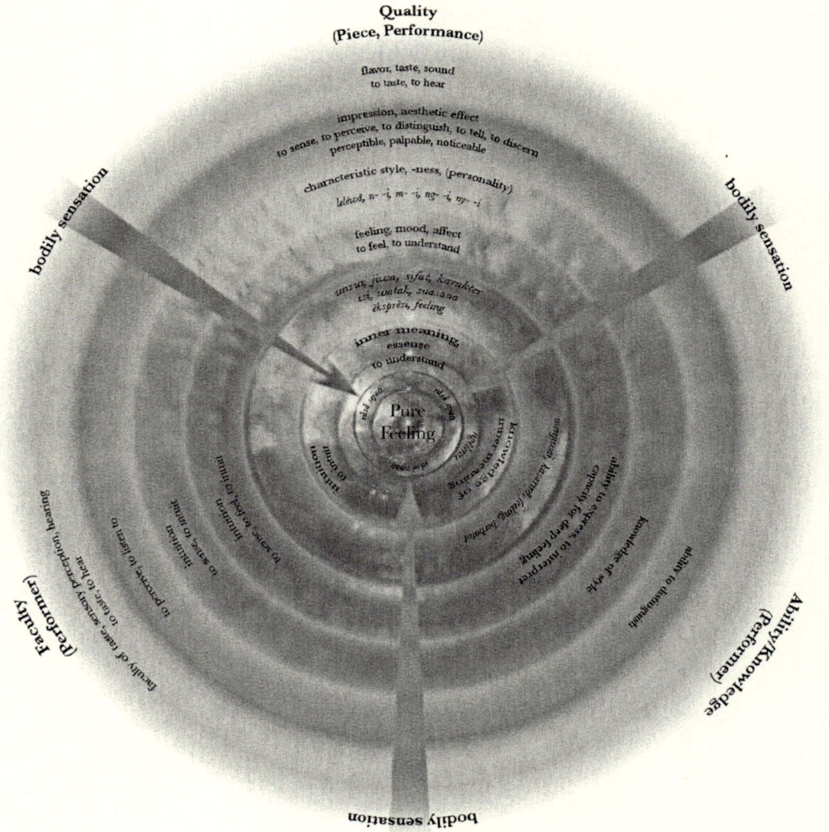
Quality
(Piece, Performance)
flavor, taste, sound
to taste, to hear
impression, aesthetic effect
to sense, to perceive, to distinguish, to tell, to discern
perceptible, palpable, noticeable
characteristic style, -ness, (personality)
feeling, mood, affect
to feel, to understand
unsur, jiwa, sifat, karakter
watak, suasana
ekspresi, feeling
inner meaning
essence
to understand
Pure
Feeling
bodily sensation
bodily sensation
bodily sensation
Faculty
(Performer)
faculty of taste, sensory perception, hearing
to taste, to hear
to perceive, to listen to
intuition
to sense, to think
intuition
to think
Ability/Knowledge
(Performer)
ability to distinguish
knowledge of style
ability to express, to interpret
capacity for deep feeling
knowledge of
inner meaning

ONE

THE MUSICAL SCENE IN SOLO

THE CITY OF SOLO

Solo is a crowded city of about half a million people.[1] It consists mostly of densely packed one-story dwellings, with storefronts in two- and three- story buildings lining many of the main thoroughfares. Situated in a rich alluvial plain near the geographic center of Java, it is surrounded by rice and tobacco fields and agriculturally based villages of various sizes. It is thus a market center for the surrounding countryside (I have heard it said that the daytime population of 700,000 drops down to 400,000 at night), and the city has one of the largest textile industries in Indonesia. All political power has been in the hands of the national government since Independence in 1945 (even city employees are national civil servants).

Historically important and still relevant to Solonese self-definition are the city's two active royal courts, which, first under Dutch control, and even more so since Independence, have served a primarily ceremonial role. Both of these

1. This chapter is meant primarily for readers who have had no direct contact with central Java or who have not read widely about Javanese gamelan traditions. Much of the material here is available elsewhere, but I know of no other overview that assembles all of the elements that will be necessary for a full understanding of what follows in subsequent chapters. The emphasis is on the situation from 1989 to 1992, my primary period of research, but some of my comments are based on a brief visit in 2003 and on six months spent teaching in Solo in 2006. I have tried to use tense to indicate whether a situation has changed or has stayed the same, but whenever I am unsure I have preferred the past tense. Marc Perlman's 1999 ethnographically rich article "The Traditional Javanese Performing Arts in the Twilight of the New Order: Two Letters from Solo" provides evocative and nicely contextualized snapshots of the Solonese musical scene in 1997 and 1998. The situation he describes, roughly midway between my departure in 1992 and my return in 2003, seemed closer to the latter than to the former. The traumatic riots of 1998 and the severe economic hardship that led up to and followed the ousting of Suharto from power made for a bleak picture at the time. This bleakness was still heavy in the air in 2003. By 2006, however, my impression was that Solo was beginning to recover, although the earthquake that was centered south of neighboring Yogyakarta brought its own challenges (primarily in the form of aiding the injured and those whose homes were destroyed just a few miles away—there was relatively little damage in Solo itself). This recovery was not only economic, but psychological and musical as well, and it seemed to me during this last stay that Solo is the most fundamentally unchanging city I know.

are housed in vast eighteenth-century palaces and are headed by sovereigns who retain the respect and allegiance of a certain proportion of the general populace. The *Susuhunan* (or *Sunan*) Pakubuwånå (currently number XIII, in a contested succession), considered the king of Solo, is the head of the senior line. His palace is the Karaton Suråkartå Hadiningrat, called the Kraton for short. The junior line is headed by the sovereign prince Pangéran Adipati Ariå Mangkunegårå (currently number IX), whose palace is the Purå Mangkunegaran (or, simply, the Mangkunegaran).

The present monarchy traces its lineage back to the prophet Mohammed on one side and the mythical heroes of the Mahabharata on the other (and, curiously, through both sides, back to Adam).[2] More recently, it looks back to a glorious past in its progenitor, the large and powerful kingdom of Mataram (founded, or rather resurrected, toward the end of the sixteenth century). Around 1745, Mataram's royal seat was moved from Kartåsurå to a new location eleven kilometers to the east.[3] The new site was a village called Sålå, which was displaced to build the new Kraton ("royal palace," from *ratu*, "king"). The place was renamed Suråkartå Hadiningrat, which is why the city still has two names, *Surakarta* and *Solo* (in their Indonesian spellings), of which the latter is more common in everyday speech.

The reason for the move was that the old palace had been occupied by a series of invaders. Kartåsurå was thus contaminated and its symbolic power as the center of the universe was rendered suspect.[4] As a result of these calamities, the *sunan*'s (monarch's) legitimacy was called into question, and several princes broke away, hoping to challenge the throne. In 1749 Pakubuwånå II died, shortly after turning control of his kingdom over to the VOC (Vereenigde Oost-Indische Compagnie, or the Dutch East India Company), in the hopes that this would secure the throne for his son. Near the end of a decade-long war of succession, a treaty was signed between Prince Mangkubumi (Pakubuwånå II's brother) and the VOC, in which the former kingdom of Mataram was divided in half; two years later the half belonging to the *sunan* was divided again. To the Sunanate of Surakarta, then, were added the Sultanate of Yogyakarta (the seat of which was sixty kilometers to the southwest) and the Mangkunegaran Principality (in Solo). Yogyakarta was later divided into the Sultanate and the Pakualaman,[5] so that both court cities each have a senior and a junior royal line.

2. See, for instance, Sindusastra 1978 and Brandon 1970:17.

3. Much of what follows is based on Houben 1989. See also Soepomo and Ricklefs 1967, Larson 1987, and Ricklefs 1981. Pemberton 1994 gives a detailed account of the move from Kartåsurå, with quotations from various Javanese manuscripts.

4. See Behrend 1989.

5. The similarity in the royal names of the four sovereigns of Yogyakarta and Surakarta is not mere coincidence. They all reflect the concentric model of kingship inherited from India: Pakubuwånå means "nail of the world or universe"; Mangkunegårå means "holding the realm in one's lap"; Hamengkubuwånå, the name of the Sultan of Yogyakarta, means "holding the world or universe in one's lap"; and Pakualam means "nail of the realm (or world)."

MUSIC AT THE PALACES

The Solonese royal houses have had no political power for some time.[6] Nevertheless, there remains a certain rivalry between Solo and Yogyakarta, as well as between the Kasunanan (the *sunan*'s palace—another way of referring to the Kraton) and the Mangkunegaran. Each court, as well as the Kepatihan (the *patih*'s, or prime minister's palace—now defunct), developed its own distinctive musical style. The differences, which are beginning to attenuate, involve(d) repertoire, to some extent, as well as characteristic ways of working out pieces (*garap*).

At least up until national independence, the court traditions were the standards that defined excellence not only in music but in all of the Javanese arts, including literature, dance, shadow puppets and puppetry, *keris*es (elaborate iron daggers), and batik cloth.[7] The last truly opulent reign in Solo was that of Sunan Pakubuwånå X (reigned 1893–1939). He had several thousand *abdi dalem* (servants and retainers), a fair number of whom were musicians and dancers.[8] Court music was distinguished not only by the quality of the players and singers, but also by the sheer size and number of the various bronze ensembles that go under the name of gamelan. Among these were (and are) certain spiritually powerful heirlooms, called *pusåkå*s, which constitute one of the ruler's sources of potency and legitimacy in the eyes of his subjects.[9]

Over the past few decades, the courts have steadily lost both in prestige and in their power to command respect, devotion, and reverence. During the 1950s, 1960s, and 1970s, many of the great court musicians were hired away by the

6. The Sultan of Yogyakarta, by contrast, is also the governor of his district. See Larson 1987 for the history and implications of this important difference.

7. Not everyone shares this view—some Javanese take a revisionist approach, claiming that the excellence of the palace arts, based on oral reports going back to the turn of the twentieth century, is something of a myth.

8. For instance, he had one hundred *bedhåyå* dancers alone (Soeratman 1989:87). (A *bedhåyå* is a sacred, courtly, choreographed group dance with abstract, esoteric symbolism; in Solo it is danced by nine—or sometimes seven—young women.)

9. At least as late as the early 1990s (and perhaps still today) the reverence afforded these *pusåkå*s was considerable. On the eve of Javanese New Year, villagers would flock into the city. A dense throng assembled in the palaces, awaiting the moment when those present could fight over the water in which the sacred gongs and other *pusåkå*s had been washed, hoping to take home some of the spiritually charged liquid for its curative powers. Equally telling is a comment made to me by one of my teachers, the late Sukanto, a habitué of the Kraton, upon whom the *sunan* had bestowed a noble title for his service to the court. He had instructed me to *sembah* every time I sat down or was about to rise from the marble floor of the main *pendhåpå* (a large pavilion, open on three sides, with a high-pitched roof). A *sembah* is an act of obeisance performed by joining one's hands as in a typical Christian prayer position, and raising them before one's face, thumbs pointing inward and fingers pointing outward (while to a Westerner this suggests an attitude of prayer, its meaning is closer to that of genuflection). According to Sukanto, it was not to the ruler (who, at any rate, was usually absent) that one paid one's respects, but rather to the *pusåkå*s that are housed in the inner chambers.

new centers of gamelan tradition—the local station of the national radio network (Radio Republik Indonesia, or RRI) and the newly formed government-run arts schools. By the time of my first visit, most of these musicians had died. Very few of the old-style *abdi dalem* are left in the courts, which have consequently resorted more and more to bringing in outside musicians.[10]

Of the two palaces in Solo, the Mangkunegaran, in the 1980s and 1990s, had maintained what were generally regarded to be higher musical standards. Several musicians (including one at the Kraton!) told me that the playing at the Mangkunegaran was technically more proficient, and it certainly did sound more polished (even foreigners with only a casual acquaintance with the tradition sensed this). This was due in part to its having always been more open both to modernization and to the outside world in general. It is quite a bit smaller than the Kraton and was visibly more prosperous.[11] Its musicians, nearly all of whom could be described as part time, were certainly not able to live on what they were paid. Yet they received far more than the merest gesture of recompense they get at the Kraton.[12]

Conversely, though, whereas the level of musicianship at the Kraton was generally weaker than at the Mangkunegaran, the participants at the former tended to be more motivated by devotion to their king and to court tradition, and by the unique atmosphere they found at the palace. This last factor should not be underestimated—one of the musicians I spoke to mentioned it as his main reason for attending rehearsals and performances there. True, by refusing to adapt to the modern world, the Kraton may have dug its own grave. But when one enters the series of portals, progressing from the monumental outer

10. For a good description of the dance situation in the Kraton in the 1970s and 1980s, see Brakel-Papenhuijzen 1992.

11. Among other things, former President Suharto's wife traced her ancestry (remotely) back to a Mangkunegårå prince, and her patronage was said to help keep the court solvent. The Kraton, on the other hand, which still nostalgically considers itself to be, at least spiritually, the center of the (now nonexistent) Kingdom of Java, is perhaps seen by the national government as stealing some of the allegiance that is its due. It is thus in the interest of the administration to limit the Kraton's resources. (There was even talk that after the death of Pakubuwånå XII no successor would be named. This, as it turned out, was not the case, although there is contention as to his legitimate successor.)

12. I do not have exact figures for the Mangkunegaran, but I am quite sure that, as of 1992, the musicians there were paid in the thousands of rupiahs for a performance (perhaps two or three U.S. dollars, which was a day's wage for a manual laborer). One Kraton musician told me he was paid the following amounts: Rp 200 (10¢—enough, at that time, for a snack or a very cheap meal) for a regular rehearsal in the big audience hall; Rp 1000 (50¢) for a rehearsal in preparation for a performance; Rp 500 (25¢—an average pedicab fare) for *Monggang* (a ceremonial gamelan played weekly) and other regular required functions. On many occasions I witnessed what I took to be a mild form of protest at Kraton events. Musicians in Java are usually paid in cash at, or immediately after, a concert. When the time came for musicians at the Kraton to be handed their allocation, which usually happened during the performance, the music was marred by unduly loud chinking noises, as they accepted their stacks of coins (the idea being, I presume, that paper money, by contrast, would have been silent).

ones to the progressively more intimate inner ones, and finally reaches the vast, infinitely calm great courtyard—with its black sand brought from the dangerous south coast, the realm of the powerful spirit queen of the South Sea; its tall, octagonal tower at the top of which each successive ruler weds the spirit queen; its three *bangsal*s (rectangular "bandstands"); its rows of slow-growing *sawo kecik* trees (a variety of sapodilla); its long, weatherworn loggias delimiting the space; and its magnificent, gilded *pendhåpå*,[13] in which the most important rehearsals and ceremonies are held (and in which, formerly, the *sunan* received his officials)—one then enters another era and leaves behind the worries and commotion of modern living. It is the only place in the city where one does not hear the almost constant revving of combustion engines, and where one feels out of place wearing Western dress.

The profound tranquility of the Kraton has a direct effect on the music played there. Sukanto (see footnote 9 and the section on my teachers at the end of this chapter) once told me that it is no longer possible to play calm pieces in a truly calm way: the world is just too *ramai* (lively, bustling, noisy, crowded). He was born in 1922, and the population of Java had nearly tripled during his lifetime. Along the same lines, Sudarsono of Kentingan once told me that everything at the Kraton is more subdued, including the colors that Kraton people wear, and that this influences the way they play. No wonder, then, that the music heard there, for all its technical faults, was often said to possess a unique *råså*, or inner feeling.

In 2006 I observed many of the ceremonial activities during the week of *sekatèn*, which celebrates the prophet Mohammed's birthday. These involve an elaborate procession, complete with gamelans and enormous decorated rice-mountains (all carried on poles), from the inner courtyard out through successive doorways and over to the royal mosque. They also include the almost continual sounding of the two massive *sekatèn* gamelans in alternation. I am happy to report that as of 2006 the Kraton, to put it crudely, still put on a great show.

OTHER INSTITUTIONAL SETTINGS

The RRI (radio station) musicians, in contrast with the palace musicians, are all civil servants, and so could, around 1990, almost live off their wages. They were probably the most technically competent musicians attached to an institution,

13. A *pendhåpå* is a large pavilion, open on three sides, with a high-pitched roof supported by many wooden columns, a bit like an enormous, elegant, banister-less front porch. The one in question was reconstructed after the original was destroyed by fire in 1985 (see Pemberton 1994:181–89, Behrend 1985, and Florida 1993:46; for photos of the *pendhåpå*, see Tirtaamidjaja 1967 and Florida 1992). Another elaborate *pendhåpå*, the "banquet hall" immediately to the south, had not been rebuilt as of 1992, and only the empty surface of its foundation remained. It has now been reconstructed, and is again being used for official dinners.

since they spent most of their working time playing or singing. Activity at RRI has diminished considerably in recent years, however, and many of its best musicians have retired. In the early days of the radio station, it was very much dominated by experts from the Kraton and the Mangkunegaran, but it gradually forged its own style of playing midway between the "classical" court ways and the more popular, modern idioms favored by the shadow-puppet troupes. Nearly all of the best-known *pesindhèns*, or female vocalists, of the cassette era worked at some point for RRI.

The other major institution, STSI (Sekolah Tinggi Seni Indonesia [National Advanced School for the Arts])—now called ISI (Institut Seni Indonesia [National Institute for the Arts])—also started out as an offshoot of the court traditions. Called ASKI (Akademi Seni Karawitan Indonesia [National Academy of Traditional Javanese Arts]) when it was founded, in 1964, it had a predecessor in KoKar (Konservatori Karawitan), now SMKI (Sekolah Menengah Karawitan Indonesia [National High School of Traditional Javanese Music]), which was founded in 1950. These two institutions (the high school and the institute), while to some extent cut off from the rest of the gamelan world, have revolutionized *karawitan*[14] in several important ways. First among them is the increased reliance on notation.[15]

Notation for gamelan music was first invented, as a result of Dutch influence, in the late nineteenth century. Before then, and for some time afterward, the music was composed, performed, and learned aurally. In and around Solo one still encounters village musicians who cannot read music, but they are relatively few, and they generally seem to regard this as a handicap. Santosa (1990:ch. 4–5) reports that, out of 175 Solonese musicians surveyed, 82 percent said that the best way to learn gamelan music was through notation or through a combination of notation and imitation. Presumably even a higher percentage would say that one ought at least to know how to read notation—being nonliterate in Java, as elsewhere, is a matter of shame. Suhartå told me that nonreading village singers, when performing in a competition, hold notation in front of them—often open to the wrong page or upside-down—hoping it will look like they are singing from it like everyone else. I have observed the same phenomenon in more relaxed settings as well.

Even though notation has existed for over a century, it took several decades before it was used as a pedagogical tool. At first it was relied upon by musicians only as an aid to memorizing the melodic outline of a piece (the only

14. *Karawitan* is the word used in Java to refer to traditional gamelan music. "Gamelan" itself refers only to the instruments—not to the music performed on them or the people who do the performing (although in English it is sometimes used in these other senses). See Perlman 1991b for more on the origin and uses of the term *karawitan*.

15. For the definitive treatment of this shift from an oral to a written tradition, see J. Becker 1980. See also Perlman 1991a and 1994, Sumarsam 1995, Brinner 1995, and Lindsay 1985.

melody that was written down). None of the more complex parts were notated, and it was certainly never used in performance. With the founding of KoKar, new pedagogical techniques were sought, with which students could learn all the instrumental parts in a relatively short time. The shift from informal to institutionalized music education had begun several decades earlier, with the establishment of music schools, for the educated classes, that were privately run by court musicians. At KoKar, however, notation was used for the first time in actually learning to play. Gradually it became more acceptable to use notation (of the melodic outline) during rehearsals and performances.[16] Nevertheless, there remains a strong oral element in *karawitan*, even when notation is used. I know from studying, rehearsing, and performing with Javanese musicians, that they relate to the written notes differently than I do, as a Western classically trained musician. Even when reading from a vocal "score" (in which all of the singers' notes are written out), they usually rely on it more as a mnemonic aid than as a blueprint to be slavishly followed. (Mistakes in the notation, for instance, do not seem to bother them.) Similarly, when I memorize from notation, my memory is entirely visual, whereas Javanese musicians seem to remember pieces largely aurally, whether they've learned them using their eyes or their ears. Moreover, talented Javanese musicians have an astonishing ability to absorb and remember the gestalt of extremely complex parts, just by listening to them in real time, even when approaching an instrument for the first time. They are not thrown off by the many variants their teachers often put in every time they repeat the same passage. By contrast, when I (and all other Westerners I have talked to about this) learn a part on a new instrument without notation, we need to sit down with an audio recording and imitate it exactly, note by note, playing and replaying the recording in bits and pieces.

It must be said that not all musicians trained at SMKI and STSI/ISI rely on notation to the same degree. Those who depend on it more are generally hindered by one of the following factors: a poorer memory than most, laziness, less time spent rehearsing and performing, or lack of experience outside school. This last point is of great importance, for virtually all the successful musicians who were conservatory trained had had a solid foundation before they began their formal schooling. This foundation was in most cases acquired the old-fashioned way: joining a group, and, over a period of years, gradually making one's way up from simpler to more complex parts. (In a traditional setting, the less-talented musicians never leave the simpler parts, or else simply stop participating.) The years spent on the simpler parts (typically *kenong* or

16. Attitudes during my main period of research were at best ambivalent. Many musicians still frowned on using notation in performance, or even in rehearsal. See, for instance, Sutton in Perlman 1992:17–18. See also chapter 4. My comparatively limited interactions with musicians in 2003 and 2006 seemed to indicate that there is less and less shame associated with relying on notation.

saron)[17] were spent watching and listening, learning the repertoire, and absorbing the musical language in much the same way that children learn languages—that is, through observation, imitation, and participation rather than through conscious analysis.

Besides new pedagogical techniques and the increased use of notation, the music schools introduced the most radical departure from accepted practice in recent history: consciously avant-garde music. As far back as anyone knows, gamelan music, like all living traditions, has been in a constant state of flux. Some aspects of current practice that may be taken for granted as permanent characteristics of the music, such as solo vocal introductions (*båwås*), the use of the *ciblon* drum[18] in palace pieces, or the linking together of pieces into long suites, were added to the tradition in the last hundred years or so. Conversely, some practices that were common in the not-so distant past have died out. And musicians have always, it seems, enjoyed trying out new, amusing, or even shocking interpretations on each other. However, the notion of creating music whose sole purpose is to be innovative, regardless of who might want to listen, may be distinct from previous developments.

Judith Becker, in her book *Traditional Music in Modern Java*, argues that some of the innovations in gamelan composition since Independence were unprecedented in kind. These included the introduction of harmony (gamelan music had been essentially polyphonic and heterophonic[19]), and of new meters that contrasted with the exclusively binary organization that had previously dominated, a redefining of the composer's role in musical creation, and the reinterpretation of the modal system. The music she analyzed, by the composers

17. The *kenong* is a large pot-gong within the gamelan that is responsible for playing a sparse time-marking part, whereas the *saron* is a one-octave, single-mallet metallophone with trough resonator. Rahayu Supanggah (in Perlman 1992) denies that there is any set order for learning, but also says that typically one starts with the *kethuk* (single-toned pot gong) and then moves on to other instruments that carry little melodic responsibility (with the exception of the drum, which has its own form of responsibility).

18. The *ciblon* is a medium-sized, double-headed drum used to accompany dance and played in most lighthearted pieces. The lively, varied patterns played on it are rapid and syncopated and incorporate a large number of distinct strokes.

19. I use these terms as a shorthand for something that is not easily described etically. By "polyphonic" I mean music that consists of several melodies that are combined into a unified whole. In gamelan music the unified whole is organized melodically (primarily around important melodic tones—sort of like a Schenkerian middle ground) rather than harmonically. It is thus debatable whether *karawitan* is heterophonic or polyphonic, since, for Western music to be considered polyphonic, it must be organized harmonically. As Perlman has pointed out (2004:62–74), in some cases relations between parts seem like textbook cases of heterophony (simultaneous variation of a single melody), but in others the parts seem too distinct to be considered mere variants of the same thing: each instrument, each vocal part follows its own norms, its own dialect (a metaphor I have borrowed from Rahayu Supanggah); some of these dialects are closer to each other than others. What is clear, though, is that harmonic considerations rarely enter into a musician's choice of what notes to play (one notable exception is on the *gendèr* [double-mallet metallophone with tube resonators]). For some of the colonialist implications of the term *heterophony* as applied to gamelan music see Perlman 2004:62 and 211.

Nartosabdho and Wasitodipuro, can for the most part be categorized as *gendhing kréasi baru* ("newly created pieces"—often shortened to *gendhing kréasi*). These pieces, while often quite innovative, are generally in a lighthearted, catchy style based on *dolanan* (children's game songs).[20]

III:2
IV:6

Even more radical than *gendhing kréasi* are the developments that go under the rubric of *gamelan kontèmporèr* (contemporary gamelan), which, according to Rustopo (1991:13–15), began in the 1970s[21] with the founding of the PKJT (Pusat Kesenian Jawa Tengah—"Arts Center of Central Java"), a government-run institution attached to ASKI that was devoted to experimentation in the arts. The PKJT was the brainchild of Gendhon Humardani, the founder of ASKI, who came to believe very strongly that the only way for the Javanese arts to survive was (1) for trained artists to bring them in line with the zeitgeist of the modern era; and (2) to raise the general public's consciousness so that it could appreciate the new art forms (Rustopo 1991:84).[22] Whereas Humardani saw this as a way of giving the "traditional" and "folk"[23] arts a new lease on life (for instance, by quickening the pace of and drastically abridging a 65-minute court dance for stage presentation), it eventually turned into an avant-garde movement not unlike the earlier ones in Europe and the United States, which had sought to *épater le bourgeois*. By the 1980s, Javanese composers were creating music that was, in Rustopo's words, "strange, non-conformist, naughty" (1991:28). The music is characterized by many of the things audiences in the West came to expect from avant-garde music in the 1960s: experimentation with timbre (unusual playing techniques), chance procedures, incorporation of the spoken word, tape sampling, the abandonment of melody as a focal point—in short, a fundamental questioning of the basic conventions of music-making, and a constant search for the new.[24]

While the *gendhing kréasi*—especially those in the style of Nartosabdho—are very much liked, and have largely achieved Humardani's goal of bringing the tradition up to date, the avant-garde composers have had virtually no impact on

20. For an excellent, concise description of *dolanan*, see Susilo 1984:151–52.

21. The English term *contemporary* seems to have entered the world of Javanese performing arts, as early as 1958, through dance (see Humardani 1991:63–64). The Indonesian term *gamelan kontèmporèr* seems to date back to a 1985 article by Hardja Susilo (Rustopo 1991:28). *Téater kontèmporèr*, on the other hand, was already common by 1979 (see Umar Kayam 1981:108ff.). For more on Indonesian contemporary music see, in addition to Rustopo 1991, Mack 2004, and Warde 2002/2003.

22. Note that these two programs are curiously at odds with each other, since it should not be necessary to train people to understand art that is culturally and socially relevant to their own lives.

23. The two were distinct for him: "traditional" arts were associated with the palaces. See Lindsay 1985:41–43.

24. And yet, during the time I was in Solo, as soon as one composer had an idea that worked, others would latch onto it. In any given year one would hear the same sorts of things, over and over, with each successive composition. This is very much the way more traditional forms of gamelan music have always been transmitted: one musician or group would have an idea, and others, hearing it, would quickly imitate it and incorporate it into their own style (Supanggah, pers. comm.). It may be, then, that *gamelan kontemporèr*, in some respects is not as radical as it purports to be.

music-making outside ASKI/STSI/ISI. Indeed, their music was never, to my knowledge, performed in a noninstitutional setting the whole time I was in Solo. They have, on the other hand, had quite an impact on the international gamelan scene, especially in England and the West Coast of the United States.

Just how much of a stylistic rupture with traditional music *gamelan kontèmporèr* represents, compared to *gendhing kréasi*, can be seen in the degree to which ensemble leaders mix the styles with older ones. Whereas *gendhing kréasi* can follow rather effortlessly and seamlessly from traditional pieces (say, in a musical suite, or in shadow-puppet accompaniment), gamelan *kontèmporèr* pieces are almost never incorporated into a traditional context. The main exception to this, if one is willing to call it a traditional context, is in the accompaniment to dance, which may call for a succession of vastly differing moods.[25] When traditional music is used within such a mercurial musical context, however, it is as if the older style of music is embedded within the new, with quotation marks around it à la Charles Ives, rather than simply coexisting on an equal footing. Consciously innovative music is often used more and more in *wayang* (shadow theater) accompaniment, which increasingly makes use of set, rehearsed sequences, instead of choosing, in performance, from an existing repertoire of expected pieces for different types of scenes.[26] But this music is rarely truly avant-garde—shadow theater troupes remain committed, by and large, to pleasing their audiences.

To summarize, then, institutions like STSI have been at the forefront of certain fundamental changes in musical practice. Some innovations, like an increased reliance on notation, have had far-reaching effects. Others, like radical stylistic experimentation, seem to be limited to a small circle of aficionados.

Lest I give the impression that STSI's primary role has been as a purveyor of Western aesthetics and as a fomenter of musical change, let me mention the other kinds of activity that went on at the school in the early 1990s. The lion's share of the curriculum was devoted to the teaching of both Kraton and Mangkunegaran styles, as well as those of Yogyakarta, Banyumas (western Central Java), West Java, and Bali. The school increasingly has sponsored research, the results of which have been made available in research reports deposited locally, national and institutional journals, and books published by the STSI press. In the early years, research was mostly carried out by instructional staff, but with the opening of the master's program in performing arts in 2000, there have been important contributions made by graduate students as well.

In the 1990–91 academic year, the four departments were *Karawitan* (gamelan and vocal music, with fifty-two instructors), *Pedhalangan* (shadow puppetry,

25. Indeed, it would seem that much of the impetus for avant-garde music originally came from its association with dance. This may have to do with the fact that, until recently, more Javanese dancers studied internationally than did musicians.

26. This trend, already noted by Perlman (1999) a decade ago, is, if anything, on the rise.

thirty-one instructors), *Tari* (dance, seventy-three instructors), and *Seni Rupa* (visual arts, twenty instructors). The teachers of Solonese music used to include older, court-trained musicians (foremost among them, Martopangrawit and Mloyowidodo), but none of those who taught at the school are still alive. Increasingly, experts from outside the palaces also give lessons at STSI/ISI. But the vast majority of instructors are ASKI/STSI alumni, growing numbers of whom have earned graduate degrees abroad.

Over the years, the school has sent musicians and dancers on tour to all parts of the globe, most frequently to the United States, England, France, and Japan. Beginning in the 1950s and continuing to the present, gamelan ensembles have sprung up in those four countries, as well as in the Netherlands, Canada, and Australia, among others. Many of the teachers for these ensembles have come from STSI/ISI. Conversely, the school has had several dozen foreign students enroll in it, or use it as a base for doctoral research (as did I). As a result of this international contact, the curriculum more and more resembles that of music schools in the United States and elsewhere.

One similarity is in the emphasis on "classical" and "contemporary" repertoire. Whereas Western music schools have tended to shun popular music,[27] STSI seemed to have banished the *kréasi* styles that were popularized by the recording industry (one exception is the *Pedhalangan* [Shadow Puppetry] Department, which included *gendhing kréasi* in its musical accompaniment classes). The omission was not accidental: one influential teacher, for instance, once dismissively referred to Nartosabdho as a "pop" composer. But Javanese—and U.S.—music schools are not simply motivated by classical-centered snobbery: there is a feeling that popular music (in all senses of the term) hardly needs an institution to either teach or maintain it.

In recent years, the primary object of disdain (and despair) of the music faculty at STSI/ISI has been another genre that blends popular idioms with elements of gamelan music, *campursari* (literally, "mixed essence" or "mixing the best parts"). Unlike for *gendhing kréasi*, their sentiments are shared with many "outside" musicians,[28] who see this relatively new hybrid genre as a threat to the very existence of more traditional—and especially classical—music. *Campursari* seems to have been invented, as early as the 1960s, at RRI, where the Western-trained *kroncong* musicians and the traditional gamelan practitioners employed at the station joined forces in a novel combination.[29] *Kroncong* is itself a hybrid genre, containing mostly Portuguese elements, and may be considered Indonesia's first national genre. Its instrumentation usually consists of various plucked and bowed string

27. See Nettl 1995. The observation is truer in performance than it is in musicology, where popular music is increasingly included.

28. See the next section of this chapter for a preliminary discussion of "outside" and "inside." It is analyzed in greater depth in chapter 4.

29. Most of my information on *campursari* comes from Supanggah 2003. See also Perlman 1999.

instruments as well as a transverse flute, all brought to Indonesia from Europe. In its Javanese version, however—called *langgam* if it is sung in Javanese—it has long had a strong gamelan influence (imitations of gamelan instruments by some of the strings, vocal ornaments, "impure" diatonic tuning, chord progressions uncharacteristic of European common practice style). Eventually *campursari* entered a kind of revival (around the late 1980s), at which time the instrumentation came to center around the electronic keyboard (of which there may be one or several), to which are usually added traditional double-headed barrel drums, as well as a variable assortment of other Western and Javanese instruments.

For the first few decades of its existence, very few people paid *campursari* any notice, but in the past few years its popularity has taken off, perhaps surpassing even that of *dangdut* (Supanggah 2003:3), an Indonesian popular genre based mainly on Bollywood film music that has been widely listened and danced to across Indonesia, particularly by working-class Muslims. Supanggah attributes its success to a variety of factors: it is more practical than gamelan music, it is versatile with respect to the repertoires it draws on, and, above all, it connotes modernity. If I dwell on it here, it is because it is perceived as draining the resources of traditional *karawitan* (gamelan music)—younger singers no longer want to get paid less to sing the harder classical repertoire, people holding rituals prefer *campursari* to gamelan music, and audiences at ritual events may even grab the *rebab* (spike fiddle) after one or two pieces to force the musicians to switch to *campursari* or *dangdut* (Supanggah, July 4, 2003).

An anecdote may serve to illustrate both its ubiquity and the resentment it engenders among some gamelan musicians. In 2003 one of the members of the music faculty at STSI was holding a ritual celebration following his son's circumcision. This was a typically large affair, with several hundred guests seated in a cavernous, rented reception hall. The music was provided by a small *campursari* group consisting primarily of a keyboardist, a drummer playing Javanese and Sundanese drums, and several vocalists. I was sitting with other musicians, who together could easily have formed a large gamelan ensemble (and would have been glad to have done so). They became increasingly irritated at the music that was provided (which, it was said, had been chosen at the instigation of the family of the celebrant's mother, over the protestations of his father). The usual order for such celebrations is USDEK: *unjukan* (drinks), *sop* (soup), *dhahar* ("eat"—a plateful of rice upon which are placed two or three dishes of seasoned meat and vegetables), *es krim* (ice cream), *kondur* (go home). The musicians I was with decided—in an act of spontaneous, unspoken, collective protest—to reverse the order of the last two items. Attendees at large events in Java, when they leave, tend to leave as a group very quickly—it seems that no one wants to be the last one. My companions started a trend that spread like wildfire, with the result that by the time the young helpers came out with the obligatory ice cream, virtually no one was left to eat it.

In this age of postcolonial studies and global ethnoscapes (to borrow Appadurai's term) it is no longer possible to think of hybridity (or synergy, or transculturation) as a special case (Appadurai 1991, Ashcroft et al. 2000). It is, in fact, constitutive of the postcolonial condition, which, because it affects both the former colonizer and the former colonized, typifies the experience of nearly every human being on the planet. And Javanese music has certainly been influenced by—or at the very least coexisted with—Western music for many generations. But there is something about *campursari* that seems particularly disturbing: almost everything that makes traditional gamelan music distinctively beautiful—its rich timbres, its nondiatonic tunings, its many layers of complex melodic interaction, its subtle manipulation of time, its profound relationship to Javanese philosophy and etiquette, its wide panoply of moods—seems to be missing from *campursari*. All that is left is its sensuous, immediately appealing side, and even that seems distorted or cheapened by the diatonic, electronically produced sounds of the keyboard. Most worrisome to those who are fond of traditional gamelan music is the way in which the Javanese elements are somehow framed as a marked case (in the linguistic sense)—although mixtures between East and West no longer shock or amuse, there is a certain self-consciousness about the way *campursari* singers use the Javanese language or include gamelan instruments other than the drums. To paraphrase Marc Perlman (1999), Javanese music has become ethnic music.

If STSI/ISI has studiously avoided certain strains of popular culture in its performance curriculum (much less so on the musicological side), this is not necessarily because of a desire to distance itself from the populace at large. In fact quite the opposite is evident in the new graduate program in *penciptaan seni* (composition/performance), which encourages students to be inspired by Indonesian traditions and to take their works back to the *masyarakat* (society, citizenry, public) (*Buku Panduan* 2005:2–3). An effort is hence made to separate modernization from Westernization. Townspeople, from whatever region of Indonesia is the chosen focus, are often included as participants in the culminating projects for the master's degree—that is, some of them help to create and perform the piece—and a major criterion in judging these projects is how the *masyarakat* responds to the event.

One other prominent institution in Solo that sponsors Javanese arts is the *Taman Budaya Surakarta* (or TBS; "Surakarta Cultural Center ['Garden,' literally]"). Its primary institutional function is as a venue for artists brought in from the outside, and it has a relatively small permanent staff. It occupies a large plot of land, not far from STSI/ISI, on the eastern edge of town. The buildings include an enclosed theater (one of very few in Solo), an art gallery, and what in 1992 was said to be the largest *pendhåpå* in Java. During the period of my research, TBS frequently sponsored *wayang*s (shadow plays), dance performances, art exhibits, drama, gamelan concerts, workshops, competitions, festivals, and conferences. It also published the occasional collection of gamelan or vocal notation.

The emphasis was on innovation, and on traditional forms that were rarely heard in a public, institutional setting. Among them were *dhalang kentrung*, an Islamic epic narrative sung to frame drums from the north coast of Java; *tayuban*, female singer/dancers accompanied by gamelan; and even dancers and musicians from the Kraton who rarely perform anywhere outside the palace. Several friends reported that, during the worst of the economic crisis, TBS was less active in its promotion of the arts and was used more as a relief distribution center for the general population. By 2006, however, it had certainly returned to its former role.

NONINSTITUTIONAL ("OUTSIDE") SETTINGS

All of the above institutions share one thing in common: they are all, among other things, helping to keep the palace traditions alive. They are also all in a position of prestige. They have access to government funding, they can hire the most highly trained teachers, they have the best gamelans and the most impressive performance spaces, and they put on the most dazzling displays of Javanese culture. As a result, the term *luar* [I] (*njåbå* [Ng], *njawi* [K]), meaning "outside," which originally referred to people, places, and practices outside the palace walls, is commonly used at all these institutions to refer to extrainstitutional artistic practices and practitioners. My sense is that the term may designate anything from "those ignorant masses who haven't had the opportunity to find out all the intricacies of the true palace style" to "those happily naive musicians who aren't constrained by all of these petty rules." It seems to be used only by people on the inside of the institution in question (most often the Kraton or STSI/ISI), or by people who have had access to "inside" knowledge, even if they are not affiliated with an institution.

In fact, the vast majority of the music-making in and around Solo is, and always has been, done by *orang luar* [I] ("outsiders"). All over the city there are amateur and professional gamelan groups not directly connected to any of the above institutions. Santosa (1990), in surveying two districts of Solo, which together cover about half the area of the city and had a collective population of about 250,000, found sixty such groups, twenty-nine of which were active at the time he collected his data. Many of the remaining thirty-one, which were inactive at the time the survey was taken, became active at various other times of the year. The most common reason for a group to stop rehearsing, besides the loss of its leader or of its rehearsal space, was the onset of the rainy season. The most common reason for an inactive group to *start* rehearsing again was the imminence of the yearly gamelan competition sponsored by RRI. Since 1992, it must be said, the incidence of the radio-sponsored gamelan competitions has been at best spotty, with it being held fewer years than not.

Each group in Santosa's study had between fifteen and thirty members, most of whom were working class, with no more than a primary education. Roughly

20 percent of those surveyed said they depended on the supplemental or primary income they got from their musical activities.

About half of all the ensembles Santosa surveyed were women's groups, although proportionally fewer of the active ones were. This undoubtedly is because many of the women's groups only performed at the yearly competitions. In fact, during my main research period (1989–92) there were usually about sixty or seventy women's groups in the citywide contest, as opposed to only about a dozen men's groups.

While the level of playing in some of the all-female groups reached quite a high standard (at least on the contest pieces), owing no doubt to increasingly cutthroat competition, women instrumentalists remained decidedly on the unpaid/unskilled end of the amateur-professional continuum. Highly skilled female instrumentalists were once fairly common, it seems, in the villages and especially in *dhalang* (puppeteer) families. The few remaining female instrumentalists with extensive performance experience are all from this sort of background.[30] Female groups entering a competition vied for the services of these expert *gendèr* (double-mallet metallophone), *gambang* (xylophone), and *kendhang* (drum) players and paid them well, just as the male groups paid their "ringers" extra. (Suhartå, who often judges competitions, was once told that it cost about Rp 750,000 [over $300]—a year's rent, at the time, for a middle-class house in Solo—for a group to get to the finals at the district level. This included money for transportation, food, and musicians' fees; it may also have included the cost of uniforms.)

Despite their ardent desire to win, women who joined gamelan groups were reputed to be motivated more by social than by musical considerations. According to several of the men who taught all-female groups, women spent more time worrying about what they would eat during rehearsals (the food did tend to be varied, plentiful, and very tasty!) and what color of costumes they would wear than about whether they had mastered their respective parts. Indeed, with the notable exception of the hired specialists, most of the women in the all-female groups I observed did not seem to take themselves very seriously as musicians. Among male musicians, the abbreviation PKK (Pembinaan Kesejahteraan Keluarga[31]) is a derogatory way of referring to a simplified way of playing or singing, suitable only for beginners. Some of this dilettantism might be

30. See S. Weiss 1993 and 1998, and Perlman 1998 for additional information on these performers. See also Kusumadilaga 1981:49, 186; Brinner 1995:88; and Keeler 1987:181.

31. "Promotion of Family Welfare," originally a government program that, under the New Order regime, was then used by the Golkar Party as a means of extending its control. Nowadays, however, the term simply refers to any neighborhood women's association. These associations engage in various activities, such as cooking or sewing lessons, small-scale lotteries (*arisan*), and gamelan music. Typically they meet at the house of one of the women, usually moving from one place to the next, except, for obvious reasons, in the case of gamelan rehearsals (Supanggah, May 6, 2006).

attributable to class differences. Whereas male musicians and *pesindhèns* (female vocalists) are typically working class, my impression is that the women in all-female groups are frequently middle class and do not generally wish to be thought of as professional musicians.

The class difference between bourgeois housewives and professional musicians is made abundantly clear in a wonderful passage from a post-Independence cookbook:[32]

> All of the foregoing recipes for Javanese desserts go under the rubric of *keleman* ("moist cakes")—all delicious, but not exactly high-class food; that is, they're not for serving to guests at a grand, formal celebration. One could serve them, but only to our fellow musicians.
>
> Actually, this is being disrespectful to our fellow musicians: why shouldn't they be served the same food as the other guests, rather than just getting snacks? Aren't they the very people who bring pleasure to the guests?
>
> Once, in Surakarta, a group of musicians staged a boycott, refusing to eat such food. As soon as the hosts realized what was happening, the musicians got served the same food as the other guests.[33]
>
> It used to be that when a hostess who was holding a ritual celebration gave orders of what to buy at the market, saying "Buy musicians' food," what she really meant was, "food not for honored guests.[34]

32. The book, by R. A. Soewarsi ("R. A.," here, presumably stands for Radèn Ajeng, or Radèn Ayu, both noble titles of low rank), was in its sixth edition in 1967.

33. In my experience, even now, musicians complain openly if they are not properly fed—whereas I've rarely heard them complain about being underpaid. During *wayangs*, *dhalangs* will inject snide (albeit indirect) comments into the dialogue if the food and drink being served to the performers is not up to snuff. According to Minarno, formerly of the Indonesian Consulate in Chicago, there are even inside musical jokes along the same lines: the drummer can play a pattern that mimics the words *wis entèk* [Ng] (it's all gone).

34. Soewarsi 1967:74. Several phrases in this passage are untranslatable. What I've rendered as "our fellow" is actually a word meaning "sibling" or "blood relative" (and, by extension, "friend"). The author is clearly not a musician, yet by using the word *sedhèrèk*, possibly for its proximity to the Indonesian word *saudara*, she is showing her solidarity with them while at the same time maintaining social distance. If she really wanted to put them on the same social plane as the reader, she would use a term of respect, such as *panjenenganipun*, rather than *sedhèrèk*, which almost has a communist ring to it (perhaps "comrade" would be a better translation). She also subtly maintains her social distance by her choice of language levels for the verb "to eat." She has been using the *krâmâ inggil* (highly respectful) word *dhaharan* all along for "food," when the people involved included the reader or honored guests. When referring to the musicians only, she switches to the plain *krâmâ* (respectful) word *nedhâ*. (Perhaps because the word *nedhâ* is relatively infrequent, she adds, in parentheses, the *ngoko* [low Javanese] equivalent, *mangan*.) Similarly, she uses the *krâmâ madyâ* (moderately respectful) expression, *boten purun*, "refused," rather than *boten remen* (*krâmâ*) or *boten kersâ* (*krâmâ inggil*). The original text follows, with the Dutch-style spelling intact (except that I've substituted *dh* for the original *d* with a dot below it, and *th* for *t* with a dot below it):

> Dhaharan tjara Djawi sadaja punika dipun wastani golonganing keleman, sadaja sarwa miraos, nanging boten kalebet ing dhedhaharan ageng, tegesipun boten kanggé njugata tamu ing kalaning tijang gadhah damel ageng-agengan. Saupami kawedalaken dados sesegah, namung dados sesegahipun sadhèrèk nijaga.

Finally, in discussing the gender makeup of ensembles, mention must be made of mixed groups. These would not be allowed to participate in an official competition since they do not fit into the two categories. The few that I knew in the vicinity of Solo tended to be in outlying villages and to have a high incidence of kinship ties among the members. One, though, was at a hospital in town. All the mixed groups I observed were just as serious about music as any of the male groups.

If the dozen ensembles I rehearsed and performed with in and around Solo, and the many others I heard about from friends, are any indication, the typical group was either centered around a neighborhood (playing a gamelan set owned by the *kantor kelurahan*—a sort of mini branch of the town hall—or by one of the wealthier citizens), a workplace, or an association (such as the Veterans' Cooperative).[35] A very few musicians had gamelans of their own and would teach groups at home. Wherever rehearsals were held, anyone was welcome to join in, especially if he or she could perform one of the more difficult parts. In the early 1990s, foreigners with chops seemed particularly welcome, but in 2006 some of my foreign friends were at times reluctant to take advantage of the privilege extended to them, intuiting some resentment that may never have been directly expressed (they sensed that if they "hogged," say, the *gendèr* some local musicians who loved to play never got the chance). A few avid musicians would belong to many groups, making the rounds throughout the week, thus filling their evenings with rehearsals and performances. The participants would chip in to pay a teacher, or he was hired by the sponsoring individual or organization.

Many of the teachers of "outside" groups are from one of the government-run institutions. A very few of them, however, are completely independent and manage to make a living by leading *bapak-bapak* (gentlemen's) and *ibu-ibu* (ladies') groups, by performing here and there, by giving private lessons to foreigners, or by some employment not related to music. They are respected musicians, however, and could easily have gotten jobs at the radio station or at one of the schools, if they had wanted. Because of their refusal to conform to the regulated life of a civil servant (and because, it must be said, of their eccentric personalities), they are seen as freedom-loving renegades embodying the true

---

Sajektosipun tjara makaten punika kalebet ngesoraken sadhèrèk nijaga, punapaa sadhèrèk nijaga boten dipun segah sami kados ingkang kanggé sugata para tamu sanès-sanèsipun, sami dipun sugata dhahar larihan, mangka nijaga punika dados golonganing tetijang ingkang ndamel suka-remening para tamu.

Ing Surakarta naté wonten golonganing nijaga ambekot boten purun nedha (mangan) sesegah ingkang makaten punika. Sareng kasumerepan kalijan tijang ingkang gadhah damel ladjeng kasugata kados sugatan ingkang kasugataken dhateng para tamu sanès-sanèsipun.

Rumijin wonten tjara, tijang gadhah damel punika, njonja rumah nalika kèngkènan blandjan dhateng peken mawi meling. Tukokna panganan nijaga, ingkang tegesipun boten ngadjèni.

35. I use the past tense throughout this section for reasons already explained, but I knew of more than half a dozen groups in 2006 that fit the same general pattern described here.

spirit of creativity. They are invariably referred to as *senimans*, a neo-Sanskrit word (*seni* [Sanskrit], "genius" + *-wan*, possessive suffix) clearly created to translate the English word *artist* (or the Dutch equivalent, *kunstenaar*).[36] But lest we assume too quickly that this Romantic view of the artist is a recent European import, let me point out that even the early-nineteenth-century *Serat Centhini* paints male musicians as recusant rakes.[37]

Rehearsals were usually held once a week. Some groups met during the day, especially the women's groups and the ones connected with work. The more serious-minded groups generally rehearsed in the evening, starting at a fairly indeterminate time—usually around 7:30 or 8:00 (or, during the rainy season, whenever the rain let up a bit). Each session would generally last about four hours, with frequent breaks for refreshments (sweet tea and light snacks) and chitchat, during which time the teacher would go over problem spots with individual participants who had had trouble during the preceding piece. Other than that, very little verbal instruction was given, and pieces were practically never stopped in the middle, even if the performers were faltering.

Experienced groups with enough repertoire would go through the normal order for evening music, progressing through the six melodic modes, and from slow-paced, dignified pieces to the gay, boisterous ones. A few expert groups would not always announce the pieces beforehand: the appropriate instrument or singer would perform the introduction for a particular piece, and the others would enter at the right point and continue through to the end, sometimes without ever knowing the name of the piece they had just played. Sukanto told me that it used to be standard practice at the Kraton, both in rehearsals and performances, *never* to announce a piece verbally. Musicians were expected to know their entire repertoire cold, and it was not uncommon for one of them, if the chosen piece was unfamiliar or simply rusty, to sweat bullets while mentally cursing the *rebab* (spike fiddle) player.

The less-advanced groups often had a blackboard upon which notation for the evening's pieces was written. Or, more commonly, photocopies of notation were circulated. Titles of pieces were always announced beforehand. Very often pieces were combined into suites (typically the more advanced the group, the longer the suite). Theoretically there is much leeway and room for surprises in the pieces to be linked together. But in practice each group tended to be fairly consistent in this regard, so that often only the first piece of a suite was announced, and anyone who had attended rehearsals regularly would know what to expect.

Each group had its own favorite ending piece, which was rarely announced, and which was usually one of the signature pieces used by the palace or radio

36. Gonda 1973, J. Becker 1994.

37. See Kunst 1973:267–68. See also Anderson 1972:7–9 for a description of "what Pigeaud called *trekkers en zwervers* (travelers and wanderers)," which included all sorts of social deviants.

ensembles at the end of their broadcasts. The closing number was always more sedate than the ones immediately preceding it and had a text that bestowed a blessing on those present, or on the nation as a whole. After the last piece, the members would disperse instantly, just as they did at any group event I attended. As these events often lasted past midnight, people had to get home so they could face the next day (which, for most people, began around 4:00 or 5:00 A.M.). In addition, nobody wanted to be left behind—a fate considered especially unpleasant in a place where the unofficial motto is *mangan ora mangan angger ngumpul* ("Food or no food, as long as you gather together," or, more freely, "Company is all the food you need").

The custom of beginning with serious pieces and ending with exuberant ones seems to be increasingly disregarded. This may be due to a decline in *priyayi* (aristocratic) sponsorship, since the most serious pieces came out of the court tradition.[38] Other factors, certainly, are the competition gamelan music faces with lively popular music of all sorts, and the perceived incompatibility of large, meditative pieces with modern life. Part of the impetus may also come from *wayang* (shadow theater), which has to compete with television and movies and so has become more and more concerned with entertainment.[39] Whatever the reason, over the past couple of decades, during rehearsals of "outside" groups, to the already ubiquitous *gendhing kréasi* in the style of Nartosabdho have been added increasing numbers of *langgams* and *gendhing Sragènan*.[40] Musicians in these groups seem to crave light, upbeat fare.

38. Calmness is associated with refinement, exuberance with crudeness. In the past, palace ensembles therefore distinguished themselves by developing their own repertoire of large, difficult, stately pieces and by avoiding the most lively ones (see Warsadiningrat 1987:129 and Supanggah 1991b). All of the traits that, other things being equal, enliven a performance—such as *kendhangan ciblon, senggakan, sindhènan, gérongan,* and *imbal*—seem to have had their origins outside of the palaces. It is possible, then, that the impression everyone has of the livelier repertoire taking over is simply a result of "outside" traditions becoming more prominent compared to the court traditions. Clara van Groenendael puts forward a similar interpretation with respect to eroticism in *wayang* (1985:177). See also the reference to Sears in the following note.

39. See, for instance, Walton 1996 and 1997, Perlman 1999, Mrázek 2005 (chapter 8), Curtis 2002, Suratno 2002, J. Susilo 1996, and Nugroho 2003. Sears (1996, chapter 6) argues that the emphasis on entertainment is not merely a reaction to mass media, but can be seen as a continuation of elements that preexisted Dutch interest in *wayang*, and were particularly prevalent in village styles. And Supanggah (2005) argues that traditional performing arts need not compete with mass media; rather, their exponents can and should make use of the media to strengthen the arts.

40. *Langgam* is a genre of popular sentimental songs in Javanese that is closely related to *kroncong*. *Langgams* are often originally composed in a diatonic scale and then transposed into *sléndro* or *pélog* for performance with gamelan accompaniment. *Sragènan* is a recent genre dating from the 1980s that incorporates, among other influences, Nartosabdho-style pieces with the *tayuban* (ritual celebration where men take turns dancing with a professional singer/dancer) and *cokèkan* (small ensemble featuring the *siter* [plucked box zither] and *gendèr* [double-mallet metallophone]) traditions from the area around the town of Sragèn (Suparno 1998/1999 and Perlman 1999).

At many rehearsals I attended, alcohol was circulated among the men (usually beer and store-bought imitation whisky,[41] mixed in a bottle), so that by the end of the evening the mood was lively indeed. At a typical rehearsal, the alcohol consumption increased as the night wore on, and this encouraged musicians to interject more and more humor into the music, and to flirt with the female singer(s), or *pesindhèn*(s). Indeed, it was this flirting that, for some, was essential to the success of the event. In the male ensembles it was considered essential to have at least one *pesindhèn* present. In some groups there seemed to be designated "*pesindhèn* finders," and on one occasion, when these had failed in their mission, the men in the group milled about restlessly without playing, until a *pesindhèn* was found. In contrast, it used to be common practice to play *gendhing bonang*[42] until enough people were present for a full ensemble. But even for pieces with *rebab* it is not necessary to have all the parts in order to make gamelan music; minimally, a drum, a gong (or gong substitute), and two or three melodic lines can suffice. Indeed, several male musicians told me that serious pieces are actually more enjoyable without a *pesindhèn* present, because most *pesindhèns* do not know how to bring out the particular mood of each piece. The *pesindhèn*'s presence in the predominantly male, heterosexual world of gamelan, then, may be valued more for the sexual interest she gives to the evening than for purely musical reasons, although her voice certainly contributes to the sexual content of the lighter repertoire. That is, while flirting is what is sought from the *pesindhèn*, this can consist of body language and repartee during breaks from the music, or it can be incorporated into the music itself.
II:2, Examples of the latter might be the *gérong*'s *senggakan* during a *pesindhèn*'s
38:38–41:39 *palaran*,[43] or instrumental interaction with the *pesindhèn*'s line—a sort of musical
IV:8, teasing—during one of her *andhegans* (cadenza-like breaks).

4:24 It is difficult to overestimate the sexual overtones of Javanese gamelan music and the dances that are associated with it. While hardly flirtatious, the songs that
II:1 accompany the *bedhåyå* and *srimpi* court dances, which are among the most sacred and awe-inspiring in the entire repertoire, are ripe with erotic content. Part of their eroticism comes from associations between the female dancers and sexual availability. Harjonegoro, an eminent batik-maker and expert on Javanese court culture, once told me that *bedhåyå* dancers were actually just glorified

41. A more traditional form of hard liquor, *ciu* (locally made rice brandy), was also sometimes used.

42. These are pieces that use the loud ensemble, without any vocalists or the softer, "front row" instruments.

43. The *gérong* is a small, unison chorus that functions as an integral part of the gamelan ensemble in a great many pieces. *Senggakans* are spontaneous-sounding interjections consisting of small snippets of sometimes cryptic text in everyday (as opposed to literary) language set to short, catchy tunes, which are used to liven up the musical atmosphere. A *palaran* is a solo vocal genre consisting of an elaboration of a verse of *måcåpat* (classical sung poetry in free rhythm) accompanied by a reduced gamelan.

talèdhèk (singer/dancer/prostitutes of former times).[44] Peggy Choy explores the historical connection between another kind of Javanese dancer and *talèdhèk*s in an article on the *golèk* dance (1984). In it she draws a connection between the *branyak* (bold, spirited) style of dancing that comes out of the *talèdhèk* tradition and Kangjeng Ratu Kidul (the spirit Queen of the South Sea), who is linked to the sacred *bedhåyå* dances in many ways.[45] For one thing, the most sacred of Surakarta dances, the *Bedhåyå Ketawang*, commemorates the sexual union between Ratu Kidul and Sultan Agung (a sixteenth-century Javanese king), and all subsequent kings in the line that culminates with the current king of Solo.[46] The dancers who perform the *Bedhåyå Ketawang* in a sense *become* Ratu Kidul during the dance, and so were also potential concubines of the king (or of another high-ranking official, should the king choose to "bequeath" one of them to him). This is why the king's own daughters, until recently, were never allowed to dance the *Bedhåyå Ketawang* (Soeratman 1989:87–88, 154–55, 176). The eroticism of *bedhåyå* dances is also quite evident in the texts of the songs, which are often esoteric, but nonetheless unequivocal in their sexual imagery.[47]

The texts used in more ordinary musical contexts also often have sexual overtones. *Senggakan*s (short, sung interjections) are perhaps the most notorious.[48] But ordinary *gérong* texts may also be about male-female relations. An example is "Kéntir-kéntir ing samodrå..." ("Adrift in the ocean..."), cited by Sastro Tugiyo (April 29, 1992; May 6, 1992), who also said that such texts have been, at various times, discouraged by the government. Other examples may be found in the texts to *dolanan*s ("play songs"), which are nominally children's songs. According to Sukanto, however, these songs are actually intended for adults, and they have double meanings that tend to the pornographic (May 12, 1992). The words to *andhegan*s (vocal cadenzas) may also be overtly or covertly sexual (an example, given to me by Sukanto, is the "Ombèn, ombèn" *andhegan* to *gendhing Perkutut Manggung*[49]).

I have mentioned how males behave at a rehearsal, but what of the *pesindhèn*s themselves? The degree to which they participate in the flirting varies from

44. This observation seems to be confirmed by Kusumadilaga (1981:179). See Walton 1996 for historical connections between *talèdhèk*s and *pesindhèn*s.

45. Choy 1984:63. See also Edi Sedyawati 1984, who makes a similar connection between the court dances and another lively and popular type of dance, *gambyong*.

46. For more on this dance, see Hadiwidjojo 1981, Brakel-Papenhuijzen 1992, and Tirtaamidjaja 1967. For its erotic content specifically, see Florida 1992 and J. Becker 1993:130.

47. See Florida 1992, and *Serat Pasindhen Badhaya* 1983.

48. I am indebted to Marc Perlman, who has collected texts to a large number of *senggakan*s, for pointing this out.

49. This *andhegan* is translated and commented on by Nancy Cooper: "Give the bird some water./I'll give it a little fresh water./Feed the singing turtledove./I'll feed it a little rice on the stalk./Early in the morning my turtledove craves milk./In the midday my turtledove craves rice grains./At night my dove craves to be satisfied./At night my turtledove increases his beauty." As Cooper points out, the sexual overtones are much more explicit in Javanese, since a common euphemism for penis is *manuk* [Ng] (bird) (1994:353–55).

person to person (as does, of course, the men's badinage). Typically, though, a *pesindhèn* will show bemusement at the proceedings, perhaps smiling coyly. If things get too bawdy, though, she might retreat into impeccable decorum (like Arletty's character Garance in the 1944 film *Les Enfants du Paradis*). *Pesindhèns* are in a sense the voices that launch a thousand ships. Generally, they are the ones who maintain self-control throughout the night (thus contradicting the commonplace that men in Java are more consistently refined, more capable of self-discipline).[50]

PERFORMANCE CONTEXTS

With the exception of the very worst ones, "outside" groups were often called upon to give hour-long live concerts at the national radio station, or to perform for a private ceremonial event, such as a wedding, a circumcision, or the thirty-five-day commemoration of a child's birth. These were the main occasions during which people could hear live gamelan music—always amplified through sound systems of dubious fidelity. (Recorded gamelan music, on the other hand, could be heard almost anywhere, almost anytime, whether coming from shops or restaurants, or from people's home radios or tape players.) If the gamelan was played at night as entertainment after the ritual itself, the music and atmosphere were very similar to what I experienced at rehearsals (in fact, the same word, *klenèngan*—a formal or informal music-making session featuring gamelan music—was often used for both). The space nearest the gamelan was usually occupied by men, who smoked and drank tea or alcohol as they sat on woven plastic or grass mats playing cards. Sometimes a nonmusician would request a particular piece or a general kind of piece, and occasionally a man (or, less frequently, a woman), typically old and toothless, would get up and dance to the music with movements distinctly related to the choreographed palace dances, but much freer. Similar, but more subdued and with fewer guests, were the monthly *klenèngans* held every thirty-five days at the house of a prominent musician or patron. All these events often lasted until 4:00 A.M. or beyond: participants told me that they forgot their cares and didn't notice the passage of time if the music and mood were good.

In 2003 there were three monthly *klenèngans* devoted specifically to the more classical repertoire (which rarely lasted past 2:00 A.M.): Malam Anggårå Kasih at SMKI, the group Pujånggå Laras at a house rented by foreigners in

50. I shall return to this topic in chapter 4. I have discussed it elsewhere as well (2002). For another take on the subject, see Sarah Weiss (1993), who bases her analysis on an article by Keeler (1990). Keeler's depiction has been broadly emended by Brenner (1995), whose view is more in keeping with my present point. Weiss has refined her analysis in a recent book (2006). See also Sutton 1984 and 1989, Cooper 1994, and Walton 1996 and 1997. Susan Walton, in particular, has analyzed the interaction between male *dhalangs* and *pesindhèns*, and what the latter have to say about it.

Lawéyan, and a get-together at the house of Rahayu Supanggah. Of these, only the first two were still active in 2006 (by then the house in Lawéyan was no longer available, and the Pujånggå Laras group often met at Supanggah's house, with the result that the two merged into one). Malam Anggårå Kasih is not strictly an "outside" group, since it is sponsored by SMKI with some donations from foreign gamelan students. Most of the participants are students and faculty from STSI/ISI. Pujånggå Laras is sponsored by a group of mostly North American gamelan musicians who wanted to do something to help keep traditional gamelan music alive. Some participants feel that the level of musicianship was higher at Rahayu Supanggah's previous *klenèngan*s, attributing the difference to the "envelopes" (cash payments) distributed at the Pujånggå Laras events (the idea being that some musicians who are not in the top tier come because they need the money). In 2006, at the Pujånggå Laras event, while the older musicians were eating (the average age is over fifty) students from STSI/ISI often took over. It must be said that the current generation of students demonstrates overall a strong desire to learn from the older generations and includes some very talented musicians. All these events are looked forward to and relished by the participants, who otherwise never have the chance to play and hear some of their favorite pieces, nor to challenge themselves with the particular difficulties the older repertoire entails.

A word should be said here about why so many Javanese performances last (or lasted) all night. People who pay attention to the teachings of *kejawèn* or "Javanese mysticism"—who probably used to include most of the population, to some degree—believe that spiritual power and self-control can only be gained through ascetic practices in which earthly desires are held in check. Foremost among these are the desire for food and sleep. As a result, it is a good thing for men to be able to stay up all night—especially on certain dates of the Javanese calendar, when spirits roam more than usual—and traditional forms of ritual entertainment are often designed to help one do this.[51]

Of all the nocturnal pastimes involving music, the most richly meaningful, the one most highly regarded, is watching a *wayang kulit*, an all-night shadow play using perforated leather puppets and accompanied by gamelan music (its name is often shortened to *wayang*, although in fact there are many different types of *wayang*). *Wayang* has been as central to Javanese culture as television has been to the modern-day United States, in its power both to entertain and to shape consciousness. It is scarcely possible to talk about Javanese politics, ethics, epistemology, psychology—or music—without reference to *wayang*. Ubiquitous, it is one of those art forms that has bridged court, mercantile center, and village.

In 1992 a good troupe cost upwards of $2,000 (U.S.) a night—more than two years' salary for most people. Consequently, paying for a *wayang* performance,

51. See, for example, Lysloff 1990.

particularly if it is by a famous puppeteer, brings much prestige, and many people go into debt as a result. Those who do sponsor a *wayang* at their home do so for the same ritual events, cited above, that they might hire a gamelan group for. In addition, companies or government agencies might put on a *wayang* for an important occasion, such as the opening of a new bank branch or the yearly Independence Day celebration.[52] If the *dhalang* (puppeteer) was popular, he and some of his twenty or so musicians could earn enough to live on solely from performing (the lowest-paid musician in a well-known troupe got around $10 a night, while the highest paid received around $30—the *dhalang*, of course, would make much more than that). In contrast, all performers in any but the top troupes—the vast majority, that is—would have to have had supplemental income.

Wayang was by far the most popular traditional art form at the time of my fieldwork. *Dhalang*s have been able to maintain its popularity by shifting the emphasis from serious lessons about life and the Javanese worldview to entertainment and often ribald humor. Jokes and lighthearted songs, as far as anyone remembers, have always been part of *wayang*; but, more and more, *wayang*s are being turned into variety shows that feature sexy *pesindhèn*s and singers of *langgam* (sentimental, often diatonic songs in Javanese), stand-up comedians (some of them literally "stand up" at one side of the screen, hovering above musicians and *dhalang* alike), and rock songs rearranged for gamelan. I once saw, in the early 1990s, a male transvestite dancer, hired for the occasion, stand up and do a shadow dance in the spot where the *dhalang* usually sits.[53] At the time these acts pushed the limits of the art form. Nowadays they would be considered rather ordinary, and additional innovations have become the norm.

Some of the more popular *dhalang*s, for instance, disregard the accepted order of scenes, so that there is no longer a long, slow build-up, in a succession of waves of increasing intensity, over the eight-hour drama.[54] A noisy battle scene might be introduced at the very beginning of the drama, right after the overture; a spectator could either think of this as interesting or engaging, or else unnecessary, unsatisfying, or annoying, depending on his or her point of view.

Another change, which has happened gradually, is the increased use of prearranged music. It used to be that one of the essential skills of *wayang* accompaniment was the ability to react instantly to what the *dhalang* called for. It was possible for an entire group to do this because certain conventions were respected, so that at any given moment in the drama musicians would choose from a somewhat limited set of possibilities (which, still, in their totality

52. For a vivid description of a typical ritual performance, see the introduction in Keeler 1987.

53. Certain conventions used to be observed in order to allow the *dhalang* to enter fully into the world of the *wayang* and to create a feeling of continuity. He was taught never to displace himself from beginning to end of the eight-hour performance—and even never to look behind him.

54. See A. L. Becker 1979 for a description of how the night was traditionally structured. And see note 39 for references that describe recent changes.

numbered into the hundreds of pieces to be started or stopped on a dime!). Nowadays it is more common for each troupe to work out in advance not only the pieces to be performed for a particular story, but also a specific arrangement of those pieces, often involving written-out choral singing.

In these innovations two things are lost: a sense of spontaneity and a beautiful simplicity predicated on making an entire world come to life out of shadows, pentatonic gamelan music, and the *dhalang*'s voice. Few aficionados would consider these recent alterations of the tradition to be improvements. Yet, so far, they have succeeded in keeping *wayang* from getting buried in mothballs. A few *dhalangs* have achieved star status, which also increases *wayang*'s mass appeal, and helps it compete with—and sometimes take advantage of—newer, glitzy diversions like television.

Other "outside" art forms that use professional musicians are *kethoprak*—a popular "folk" theater form whose plots revolve around Javanese historical figures—and *wayang wong* [Ng] (*wayang orang* [I], literally, "people puppets")—a more court-based theater tradition with mythological stories, in which the actors occasionally sing and dance.[55] *Wayang wong*'s popularity has declined steadily over the past several decades, perhaps because the narration and dialogue use many difficult, archaic words, and because the plot moves more slowly than in *kethoprak*. The primary venues in Solo are the auditorium at RRI and the theater in the Sri Wedari amusement park, which was formerly connected to both the Kraton and the Mangkunegaran; since Independence it has been run by the city of Solo (Susilo 1984:119). *Wayang wong* was officially created by Sultan Hamengkubuwånå I of Yogyakarta in the mid-eighteenth century (Soedarsono 1984:19).[56] It is important to note that official, court-centered histories usually ascribe a court origin to all of the court arts, whether they were actually first practiced inside or outside the palace walls. *Wayang wong* certainly reached its apogee at the Kraton in Yogyakarta and the Mangkunegaran in Solo. *Wayang kulit* also had a strong palace tradition, which is now all but defunct. In recent decades, in Solo at least, both *wayang wong* and *wayang kulit* have flourished more outside of the palaces than in, and so may be thought of as "outside" traditions.

Choreographed dancing with gamelan accompaniment is frequently performed on a small scale at weddings. The larger-scale choreographies are staged

55. For a thorough treatment of *wayang wong* in Yogyakarta, see Soedarsono 1984. See also Lindsay 1985. For an excellent, concise introduction to the art form and its history, practice, performance context, and musical accompaniment, see Susilo 1984.

56. According to Kusumadilaga, though, *wayang wong* was created in 1731 in Surakarta, at the urging of a "woman of European ethnicity" (1981:168). But what he describes was a masked dance, which must have corresponded either to the modern-day *tari topèng* (performed by silent, masked dancers), or *topèng dhalang* (which used to be performed, during *wayang*'s off-season, by masked *dhalangs*, who occasionally lifted their masks to speak). In either case, even though Kusumadilaga's *wayang wong* was *wayang* (mythico-historical drama), and even though it was *wong* (people), it was probably not what today is called *wayang wong*.

mostly in institutional settings. As in the case of music, institution-sponsored dances carry on the court tradition (unless they are consciously avant-garde or folk inspired). At the broadest level, court dances were divided into three categories: female, male, and theatrical (Brakel-Papenhuijzen 1995:24 ff.). Female dancing meant primarily the sacred, ritual *srimpi* and *bedhåyå* ensemble dances, though the "outside" *golèk* and *gambyong* dances were cleaned up and stylized, and incorporated into the court tradition as well. Male dancing meant warrior dances—stylized enactments of battles. Aside from *wayang wong*, theater forms that involve dance include *langendriyan* (the Javanese answer to opera, in which the actors dance as well as sing) and *wayang topèng* (masked dance drama). A more recent, fast-paced form of danced theater, *sendratari*, or *drama tari*, draws on all of these older forms to tell a historical or mythological story. According to Brakel-Papenhuijzen (1995:51), it was modeled on ballet. Frequently, excerpts from any of these theatrical genres are performed as set pieces, either with live or recorded music. Such excerpts may be performed in institutional or "outside" settings (mainly at weddings).

While the number of tourists visiting Solo is nowhere near the multitude that streams through Yogyakarta and Bali, tourism does play a role in maintaining the traditional arts, especially at the palaces. Throughout the month of September 1991, a spectacular Kraton Festival was held, in the hopes of attracting more tourists to Solo. Superb concerts of many traditional performing arts were held at both palaces. The event was attended by goodly numbers of Indonesians and a few foreign tourists. It introduced the court arts to many people (Javanese and foreign alike) who otherwise would not have known them firsthand. And yet, I couldn't help feeling a certain sadness. Three of the *sunan*'s daughters and a fourth Kraton dancer performed a *srimpi* dance at the Mangkunegaran (the *other* palace—a place where, to my knowledge, they had never danced before). The throngs of people were milling about, hovering around the perimeter of the dance area as if at a carnival, while the four dancers performed the long, exquisite, meditative choreography of the sacred dance *Anglir Mendhung*. Similar incongruities occurred at a royal wedding that was also held at the Mangkunegaran. This time, folding chairs and food were provided for all 4,000 guests. This was a formal, ritual event; yet, in the middle of the procession there were foreign tourists, in shorts, taking pictures from the most obtrusive spots.

A more successful incorporation of foreign visitors into the artistic scene has been the regular series of dance performances at the Mangkunegaran for wealthy Dutch and Japanese tourists. In 1992 these were given about once a month, always in the evening, when the palace was nearly empty. The guests, numbering about thirty, were served dinner, and then led out to the great *pendhåpå* for the performance, about which they were briefed by a Dutch-speaking member of the Mangkunegaran family. One of the very positive effects of these performances was that they helped to revive the almost lost *wirèng* and *langendriyan* dances in the Mangkunegaran style, and that they provided extra income for both musicians and dancers alike.[57]

BLURRED BOUNDARIES

In the preceding description of music making in Solo I set up various oppositional categories: institutional/"outside," court/school/radio, classical/popular, amateur/professional. In doing so, however, I underemphasized the fluidity between them. Indeed, there is a great deal of interaction between and overlap among all of the gamelan groups in Solo. Many of the musicians I saw at the Kraton also showed up at the Mangkunegaran, and some of these were also employees at the City Hall, at RRI, or at the *wayang orang* theater in Sri Wedari Park. Between one "outside" group and another, again, I often saw some of the same faces reappearing; many of these were also to be seen at the above-mentioned institutions.[58]

There is a Javanese saying, "Désâ måwâ cârâ, negârâ måwâ tâtâ" [The village has its ways, the city its etiquette]. This was quoted to me by the late Mloyowidodo (May 2, 1992), who had begun his career as a Kraton musician in colonial times. He was quick to point out that neither one is superior. The *cârâs* (ways) of the village cannot simply be dismissed as *kasar* (coarse) or *lugu* (simple, straightforward), although, at least materially, the Kraton is unquestionably more *alus* (refined). One of the anthropologist Walter Williams's interviewees, an older singer who grew up in an impoverished, remote part of central Java, described her nonliterate father's reaction to her decision to leave home as follows: "He did not really want me to leave, but he was always so smooth [*alus*] and indirect about the way he expressed himself" (1991:112). This strikes me as highly plausible: I was always treated more respectfully by strangers in the village than in the city, even though my presence as a "Dutchman" was probably more intrusive in the village. In terms of etiquette, Javanese peasants are much more *alus* than they are made

57. A *wirèng* is a mock battle dance, whereas *langendriyan* is a dance drama in which the dialogue is sung by the dancers themselves. See Daryono 1999 for a detailed overview of these tourist performances. He also concludes that their overall effect has been positive.

58. In the later 1980s and early 1990s the most isolated of all institutions was not the Kraton, but STSI. This is partly because of its location—on the extreme eastern edge of town—but also because the students and teachers there were kept so busy with their various duties. Indeed, many of the teachers were out of touch with the "outside" music-makers and had difficulty joining in with the groups that were on their level of musicianship, simply because the STSI musicians hadn't kept up with recent developments and had also forgotten some of the older repertoire that they had learned as students. On the other hand, they did and do often fill out the ranks for palace rituals (see Devereaux [and Hastanto] 1989). As of 2003 and 2006 STSI/ISI was much less isolated musically: the more ambitious students were participating in various "outside" groups around town, and there were proportionally more "outside" musicians teaching at the school.

out to be. Moreover, some of the most *kasar* linguistic behavior I have witnessed has been inside the Kraton, when people of high status were addressing their social inferiors. In sum, it is an oversimplification to equate "*alus*ness" with the palace, and "*kasar*ness" with the village.

But even demographically, the dichotomy between city folk and country folk has never been rigid. At least as far back as the early nineteenth century, when the extraordinary 3,500-page manuscript of the *Serat Centhini* (an "encyclopedia" of Javanese customs) was written—and certainly in the twentieth century—the court arts have been influenced by "country ways," and vice versa.[59] Many of the servants and courtiers, including performers, have had country roots. Back when the prestige of the courts was at its zenith, if a ruler heard of a superb musician, dancer, or puppeteer out in a village somewhere, he would make sure that that person ended up in his service. Such people maintained ties with their families in the country, much as those who live in the nation's capital, Jakarta, retain strong regional identities and attachments. Indeed, practically all Solonese seem to have some relation in the country whom they visit from time to time. Thus, not only were the court arts enriched by "outside" influences, but the villages often imitated the palace styles as best they could, although they never had full access to "inside" ways.

Other distinctions for which there are no clear dividing lines are the oppositions between rehearsal and performance, amateur and professional musicians, and classical and folk traditions. In the European tradition, a prototypical rehearsal has the following traits: its primary purpose is improvement rather than enjoyment; there is usually no audience; musicians talk about the music while it is going on or during breaks; pieces are rarely played from start to finish without stopping; and concert dress is usually not worn. A prototypical concert has the opposite traits.

But in the gamelan tradition, pieces are rarely stopped in rehearsal; the primary purpose seems to be for enjoyment rather than improvement; there is very little talk about the music, except during breaks between pieces; and participants might wear the same dress as for a performance. A concert is distinguished mainly by the presence of an audience. Yet there, too, there may be ambiguity. In the Kraton, for instance, the night before the yearly enthronement commemoration, musicians played *gendhing bonang* (long pieces with no "soft-style" instruments). The one time I attended, a few Japanese gamelan students and I were the only people listening, yet this was a highly formal affair. Conversely,

59. See Sears 1986 and 1996; Sedyawati 1984; Soeratman 1989:97–99; Mardusari 1987; Supanggah 1991b; Brakel-Papenhuijzen 1995:30–31; and Siregar [1990?]:109–16. I am also basing these statements on personal communications from musicians, in particular Rahayu Supanggah, who headed an oral history project in the Solo area.

when a group "rehearses" in someone's home, neighbors might come by to enjoy the music. There is much variety, however. The distinction between rehearsals and concerts is clearest at the music academies, which have adopted somewhat Europeanized styles of rehearsing and performing.

With amateurism and professionalism, again, there is more of a continuum than in the European tradition. Very few musicians support themselves entirely from performing. *Wayang* musicians accompanying a famous *dhalang* (shadow puppeteer) come close, as do those at the national radio stations; almost all of these are very highly skilled. In contrast, some musicians are never paid, never achieve much proficiency, and yet continue to participate in a group. Most musicians fall somewhere in between. The dual criteria of skill and income can be used, then, to establish endpoints on the continuum. But where the distinction really breaks down is in the composition of groups: "amateur" and "professional" musicians usually rehearse or perform together. This is made possible by the wide variation in the degree of complexity of the various parts.[60]

The terms *classical* and *folk*, like all music terms, are embedded in a particular cultural and historic context. Both are terms that have been used for different purposes, and with many different meanings. The prototypes conveyed by the terms as they were applied to European music are, on the one hand, an urban, elite, written, trained, complex, cosmopolitan, professionalized, evolving, composer-oriented tradition; and on the other, a rural, working-class, oral, untrained, simple, localized, amateur, unchanging, anonymous tradition.[61] Just how well these prototypes correspond to actual European (and, by extension, Western) practice is debatable (especially regarding the folk prototype).[62] With Javanese traditional music they are well-nigh useless. Gamelan music is found both in the cities and in the villages (though there are certainly stylistic differences between the two, and some differences in repertoire); it is music both of the educated elite and of the unschooled poor; it used to be an oral tradition, but now has a mixture of oral and written traits; some very good musicians are formally trained, some are not; some pieces are marvels of simplicity, some are complex by any standard; there have been minutely localized traditions, but increasingly there is transregional standardization; there is no sharp divide between the professional and the amateur; the tradition has continually evolved, undergoing

60. Whereas in the European tradition amateur and professional instrumentalists do not often mix, this is not as true of vocalists. See, for instance, Smith 1998. Indeed, one could argue, as does Smith, that the distinction is often very murky, even in the world of Western classical music.

61. See Bruno Nettl's entry on "Folk Music" in the *New Harvard Dictionary of Music* for an impressive attempt to define this protean concept.

62. For one thing, as in Java, European folk and classical spheres turn out not to be as separate as they once seemed. Increasingly, musicologists have looked into the points of contact and mutual influences between vernacular and learned traditions in Europe. Outstanding examples are Charles-Dominique 2007, Macchiarella 1995, and Salmen 1983 [1971]. See also the extensive literature on the pastoral trope in eighteenth-century music.

countless shifts in fashion, and yet, until recently, music of the past was not sharply set off from music of the present; and, finally, while composers' names are rarely mentioned or put at the top of a notated part, the composers of many pieces in the repertoire (or at least the sovereigns for whom the pieces were composed) are identified in oral accounts.[63]

NON-GAMELAN MUSIC IN SOLO

Karawitan (traditional gamelan music) is only one of many kinds of music produced and heard in Solo. In fact, some people grow up in Solo without ever paying the slightest attention to the music of the gamelan. Here, then, is a very brief overview of a few of the kinds of music that I observed during my three years there.[64] I will not discuss these further in the book, but they must be mentioned to avoid giving the impression of a homogeneous culture with a single musical tradition.

In my neighborhood, the most frequently heard live music was that made by teenagers sitting on the front stoop, strumming on a guitar, and singing Indonesian pop songs. There is a huge pop music industry based mostly in Jakarta (Wallach 2008), in which I am including various rock genres, some of which tend to have niche markets. These had and have local representatives as well (Suranto 1995, Perlman 1999), and they have kept up with global trends with the now-expected speed of the electronic age. Occasionally an Indonesian rock group would come through Solo and give a big, highly amplified concert that could be heard a mile away. Sometimes foreign groups of various kinds would also come through on tour. For instance, I heard an Australian "world beat" group that gave a free concert at STSI as well as a Dutch classical vocalist and pianist at a privately run arts center in town. Sometimes there would be a festival in which musical groups from other regions of Java or from other islands would perform. Another kind of non-Javanese music was that catering to the minority Chinese population. I once heard Buddhist ritual music being played at a Chinese funeral in the old Chinese part of town. Much more common was Chinese karaoke, which was sung at expensive Chinese restaurants (where Indonesian and English—and, much more rarely, Javanese—songs were also mixed in). Yet another kind of singing in a foreign language is *tahlilan* and *yasinan*, a kind of monotone Arabic chanting done on ritual occasions. Strictly speaking, I suppose, these are not music, as they are both prayers, consisting in reading selected verses from the Kur'an. They are, however, musical, and at least one participant in a *yasinan*

63. See, for example, Warsadiningrat 1987, which is subtitled *Serat saking Gotèk* (Written Based on Oral Reports).

64. For a good overview of the various genres of *recorded* music commonly heard in Solo up through the 1980s, see Yampolsky 1987. And for more recent genres heard around Solo, see Perlman 1999.

group told me that for him it was, indeed, a form of musical art. During my principal research period, in the world of gamelan musicians it was rare to hear either genre. In 2006 it was extremely common—one indication of the increased Islamicization of Indonesia, acknowledged by all.[65]

There are also several kinds of traditional Javanese music not performed on gamelan. (I will not describe *tembang* [Ng]—traditional Javanese singing—here, as it is often included in *karawitan*, and will be discussed elsewhere.) One kind of ensemble, which I heard in monthly live broadcasts from the national radio station, is called *larasmadyå* [J]. It consists of mixed choral singing in octaves (either using *måcåpat*[66] texts or Islamic poetry—in which case it is called *santiswaran* [J]), accompanied by frame drums (*terbang* [J,I]), a pair of hand-held bronze or iron tubular bells (*kemanak*), and a *ciblon* drum.[67] In the villages, if funds are short, it may replace a gamelan concert (*klenèngan*) or *wayang* on ritual occasions. Most of the groups that sang at the radio station were from the vicinity of Klathèn (often spelled Klaten), a town between Solo and Yogyakarta. I knew of only two groups in Solo that rehearsed regularly, one of which was at the Kraton.

Siteran, also a gamelan substitute, is a portable ensemble in which one or several zithers play approximations of the instrumental lines in a gamelan piece, along with a *ciblon*, singers (some of whom may be doubling as instrumentalists), and a gong substitute. This is a common form of itinerant music making (*barangan* [J]), for which the gong substitute is a blown gong (*gong bumbung* [J]—actually, a form of low-pitched trumpet that imitates the sound of the gong) rather than the less portable *gong kemodhong* [J] (a pair of bossed bronze plates that create acoustic beats when struck together and are suspended over large resonators). Another kind of door-to-door music is that afforded by the lively drumming of monkey trainers, who put on shows for anyone who wants to pay them a small fee. This is called *tlèdhèk kethèk* (monkey dance). Along the same lines, the intra- and intercity buses are commonly boarded by itinerant musicians who, for the most part, plucked or strummed lutes of various shapes and sizes, which are sometimes amplified with much distortion.[68] The array of homemade instruments is astonishing, and many are no doubt unique.

Kroncong groups are somewhat rare and less visible than gamelans, but there was one in the early 1990s that rehearsed in a *Satpam* (security guard) station not far from my house. In 2006 there was an excellent small *kroncong* group that

65. See, for instance, Perlman 1999 and Murtioso 1998. For general overviews of Indonesian Islam in recent years see Beck 2003 and Fealy and Hooker 2006.

66. *Måcåpat* is a category of classical Javanese verse. Its original context is poetry that one sings as one reads. However, texts in *måcåpat* meters are used in a variety of other musical contexts.

67. The *ciblon* is a medium-sized, double-headed, hand-played barrel drum associated with dance accompaniment.

68. For a description of bus music in an area not far from Solo, see Santoso 1995.

performed at a famous *warung* on the south side of town.[69] Like gamelan music, *kroncong* is now considered old-fashioned (Supanggah 2003), and, as previously mentioned, the two have merged into *campursari*, which has greatly overtaken them both in popularity. Supanggah (2003:1) estimates that nearly every village now has a *campursari* group. In his district just outside the city limits of Solo, there were three gamelan groups that rehearsed weekly on the gamelan at his house (an unusually large number nowadays for any neighborhood) and no *kroncong* groups, whereas there were five *campursari* groups (probably not an unusually large number).

During my period of research, in most neighborhoods men took turns on the night watch (*ronda* [I]), walking through the streets in small groups between midnight and 3:00 A.M. As they proceeded, they played percussive rhythms similar to the clapping patterns used in gamelan music, which they performed on bamboo sticks of various lengths. Finally, I must mention the sounds of the street vendors, which, though perhaps not intended as music, filled my neighborhood day and night. Aside from the vocal calls (such as a piercing, slowly falling *saaaaaaaaa-tééééééé*, reminiscent of the Kraton *bedhåyå* singers), there were, among others, a smallish gong (ice cream); a high, clanging bell (coconut ice cream); a steam whistle (*puthu*, a sweet rice and coconut snack); and a hollow clacking sound (noodles).

A NOTE ON "TRADITION"

In the foregoing I have used the word *traditional* several times. Since the remainder of this study focuses on traditional music, an explanation of why this is so, and what I mean by the term, is in order. The term has been problematized by innumerable authors, and it cries out for clarification. With respect to Javanese culture, penetrating critiques have been made by Florida (1993 and 1995), Pemberton (1994), and Lindsay (1985), and by the British dance ethnographer Hughes-Freeland (1993). The straightforward use of the term has been called into question because of the political uses to which "tradition" is put; because it is not always clear what is "traditional" and what is not (for one thing, many "traditional" practices turn out to be of recent or foreign origin); and because of the selective nature of what is presented as "traditional." Pemberton, in particular, has shown how "traditional" Javanese culture was created in reaction to the Dutch presence, and how this notion was used by the New Order regime (1966–98) to maintain the status quo. One could argue, though, that whatever forces shaped "traditional" Javanese culture, and however different pre-colonial Java may have been from what resulted from Dutch contact, this is now what is thought of as Javanese.

69. A *warung* is an inexpensive open-air food stall; this one was larger and more stationary than most.

It is likely that people in every culture intuitively agree as to what is traditional and what is not, though they may argue about the fine points. The Solonese certainly fit this pattern. Everyone agrees that *bathik* is traditional—though some say that *lurik* (a coarser, handwoven striped cloth) is even more traditional, even more Javanese; blue jeans, on the other hand, are not even in the running. *Traditional* is thus a handy way of reflecting a distinction that people make in practice, and no one has offered a suitable alternative. And because it reflects a conception of the arts held by the people I spoke with, I use it freely, without supercilious quotation marks.[70]

I believe, following Wittgenstein, that one can use a word without being able to define it. Nevertheless, because I might otherwise be misunderstood, I will try to circumscribe my use of the term *traditional*. The closest I can come to a definition is "Any shared practice (a repertoire, a style, a context, a medium) that is *perceived* (1) as having *persisted* through several generations (cf. the Latin *traditio*, from *tradere*, "to hand over," "to entrust," "to bequeath")—or, more specifically, as having predated living memory or Independence; and (2) as being *characteristic of* (and not necessarily *unique to*) the group of people in question (a family, a town, a linguistic group)." This definition attempts to reflect ordinary Javanese and English usage while at the same time answering some of the concerns of the above-mentioned critics. Note that there is nothing here about the *actual* origins of the practice, nor the degree of change that the practice has undergone. What concerns me is the *perception* of age, continuity, and group identity, not the actual timelessness or boundedness[71] (which we can assume are always fictional) of the tradition. I will leave to others the important work of analyzing *why* a practice might or might not be perceived in this way.

There is no point in hiding the fact that in general I prefer traditional music to modern hybrids, for reasons I will not go into here. But the answer as to why I have chosen this focus—despite increasing discomfort, among ethnomusicologists, with representing the Other as stuck in a static loop of unchanging ways—has to do more with particularities and happenstance than with an ideological or theoretical stance. The traditional music of central Java is especially

70. For a lively exchange on the self-conscious use of quotation marks, see Harold Fromm's contribution to *"Race," Writing, and Difference*, and Henry Louis Gates's reply (1986). Gates's well-argued position on "race" is close to that of Florida's on "traditional." Florida explains her use of quotation marks as follows: "I will use the semifictional categories 'traditional Java' and the 'modern world,' not as substantive entities but as fragile constructs that serve to delineate differences between conceptual orders that emerged in time through history" (1995:10). I might add that one other reason for using the quotation marks is to show that one is giving the English equivalent of the Dutch loan word *tradisi* as used by Indonesians in a particular context. Note that it is precisely because of this connection that I have chosen to remove the quotation marks (not unlike Marcel Duchamp's "Mona Lisa, Shaved"): I find ordinary usage of *traditional* and *tradisi* to be quite close to each other, and so the English word works just fine as an approximation for the conceptualization I encountered.

71. I am using this word as it has been used in anthropology for the past thirty years or so to refer to the way cultures have often been written about as almost hermetically bounded wholes.

rich in repertoire and in interpretations of this repertoire; its sounds are especially distinctive (and, to me, uniquely satisfying). Moreover, it is a kind of music into which I had already been initiated before I began my fieldwork. This in itself is not free from political overtones: why, for instance, was central Javanese *karawitan* among the first non-Western musics to be incorporated into music departments in the United States, starting in the late 1950s? That said, I did not join a college gamelan group because it represented the "high cultures of the East," but simply because it was there. In a sense, then, there was a well-beaten path that led me to Solonese gamelan music.

The fact that many ethnomusicologists before me have already written about this tradition has its downsides, to be sure: What about all of the lesser-known musics of Indonesia? And what of the nontraditional musics that have arisen in response to modern living conditions? Yet it has the distinct advantage of allowing for a selective, focused study that is somewhat freed from the descriptive exigencies of a first encounter. In other words, it is thus more feasible to do a study that goes into the same kind of depth and specificity that musicologists have long applied to Western art music.[72]

WHERE MY TEACHERS FIT IN

Since I have represented my teachers' individual voices throughout the book, I would like to introduce them one by one: they are the characters around which my narrative is woven. I will include here only the ones whose conversations I have cited extensively.

My principal singing teacher, as mentioned above, was Suhartå (born c. 1945). He grew up in Delanggu, a town several miles southwest of Solo. Both his parents sang: his mother at home, his father with local gamelan groups. He graduated from SMKI in Solo, studied in Yogyakarta for a year, then entered ASKI in Solo a few years later. I have thirty-five one-hundred-minute tapes with him in Indonesian with occasional forays into Javanese.

My *rebab* teacher was R. M. Sukanto Sastrodarsono (1921–94). He was of noble birth and grew up in one of the old neighborhoods surrounding the Mangkunegaran Palace in Solo. He completed a Dutch education through the end of junior high school (*mulo*), and first learned *karawitan* mostly in his own neighborhood. When SMKI opened in 1950 he was hired in the research division. He continued to study *karawitan* from the eminent palace musicians who taught at SMKI. Later he taught for many years in the United States. Upon his return to Indonesia, he was active in maintaining the musical activities at the Kraton, and, as a result, in 1989 was given the title K.R.M.T. Bojrodiningrat by

72. See, for instance, Dell Hymes's division of ethnography into three stages: systematic, topic oriented, and hypothesis oriented (1996:4–6).

Susuhunan (King) Pakubuwånå XII. I have roughly eleven ninety-minute tapes with him in Indonesian sprinkled with Dutch, English, and Javanese.

One of my first gamelan teachers, Rahayu Supanggah, is a consummate performer, composer, and ethnomusicologist. We first met in Paris in 1981, where he was working on his doctorate, after having taught in Java and Australia. He was born into a puppeteer family in 1949 and grew up in the villages of the hilly Boyolali area to the west of Solo. By the time he attended SMKI he had already absorbed much musical know-how. He received his Sarjana (bachelor's degree) in karawitan from ASKI in 1978, where he taught for many years, becoming the head of the then-named STSI in 1997. Subsequently he was the founding director of the graduate program in performing arts at STSI/ISI, a position that allowed him, to a greater extent, to pursue his international career as a composer and musician, primarily for theater and dance productions. He remains on the teaching faculty of ISI, but most recently he has put more of his energies into writing, composing, and performing, for which he travels widely and often. I have no tapes of the two of us from my main period of research, but I do have several dozen pages of fieldnotes of our conversations. Our language of communication has shifted over the years (first French, now mostly Indonesian).

My relationship with Sudarsono was primarily as a member of his various gamelan groups. I also studied drumming and *senggakan*[73] with him privately, and had several sessions just of conversation. He was born in Boyolali in 1948 (he and Supanggah knew each other as children). He attended SMKI and ASKI, where he studied with several eminent court musicians. Uniquely among my teachers, he has never been a civil servant. He taught several gamelan groups, some of them consisting of all women, some of them mixed (one of them was unusual in that both men and women played instruments together, in almost equal numbers). He continues to teach at least one mixed group that I joined briefly in 2006. He has been a mentor to many foreigners studying *karawitan* in Solo and has always welcomed them into his ensembles. I have roughly four one-hundred-minute cassettes with him in fast-paced Indonesian.

The remaining four teachers are all from an older generation (roughly the same age as Sukanto), and I approached all of them, towards the end of my stay, not as a *karawitan* student, but as a researcher. R. T. Mloyowidodo (1911–97) was known for several years as the oldest living musical expert in Solo. He was particularly admired for his astonishing memory (several hundred pieces memorized backwards and forwards) and for his outstanding *bonang*

73. As already mentioned, this is a kind of sung interjection with lighthearted lyrics. It appears to come quite naturally to Javanese musicians but was very difficult for me (I could rarely catch the words, and I rarely knew when it was time to put in a *senggakan*). I am probably the first person in Solo ever to take private *senggakan* lessons (a dubious honor, to be sure).

playing.[74] He came from a family of court musicians, and he himself was hired at the Kraton under Susuhunan Pakubuwånå X (reigned 1893–1939). After leaving the court he taught at SMKI and STSI. He was an instrumentalist at heart, utterly uninterested in vocal music, but otherwise eminently knowledgable and articulate. I have one and a half one-hundred-minute tapes with him in Javanese.

Sutarman Sastråsuwignyå (1920–2000—also known as Sutarman Pråjånagårå), acknowledged to be the foremost expert on Solonese vocal music, was born in the same neighborhood as Sukanto. His father, whom he rarely saw, was a minor aristocrat and a good musician. As a teenager Sutarman was a singer of *kroncong*, but then realized that he could excel if he switched to *karawitan*. He worked at SMKI for many years as a teacher and researcher, but did not teach at any of the government schools after 1973. He had a complete gamelan at home, where he gave private and group lessons. I have just over three one-hundred-minute cassettes with him in Indonesian with some Javanese.

Sastro Tugiyo (1922–2002) was regarded by many as the best *båwå* singer of his generation.[75] His voice can be heard on countless commercially recorded cassettes. In addition, he was an accomplished instrumentalist. He learned the rudiments of *karawitan* as a boy in Delanggu (the same town Suhartå is from), but once a week he attended the then-recently opened *karawitan* school in Solo called Kawruh Kaniyagan (KåKå—not to be confused with KoKar). This school was only for aristocrats, but Sastro Tugiyo was able to tag along with a friend of his who was of noble birth. Just before the Japanese invasion, he did a stint teaching *karawitan* in Borneo. In 1959 he joined the RRI, retiring in 1981. He traveled abroad once to Japan (with Mloyowidodo). As of 1992 he still sang occasionally and taught amateur gamelan groups. I have four-and-a-half tapes with him of varying lengths, in Indonesian.

Last, but not by any means least, Sudarsono Wignyosaputro (1927–2003) was well known as a teacher of gamelan and vocal music (less so as a performer). His grandfather was a court musician, starting with the reign of Susuhunan Pakubuwånå IX (1862–93). Wignyosaputro received a public Dutch education and taught elementary school for many years. Having learned the basics of *karawitan* at home, as a young man he continued his musical education informally at SMKI. He taught vocal music part time at STSI. I have two-and-a-half one-hundred-minute cassettes with him in Indonesian and Javanese.

Let me close this chapter with a few observations about my teachers in general. Nearly all of them were male. They were all married and had all raised children. They were all literate, some more profoundly so than others. Their levels of formal education ranged from grade school to graduate school, but this

74. The *bonang* is a two-octave, gong chime played with a pair of cylindrical padded mallets.
75. A *båwå* is an extended solo vocal introduction to a gamelan piece.

range is deceptive: nearly all were quite intellectual, in the sense of being given to theorizing.[76] Most of them had been born into poor families; a few had *priyayi* (aristocratic) backgrounds (although this is no guarantee of wealth). Some were from the village, some from the city, but all had received extensive musical training in Solo proper. Most of them were affiliated with one of the major music institutions, and none of them seemed to consider themselves to be *orang luar* [I] ("outsiders"), although most of them had grown up in an "outside" musical environment, that is, in a village setting far removed from a centralized institution.

My teachers' ages fell into two broad groups: those who were old enough to remember the reign of Pakubuwånå X (reigned 1893–1939), and those born around 1945, the time of Independence. The first group included some court musicians, while the second group was made up entirely of people who had studied at SMKI and ASKI.

All of my teachers were at least bilingual (in Javanese and Indonesian, usually with Javanese dominating). Several of them spoke three or four languages fluently. All of them, I believe, had been abroad at least once. They were not generally drawn to any musics besides *karawitan*, although a few had had experience performing some Western-influenced music when they were young.

Of my teachers involved directly in my research, two were Christian. The rest were mostly "Islam KTP" ("identity-card Muslims"). This means that they had to choose a religion for their identity cards, and since the default religion is Islam, that is what they put.[77] They drank alcohol quite freely and I never knew them to worship at a mosque. If they fasted it was either for Javanese reasons or out of solidarity with those who were fasting out of religious conviction. Two of my older teachers, both *priyayis*, practiced *kejawèn* (Javanese mysticism) regularly; the others also probably did as well, but less regularly.

Finally, all of my teachers had dedicated their lives to performing, understanding, and teaching *karawitan*, and they all shared their expertise with unceasing grace and generosity.

76. Geertz, too, has remarked on how surprised he was to be constantly launching into deep metaphysical discussions with people who had almost no formal education (1976 [1960]). Be that as it may, many Javanese musicians are not theoretically inclined, especially those among the rank and file.

77. Over the past decade, at least, performers have been showing more and more signs of Islamic piety (*pesindhèns* wearing Muslim clothing, Islamic content in *wayangs*, and the like)—see, for instance, Murtioso 1998 and Perlman 1999. During my main research period there seemed to be a certain tension between gamelan aficionados and devout Muslims: one American friend who lived in a predominantly Muslim neighborhood had to stop having rehearsals at his house during the month of Ramadan, for example.

TWO

THE TASTE OF MUSIC

Rasaning Gendhing

The meaning of the Javanese term *råså* [Ng] is one of the most elusive in the Javanese language for a nonnative speaker to grasp. It is used in different contexts to mean vastly different things; it is used in similar contexts to mean subtly different things; and it is tied to highly developed theories of cognition that do not match up very well with modern European and North American notions of how the mind works.[1] The closest all-purpose translation is "feeling."[2] In most musical contexts, this is not a bad approximation, though it can be misleading. *Råså* (in music) may also be translated as "sensation" or "inner meaning." But it sometimes means "the ability to express or perceive feeling or inner meaning," or "the faculty through which these are perceived" ("intuition").

In Sanskrit, the language from which *råså* derives, the word's usages are many and varied. They include the following: "sap," "juice," "essence," "marrow," "potion," "milk," "serum," "mercury," "semen," "myrrh," "mineral," "gold," "green" "onion," "resin," "flavor," "the faculty of taste," "fondness," "pleasure," "aesthetic affect," "sentiment," and "disposition" (Monier-Williams 1979 [1899]). Of these, "essence," "mercury," "flavor," "the faculty of taste," "aesthetic affect," "sentiment,"

1. See J. Weiss 1977 for the most complete account in English of Javanese theories of cognition. Discussions of *råså* in various Javanese contexts may be found in Sastrapustaka 1953, Geertz 1976 [1960], Padmosoekotjo [1960?], Hadiwijono 1967, Gonda 1973, J. Weiss 1977, Uhlenbeck 1978, Howe 1980, Mulder 1980, Stange 1984, Boow 1988, Magnis-Suseno 1988, Mulder 1989, Humardani 1991, J. Becker 1993, Florida 1995, Walton 1996, Hughes-Freeland 1997a, Grave 2001, Hardjana 2003, Marianto 2003, Nugroho 2003, S. Weiss 2003, Purwadi et al. 2005, Waridi 2005, Sulastuti 2006, and S. Weiss 2006.

2. Both Hughes-Freeland (1991:359–60) and Florida (pers. comm.) have suggested "sense" as an all-around translation. This, indeed, has connotations of sensation and intuition. But "feeling" has those same connotations as well. The difference is that, whereas "feeling" emphasizes emotion, "sense" emphasizes meaning—both of which are essential components of *rasa*. But in a musical context, "sense" simply does not usually work as a translation: what would be the "sense" of Mozart's G Minor Symphony, or *gendhing Gambir Sawit*? I suggest that, for musical compositions, "feeling" also encompasses meaning, since in both Java and the West, musical meaning is often equated with musical affect.

and "disposition" have all been retained in modern Javanese. Additional common usages are "inner meaning," "speech," and "refined perception." In literary Javanese it also means "mystery" or "secret," albeit often with a different spelling. In this sense it derives from a different Sanskrit etymon, *rahasya*, but in Javanese mystical writings the two are blended into a single concept (Gonda 1973:256).

Depending on the vocabulary set, the word may take on different forms; and there are many closely related words formed by adding prefixes, suffixes, and infixes, of which only a small handful are relevant to music talk.[3]

The Indonesian word *rasa* is not always an exact translation of the *ngoko råså*, since Javanese people often insert the *ngoko* word into an Indonesian sentence. The same may be said for the *krâmå* version of the term, *raos* (see, for instance, Sastrapustaka 1953:10). When *råså* is used in either an Indonesian or a *krâmå* context, it seems to carry metaphysical overtones that *rasa* and *raos* fail to convey. But this may be splitting hairs, and in many contexts native speakers would probably think of the three versions (*rasa* [I], *råså* [Ng], *raos* [K]) as variants of the same lexeme. For the most part, throughout the book I have used the Indonesian word *rasa* as a kind of unmarked, all-purpose term, and *råså* when I wish to emphasize its "Javaneseness," particularly as it relates to mysticism.[4]

Rasa may be turned into a verb by adding affixes. Transitive verbal forms ("to feel," "to understand") are *merasakan* [I], *ngrasakaké* (or *ngrasakkê*) [Ng], and *ngraosaken* [K]. The corresponding passive forms ("is felt [by X]," "is understood [by X]") are *dirasakan* [I], *dirasakaké* (or *dirasakkê*) [Ng], and *dipunraosaken* [K]; whereas the accidental passive forms ("is felt," "is noticeable") are *terasa* [I], *kråså* [Ng], and *kraos* [K].

Poerwadarminta, in both his Indonesian and his Javanese monolingual dictionaries, begins his entries for *rasa* with the sense of taste. This appears to be the most basic, literal meaning for speakers of both languages. It is worth quoting from both dictionaries.

Baoesastra Djawa (Javanese Dictionary):

[outer:]	I. 1 the quality of something when it strikes the tongue: *rasa pedhes* [spicy-hot], *pait* [bitter], *getir* [tart, acerbic, bitter], etc;
[middle:]	2 the quality of something when it strikes the body or the heart: *rasa keri* [tickling sensation], *rasa soesah* [sorrow], etc.;

3. For a more comprehensive catalogue of these offshoots, see Geertz 1976:239, Uhlenbeck 1978:161–75, and Horne's *Javanese-English Dictionary*.

4. I ask for the reader's indulgence if upon occasion I have been inconsistent; I am fairly certain that this would scarcely be noticed by most native speakers of Javanese, and so should cause no concern. While on the one hand the Javanese language seems to delight in a luxuriant and astonishingly precise vocabulary, on the other hand it enjoys great fluidity, particularly with regards to spelling. In fact, the symbol /å/is not normally used in Romanized Javanese texts, since a native speaker would automatically know which /a/'s are to be pronounced *a* (as in f*a*ther) and which should be *aw* (as in l*aw*), and the Javanese script does not have a separate character for the two sounds. I have used /å/for the benefit of non-Javanese speakers.

[inner:] 3 inner meaning (in *ngèlmu batin* [Javanese psychology/metaphysics], etc.).

[senses I.4, II, III, and IV are not used in referring to music, and so are omitted here]

Kamus Umum Bahasa Indonesia (General Dictionary of the Indonesian Language):

[outer:] I: 1 that which is experienced by the tongue or the body (when touched by something): *a sweet (bitter, hot, sour, etc.) rasa; a smarting (sharp, aching, sore, etc.) rasa; my feet have the rasa of being stabbed by needles;*

[outer:] 2 the quality of an object, etc., that gives rise to a rasa in sense 1: *sugar and honey have a sweet rasa; this medicine has a rasa like that of fish oil;*

[middle:] 3 that which is experienced by the heart or mind (when the senses perceive something); the condition of the heart or mind (in regards to something): *rasa sedih* [sorrow] (*susah* [sorrow], *kecewa* [disappointment], *pilu* [being moved], *senang* [being pleased], etc.); *rasa hormat* [respect] (*takut* [fear], *cinta* [love], *sayang* [affection], *iba* [compassion], etc.);

[mid./inner?:] 4 judgment (in the mind or heart) of good or bad, right or wrong, etc.; opinion: *rasa adil* (sense of fairness); *pada rasa saya* (in my opinion).

[senses I:5, I:6, I:7, and II are not used in referring to music, and so are omitted here]

Poerwadarminta organizes his definitions according to a Javanese psychological model in which a person's outer core (*lahir*) consists of the five senses; the middle core is where emotions, thoughts, and desires reside; and the inner core (*batin*) is the heart, which is the realm of "pure feeling" (or intuition—there is no adequate translation) divorced from the senses. Whereas in his Javanese definition the innermost level is "inner meaning" (*pathining teges*) or metaphysical reality, in his Indonesian definition it is "judgment" (*pertimbangan pikiran [hati]*). But since the heart is both what perceives inner meaning and what makes ethical judgments (that is, it allows one to see truth, to know directly what is right), both definitions are linked through a common Javanese theory of cognition.

Yet in neither definition does Poerwadarminta mention *råså sejati* (genuine/pure feeling). This rather specialized notion, of an extrasensory faculty of perception that intuits invisible essences, has been explored by authors interested in courtly or mystic interpretations of *råså* (Zoetmulder 1995 [1935]:182ff., Sastrapustaka 1953, Hadiwijono 1967, Howe 1980, Stange 1984, A. L. Becker

1993, Florida 1995, Grave 2001).[5] Many Javanese people see *råså sejati* as being characteristically Javanese. It is in this sense of "intuition"—and in the closely related meanings, "essence," "perception of essence," and "deep understanding"—that Javanese speakers often prefer *råså* [J] to *rasa* [I] when speaking Indonesian.

A stereotype one hears over and over in Java is that Western thought is guided by rationality, by concern for the material world; whereas Javanese thought is guided by intuition, by concern for the spiritual world, by *råså*.[6] Like all stereotypes, this is far too simple a picture. Many of the decisions Javanese musicians make are, in fact, guided by analyzable principles, which they are sometimes eager to discuss. But their subtlest—perhaps their most aesthetically important—decisions are ascribed to *råså*. This is certainly evidenced in the following report, by Suhartå (May 6, 1991), of Pak Pådå's[7] advice to him: "Javanese art—*karawitan*—is not like mathematics; it has to do with *rasa*. So, for example, 10 does not have to be 2 x 5."

Perhaps because very few living musicians are from *priyayi* (aristocratic) backgrounds, or perhaps because most of my discussions were in Indonesian, the more mundane senses (outlined in Poerwadarminta's definitions) predominated in the music talk I heard. These are the senses that I focus on most in subsequent chapters.

In exploring further how Javanese musicians use the word *rasa* here, I loosely follow Poerwadarminta's progression from the *lahiriah* [I] (outer) to the *batiniah* (inner), or, to put it slightly differently, from the *wadhag* (visible, corporeal) to the *alus*[8] (subtle, invisible, spiritual). Figure 2.1 is reproduced from Yoder 1987. It is a representation of the human psyche that Yoder saw hanging on the wall of Djojodihardjo, his principal teacher in matters of Javanese religion. The outer layers (the emotions and the senses) are relatively self-explanatory. The inner layers, however, require some elucidation. What Yoder translates as "the will" (*kerså* [KI,J], also spelled *kerso*),[9]

> is the seat of personal identity in human personality which can also be spoken of as the *jiwa* (soul). . . .
>
> But the *jiwa* is not the essence of a person. The inner core of a person, understood in terms of Javanese psychology, is the *cipto*, the unconscious will. (1987:220–21)

5. Although Sastrapustaka uses the term *råså sejati* (1953:8), he does not define it in its mystical meaning, but rather as the sixth sense, or "feelings of the heart" ("joyful," "troubled," etc.).

6. See J. Weiss 1977:265–67 and Bonneff 1976.

7. I do not have much information about Pak Pådå. When I was told about him in 1991, he was of an older generation but still alive. He was not a musician but a "paranormal" (someone able to perceive and communicate with the spirit world). Because of his highly developed *råså*, he was able to intuit the deeper meanings of music that ordinary musicians were blind to.

8. See chapter 3, pp. 65–66, for Clifford Geertz's gloss on this wide-ranging, fundamental word.

9. Weiss's principal teacher, the aptly named Dwidjo Sukarso (Sukarso = Karså), felt that *karså* (or *kerså*), though normally thought of as a *krâmå inggil* variant of the *ngoko* word *karep*, was quite distinct, at least when used as a psychological term. It can thus be used in all speech levels when referring to desire as an abstract faculty (J. Weiss 1977:242–43).

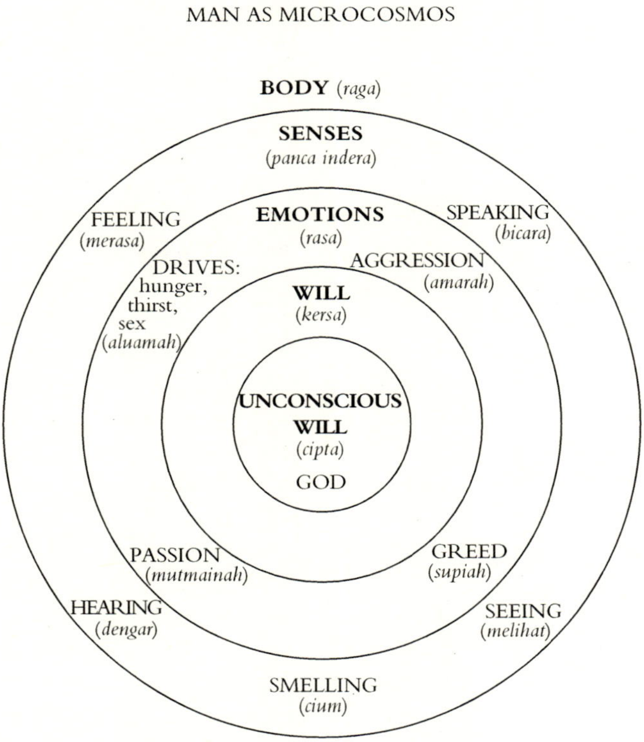

FIGURE 2.1. "A Javanese analysis of the human makeup." Based on Yoder's redrawing of an image displayed in the home of his teacher, Suhadiweko Djojodihardjo in Pati, Central Java (Yoder 1987:220).

I distinguish between *rasa* as (1) a quality of a musical object (a performance, a *gendhing*) or its effect on a perceiver;[10] (2) a mental capacity that is gained largely through experience; and (3) a faculty of perception that is innate but may be fully utilized only through training. In each case I will progress from the outer to the inner. Figure 2.2, which is meant as a guide to the discussion that follows, summarizes both of these analytical dimensions (the kind of thing *råså* is and its degree of depth), and is my attempt to make sense of the word as it is used in musical contexts. I have based these remarks on fieldnotes, recorded conversations, and published writings by Javanese musicians. More specifically, I have pored over some 150 oral citations by Javanese musical experts, culled from my transcriptions of recorded conversations.

10. I am conflating stimulus and percept here, though there are reasons not to. Poerwadarminta distinguishes between the two in his Indonesian definition, but not in his Javanese one. I am ignoring the distinction because musicians do not seem to observe it in casual speech, although they may emphasize it when waxing philosophical (see chapter 6).

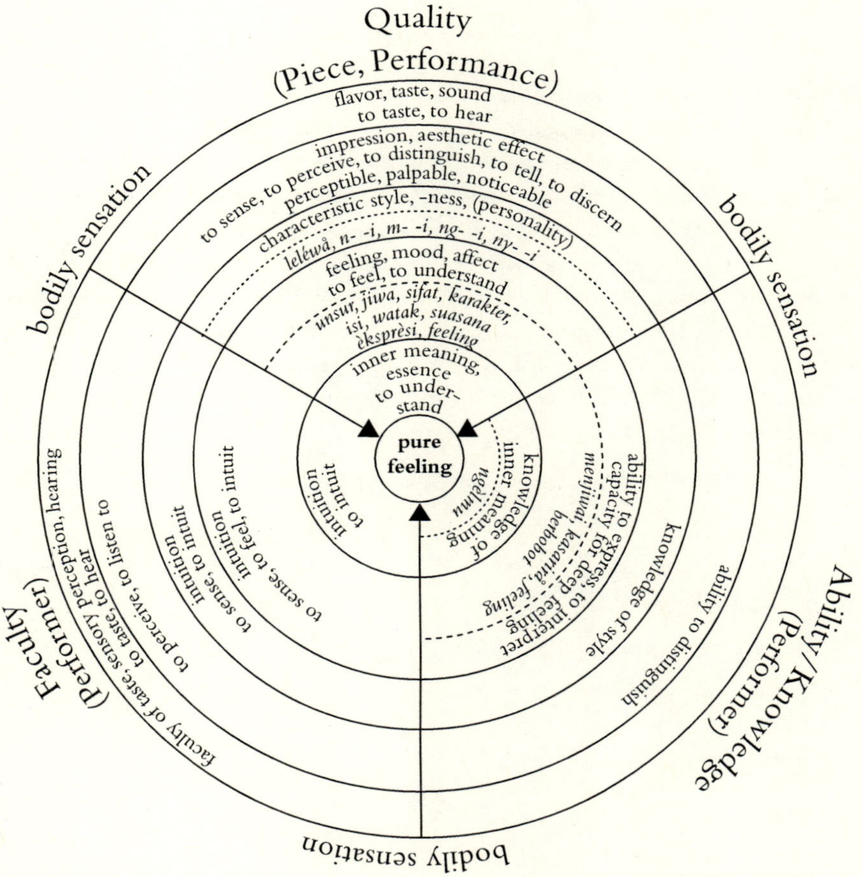

FIGURE 2.2. One way of thinking about *råså*. This is based on lexicographic analysis of mostly oral citations from Javanese musicians, as well as on various analyses of Javanese theories of perception. The concentric circles represent levels of perception, from most bodily or physical to most abstract; these can also be interpreted as layers of the human psyche. At the center is *råså sejati* ("genuine" or "pure" feeling/sensing), a kind of sixth sense that may bypass the other five. The three radial divisions represent three different but overlapping usages, each of which reflects an ontological category. The words in parentheses are the things that *råså* pertains to in each ontological category. Within each concentric circle are English-language translations for *rasa* or *råså* in the sense of that particular intersection of perceptual level and ontological category. Where there is a dotted line, the words below it are Javanese or Indonesian synonyms for the meaning in question (note that some of these are borrowed from English or Dutch). The prefixes and suffixes apply to adjectival *rasa* terms used to describe a piece or performance (usually the latter).

RASA AS A QUALITY

When Poerwadarminta's first definition of *rasa*, "taste," is applied to music, the word then becomes more self-consciously metaphoric than in its other meanings. The perception of music is thus likened to the perception of flavor or texture on the tongue. In the conversations I recorded, this came up mostly in abstract discussions of the nature of musical rasa—theorizing about the process by which it is imparted, and what the variables are (see chapter 6). But food metaphors abound in music talk, from the naming of compositions, to comparisons between melodic ornamentation and cooking spices (*bumbu* [I,J])—or between a performance's polish or finish and "ripeness" or "doneness" (*mateng* [J], *mentah* [J,I]).[11] A little closer to home is the use of many *rasa* terms borrowed from the domain of taste:

cemplang [I], *kembå* [J], *sepå* [J] (insipid)

langu [J] (rank, pungent)

énak [I,Ng],[12] *sedhep* [J] (delicious)

empuk [I,J] (soft, tender)

renyah [I,J] (crisp)

manis [I,K], *legi* [Ng] (sweet)

getir (sour [J], bitter [I])

pait [I], *pahit* [J] (bitter)

pedas [I], *pedhes* [J] (hot, spicy)

Shifting over to the sense of hearing, *rasa* refers to an aural sensation, to the sound (of something). And moving slightly inward we get to "an impression," "an aesthetic effect." *Rasanya kecil sekali* [JI] might be translated as "it sounds really high." The phrase *rasané bédå* [Ng], in speaking of a melodic variant, could be rendered "the impression is different." And *rasané kåyå båwå waé* [Ng] is approximated by "it sounds like a *båwå* (but shouldn't)." The transitive verb form, *merasakan* [I], in this usage becomes "to sense," "to perceive," "to hear," "to distinguish," "to tell," "to discern." Besides the more common verbal affixes, the accidental passive prefixes *ka-* or *k-* [J] (*ter-* [I]) may also be applied in this sense. K*råså* thus can mean "perceptible," "palpable," "noticeable."

11. See Benamou 2006 for a fuller exploration of food metaphors in Javanese music talk.

12. In Indonesian there is only one word for both "delicious" and "comfortable," while in Javanese these are usually distinguished: *énak* (Ng) or *écå* (K) versus *(ke)pénak* (Ng) or *sekécå* (K). Since most of my conversations were in Indonesian, it is not always clear which meaning of *énak* was meant. When listening to musicians speak in Javanese about music, I only remember hearing the word for "comfortable" (*pénak*) and never "delicious." Nevertheless, the Indonesian word was occasionally used in the context of a food metaphor, so "delicious" is a possible translation.

Getting a little further from the realm of pure sensation, moving towards the more subtle one of "pure feeling," we come to *rasa* as a characteristic style. The best translation here is often the suffix *-ness* applied to the style in question. *Rasa Jawa* [I] could thus be rendered "Javaneseness," and *rasa mérong* [JI], "*mérong*-ness."[13] The second term in these noun-modifier pairs is usually a genre or a geographic region. This sense of *rasa* is akin to "essence," but more superficial. Supanggah (1988a) uses the word *leléwå* (character, nature) in precisely this sense. I have never encountered a corresponding verb form.[14]

Moving ever inward, we find *rasa* being used to refer to a particular "feeling" or "mood" in the music.[15] Thus, *rasa gendhing* [JI] (or *råså gendhing* [Ng], *rasané gendhing* [Ng], *rasaning gendhing* [Ng], *raos gendhing* [K], *raosipun gendhing* [K], *raosing gendhing* [K][16]) means "the feeling of a piece of gamelan music." "Feeling," here, can either be an emotional state (such as *sedhih*), an atmosphere(such as *ramé*), a character trait (such as *gagah*), or some other descriptive term (such as *seger* or *kaku*).[17] When this is made into a verb—*merasakan* [I] (*ngrasakaké* or *ngrasakké* [Ng], *ngraosaken* [K])—it simply means "to feel." Either a piece or a performance of a piece can have *rasa* in this sense. The object of the verb, however, is more commonly a piece. (It seems to require more skill to "feel" a piece, which is more abstract and hence more ineffable, than it does a performance. And it is more usual to talk about the more problematic case.) For the purposes of this study, I have taken this sense of *rasa* to be primary: chapters 3, 5, 6, and 7 focus primarily on *rasa gendhing*. (Chapter 4, on the other hand, is mostly about *rasa* as intuition or deep understanding.)

The most profound, esoteric meaning of *rasa* as a quality is "inner meaning," or "essence." In literary texts, the *su-* prefix is likely to be added, to form the

13. The *mérong* is the first, calm section of a medium-large to long gamelan piece.

14. For this, one has recourse, in Javanese, to applying the n-/ng-/m-/ny- prefix and the -i suffix directly to the thing whose essence is (or isn't) being expressed: *mbawani* (to be truly *båwå*-like), *nyindhèni* (to be *sindhèn*-like).

15. Interestingly, in Ewe aesthetics, according to Fiagbedzi, the level of feeling is also considered to lie two levels down from sensation, with the level of distinguishing or perceiving in the middle:

> Aesthetic experience may thus be said to operate at three levels of (1) *seselelãme* or *seselefutome* (i.e. sensation or direct sense impression, either physical and/or psychological), (2) *sidzedze nu* i.e. cognition or perception (lit., the process or act of mentally placing, recognizing or knowing of, a thing) and (3) *seselelãme* or *seselefutome* (emotion, i.e., affective reaction to a thing or situation). (2005:11)

Note that, although there is a separate term for the second level, the same term is used for the first and third levels (as in Javanese and Indonesian). Even though the Ewe have traditionally lived in the coastal regions of Togo and Nigeria, and so some distance from the predominantly Muslim regions of West Africa, it is tempting to speculate whether there isn't a Sufi connection here.

16. The suffixes *-nya*, *-né*, *-nipun*, and *-ning* may be roughly translated as "of." They emphasize the possessive relationship between *rasa* and *gendhing*, which is already expressed by their juxtaposition. That is, *rasa gendhing* already means "the *rasa* of a *gendhing*" even without the suffixes.

17. Rough equivalents for these *rasa*s are as follows: *sedhih* [J] (sad); *ramé* [J] (bustling); *gagah* (manly); *seger* [J] (refreshing); *kaku* (awkward). Note that some musicians distinguish between an atmosphere and the *rasa* associated with it.

related word *suråså* [Ng]. The *suråså* of a *gendhing* is something ordinary people have to search for (by pondering a *gendhing*'s title, for instance): *golèkånå surasaning lagu* (seek the essence of the melody) (Martopangrawit 1972:59). People who are spiritually developed, who are aware of the spirit world (*alam alus*), can sense it directly. These people are frequently nonmusicians (for instance, Pak Pådå, quoted on p. 43). I have heard many illustrative stories that revolve around a *klenèngan* that was held at the house of Pandji Soetopinilih every eve of *anggårå kasih*.[18] Suhartå gave me a fairly full account (March 26, 1992) of the one time he had attended. The lights were put out, and *gendhing Gambir Sawit* was
II:2 played in darkness.[19] Afterwards there was a discussion. The young musicians all felt that it had been a high-spirited piece—the usual interpretation—and had put in all sorts of vocal interjections to liven it up. The older people who were present, however, concurred that the inner meaning of *Gambir Sawit* had revealed itself to be *lemeng*[20] (happy on the outside, but troubled on the inside—like someone being compensated for a loss).

In all these uses of *rasa*, the object of perception has been either a performance or a piece. There is one sense, however, in which the quality being perceived belongs to a person. For example, Suhartå once said that *pélog limå*—a particularly "heavy" or serious melodic mode—was "well-suited to [his] *rasa*" (May 2, 1992). The meaning of the word in this case is very close to "personality" or "disposition." This usage is rare, since there are better words in Javanese and Indonesian for personality.

RASA AS AN ABILITY

Rasa as a mental or spiritual capacity ranges from the ability to distinguish between various styles to knowledge of inner meaning (I have not heard it used for the ability to taste or to hear in a musical context).

According to the German theologian and Javanist Franz Magnis-Suseno, an essential component of Javanese *råså* is knowing one's place in society and in

18. *Anggårå kasih* is a ritually important day of the Javanese thirty-five-day month, associated with Ratu Kidul, the powerful spirit "Queen of the South."

19. This practice, called *muryo raras* (various spellings, meaning uncertain; may mean "in order to feel harmonious"), is still occasionally carried out, especially as a sort of prayer for musicians who have recently died or are in ill health. One place where it happens frequently is at the monthly *klenèngan* (music-making session) at SMKI (Indonesian High School for Javanese Performing Arts), which is held (coincidentally?) on the eve of *anggårå kasih*. Waridi (2005:313–23) and Perlman (1994:349) describe the *muryo raras* sessions held at Prince Kusumåyudå's house in the 1920s.

20. I have not found a dictionary definition that is anything close to Suhartå's. The word *remeng* (dark, murky) is a much better match, but there is no mistaking the "r" on the recording for an "l." Nevertheless, in many words the two letters are more or less interchangeable (*luruh* and *ruruh, laras* and *raras*), and so Suhartå's *lemeng* might indeed be a variant of *remeng*. See also the section on "Mixed *Rasas*" in chapter 3.

the universe (1988:156ff., 197ff.). Indeed, he claims that Javanese ethics in general revolve around *råså* in the sense of understanding. An adult Javanese not only knows what is appropriate intellectually, but also feels it intuitively as a result of socialization. *Råså* is what prevents one from openly disagreeing with a superior, or from asking that a borrowed object be returned (which would be petty),[21] or from admitting that one is hungry when one is an unexpected guest. All these actions (or inactions) are intuitive rather than the result of calculation—it just wouldn't *feel* right to do otherwise. Yet they involve understanding as well: one must know what will maintain social harmony in order to act suitably. (While *råså* is what guides one's actions, the expression that is most often used in these circumstances is a sort of negation of the opposite of *råså*: *ora tegel* (Ng)—" [I] couldn't bring myself to do it," in other words, "[I] didn't have enough lack of *råså* to do it.")

Being able to express the right feeling musically, then, depends not only on knowing how to produce the right effect through details of *garap* or "interpretation," but also on sensing what is appropriate to a particular situation.[22] This might mean, for instance, knowing when to sing plainly or to let loose with ornaments, depending on whether a piece were solemn (*regu*) or jovial (*bérag*), or on what the genre or context called for. One is guided by feelings, but feelings learned through socialization of what is appropriate to a social context or musical mood, and it is the relational nature of these feelings that is regarded as particularly Javanese.

As far as I know, there is no verb form corresponding to musical *råså* in this sense. There is, however, a synonym, *jiwa* [I] (soul, spirit), which has a corresponding verb form, *menjiwai* [I], "to express the *jiwa* of" (see subsequent discussion of synonyms).

The capacity to have deep feelings is something Sudarsono often spoke of with me. For him, listening to a musician who lacks this capacity but is otherwise competent is like looking at someone who is good looking but, for some inexplicable reason, is not attractive. For a musician to have *rasa* in this sense, he or she must play or sing with *greged* (dynamism, vigor); it is not enough just to be in tune and in the right place at the right time. Sudarsono's ideas about playing with feeling struck me as being particularly close to nineteenth-century European notions of musicality that are still prevalent (feeling, *Gefühl, Ausdruck*, expression, and the like), but perhaps with less of an emphasis on subjective emotion. The similarity is underscored by his occasionally using the English word *feeling* instead of *rasa*. A *gendhing* might have deep feeling, too. A profound *gendhing*, for Sudarsono, is typically one that is simple and yet never tiresome.

21. See Keeler 1975:98–99.

22. Cf. the following view, by an expert on *wayang* iconography: "According to Suhatmanto, the key to achieving *rasa* lies in the presence of correctness and appropriateness in a given work." Sedyawati 1981:20.

The deepest sort of mental capacity is knowledge of inner meaning, or *ngèlmu* [J]. This kind of knowledge can be passed on from an *empu* (master), but more likely is the result of one's having developed the faculty of *råså* as intuition, which will be discussed shortly.

RASA AS A FACULTY OF PERCEPTION

When we speak of *rasa* as a faculty of perception, we have drifted quite far from the English word *feeling*. Nevertheless, when *rasa* refers to the outer sensory faculties of taste and hearing, it is easily assimilated into modes of thought associated with the English language: the terms "sensory perception," "taste," or "hearing" are quite close to this meaning of *rasa*. Not so, however, of the deeper faculty of intuition. This is an extrasensory faculty of perception, through which the properly trained heart can "feel" essences directly. Paul Stange, in his oft-quoted account of how *råså* functions within the precepts of the *Sumarah* mystic movement, describes the faculty thus:

> Rasa is at once the substance, vibration, or quality of what is apprehended and the tool or organ which apprehends it. . . .
>
> Within Sumarah "rasa" is considered an organ or constituent of our psychology in precisely the same sense as "thought" is. In fact it is commonly said that "mind" is the tool through which we register and process information received through the five senses from the outer world, *alam lahiriyah*, while "rasa" is the tool through which we apprehend inner realities, that is[,] alam *batiniyah*. (1984:119)

Stange's characterization of *råså* as an organ helps to clarify an otherwise opaque statement by Mloyowidodo. I quote it at length not because it is typical, but rather because such ways of talking have become rare, and this is a usage of *rasa* that I do not dwell on in the remainder of the book. Nevertheless, it is (to quote Stange out of context) "profoundly rather than incidentally Javanese." Mloyowidodo was born in 1911, and had been a court musician before Independence. His professed religion was *kepercayaan* [I], which literally means "belief," but which he was using as an oblique term for *kebatinan* [Ng, I] or *kebatosan* [K]: Javanese mysticism, science of inner life (literally, "interiority"). According to Supanggah, his way of thinking was typical of his generation but is now all but extinct (April 12, 1992).

> MW: So, way back when I was learning from the old generation, they told me, "if you're playing ['facing'] the gamelan, you have to meditate." Meditate focusing on the gamelan, that is. So I concentrate on what I'm playing. If it's *rebab*, I just concentrate on that. I don't glance around to see what else is going on. If I play *bonang*, same thing. Because you have to follow the *gendhing*, you have to follow the *wiled* [improvised melodies]. If my thoughts wander, it goes awry, it falls apart. So when I play, I'm in a state of meditation. That's how I'm able to attract ["pull"] those

who are listening. [...] Their *raos* [K] (*råså* [Ng]) can be pulled. From one *raos* to another. [...]

MLB: Just now you said that playing has to be like meditation. When you were studying *karawitan* did you also study meditation?

MW: Yes. On the side. Along the way. [...] But I didn't actually study it—those who knew a lot about it...gave advice. So when you played...well, like me, like Pak Martå[23]—the oldest generation—we're sure to pay a lot of attention to it. Because of my meditation...you are drawn by my meditation. Without realizing it you're drawn by my *raos*. Let's say you're listening to a *klenèngan*—if you're not listening you won't be drawn in—but if you've come just to listen, and the players are all of my generation, you're going to be drawn in. That doesn't necessarily mean that my playing is good, though. But you're drawn by my meditation. I've pulled your *raos* with my *raos*. That's what you call *kebatosan*! That was in the old days! Nowadays, it's no longer... [*laughs*]

The most puzzling passage in the above quote is the one in which Mloyowidodo says "I've pulled your *raos* with my *raos*." There seems to be a shift from "your faculty of perception" to "my ability." But is there?[24] Stange's notion of an *organ* of perception might work for both, and the following discussions of vibrations by Javanese experts in metaphysical knowledge show how:

In meditation like this we make use of or receive the waves of nature. Thus, we can receive the waves of nature and we can cause waves to vibrate in nature around us. Nature also records waves. But, on the other hand, we can also record or receive the recordings of nature. It depends on our sensitivity towards the vibrations. What I mean when I refer to rasa is how sensitive our rasa is. We can receive the waves of nature with our rasa and we can also cause waves to vibrate outside ourselves. (Suwondo, quoted in Howe 1980:76)

If a person studies *kabatinan* [also spelled *kebatinan*], he knows that *cipta* [capacity for thought], *karsa* [desire], and *rasa* [capacity for feeling] have vibrations. The vibrations from these three elements constitute the vibrations of a person's feelings. Thus, a person's feelings and intentions can penetrate into the invisible world. People who have already studied this spritual world also possess feeling and vibrations, and if these enter into it, they all flow into the same place. Your feelings and my feelings become one

23. Martopangrawit (1914–1986), generally considered to be the foremost Solonese musician of his generation. Like Mloyowidodo, he grew up in a family of court musicians.

24. Another example where these Western distinctions seem misleading is in the expression *adu råså, adu semu* [Ng], which Sukanto translated as "an interaction of feeling, an interaction of suggestion." *Adu* (to pit against each other) has the same transformative quality that *tarik* or *dudut* have in the quote from Mloyowidodo (Supanggah glossed it as an "inner dialogue through body language and feeling, for the purpose of attaining a common goal" [pers. comm., August 12, 2009]). Once again, Sufi ideas about music are evoked here: *hâl* in Persian music, which in many ways overlaps with musical *råså*, seems to be sometimes used in somewhat similar ways: they both may refer not only to a listener's affective state but at the same time to a musician's skill in bringing it about (During 2001, chapter 3). Interesting parallels might also be sought in the Arabic terms *ṭarab* and *iḥsās* (Lambert 1997, chapter 10; Racy 2003; Lambert 2004). I am indebted to Mary Hunter for pointing out the possible Arabic parallels.

in the spiritual world. If I can look into it, I can guess yours. (Dwidjo Sukarso, quoted in J. Weiss 1977:287)

Before leaving this topic, a final brief note about parts of speech: *rasa* in the sense of a faculty of perception, whether sensory or extra-sensory, is very common in its verbal forms, in which case it means "to taste," "to hear," "to listen to," "to perceive," or "to intuit."

SYNONYMS FOR *RASA*

Whereas *rasa* itself has multiple meanings, there are also multiple terms that cluster around the word in its various usages. Some common words that are used synonymously with what I am calling the primary sense of *rasa* in music talk ("affect," "mood," "feeling") are

unsur [I] (element),

jiwa [I], *jiwå* [J] (soul, spirit),

sifat [I], *sipat* [J] (nature, attribute),

karakter [D,I,J] (character),

watak [J,I] (personality, character),

isi [J,I] (content),

suasana [I], *swasånå* [J] (atmosphere).

Less common are the loan words *èksprèsi* [D] (expression) and *feeling* [E]. The sheer number of synonyms is one indication that this sense is somehow more basic to aesthetic discussions than the other senses—one or another of these terms comes up again and again in conversation with musicians. Several of these words deserve special mention.

Unsur (I), a term that was used most notably (but not exclusively) by the influential singing teacher Sutarman, literally means "element," "constituent." Sutarman's examples of *unsur gendhing* correspond exactly to the sort of thing others call *rasa gendhing* (although there are other idiosyncracies in the specific terms he uses for the various *unsurs*).

Suasana [I] (*swasånå* [J]) means "situation," "atmosphere," "mood," and is hence most often used in connection with *wayang* (shadow theater) or some other dramatic form, such as dance drama. Some musicians distinguish between the *suasana* of a dramatic scene and the *rasa* of the music that contributes to it, while others freely substitute the first term for the second.

Watak (J,I) means, roughly, "innate personality"—the part of one's personality that one can't do anything about.[25] *Wataké yå ngono* would mean something like

25. See J. Weiss 1977:59–67.

"that's just the way s/he is." While this word is usually used for people, it is sometimes used to refer to the characteristic mood of a piece of music (i.e., its character). In fact, musicians often talk about pieces as if they were people: just as some people are harder to get to know, while others—perhaps with a sunnier disposition—are more approachable but more superficial, so, too, pieces can be deep and inscrutable, or lighthearted and appealingly unambiguous. And, just like people, *gendhings* can come across very differently depending on the circumstances. That is, the musicians can give them a wide variety of moods, depending on the musical treatment they choose for a particular occasion (see chapter 7). Sometimes this brings out the "true" nature of the *gendhing*, sometimes it is said to go against it. Another way in which *rasa gendhing* is related to *watak* is in the specific terms used: many *rasa* terms are not so much emotions as they are personality types or human behavioral traits (e.g., manners of speaking, dressing, walking). Examples are

bregas (dapper)

sigrak (energetic, agile)

trègèl (impetuous, vivacious)

alus (genteel, soft-spoken)[26]

gagah (handsome, manly)

mrabu (regal)

prenès (coquettish)

luruh (humble)

branyak (brash)

lanyapan (erect of posture and direct of gaze)

wingit (spooky, spectral)

manis ("sweet," dark-skinned and attractive)

rongèh (fidgety)

sarèh (calm, relaxed).

A close synonym for *watak* is the Dutch loanword *karakter* (I), "character." This is used mostly in writing by conservatory-educated musicians. Both *watak* and *karakter* are very often employed to describe the differences between the various *wayang* characters, for which the terminology overlaps considerably with both music and dance descriptors: *alus, gagah, luruh, branyak, lanyapan.*

Like *watak, jiwa* [I] (*jiwå* [J]) is often used to refer to a *gendhing*'s true nature.[27] And, like *watak*, it can refer to a performer's personality. Literally, it means

26. *Alus* has other, related meanings in other contexts (see chapter 3).

27. Sometimes it is used with the *ke- -an* or the *pe- -an* circumfixes. However, both *kejiwaan* and *penjiwaan* seem to be interchangeable with *jiwa* in this context. In ordinary conversation it is quite common to drop many of the affixes, and so one might surmise that *jiwa* is simply a more informal

"soul," and so is close to "essence," though it usually has the more prosaic meaning of "mood" or "affect." It is more common in its verbal form, *menjiwai* [I], which, according to a standard Indonesian-English dictionary (Echols, Shadily, et al. 1989), means "inspire, be the soul of." When a musician says *kurang menjiwai*, however, he or she means "[s/he] fails to bring out the proper affect."[28] The closest Javanese equivalent, *njiwani* [J], seems to be rarely used (I've never heard it in this context). Not quite as uncommon, perhaps, is the Javanese synonym *kasarirå* (to be overcome, i.e., to become one with, to take into one's body). Martopangrawit, in a didactic poem, uses *kajiwå* [J], apparently to mean "assimilated" or "internalized": *rerasen nganti kajiwå* (dwell on [the essence of the melody?] until you have assimilated it) (1984 [1975]:242).

While Geertz claims that in *rasa* "feeling and meaning are one" (1976:239), I prefer to see "feeling" and "meaning" as different levels of *rasa*. Nevertheless, I will admit that there is a fine line between them. In fact, *jiwa* can be used for both.[29] A more common synonym for *rasa* as inner meaning, however, is *isi* (I,J), which means, literally, "content(s)."[30] *Jiwa* and *isi* are tied in other ways, though, since *isi* can refer to the spirit that inhabits a revered heirloom, such as a *keris* (dagger) or gong. *Isi* can also refer to the content of a poem, and, by extension, both to the referential meaning in a *gendhing* title (for instance, a low melodic
I:1 range in the piece *Kombang Mårå* ["The Bumblebee/s Arrive/s"]) and to the affective content of a piece.

ON THE PERILS OF TRANSLATION

In the discussion above, I divided the usages of *rasa* into various categories. This was to show the array of meanings the word can have in musical discussions, and the differences between *rasa* and any one English translation of it. But one may well ask to what extent these various meanings are discrete in Javanese or Indonesian. In trying to sort my various citations of *rasa* into distinct senses, I kept coming up against the problem of where to place them—even those that

---

variant of the longer forms. Note that this is a highly unusual usage of *kejiwaan* (it is not listed in any dictionary, as far as I know), which usually means "spiritual," "psychological," "spirituality," or "psychology." Similarly, *penjiwaan* is not even listed as a possible form. So either this usage is a case of hypercorrection—a fancy substitute for *jiwa*—or else affixation is being used creatively to extend the lexicon. *Kejiwaan* or *penjiwaan* might thus mean either "something related to *jiwa*"—"mood," for example, or "spirituality" (compare *gunung*, "mountain," and *pegunungan*, "foothills")—or "knowledge of *jiwa*" (compare *keturanggan* [J], literally, "knowledge of horses;" or *pedhukunan* [J], "witchcraft").

28. The Indonesian me- -i affix pair, and its Javanese equivalents, can be used intransitively to mean "to have the quality of x" or "to become x." See footnote 14, above.

29. In Indonesian, more than in Javanese, *jiwa* can have the same meaning that the English *spirit* has in "the spirit of the law." The Dutch *geest*, "spirit," can be used in this same way as well, and one must wonder whether this isn't more than just a coincidence.

30. For additional confirmation of the connection between *isi* and *rasa*, see Boow 1988:89.

had at first seemed to be obvious examples of one usage or another. I was beginning to have what seemed like a perfect example of Quine's indeterminacy of translation thesis. His thesis, as stated in *Word and Object*, is that "manuals for translating one language into another can be set up in divergent ways, all compatible with the totality of speech dispositions, yet incompatible with one another" (1960:27). One of the consequences of this is that a non-native speaker can never be sure whether he or she has "gotten it right."

In a less hypothetical way, Eleanor Rosch Heider (1972) has shown how it is possible to use color terms in a newly acquired foreign language and be systematically wrong without realizing it. She then demonstrates a clever way of discovering native categories while removing the cultural blinders that can get in the way. Even though Heider, in the end, is more optimistic about the foreign researcher's ability to uncover "the system" (at least for measurable things like color), both she and Quine seem to feel that there is a right answer to the question "does *this* mean *that*?"

The problem has been stated more congenially by Nida:

> (1) no word (or semantic unit) ever has exactly the same meaning in two different utterances; (2) there are no complete synonyms within a language; (3) there are no exact correspondences between related words in different languages. In other words, perfect communication is impossible, and all communication is one of degree. The statement of equivalences, whether in dictionaries or in translations, cannot be absolute. We are faced, therefore, not with a problem of "right or wrong" but with "how right" or "how wrong." (1975:5)

What all three authors would agree on is that translation can cover up misunderstandings that one may never be aware of. This point is emphasized by A. L. Becker:

> The unavoidable problem we face in understanding a distant language is that our understanding begins within the bounds of our own language, and, although we can try very hard to overcome this problem and with new experiences go beyond these bounds, we remain to the very end outsiders engaged in a utopian task—one of those many human tasks in which we must always settle for approximations. (1995:231–32)

To return to the question of how discrete the various usages of *rasa* are, it may be that I can never really know. It may be, too, that it is different for different native speakers, and that there is no definitive answer. It does seem, though, that *rasa* is more like the English word *love* than it is like *case*. One can distinguish between many kinds of love (motherly love, Christian love, romantic love, sexual love, a penchant for something). But these meanings often overlap considerably. The meanings of *case*, on the other hand (court case, violin case, case of beer, to case a joint, grammatical case, in case), are kept quite distinct: there is rarely any ambiguity as to which is meant.

Stange, who has probably gotten as close as any English speaker to "getting it," certainly feels that the meanings of *rasa* overlap:

> Because rasa links the physical sense of taste and touch to emotions, the refined feeling of the heart, and the deepest mystical apprehension of the ultimate, it provides a continuum which links surface meanings to which anyone can relate to inner levels of experience which normally, at least within our context, appear discontinuous. (1984:127)

The key, here, is that these meanings *appear* to English speakers—because of their language and the "prior texts" they have in it—to be discontinuous.[31] We would do well to heed this warning. In the pages that follow, it must be remembered that when I translate *rasa* as any one of the many approximations I have found for it, others might do just as well. It is thus essential, when encountering any particular instance of the word in its various forms, to keep in mind *all* of its connotations, as well as its theoretical underpinnings. As the philosopher Wittgenstein has put it, "to understand a sentence means to understand a language" (1958, §199).

IN A WORD

The foregoing has been, admittedly, necessarily dense in places. Here, then, are a few points worth retaining. *Rasa*, in its various manifestations, can be either a noun or a verb. As a noun it can refer either to a perceptible quality or to a mental faculty; as a verb it means "to sense," "to feel," "to understand," or "to intuit." These, and all other relevant meanings of *rasa*, can be placed along a psychological continuum, from "outer" to "inner"; that is, from the realm of bodily sensation to that of pure intuition. Finally, the most common acceptation, in a musical context, is "feeling" or "affect," though its many other senses are often hovering nearby.

31. See A. L. Becker 1995 for various formulations of what he means by *prior text*. Very roughly, it is an accumulation of particular, contextually embedded linguistic memories, which may be personal or cultural (that is, shared). Some related concepts are word associations, connotations, and contextually rich usage. Prior text is not unlike the corpus of citations from which lexicographers derive their definitions, but it is likely to include a great many more oral than written instances, and the contexts of these citations are likely to be more fully remembered.

THREE

THE CLASSIFICATION OF *RASA GENDHING*

The way people habitually describe music is part of what DeNora calls (following Meyer 1967) their *preparatory set*, which consists of "those things that may dispose the listener to hear and thus respond in one way rather than another" (2003:105). In other words, hearing or overhearing music being discussed authoritatively in *this* and not *that* way affects how one hears it, and this is true whether one is a child or an adult, whether a cultural insider or someone who did not grow up surrounded by the musical tradition in question. By attending to insiders' descriptions, then, anyone can begin to acquire an appropriate preparatory set for a given music. But, as I hope to have demonstrated in the previous chapter with the word *rasa*, it is not enough merely to list Javanese musical descriptors and their translations. Understanding how these terms relate to each other and to nonmusical words—both hierarchically and associatively—is essential to understanding Javanese responses to music. It is with this goal in mind that I propose to explore *rasa gendhing* (mood categorization as it relates to the gamelan repertoire) in the discourse of Javanese musicians.

ON THE DANGERS AND DIFFICULTIES OF GENERALIZING

Trying to represent how Javanese musicians classify the *rasa*s of *gendhing*s is like trying to describe the system by which Americans classify people by personality, for there is no single system in the minds of Javanese musicians. The first difficulty one encounters is that the terminology is not standardized. While one person might say *memelas* to describe a certain kind of sadness, another (or, indeed, the same speaker on a different occasion) might use *trenyuh* to describe what appears to be the same quality in the same piece of music. Conversely, a single term might be used differently by two different speakers.[1] The linguist Charles Hockett put the problem thus:

> There are few aims which might lead us to study a single idiolect in detail. Usually we are concerned with the by-and-large habits of some group of people. Yet the notion of idiolect is important, because in the last analysis a language is observable only as a collection of idiolects.... We cannot directly observe the by-and-large speech habits of a whole community. We cannot even observe the *habits* of a single individual: all that is directly observable is the speaking *behavior* of individuals (or its physical results, such as written records); all the rest must be inferred. (1958:321–22)

In what follows, then, I remain wary of presenting a pat, ossified schema, in view of the complexity of the speaking behavior of the individuals in question. (I am particularly concerned that the model I construct here might be taken as a kind of orthodoxy [cf. Barthes's *doxa*], by cultural insiders.)[2] Yet I feel it is my duty to represent, somehow, this characteristically Javanese way of regarding musical affect, and in doing so I will be moving back and forth between the particular and the typical, between the actual and the ideal.

The problem of matching up individual variations in usage, however challenging, is not insurmountable—if it were, the field of lexicography would be a complete sham. It is complicated, though, by the fact that the terminology used spans four languages (Javanese, Indonesian, Dutch, and, occasionally, English).[3] The Javanese lexicon itself is split into two or more vocabulary sets for certain items (see Technical Notes), although the equivalents are usually quite direct between speech registers.[4] Which language is used depends on

1. Many linguists have made a case for saying that the meaning of an utterance does not inhere in the words and hence is never fixed. Concomitantly, there is never perfect congruity in word meaning from speaker to speaker, and from speaker to hearer. Adrienne Lehrer (1983) has pointed out how scientific terminology is a special case in which complete consensus about word meaning is explicitly sought, and in some measure achieved. *Rasa* terms are not meant to be scientific.

2. During my return visits to Java in 2003 and 2006, it became clear that an earlier version of this book (1998b) had indeed had an impact on what Javanese researchers were saying about their own traditions (cf. Bantolo, Sulastuti, Waridi, Suraji, Nugroho). Indeed, it had been used as a core reading for research seminars in the M.A. program in performing arts at STSI Surakarta. I have been gratified to see, however, that so far no one has taken any of my lists of *rasa* terms to be in any way definitive, drawing up instead new lists that overlap with but do not duplicate precisely what I have set forth in this chapter.

3. Examples of English words are *feeling, show* (used adjectivally), *simple*, and *rilèks* (relaxed). If one includes written documents, we must count French as a fifth language, since there are now two doctoral dissertations in French by Javanese musicians, both of whom discuss musical *rasa* (Supanggah 1985, Soetarno 1978).

4. There are at least two exceptions to this. One is when a single *krâmâ* word substitutes for several *ngoko* words, as in *sampun* [K] for both *âjâ* [Ng] (don't) and *uwis* [Ng] (already). The other is when either the *ngoko* or the *krâmâ* word is used in a special sense, and so the one form is used regardless of the language level being spoken at the moment. This seems to be the case, for some speakers at least, with *tembang* [Ng] (Javanese song) and *sekar* [K] (Javanese song in classical verse forms), and, as already mentioned, with *râsâ* [Ng] and *raos* [K].

who is being addressed, as well as on the education, social status, generation, and degree of exposure to foreign cultures of the speaker. Often speakers will mix languages in the same sentence to make subtle shifts of meaning; to reinforce a point; to sound more learned, respectful, or familiar; or simply to add variety.

Terminological difficulties are compounded further by the open-endedness of the vocabulary set. That is, musicians might expand the lexicon at will, mostly by taking a term from some other lexical domain and applying it metaphorically to music.[5] Do such creative uses of language have a place in a study of musical terminology? In introducing his discussion of Javanese music theory, Perlman warns us not to confuse technical terms with "casual turn[s] of phrase and flight[s] of fancy" (1994:18). According to Leonard Bloomfield, for a term to be used scientifically, its meaning must be "fixed by an agreement of definition, which receives explicit formulation and strict adherence."[6] To be sure, there have been attempts to create denotative lexicons for music.[7] But music theory is not science. And in the case of *rasa gendhing* I know of no attempt to legislate meaning. Central Javanese musicians use *rasa* terms in a variety of contexts, but they rarely define them or try to resolve differences in usage. And, while they seem to agree universally that pieces may be classified according to affect, their classifications are rarely laid out in toto and have not been codified in writing to the extent that they have in, say, Indian aesthetic theory. We would thus search in vain to find anything approaching a set of denotative, scientific terms. Perhaps one could define a "technical term" less stringently. For example, we could posit that a technical term must, at the very least, have a single qualified speaker who consistently uses it in an explicitly unambiguous way. The question, in our case, is whether a term needs to be technical for it to tell us something about the way Javanese musicians conceptualize their music.[8] I deem any term used by any knowledgeable native speaker to be worthy of study.

If there is interpersonal variation in the terms used to describe musical *rasa*s, there is also variation in reactions to a piece of music. What one person finds funny, another might find coarse. Furthermore, there might be subtle differences of perception that are impossible to verify. It's the old problem of knowing whether the sensation one person has of "blue" is the same as another's—it

5. See Lehrer 1983:16–29, 48–50, 217–18 for a discussion of how language users extend vocabularies.

6. Bloomfield 1939:256, quoted in Lehrer 1983:153.

7. Exact denotation is, however, rarely achieved. One need only look up a representative sample of terms in any of the standard dictionaries of music to realize that usage of musical terms in European languages has always been rather slippery. (Try, for example, *andante*, or *appoggiatura*, or *heterophony*, or *falsetto*.)

8. Lehrer, in *Wine and Conversation* (1983), amply demonstrates the usefulness of studying nontechnical vocabulary.

is not enough simply to see whether these two people apply the same word to the same stimuli. Similarly, when I say that I find a certain piece to be majestic and you agree, we can never really know if we experience it in the same way, though we might come close to an understanding by describing our experience in greater detail. This is something one of my teachers was acutely aware of. When I asked the noted gamelan and singing teacher, Wignyosaputro (born 1927), about *rasa gendhing*, his very first words were as follows:

> For me, *rasa*, as it applies to Javanese music, is relative: [it depends on] who is doing the perceiving/feeling/tasting. I'll give an example. For instance, physical *rasa*—we're not talking about sound, here—you know, chilies. Most people say that chilies are "hot": "*lombok 'ki pedhes*" [Ng]. But you have to take into account the kind of chili and who is tasting it. One person's sense of taste is going to be different from another's. In Javanese there's a saying that goes like this: "*Your* saliva is not *my* saliva." And, "*your* gait is not *my* gait." (June 19, 1992)

Wignyosaputro goes on to point out that the *rasa* of a piece is going to depend, also, on the particular performance. The reason this is particularly true of *gendhing*s is that they are much more protean than, say, nineteenth-century symphonies; they are much more akin, in this respect, to jazz tunes. A useful analogy is that of a recipe: one might recognize a cheesecake, whether it has a graham-cracker or cake-crumb crust, whether it is made with gelatin or by baking, whether it has a topping or not, etc. Similarly, the piece *Pangkur* is still
III:4 *Pangkur* even though performers may choose from an array of melodic, rhythmic, and timbral treatments. We shall revisit Wignyosaputro's theories in chapter 6.

The situation is complicated still further by the metaphorical nature of *rasa* language. While a statement about the *rasa* of a *gendhing* is primarily about musical affect, it may also imply features related to any of the following parameters:

length, age, accessibility, or degree of difficulty of the piece

gender

tempo and rhythm, dynamics, tessitura, melodic mode

liveliness, ornateness

time of day (order in a program)

refinement, social class.

These connotations must be included in any classificatory scheme if we are to understand how this complex lexicon is structured. The problem is that mapping *rasa*s according to these various parameters does not result in complete congruence. That is, two *rasa*s that are closely related in one sense might be quite distant from each other when viewed from a different perspective. And all of this, too, is subject to personal variation.

Our task is to tease out some kind of sense from these complex webs of words. Despite their many personal differences, we would do well to remember that Javanese gamelan musicians living in and around Solo share a great deal with each other. They share a repertoire of several hundred pieces, all of them in the *sléndro* or *pèlog* tunings (or, rarely, a mixture of the two). They share certain associations with various pieces in that repertoire (with *wayang*, for instance, or weddings, or late-night revelry). They eat rice. They inhabit a similar physical space: a world of dense neighborhoods—of mostly one-story brick or thatched houses with steeply pitched tile roofs—traversed by motorcycles and pedicabs and dotted with banana trees. But most of all, they share a language. And that language carries with it certain patterns of dividing up the world, even if no two speakers use the language in precisely the same way.[9]

METHODOLOGY

While I have tried to draw up my most general scheme in such a way as to correspond to as many explicit classifications as possible, I did not derive it directly from them but from a large number of comparative statements (see the subsequent section, "Five Continua"). This scheme does not reveal the structure of the Javanese mind, as it were. Nor does it show us the richness of the *rasa* vocabulary in all its breadth and subtle variability (for instance, certain "stray" *rasas* had to be excluded). What it does show are the links and distinctions I have noticed between a few key words as demonstrated in their actual usage, and, it is to be hoped, something about how Javanese musicians experience their music.

The twenty or so explicit classifications of *rasa gendhing* that I either found in the literature or was given orally are really just lists of principal *rasas*. By analyzing statements musicians use to compare or define *rasas*, however, we can go beyond this to construct what Adrienne Lehrer (1983:4) calls the "lexical structure" of the vocabulary set. To do this, I extracted roughly 650 propositions from recorded conversations with musicians. Each of these propositions might represent anywhere from a single sentence to about a paragraph's worth of speech. When I say "extracted," I mean that I took a comparative statement (or a group of them) and encoded it (or them) with a number of symbols that stood for things like "is the same as," "is incompatible with," or "lies along a continuum with."[10] This procedure produced great concision and allowed me to compare many statements at a glance. The symbols, however, were thrice removed from the original utterance: they represented abstractions of my abridged transcrip-

9. See George 1990, and footnotes 1 and 5, above.

10. See Benamou 1998b for more specifics.

tion of a recording of the speakers' voices. Thus, in many instances, I had to go back and reexamine the transcription to check a particular point.

Of the many statements I collected on tape, some were *elicited*—that is, they were direct responses to questions of mine (usually along the lines of "Is *regu* [stately] the same as *wibåwå* [commanding]?" or "What musical features contribute to a feeling of *tlutur* [sad]?"). Some were only *incidentally* elicited in that they arose as part of a natural train of thought during the course of a long answer to a question. Many, however, were relatively *unprompted*, in that they were occasioned by something other than a query, such as a recorded performance, or a private *rebab* or singing lesson in which I was being corrected or my teacher was demonstrating several different performance styles. Nearly all these comments were directed at me, so that there was probably a larger proportion of Indonesian terms (relative to Javanese) than would ordinarily be the case in exchanges between two Javanese musicians. (This is not, however, a foregone conclusion. Most of my lessons and discussions took place in Indonesian, even though most music in Solo is in Javanese. Nevertheless, my teachers typically would break out of Indonesian and use a Javanese term whenever they were talking about *rasa*. Ironically, though, the few musicians I spoke to in Javanese often reverted to *Indonesian* and *Dutch* in the same places where younger musicians inserted *Javanese* into their Indonesian!)[11] Towards the end of my initial period of research I was able to follow conversations amongst Javanese musicians in a more usual setting (e.g., during a rehearsal or after a competition). In comparing these to my taped conversations, I did not find glaring differences in usage.

Approximately 65 percent of the statements I examined came from my principal teacher, Suhartå (well over half of my interview and lesson tapes were from him). This means that his particular idiolect figures heavily in my characterization of Javanese music talk. I am not sure there is such a thing as a typical Solonese musician, so I hesitate to say that he is one of them. At the least he is not conspicuously atypical. He circulated widely enough as a young man to have picked up ways of talking about music from different corners of the Solonese scene. He is familiar with courtly ways as well as with village ones, with institutional settings as well as more informal contexts. Moreover, neither an elder nor an upstart, he belonged to a sort of intermediary generation at the time of my fieldwork.

Because of the many contingencies in the way I collected my data (I spoke with certain people and not others, under certain conditions and

11. Much more could be said about the import of choosing one vocabulary set over another. For a fascinating account of the reasons Javanese speakers might choose Indonesian over Javanese, see Wolff and Poedjosoedarmo 1982, chapter 3. (I am calling them "vocabulary sets," here, to emphasize the way in which one language is inserted into another, just as *kråmå* is inserted into *ngoko*.)

not others, and it was I and not someone else doing the research), I do not want to pretend that my empirical method is objective in the sense of being entirely replicable by any other trained researcher. At the very least it forced me to scrutinize closely these conversations with my teachers. At best it affords a valuable supplement and possible corrective to my more impressionistic conclusions: even admitting that ethnography will never be a hard science, it ought to rest on *something*, and whatever that something is, it ought to be carried out as thoroughly and meticulously as time and patience will allow.

FOURTEEN KEY TERMS

In presenting my cognitive maps of the *rasa* lexicon, I will focus on certain key terms. These are words that I sensed were particularly salient. My intuitive selection was confirmed by a rough statistical analysis of the recorded and written corpus. In performing the tabulation, I counted as a single term Indonesian and Javanese equivalents, as well as *krâmâ* and *ngoko* variants, if these were clearly used interchangeably. Perhaps it would be less confusing to call these *lexical sets.* The fourteen most common lexical sets, in decreasing order of frequency, are listed below.

prenès [J], *mrenès* [J]—flirtatious, coquettish

gagah[12] [I,J]—manly

sedih [I], *sedhih* [J]—sad

bérag [J]—exuberant

regu [J]—stately, regal

susah [Ng,I], *èmeng* [KI]—sad, troubled

gembira [I], *gambirâ* [J]—happy

gecul, nggecul [J]—jocular

wibâwâ [J], *berwibawa* [I]—imposing

ènthèng [J], *ringan* [I]—light

sereng[13] [J]—tense, heated

énak [I,Ng], *pénak* [Ng], *sekécâ* [K]—easeful

12. This is one case where my reliance on Suhartâ may have skewed the numbers considerably. I found him to be more preoccupied with gender in performance than most other musicians. In particular, he was very concerned that male singers should sound masculine. Clearly, this is of less concern with instrumental music.

13. This term is used quite often for vocal music, less so for instrumental music. If I had spoken primarily to instrumentalists, I'm not sure it would have made the list.

klasik [I,J], *klassiek* [D]—classic, noble, arcane

anteb (*manteb*) [J], *berat* [I]—heavy

These fourteen lexical sets are significant for reasons other than just their frequency of use. All were used by at least three speakers or authors (typically far more than that). Also, nearly all of them could be considered prototypical of *rasa gendhing* terms.[14] In addition, they often led to or from less frequent *rasa* terms in the course of a discussion. And, finally, they are for the most part at a medium level of specificity—what the psychologist Eleanor Rosch calls the "basic level."[15] Indeed, there seems to be some evidence that, across cultures this generic level (as opposed to that of a realm or a species) is cognitively more fundamental: we tend to think "cat" more readily than "Siamese," when presented with an image of a Siamese cat; or "book" more readily than "folio" (this is, of course, entirely dependent on context, but the principle does seem to apply to responses to the question, "What is this called?").

Within this middle level of fourteen key terms there are further distinctions to be made: some of the terms are broader than others. In the middle of the middle level lie six basic terms, which show up on many of the lists of principal *rasa*s given by musicians; and if one includes synonyms, they are even more ubiquitous (see Appendix A). They are *regu, sereng, sedhih, prenès, bérag*, and *gecul*. These six terms can be arranged along several continua, depending on which parameter is being used to compare them (see below). Moreover, they may be grouped, according to these and other parameters, into a number of binary oppositions. Such broad categories occur at what Rosch calls the "superordinate" level. Finally, the six basic terms represent clusters of terms that are related by a series of family resemblances (in Wittgenstein's sense), at the "subordinate" level. We thus have three different sorts of cognitive maps. I will present these from the broadest to the most specific.

14. Much of my discussion of key terms is inspired by Heider 1991. Heider explains prototypicality thus: "Prototype theory of categories has been developed in response to . . . categories that lack absolute boundaries, and whose constituent elements are better or worse members of the category" (1991:42). He warns against assuming that the most frequently used terms are also the most prototypical (1991:29). My sense, based on what I could gather from listening to my field recordings and from Appendix A, is that most of these fourteen terms *are* prototypical *rasa-gendhing* terms. I am not sure what the results would have been had I applied, in the field, Heider's ingenious techniques (which are based on Rosch's work) for determining prototypicality.

15. Lakoff (1990, chapter 2) provides an excellent summary of research in this area. He introduces basic levels thus:

> Categories that are cognitively basic are "in the middle" of a general-to-specific hierarchy. Generalization proceeds "upward" from the basic level and specialization proceeds "downward." . . . Basic-level categories are functionally and epistemologically primary with respect to the following factors: gestalt perception, image formation, motor movement, knowledge organization, ease of cognitive processing (learning, recognition, memory, etc.), and ease of linguistic expression. (13)

BINARY OPPOSITIONS

I first realized that there might be two overarching categories of *rasa*s when, in asking about which singers were right for which *rasa*s, there seemed to be really only two kinds of voices. Again, using the notion of a key term—one that is often used, is prototypical for voice types, and seems to lie at the center of a whole cluster of terms—we might call these two categories *luruh* ("humble") and *trègèl*[16] ("agitated, fluttery"). The *luruh* voice type, characterized by a slow vibrato and a preference for relatively unadorned melody, is appropriate for "sad" (*sedhih*), "imposing" (*regu*), or "tense" (*sereng*) pieces. The *trègèl* voice type, on the other hand, characterized by a fast vibrato and great agility, is more appropriate for "coquettish" (*prenès*) and other lighthearted pieces. (For the remainder of this discussion on dualities I will occasionally use English words to stand for a whole host of Javanese and Indonesian terms. In many cases there is no unique Javanese or Indonesian word that stands out as archetypal. In others there is only a multiword expression, or even a whole description in which certain connotations were made clear.) The word *luruh* evokes *wayang* characters with a lowered head and downcast gaze. They are humble, refined, and poised, in contrast to less refined characters, who are brasher, less restrained, and coarser in appearance and behavior. The primary associations of *trègèl*, on the other hand, are femininity and activity; by extension, greater humility is associated with masculinity and calmness. These oppositions are summarized in the top part of table 3.1.

Out of all the dyads evoked in table 3.1, three pairs stand out as fundamental, as they each link up with a large cluster of related dualisms. These are the *alus/kasar* (refined/coarse), the *anteb/ènthèng* (heavy/light), and the *gagah/kenès* (masculine/feminine) pairs. The first of these is amply discussed in Geertz's *The Religion of Java* (1976/1960:232). His gloss is worth quoting at length, since certain elements of it will reappear in other binary oppositions of *rasa*s:

> Peasant and king, center and periphery, pinnacle and base, God and animal, sacred and profane—these were, and, with some reinterpretations, are now the coordinate termini of the *prijaji*'s [i.e., aristocrat's] metaphysical and social measuring rod, termini summed up in a pair of concepts central to the *prijaji* world-view: *alus* and *kasar*.
>
> *Alus* means pure, refined, polished, polite, exquisite, ethereal, subtle, civilized, smooth. A man who speaks flawless high-Javanese is *alus*, as is the high-Javanese itself.

16. While *branyak* is a more exact antonym, *trègèl* is more common in this context. It is, however, apparently uncommon in nonmusical circles—it appears only rarely in Javanese dictionaries, and even then it usually figures in a compound word with a quite distinct meaning. The closest definition, for our purposes, is in the *Kamus Basa Jawa*, which defines *trègèl* as *grusa-grusu*, for which Robson and Wibisono give "to act impetuously."

TABLE 3.1. Some binary oppositions related to the humble/brash and heavy/light dichotomies. Note that not all items on the left are related to each other, nor are all those on the right.

regu, sereng, sedhih **(imposing, tense, sad)**	***prenès, bérag, gecul*** **(coquettish, exuberant, jocular)**
humble (*luruh*)	**brash (*trègel*)**
alus	*kasar*
refined	coarse
calm	active
decorous	unruly
controlled	unrestrained
plain	fancy
straight	curvilinear
courtly	rural
smooth	rough
conjunct	disjunct
even (homogeneous)	uneven (contrasting)
ordered	disorderly
heavy (*anteb, berat*)	**light (*ènthèng, ringan*)**
low	high
solemn	gay
sad	humorous
serious, powerful	frivolous, effeminate, flirtatious
serious, powerful	jocular, waggish, macho
resolute, vigorous	lackadaisical
masculine	feminine
virginal, ascetic	sexualized, flirtatious
old (ancient)	new
old (mature)	young
early evening	late night
inner	outer
deep	surface
spiritual	corporeal
inscrutable	accessible
difficult	easy

A piece of cloth with intricate, subtle designs painted onto it is *alus*. So is a smooth stone, a dog with his hair petted down, a far-fetched joke, or a clever poetic conceit. God is, of course, *alus* (as are all invisible spirits), and so is the mystical experience of Him. One's own soul and character are *alus* insofar as one emotionally comprehends the ultimate structure of existence; and one's behavior and actions are *alus* insofar as they are regulated by the delicate intricacies of the complex court-derived etiquette. *Kasar* is merely the opposite: impolite, rough, uncivilized; a badly played piece of music, a stupid joke, a cheap piece of cloth. Between these two poles the *prijaji* arranges everyone from peasant to king.

While Geertz, in his inimitable pithiness, might have overstated the case,[17] there is no question that the *alus/kasar* opposition is a fundamental distinction. In fact, according to Santosa (2001:273), Javanese villagers who are not necessarily musicians have only those two verbal categories for distinguishing musical *rasa*s. Among the musicians I talked to, the *alus* affects can be linked to the following cognitive areas: humility, courtliness, majesty, power, masculinity, asceticism, inner knowledge, inscrutability, solemnity, seriousness, decorum, plainness, straightness, smoothness, melodic conjunctness, evenness of rhythm and volume, and calmness. The *kasar* cluster, on the other hand, consists of brashness, "villageness," "commonness," femininity, overt sexuality, shallowness, accessibility, gaiety, frivolity, lack of restraint, roughness, melodic "disjunctness," abruptness of tempo or volume, and activity. (Note that, while plainness is strongly associated with "*alus*ness," ornateness is not particularly *kasar*.)

The second major cluster pair associated with the *luruh/trègèl* opposition is that between "heavy" (*anteb* [J], *abot* [Ng], *awrat* [K], *berat* [I]) and "light" (*ènthèng* [J], *ringan* [I]). Many of the senses of the two English words apply (although there do not appear to be any negative associations with *anteb* as there sometimes are with "heavy"). Thus, along with weightiness go seriousness and difficulty, while lightness has elements both of levity and ease. ("Ease," here, refers both to the acts of listening and performing.) Pieces that are "heavy" tend to emphasize the low register, and are often played during the first part of a *klenèngan*, or playing session—usually in the early evening. Pieces that are "light," on the other hand, tend to be higher, and are often played later—usually in the late evening on into the early morning.

Aside from *alus/kasar* and *anteb/ènthèng* there is a third major binary opposition, namely masculine and feminine.[18] For this one, however, we will have to reconfigure the six basic *rasa*s listed at the top of table 3.1, in which *regu* (stately), *sereng* (tense), and *sedhih* (sad) were grouped together as "heavy"; and *prenès* (coquettish), *gecul* (jocular), and *bérag* (exuberant) were grouped together as "light." In contrast, the typically masculine *rasa*s are the ones at both ends of the

17. Javanese people do frequently define their own culture in terms of its *alus*ness, and one does hear the two words *alus* and *kasar* frequently used to summarily judge someone or something. But I'm not so sure the opposition is as quintessentially Javanese as it's sometimes made out to be. A very similar notion is just as prevalent among bourgeois Europeans (whose culture, after all, had a fair amount of impact on colonial Javanese), or in certain areas and classes of the Midwestern and Southern United States, where gentility is highly prized (my grandmother, for instance, who was from Iowa, was just as indirect and reserved, just as appreciative of subtlety and finery as any upper-class Javanese). For a somewhat more complex view of this duality—in which *alus* and *kasar* are not so value-laden, see Benedict Anderson's *Mythology and the Tolerance of the Javanese* (1965). For the definitive treatment to date of *alus*ness in Javanese dance, see Bantolo 2002. Significantly, the opposite of *alus* in that context is not *kasar* but *gagah* (virile).

18. For a more extensive discussion of gender as it relates to *alus*ness in music and other Javanese arts, see Benamou 2002. S. Weiss 2006 also contains relevant passages.

heavy-light spectrum (*regu, sereng, gecul, and bérag*), whereas those with more feminine connotations lie in the middle, with *prenès* being perhaps more quintessentially feminine than *sedhih*. *Alus* men, because of their mystical practices,[19] are generally perceived as more *alus* than *alus* women. One might thus expect the *alus rasa*s to be masculine, the *kasar* ones to be feminine. But no sane woman is as *kasar* as a *kasar* man. Consider, for instance, the following exchange:

> MLB: Mrs. X is pretty *kasar*.
>
> H: [...] and she's a woman!—if she were a man, s/he'd be even more [so] ... (Suhartå, April 9, 1992)

When it comes to rowdy behavior, then, men get the prize. And yet the extreme "*kasar*ness" of a group of drunken Javanese men has been left out of most scholarly accounts of how gender is linked to notions of "*alus*ness." A key example is Ward Keeler's perceptive analysis (1987, 1990), which emphasized the way Javanese men's higher social status (relative to that of women) confines them to greater decorum. This view of gender in Java (male = *alus*, female = *kasar*), which comes out of Benedict Anderson's portrayal of power (1990 [1972], chapter 1), is echoed in S. Weiss 1993 (but then revised in Weiss 1998 and 2006).[20] We will come back to this in the section entitled "An Aesthetic of Interiority" in the next chapter. To reiterate, then, with respect to musical *rasa*, masculinity lies at either end of the *alus* ↔ *kasar* continuum, with femininity in the middle.

Femininity is linked, musically, to curving lines and ornateness, as opposed to straightness and a lack of adornment.[21] Intricacy (for instance, in the fine batik cloth Geertz refers to in the quote above) is actually *alus* in a certain sense; but austerity (for instance, as it applies to the *wayang* character Yudhistirå) may be perceived as even more—sometimes *too*—*alus*.[22]

There remains an important binary opposition not yet mentioned because it does not often appear explicitly in Javanese musicians' discourse about music

19. Suzanne Brenner (1995) and Suryo Negoro (2000) have documented current cases of female asceticism in central Java. But the common perception of Javanese men, at least, seems to be that women as a class are incapable of being interested in, understanding, or achieving mystical knowledge. The stereotype calls to mind Immanuel Kant's distinction between the masculine "sublime" and the feminine "beautiful": "Deep meditation and a long-sustained reflection are noble but difficult, and do not well befit a person in whom unconstrained charms should show nothing else than a beautiful nature" (Kant 1960 [1763], quoted in Wiseman 1993:172).

20. For analyses that concur with my findings, see Brenner 1995 and Hughes-Freeland 1995. Interestingly enough, my conclusions were drawn independently, before these two studies were published.

21. I have countless attestations of this with reference to vocal music, a great many of them from Suhartå. For instrumental music, see S. Weiss 2006:120–21, 124.

22. Simplicity in the melodic line, though, when it results from machismo, can be *gagah* ("masculine") or *kau* ("awkward, stiff, ungainly"); when from lack of skill, it is either unintentionally humorous or just plain unpleasant.

(it is more frequent when discussing dramatic situations). The categories in question are those of "cold" and "hot." But the temperature differential in this context applies not merely to the state of a physical object, it also refers to the sensation a body feels when coming into contact with certain elements and, by metaphorical extension, to an atmosphere or mood. This conception seems to derive from Javanese humoral theory (which is a mixture of indigenous, Indian, and Arabic elements), in which virtually all foods can be classified as heat-producing or cold-producing, regardless of their actual temperature.[23] In contrast to what I have published elsewhere on the subject (Benamou 2006, Benamou and Supanggah 2006), I now believe (following a 2007 conversation with Supanggah) that temperature metaphors are applied to music only sporadically and somewhat inconsistently. While synonyms for *hot* are used in describing, say, a social atmosphere, I know of no instance in which they are applied to music directly. Synonyms for *cold*, however, are not rare in describing music. They may be grouped into two clusters: "chilling" and "refreshing," with similar connotations to these two English words.

FIVE CONTINUA

In representing the relationships between what I am calling the six basic *rasa* terms (*regu, sereng, sedhih, prenès, bérag*, and *gecul*), I have decided against drawing a single cognitive map. Instead, I shall trace a series of continua, each relating to one or two of the most important dualities just discussed. These continua were derived in the manner already discussed under "Methodology," above, from musicians' statements. They are thus meant to represent Solonese musicians' perceptions generally, although there would undoubtedly be numerous disagreements in any given case. For some, I had very little to go on, and made my best guess, based on the overall picture of what I had gathered about the terms in question.

This exercise will give us a chance to explore further the binary oppositions outlined above, and, in some cases, where the cognitive maps line up, to find further links on the level of the dichotomous connotations themselves. For example, in the first continuum below, it would seem that the "heaviness" of a piece is closely related to its perceived age, since the ordering of the terms is the same for both.

I do not wish to imply by choosing the word *continuum*, here, that one *rasa* shades into the next in a continuous progression of emotional states (see

23. Laderman 1984 gives a nice summary of Malay humoralism, and attempts to tease out its indigenous, Indian, Arabic, Chinese, and Greek elements. Much, if not all, of what she says would seem to apply to Javanese humoralism as well. For interesting parallels in West African cultures, which are at best distantly related to Java, see Thompson 1973.

Appendix A, item 32). This is perhaps apparent in the way specific *rasa*s shift positions from continuum to continuum. What I wish to bring out, rather, is how different *rasa*s relate to each other comparatively, with respect to a set of culturally significant parameters.

1. Heavy ↔ Light, Old ↔ New

regu ↔ *sereng*(?) ↔ *sedhih* ↔ *prenès* ↔ *bérag* ↔ *gecul*

FIGURE 3.1. Continuum from "heavy" to "light," and from old to new.

As *rasa gendhing* lies chiefly in the realm of affect, I shall start with the opposition that most clearly has to do with feelings, namely "heavy" (*anteb* [J]) vs. "light" (*ènthèng* [J]), or, in a less literal translation, serious versus gay. This distinction is perhaps the most fundamental of all, and is the closest equivalent—for musical compositions—to the two basic voice types of *luruh* and *trègèl*. In figure 3.1, I have arranged my six terms from most serious (*regu*) to most mirthful (*gecul*).

Ènthèng has a number of synonyms:

ringan [I] (light)

gembira [I] or *gambirå* [J] (happy)

sigrak [J] (agile)

bérag [J] (exuberant)

prenès [J] (coquettish).

Note that, whereas *bérag* and *prenès* can also refer to more specific *rasa*s within this general category, they are so basic that they are often used more generically to refer to the entire cluster of affects (just as *elm* can refer specifically to the species *Ulmus americana*, to it and any of its relatives in the genus *Ulmus* [English elm, slippery elm], or to the family *Ulmaceae*, which includes hackberries and zelkovas as well as the elm genus).

In contrast to *ènthèng, anteb* has no close synonyms outside of the immediate lexical set, *anteb/manteb/berat*. The Indonesian equivalent, *berat*, means "weighty," "serious," and "difficult." Only the first two of these meanings are expressed in Javanese by *anteb*, and only the first and third by *abot* [Ng] (*awrat* [K]) (see table 3.2). While *abot* is not really a *rasa* term per se, pieces that are *anteb* are often *abot* (difficult) as well.

The only other continuum that is a good match for *anteb* ↔ *ènthèng* is old ↔ new. By that I mean that "old" affects tend to line up with "heavy" ones and "new" ones line up with "light" ones. In other words, great seriousness seems to be associated with great age. This is reflected in the term *gendhing*

TABLE 3.2. Berat/anteb/abot.

	berat	*anteb*	*abot*
weighty	X	X	X
serious	X	X	
difficult	X		X

klasik (J, JI, D),[24] which matches up quite closely with *gendhing anteb*. Conversely, the newer pieces (*gendhing kréasi* [D,I,J]) all edge toward the *ènthèng* side of the spectrum (even those that are *sedhih* are generally "lovelorn" [*kasmaran*]—and hence closer to *prenès*—than they are truly despondent). Another way of putting it is that recent, frequently performed compositions are mostly lighthearted, flirtatious, or at best wistful in nature.

Significantly, at least one Javanese author (Sutarno) has mixed the two parameters of age and degree of heaviness in constructing his typology of *gendhings*. His list, with the exception of *gending keramat*, follows the progression from "heavy" to "light":[25]

> 1. GENDING KUNA (KUNA: old) . . . 2. GENDING ALUS (ALUS: refined) . . . 3. GENDING SEDIH or TRENYUH (sedih: sad) . . . 4. GENDING PRENES (PRENESAN) Melodies with erotic or joyous sentiments . . . 5. GENDING GECUL (gecul: comic) . . . 6. GENDING KERAMAT (keramat: sacred) . . . 7. GENDING POPILER (Pop: modern) . . . 8. GENDING DOLANAN (dolanan: to play) . . .[26]

2. Large ↔ Small, Difficult ↔ Easy

regu ↔ *sedhih* ↔ *prenès* ↔ *bérag* ↔ *gecul* ↔ *sereng*

FIGURE 3.2. Continuum from "large" to "small," and from difficult to easy.

Also closely bound up with the idea of *gendhing klasik* is the notion of *gendhing* size, which forms a second, closely related continuum (see figure 3.2), which differs from the first only in the placement of *sereng* (tense). The most *klasik* of *gendhings* are not only old, but very large, in the sense of being composed in an extended form with a long gong cycle. (Though, in fact, the oldest *gendhings* of all—those played on the gamelan *pakormatan*, the archaic ritual palace ensembles—are probably very "small," with short gong cycles.) Partly because of their size, the largest

24. See, for instance, Lindsay 1985.

25. Indeed, his list seems to have been drawn up rather intuitively rather than as the result of careful deliberation. Nevertheless, there is, with that one exception, a definite pattern to it.

26. Sutarno 1978:37–39. Original text in French interspersed with Javanese terms. The translation from the French is mine. I have preserved Sutarno's inconsistent capitalization and lack of italics.

gendhings are almost never played.[27] The fact that they are rarely "brought out to be aired" (*dipunisis* [K]) adds to the impression of age: it makes them feel less contemporary than older pieces that are constantly played, and only very old musicians can remember how to play them. Middle-aged musicians I talked to refused to comment on the *rasas* of large *gendhings*, protesting that they had never "experienced" them. To clarify, "size" here refers not to how long a performance takes from start to finish, but rather to the time elapsed between strokes of the large gong. In the largest palace *gendhings* this is a very long time indeed (ten minutes or more in a moderate tempo level—longer than most symphony movements and twice or three times the length of most popular songs).

Warsadiningrat (b. 1882), in his treatise on gamelan history explicitly links *gendhing* size with *rasa*. He says that at the time of Sultan Agung (1613–45), there were four types of *gendhing* being played at the palace: (1) *gendhing ageng* ("large pieces"); (2) *gendhing tengahan* ("medium pieces"); (3) *gendhing alit* ("small pieces"); and (4) *gendhing prenès* ("coquettish pieces") (1987 [1943]:71). (Note that *prenès* is not a *gendhing* size at all, but an affect. This mixing of parameters in classifications is quite common in Javanese music theory.) He goes on to explain how the three sizes (*ageng, tengahan*, and *alit*) are related to character:

> *Gendhing ageng* refers to *gendhing kethuk 4 kerep, minggah kethuk 8*,[28] that is, long *gendhings*, with many *céngkoks* [musical phrases], and whose *wileds* [melodic patterns] are consistently *regu* [stately].
>
> *Gendhing tengahan* refers to *gendhing kethuk 2 kerep, minggah kethuk 4* (or else going to a *ladrangan*), that is, *gendhings* whose *céngkoks* [melodic formulas] and *wewileds* ["surface" melodies] are *sekécå* ["comfortable," pleasing, easy to play].
>
> *Gendhing alit* refers to *gendhing ladrang* along with *ketawangs*,[29] whose melodic variations are easy [to figure out]. They are somewhat *regu*—not *prenès*.
>
> *Gendhing prenès* (or *prenèsan*) refers to those *gendhings* that have the power to bring joy to one's heart, [to make one] content and happy, ever glad.
>
> There's another kind, *gendhing gecul* (or *geculan*), of the crude type, whose *rasa* is thoroughly comic or jocular.[30]

27. For an account of how the most revered literature in Java is rarely read because of its purported difficulty, see Florida 1987; 1995, Introduction.

28. This designation of gong-cycle structure and size indicates the number of *kethuk* strokes per *kenong* unit (the *kethuk* being a small, dull-sounding pot-gong, and the *kenong* a large, resonant one of major structural importance). *Kethuk 4 kerep* applies to the *mérong*, or opening section of the *gendhing*, whereas *minggah* means the second half, in which the number of *kethuk* strokes usually doubles. I say "usually," because some *gendhings* go to a *ladrang* (or *ladrangan*) form in the *minggah* (see following paragraph and the following footnote). *Kerep* [Ng] means "frequent" (once every eight beats), while *arang* [Ng] (*awis* [K]) means "rare" (once every sixteen beats).

29. A *ladrang* or *ladrangan* is a small-sized *gendhing* with two *kethuk* strokes and eight beats per *kenong* stroke. Since there are four *kenong* units per gong, that makes for a gong cycle of thirty-two beats. A *ketawang* is a *gendhing* with a sixteen-beat colotomic structure that is almost identical to the *ladrang*'s, but with two *kenong* units per gong cycle rather than four.

30. The edition I used is the transliteration published by STSI Surakarta in 1990. This passage is also translated in Becker and Feinstein [1987:92–93].

Since the only possible *gendhing* sizes are small, medium, and large, the *gendhing prenès* and *gendhing gecul* must overlap with at least one of the other three categories (most likely the second, if we are to take their characters at face value). This is one indication that the one-to-one correspondences laid out for the three different sizes are probably a little too pat. In current practice, at least, there are many exceptions, although this is one area where things could have changed since Warsadiningrat's time.[31]

Toward the end of my first discussion about *rasa gendhing* with Mloyowidodo, he recapitulated the range of *rasa*s he had outlined earlier, making absolutely clear how it fit in with *gendhing* size. The progression was as follows: *klassiek ageng* (large-sized classic), *klassiek tengahan* (medium-sized classic), *nges* (moving), *memelas* (piteous), *bérag alus* (refined exuberant), *bérag sanget* (very exuberant), *gecul* (jocular), *gecul sanget* (very jocular), *lancaran* (a category of pieces with a very small gong cycle), *ayak-ayak* (a category of extremely "small" pieces), *srepeg*[32] (a category of even "smaller" pieces), *sampak* (the "smallest" pieces in the repertoire). In another formulation, the list began with *klassiek berat*, then *klassiek ènthèng* (see his explicit classification by *rasa* on p. 80). The implication here is that *klassiek ageng* and *klassiek berat* are equivalent, as are *klassiek tengahan* and *klassiek ènthèng*. Mloyowidodo knows Warsadiningrat's work backwards and forwards,[33] and his typology almost certainly derives from the older musician's. But these are not the only two authorities to make the connection between *gendhing* size and *rasa*: at least four other musicians I talked to made the same association, but none as systematically as Warsadiningrat and Mloyowidodo. Another thing that distinguishes the two older musicians' formulations from the others is that, for them, heaviness alternates with lightness as we go from big to small (for Mloyowidodo this is more evident in figure 3.13). For most of the others the relation is a bit simpler: the most serious pieces are very large; in other words, size in and of itself confers weight.

Large, heavy, old pieces are also considered the most difficult in the repertoire, and this, too, is reflected in figure 3.2. The obvious reason is that musicians have to remember a lot of notes, and must keep track of where they are without the help of frequent and distinctive oral cues: they do not use the *kempul* (medium-low hanging gong), and the strokes of the *kenong* (medium-high pot gong) are spaced very far apart. The less obvious reason is that, because of their courtly origins, these pieces are replete with interpretive idiosyncrasies designed to keep "outside"

31. We know from oral history that the proportion of pieces that are performed with *gérong* (unison male chorus) has increased markedly in living memory. This is important, since the *gérong* part, except under special circumstances, automatically lends an air of levity to the proceedings. As a matter of fact, it was precisely in complaining about that particular development that Mloyowidodo made the comment quoted in the next paragraph.

32. The first time through the list, *srepeg* was inadvertently placed ahead of *ayak-ayak*. Mloyowidodo corrected himself very soon afterwards.

33. When STSI came out with its new transliteration in 1990, Mloyowidodo was the first to notice that certain sections had been omitted by mistake.

musicians from being able to play them successfully.[34] Recall that *anteb* [J,I] (heavy, substantive) is linked to *abot* [Ng] (heavy, difficult) through the Indonesian *berat.*

3. Alus ↔ Kasar, Calm ↔ Lively

sereng(?)
regu ↔ *sedhih* ↔ *prenès* ↔ | ↔ *gecul*
bérag

FIGURE 3.3. Continuum from *alus* to *kasar*, and from calm to lively.

As will be clear by now, closely related to the two previous continua is that between *alus* (refined) and *kasar* (coarse, crude) (figure 3.3). It, too, differs from the previous two only in the placement of *sereng*, which is not as *kasar* as *gecul*, but, because it has an element of anger, is more *kasar* than *prenès*.[35] This ordering also works for the continuum that lies between the poles of *tenang* [I] (calm) and *ramé* [J] (lively), pointing up the element of spiritual development and inner composure in one of the primary meanings of *alus* (Benamou 2002).

4. Masculine ↔ Feminine

sereng *bérag*
regu ↔ | ↔ | ↔ *prenès*
gecul *sedhih*

FIGURE 3.4. Continuum from masculine to feminine.

Because of the complex distribution of masculinity on the *anteb* ↔ *ènthèng* scale, the gender continuum requires a diagram unto itself (figure 3.4). Note that, of my six basic terms, *prenès* is the only distinctly feminine one. Gamelan music truly is a man's world—at least as it is conceptualized by male musicians. The gender continuum is discussed at length in the earlier section on binary oppositions (see also Benamou 2002).

34. See Perlman 1994 and Supanggah 1985. It should be mentioned, however, that it is possible to construct a revisionist interpretation that questions these courtly origins to begin with. Indeed, Supanggah now believes that nearly every aspect of palace-style music originated in the villages, since the musicians were largely recruited from outside the palace, and there was a highly developed and far more dynamic musical scene in areas such as Gombang and Purworejo (pers. comm.).

35. *Sereng*: "tense." *Gecul*: "jocular." *Prenès*: "coquettish." The placement of *sereng* is, in fact, the only thing separating these first three continua. See the section in this chapter on explicit classifications (pp. 79–82) for an explanation of why this might be so.

5. Plain ↔ Ornate

regu ↔ *sereng* | *sedhih* ↔ *gecul* ↔ *bérag* ↔ *prenès*

FIGURE 3.5. Continuum from plain to ornate.

Our fifth ordering, illustrating the *plain* ↔ *ornate* continuum, differs from the previous one only in the placement of *sedhih* (sad). This affect belonged further to the right in figure 3.5, because it edges towards the feminine. But to perform sadness musically one must choose patterns that are not too ornate, and so the term must be moved towards the left in figure 3.5, closer to the plain end of the scale.

SIX CLUSTERS

One way of clarifying the way our six terms relate to the binary oppositions discussed so far is to present the terms individually, showing some of their respective associations. In figures 3.6 through 3.11, I have arranged their associated *rasa* terms in a circle, like spokes of a wheel. In so doing, I have kept related terms near each other on the wheel, so that one meaning shades into the next. Unlike Hevner in her famous adjective circle (1936, Benamou 2003), however, I have not attempted to place opposites across from each other (indeed, there is very little, within a single wheel that is oppositional). In one case (*regu*) it was possible to continue around the circle without a break, in the others no such continuity was possible: a gap in the spokes indicates that the terms on either side of the gap are not related to each other. Included are only those terms for which I have documented an explicit association *between terms*. This means, for instance, that, although musicians contrast *bérag* (exuberant) with *alus*, thereby linking the former with *kasar* (see figure 3.3), *kasar* does not appear on the *bérag* wheel because I never documented the two words being directly linked in conversation. Another difference between the continua and the clusters is that the clusters show not only associated affects, but subsidiary ones as well. For instance, the *sedhih* wheel shows eight different shades of sadness (moved, commiserating, pained, grief-struck/despondent, confused, troubled, in love, yearning, and lonely).

What both the continua and the clusters show are some of the connotations that *rasa* terms have. For instance, if one is told that *gendhing Laler Mengeng* is *sedhih*, this entails much more than sadness: it is a "heavy," relatively difficult piece, which should be played plainly; it is not particularly masculine, but it is quite *alus*, quite calm. These connections, of course, only scratch the surface of the entire range of connotations that the words have for Javanese musicians—what A. L. Becker calls their "prior texts." But associative meanings are nonetheless essential to understanding what Javanese musicians say as well as the

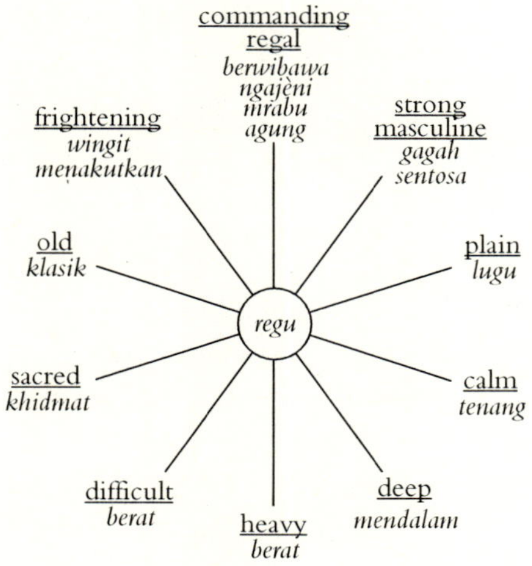

FIGURE 3.6. *Regu* cluster.

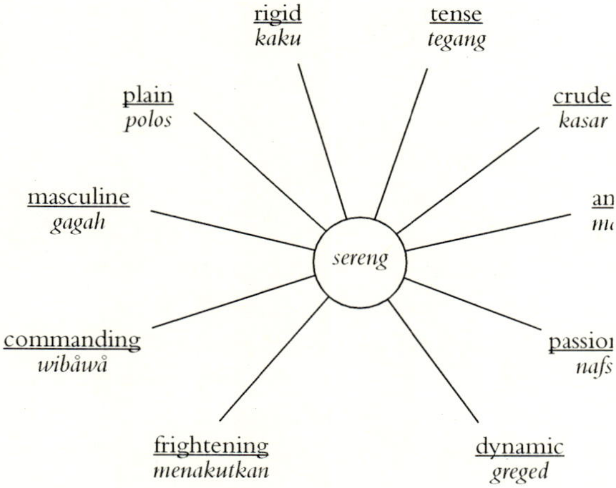

FIGURE 3.7. *Sereng* cluster.

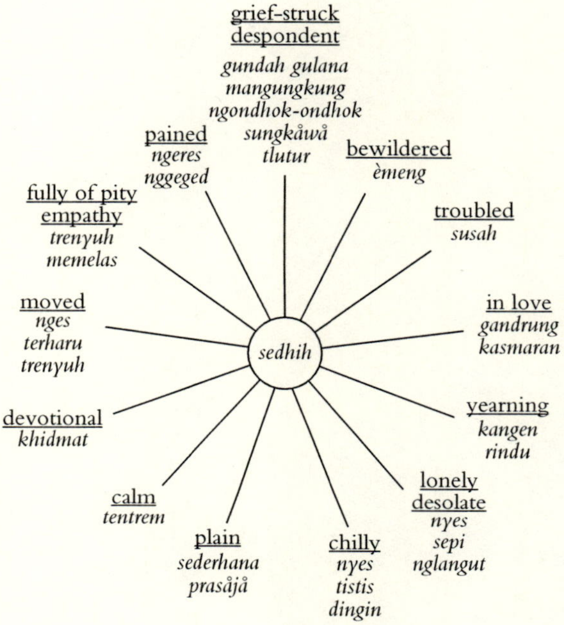

FIGURE 3.8. *Sedhih* cluster.

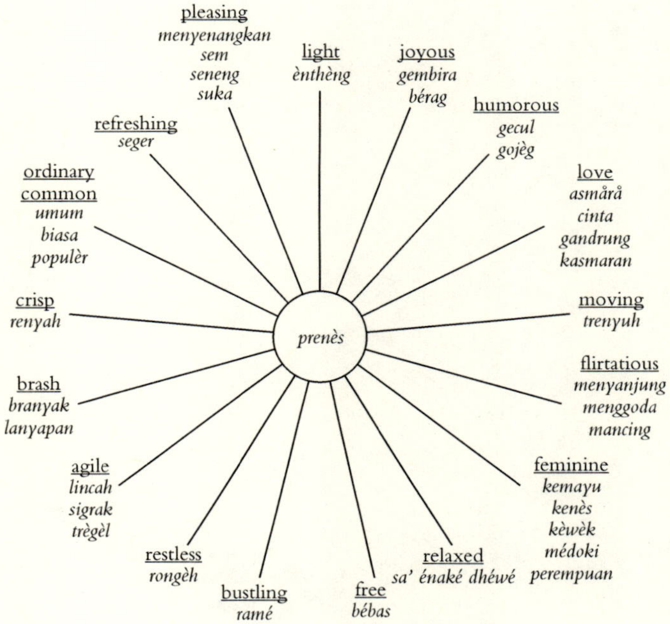

FIGURE 3.9. *Prenès* cluster.

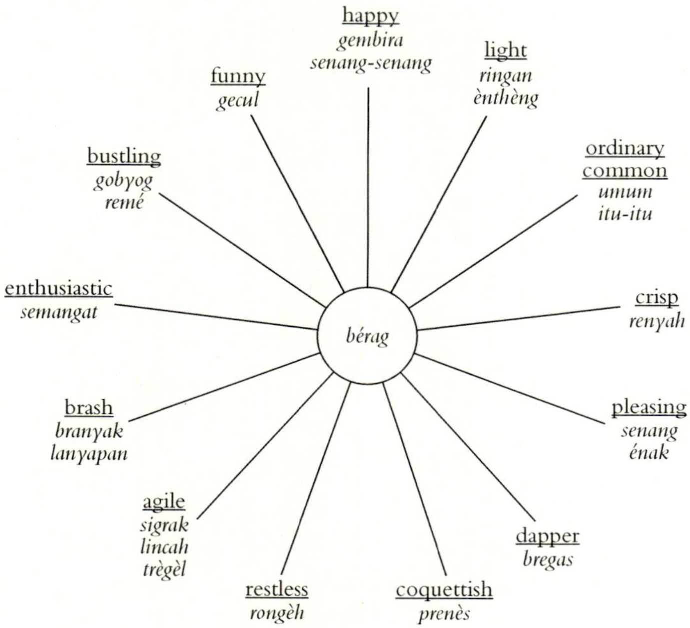

FIGURE 3.10. *Bérag* cluster.

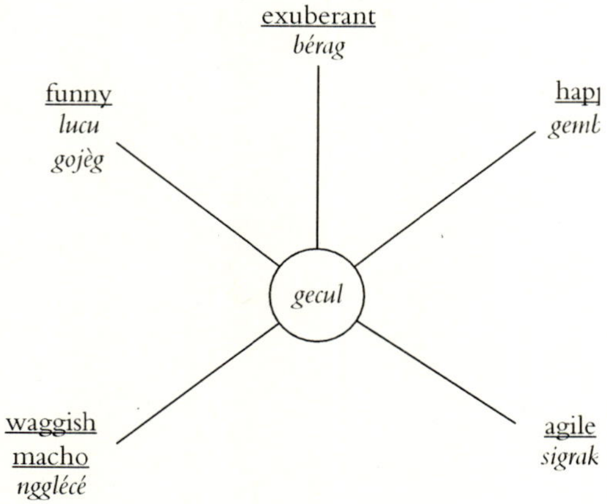

FIGURE 3.11. *Gecul* cluster.

affective content of their music. That is, they point up just how insufficient the one-word glosses are that I have provided in parentheses throughout the book. This is perhaps the sort of thing Roland Barthes had in mind when he admitted having had a certain

> pessimisme constant à l'égard de la traduction, affolement devant les questions des traducteurs, tant ils paraissent souvent ignorer ce que je crois être le sens même d'un mot: la connotation. [constant pessimism about translation, a panic when faced with translators' questions, who seem to have missed entirely what I consider to be the very meaning of a word—its connotations.][36]

THREE EXPLICIT CLASSIFICATIONS

In order to see the degree to which the foregoing construction may or may not be representative, let us look at several typologies of *rasa gendhing* as presented to me in conversation. I will limit myself to the three people who were quite confident that their initial lists were exhaustive.[37] Significantly, all three were among the oldest musicians I talked to. On the first line of each diagram, below (figures 3.12 through 3.14), I give each speaker's initial response to the question, "What kinds of *rasa gendhing* are there?" After they had given me their respective lists, I asked them if there were any other *rasa*s, and they all said that any other terms would duplicate ones already mentioned. As each conversation progressed, however, all three used *rasa* terms that were not on the original list, usually in a context that made it possible to see how these were linked to the original set. Thus, even when musicians are quite rigid in their theoretical expositions, in actual practice their language is considerably more fluid. Below the first line of each diagram I have indicated those terms that were later linked to the original categories. While the three diagrams are meant to represent explicit formulations, they are thus partially pieced together from various segments of a conversation. As such, they are an attempt to render synchronically and panoptically what was actually diachronic and fragmentary. The first of the three (figure 3.12) is the closest to the idealized schemes presented in the continua above. Note that while Wignyosaputro sees a clear divide between the "light" *rasa*s and the "heavy" ones, Mloyowidodo sees the opposition more as a

36. Barthes 1975:119. In view of the sentiments expressed, I have given the French original first. An example of what he is talking about may be found in the word *affolement*, which I have translated as "panic," but which is allied to the word *folie* (madness, folly, extravagance), and rhymes with the equally related *raffolement* (infatuation). To these associations one could add the gay slang word *folle* (queen), which, while far fetched, is perhaps not completely irrelevant in view of Barthes's openness about his same-sex orientation.

37. For a comparison with other classifications by Javanese musicians, either open or closed, oral or written, unidimensional or multidimensional, see Appendix A.

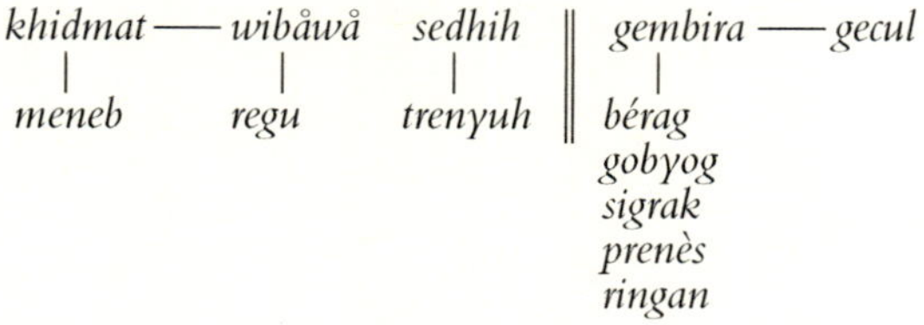

FIGURE 3.12. Wignyosaputro's classification of *rasa gendhing*.

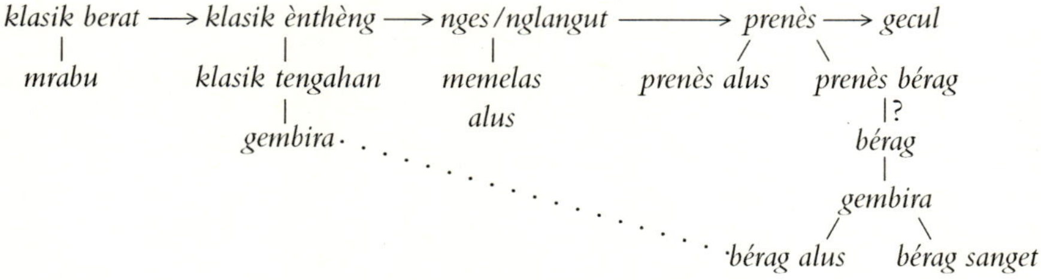

FIGURE 3.13. Mloyowidodo's classification of *rasa gendhing*.

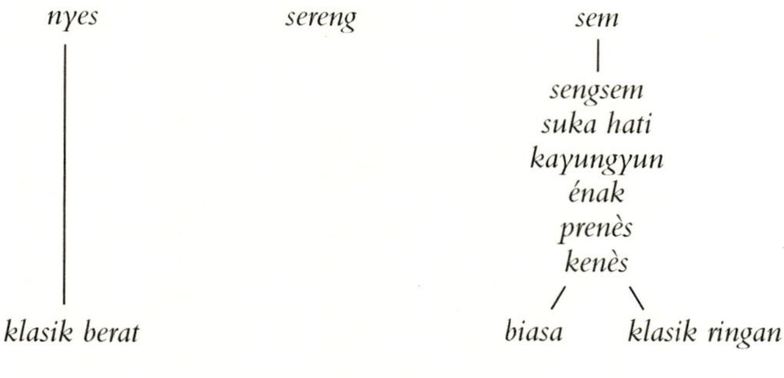

FIGURE 3.14. Sutarman's classification of *rasa gendhing*.

alus: refined; **bérag**: exuberant; **berat**: heavy; **biasa**: "ordinary," lighthearted; **énak**: "comfortable," pleasing, leisurely; **ènthèng**: light (lightweight); **gecul**: jocular; **gembira**: happy, cheerful; **gobyog**: bustling; **kayungyun**: madly in love; **kenès**: coquettish, hyperfeminine; **khidmat**: devotional; **klasik**: classic(al); **memelas**: compassionate; **meneb**: settled, calm; **mrabu**: regal; **nges**: moving; **nglangut**: melancholy; **nyes**: cold, lonely; **prenès**: coquettish; **regu**: stately; **ringan**: light(weight); **sanget**: very; **sedhih**: sad; **sem**: enchanting; **sengsem**: same as *sem*; **sereng**: tense, stern, heated; **sigrak**: buoyant, agile; **suka hati**: delighted; **tengahan**: in-between; **trenyuh**: affecting; **wibåwå**: commanding, imposing

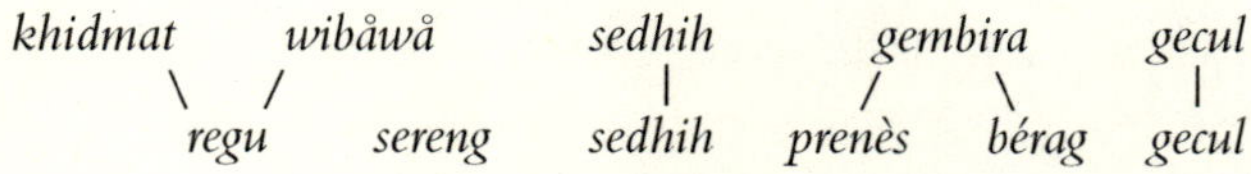

FIGURE 3.15. Comparison of Wignyosaputro's classification with my six basic *rasas*.

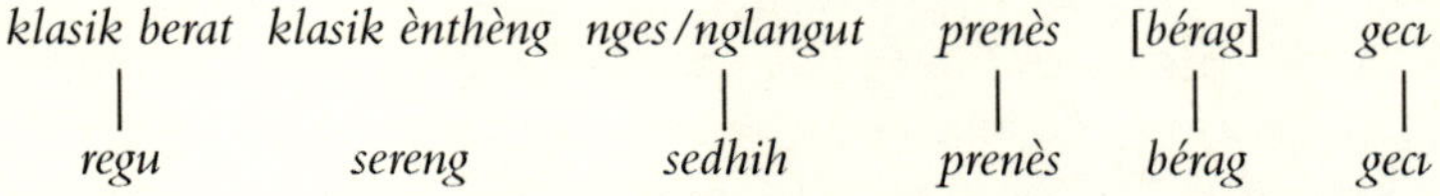

FIGURE 3.16. Comparison of Mloyowidodo's classification with my six basic *rasas*.

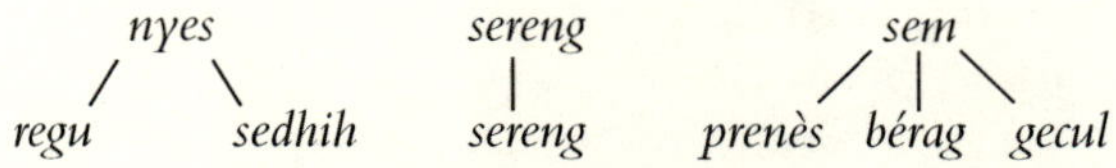

FIGURE 3.17. Comparison of Sutarman's classification with my six basic *rasas*.

continuum between two poles. Sutarman, on the other hand—ever the non-conformist—has a triangular scheme that resists bifurcation.

I am now going to take these three musicians at their word—that any other terms are mere synonyms—and show how these apparently divergent classifications can all be linked rather closely to my six basic *rasas*. In figures 3.15, 3.16, and 3.17, I have used vertical lines to indicate these links between my terms and those of Wignyosaputro, Mloyowidodo, and Sutarman. In many cases there is very nearly a one-to-one correspondence. In others there is merely a difference in classificatory level. Only two terms on the combined lists do not seem to have appropriate matches (in figures 3.15 and 3.16 there are no vertical lines attached to them): *klasik ènthèng* and *sereng*. Mloyowidodo's *klasik ènthèng* is difficult to place because it combines venerableness and medium size with levity: it belongs with *bérag* in terms of mood but is closer to *regu* in terms of size and age. As for *sereng*, this is a particularly problematic *rasa*, as I had found in drawing up my continua. It is often left out, perhaps because it is associated above all with *gendhings* that have extremely short gong cycles. These pieces play major roles in accompanying dramatic forms (dance, *wayang*, theater), but are relatively unimportant in a concert (*klenèngan*) setting. The quality of being *sereng* is also strongly associated with two common vocal genres, *palaran* and *ådå-ådå* (indeed, these may be archetypal).[38] This is perhaps why Sutarman

II:2 and 3 for palaran; IV5 for ådå-ådå

38. *Palaran* may be defined as unmetered singing of *måcåpat* poetry accompanied by a *srepegan*-like, metered gamelan part. *Måcåpat* is sung verse using indigenous poetic meters, each of which has a number of traditional tunes associated with it (these tunes are drawn out with melismas in *palaran* singing, though to reinforce a *sereng* mood the melismas would be limited). S*repegan* is a genre of

includes the term as one of his three primary *rasa*s (or *unsur*s, as he calls them), since he is principally a vocalist, whereas instrumentalists tend to omit it entirely from their lists.

If my analysis is correct, then, the three explicit classifications shown in figures 3.12 through 3.14 overlap considerably with each other, and with the more generalized six-way categorization that I have abstracted from all of my teachers' comments. Indeed, as figures 3.6 through 3.11 show, my six basic terms cover, in one way or another, a good many of the commonly used *rasa* terms, which cluster around them. This unity in diversity is neatly summarized in the following exchange I had with two of my teachers:

> WIGNYOSAPUTRO [SPEAKING TO MARC BENAMOU]: Don't assume that everything I tell you is right. And if you go ask someone else, you'll get a different . . . viewpoint. This is only my own personal point of view.
> SUHARTÅ: But there's a lot of agreement. [. . .] You [Marc] happen to be asking around in a Solonese milieu, so people use the same terms. If you were to go to Wonogiri, or Klatèn,[39] maybe you'd find that they use some words a bit differently. (June 19, 1992)

MIXED *RASAS*

In discussing classifications of *rasa gendhing*, I have perhaps given the impression that each *gendhing* has a single *rasa*, the way movements in baroque pieces are said to express a single affect. In the case of Javanese music, as in much baroque music, this is an oversimplification. *Rasa*s may be mixed in one of two ways: sequentially or simultaneously. In the latter case they may either have a complex, named *rasa*, or they may lie somewhere between two named *rasa*s. The musicians with whom I talked about this generally denied that *rasa*s could be mixed into a single passage, but at other times, in describing specific pieces, at least one of them spoke as if they could. First their general statements:

gamelan music, used typically in shadow-puppet plays for traveling or fighting. It has extremely short gong cycles, which give it a heated or tense feel. *Ådå-ådå* is an unmetered song, voiced by the puppeteer in a shadow play (but sometimes used in other contexts), usually with a rapid delivery, accompanied by a solo *gendèr* (double-mallet metallophone with tube resonators), which emphasizes key notes of the song using busy-sounding, repetitive holding patterns. During *ådå-ådå* the puppeteer raps rapidly and continuously on the puppet box with a special wooden beater, and occasionally the drum and one of the gongs are sounded to give weight to the ends of phrases. Like *srepegan*, it is typically used in moments of excitement or conflict.

39. These are towns within a twenty-mile radius of Solo.

H: A lot of *gendhings* are "complete." They might have a little sadness, a little happiness—so one *gendhing* would have several different *rasas*.

MLB: You mean, now it's happy, now it's sad; or they're mixed?

H: Mixed... yes, some are mixed.

MLB: I mean, at this one moment, aside from happy it's also sad, at the same time? [...] Or there are parts that are—

H: Right, there are parts. This one—this *gåtrå* [four-beat unit] has to be played with *minir* [sadly]... this *gåtrå* should be *biasa-biasa* [lighthearted]... [this one] has to sound *regu* [stately], for instance, it has to sound *berwibawa* [commanding]... this *gåtrå* is a bit *sigrak* [energetic], and so on. (Suhartå, March 26, 1992)

Gendhings consist of parts that are strung together: there's the *mérong* [first, calmer section], and there's the *inggah* [second, livelier *section*]. If the *mérong* was *khidmat* [calm, reverential], even though the piece as a whole is *khidmat*, the inggah then has music that's neither *khidmat* nor gay. That's how you get it to sound *regu* [stately]. Take, for example, *gendhing Rårånjålå, laras pélog pathet limå*: the *mérong* is really *tenang* [tranquil], but the *inggah*—even though it's part of a *gendhing khidmat*—is a bit *bérag* [exuberant]. So, composers of *karawitan* aren't monotonous; they don't make *gendhings* that are *khidmat* from the *bukå* [intro] right up to the *suwuk* [final gong phrase]. If this part here is *khidmat*, then the *inggah* will be made a bit *kenceng* [fast, taut]. It's like when a "thing"[40] gets hard. This here is flaccid, this here is taut. [*Laughs.*] That's the way it usually is. (Wignyosaputro, June 19, 1992)

MLB: Let's say you've got *sem* [pleasing] and *sereng* [heated] [...]; can they be mixed in a single melody?

T: No, they can't. [...] They can't. So, let's say, for instance, you've got one, two, three, four, five, six lines that are *sem*. Then you have one, two that are *nyes* ["chilly," "lonely," sad]. Then it goes back to *sem*, and so on. (Sutarman, June 24, 1992)

I was given many specific examples of *rasas* mixed consecutively. The one piece that was consistently cited as being almost chameleonlike in its mutability from beginning to end was *Elå-Elå Kalibeber*. A cursory glance at the notation I:2 for the *balungan* (reference melody) shown in figure 3.18 will tell why: the rhythm, atypically for a gamelan piece, is extremely variable, going from long held notes (indicated by dots), to beats, to half-beats, to quarter-beats, and back. For comparison, see *Gambir Sawit* (figure 3.19), whose relatively regular rhythm II:2 is more usual. Each change in rhythm in *Elå-Elå Kalibeber* corresponds more or less to a change in affect, and this is one of the reasons it is considered to be among the most musically challenging *gendhings* in the entire repertoire. In most pieces it is possible to take one's cue from other musicians (more so on some melodic parts than others), so that collective memory is always more

40. *Barang* (thing) is a common euphemism for the genitalia, not unlike *private parts* in English, but more ambiguous.

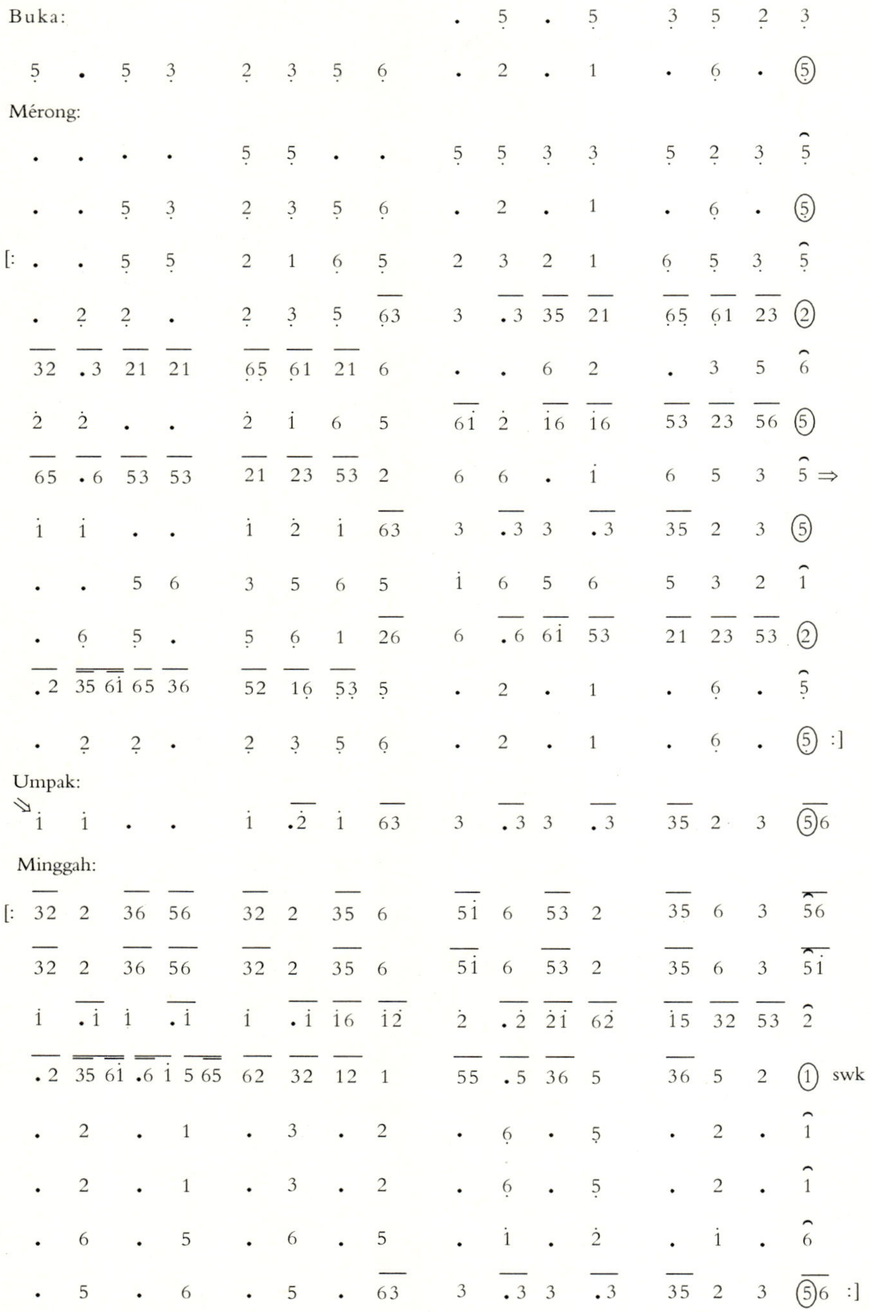

FIGURE 3.18. *Gendhing Elå-Elå Kalibeber, kethuk 2 kerep minggah 4, laras sléndro pathet sångå* (as recorded on *Gamelan de Solo*, disc 1, track 2; see also Mloyowidodo 1976, vol. 1:90–91 and Gitosaprodjo 1992:26–27).

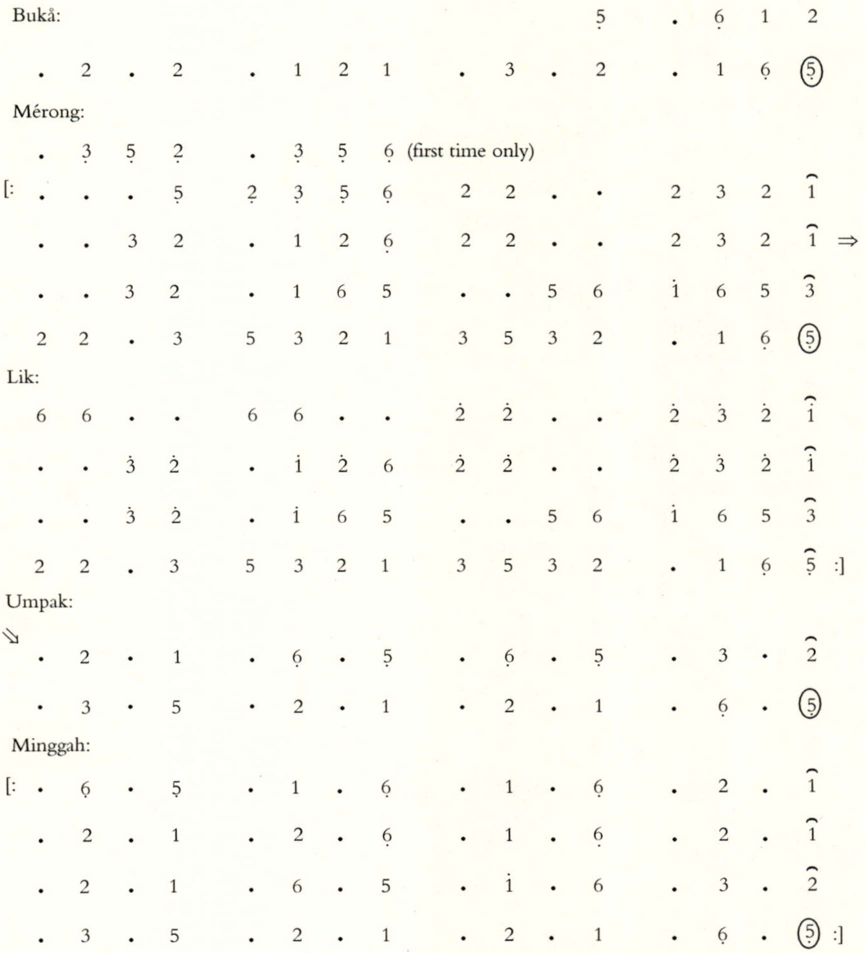

FIGURE 3.19. *Gendhing Gambir Sawit, kethuk 2 kerep minggah kethuk 4, laras sléndro pathet sångå.* (Mloyowidodo 1976, 1:[82]–83).

complete than individual memory (Brinner 1995). In this piece, however, to get the *rasa* right, each musician must know the *balungan* well enough to anticipate all of the sudden changes, at the risk of being left behind.

When Sutarman mentioned that his three *unsur*s (*rasa*s) were sometimes mixed in a single piece, I asked him for examples. After a couple weeks of thinking about it, he produced the following list:

1. *Dhandhanggulå, barang miring*: *nyes* mixed with some *sereng*
2. *Sinom Wénigonjing, pélog barang*: *sereng* mixed with some *sem* 1:3

3. *Ladrang Dirådåmetå, sléndro nem*: *sem* mixed with some *nyes*

4. *Ketawang Sukmåilang, sléndro manyurå*: *sem* mixed with some *nyes*

III:4 ◉ 5. *Båwå Sekar Ageng Banjaransari, pélog barang*: *sem* mixed with some *sereng*

One musician not mentioned above, Rahayu Supanggah, also gave a particularly clear example of consecutively varied *rasa*s. I had asked about the *rasa* of a whole piece and was given a detailed, part-by-part analysis. Supanggah's analysis of *gendhing Titipati* is presented in full in chapter 7.

An example of an inherently mixed *rasa* is *lemeng* [J]. Suhartå defined it as "overcast," or "like the atmosphere before war is about to break out."[41] Musically, it is a combination of fear and sadness, neither of which is immediately apparent. Suhartå said, "It's like someone who's been given compensation for a wrong committed against him: he might look happy, but actually his heart is sad" (March 26, 1992). I have only heard this used by Suhartå (Supanggah, who is about five years his junior, had never heard of this term), who told me that, according to the late musicians Martopangrawit and Pandji Soetopinilih as well
II:2 ◉ as the "paranormal" Pådå, *lemeng* is the true *rasa* of the piece *Gambir Sawit* (figure 3.19), which is usually described as *prenès* (coquettish) or *bérag* (exuberant). In other words, it is outwardly cheerful but with an underlying sadness (unbeknownst to most of the younger generation of musicians). While this is the clearest case I could find of a mixed *rasa* in a composition, musicians, when defining *rasa*s, often described them as a combination of emotions.

On several occasions Suhartå described the *rasa* of a single passage as consisting of two *rasa*s that are normally thought of as entirely distinct, or even incompatible. Once during a lesson (June 19, 1991) he demonstrated two ways of singing a short phrase:

3/1 ◉ 7̣ 2 ^3 ^^2 7̣

7̣ 2 3̃ 2 7̣

The first version he described as *lelah* [I] (listless). But the second one he called "somewhat *gagah* [manly], *prenès* [coquettish]." Yet Suhartå usually contrasted *gagah* with *prenès*—was this a case where they were both mixed into a single *rasa*? Probably not. It is more likely that this *wiledan* (way of ornamenting a line) could work for either one. What seems to unite them in this case, is that they both stand in opposition to relaxation or lack of energy. That is, this particular *wiledan* has *greged* (oomph, drive), and so is simultaneously more *gagah* and more *prenès* than the other one, which is too lackadaisical to be either (see Appendix A, item 32 for possible confirmation of this interpretation).

41. See footnote 20 in chapter 2. Poerwadarminta gives "at a constant heat" as a definition for *nglemeng* (a variant of *lemeng*—the *ng-* prefix, here, serves an adjectivizing function). This seems to be unrelated to the musical use of the term.

On another occasion he characterized *palaran Durmå*, sung in *minir* (*pèlog*-like intervals in the vocal part with *sléndro* instruments), as *gagah* but also *sedhih* (sad). In this case, it is possible to imagine the two sentiments being melded into one. And, in fact, he summed up the *rasa* with the word *kegetir* [J,JI] (sour [J], bitter [I]).

I would like to return briefly to the notion that a *gendhing* may have more than one *rasa*. Both Wignyosaputro (see quote on p. 83) and Suhartå told me that for anything larger than a *ladrang* this is in fact the *norm*:

> For *gendhings* that are *kethuk 2* or bigger,[42] it's hard to find ones that are, say, 75% *prenès* [lighthearted]—they're usually mixed. In other words, they might be part *prenès*, part *sedhih* [sad] [...]. You're not going to find one that's all *prenès*. They don't exist. Well, they do, but... those for which you can say the *rasa gendhing* is clearly *gecul* [jocular], say, are *ladrangans*. For *ladrangans* or *lancarans*, you can say with confidence, "*that* one's *gecul*," "that one's whatever," "that one's troubled"—it's really clear because the pieces are so small. But for *gendhings*, on the other hand, it's harder. (Suhartå, March 26, 1992)

This is significant in that it goes against the notion—commonly held in the West—that "Eastern" music is essentially static.[43] Within Javanese music there are, to be sure, pieces that are strikingly repetitive in their cyclicity, but they occupy a relatively small part of music talk in Java, and probably also of musicians' attentions.[44] Yet in the early part of the century, both Dutch writers and Javanese experts writing for a Dutch audience perpetuated the stereotype of stasis:

> Eastern music amounts to the expression of one or a few sentiments, whereas Western music usually means a multiplicity of emotions. Eastern music is concentration-music, and is, in essence, contemplative; Western music, barring exceptions, is essentially emotional. (Soorjo-poetro, quoted in Kunst 1973 [1934]:120)

A generation later, Soorjo-poetro's comment is echoed by Sindoesawarno, the founder of the first conservatory of *karawitan*, who, like Soorjo-poetro, had studied Western music:

42. "*Kethuk 2*" means that there are either sixteen or thirty-two *balungan* beats per *kenong* unit. Larger yet would be *kethuk 4* or *kethuk 8*, with a maximum of sixty-four *balungan* beats per *kenong* unit. By comparison, a *ladrang* (or *ladrangan*) has eight *balungan* beats per *kenong* unit, and a *lancaran* has four (although in practice it often sounds more like two).

43. Consider, for instance, the way René Daumal (1982 [1931]:21) portrays the typical French bourgeois reaction to a concert of Indian music: "The music of those people babbles, like their philosophy, always the same measure or the same proportion, for hours or for centuries, all the same monotone." We can surmise that the Eurocentrists against whom he inveighs would have much the same thing to say about Javanese music.

44. For more on the split between cyclicity and linearity, see Hoffman 1978, Maceda 1986, Benamou 1989, and Basset 2004.

> Like Indian, Arab, and Chinese melodies, *lagu* [tunes, melodies] in *karawitan* always center on a single emotion or a certain idea that is manifested by the *lagu*.... The musician must know the characteristics and nature of each *lagu*, and to which class of emotions it belongs.... Musicians divide pieces according to mood and use.... From this classificatory scheme we can... see that a given piece can express only one type of emotion. (Sindoesawarno 1984 [1956–59]:393, 397)

Contrast these statements with the following Westward-directed comment by Suhartå:

> Perhaps Western music is also like [Javanese music]: in a performance of a single piece, not everything will be sad, in minor; some of it will not be sad; perhaps some of it has a rushed feeling; or a disoriented, depressed feeling. Perhaps that's the way all art is. (April 8, 1992)

EMICS AND ETICS

In this chapter I have used my observations of Javanese musicians' verbal behavior to draw conclusions about their conceptual categories for musical affect. I have tried to show (1) what the range of *rasa*s is in Javanese music talk; (2) how musicians group these *rasa*s in various ways; (3) that there are clear patterns of synonymy within an almost bewildering variety of terms, and hence a fair amount of consensus; (4) that connotations—links to other words, to other categories of thought—are essential to the meaning of *rasa* terms; and (5) that different *rasa*s may be combined within a single piece.

More generally, I hope to have demonstrated here and in subsequent chapters that attending to the lexicon of musical affects—and, more importantly, to how that lexicon is structured—can lead to an understanding of how Javanese musicians experience their music. No amount of formal analysis alone will reveal that a certain *gendhing* or performance is *wingit* (spectral) or *prenès* (lighthearted). And to understand all that that implies, one needs to know how these terms fit into the larger linguistic picture. It is especially important for cultural outsiders to see how *rasa*s are linked to each other. This can lead, concomitantly, to an understanding of the structure of Javanese emotion categories in general. For example, one of the major varieties of sadness in Javanese music is *kasmaran* [J,JI] or "smitten" (figure 3.8). The notion that, for Javanese speakers, love and sadness are closely linked is confirmed by Karl Heider (1991), who found that love-related emotions in Indonesian tended to fall within the sad clusters for the fifty Minangkabau and fifty Javanese people he queried (1991:14). This is in marked contrast to the fifty American subjects whose idiolects were studied by Davitz (1969), for whom the word *love* was clearly linked to happiness.[45]

45. Kövecses (1990) also found that happiness was a usual component of love for English speakers.

Some ethnomusicologists, following certain developments in linguistics, feel that it is the implicit features of a musical system that are the most significant, and they have devised various clever ways of seeking out underlying regularities.[46] I do not deny that there are limits to what music talk can reveal. Javanese musicians themselves resist making precise correspondences between affect terms and listeners' feelings, and between those same terms and pieces of music. Indeed, many of them insist that words can only loosely convey the actual character of a piece of music. But this is not the same thing as saying that music talk is largely irrelevant, and that basic musical processes can be discovered without recourse to language. While I am certainly not claiming that what musicians say is the only clue to what is going on in their minds, I do believe that it is the best starting point—especially when coupled with hands-on experience in the field—in the search for musical meaning.

Defenders of nonverbal experiments as a means of discovering musical structure (and hence of musical meaning) have explicitly or implicitly carried out etic analysis as a corrective to what they see as an overreliance, in emic analyses, on insiders' verbalization. But emic analysis, as Pike conceived it, does not simply consist in reporting insiders' speech: it is a researcher's attempt to come up with a model that "is built up from principles derived from, rather than forced upon, the data" (Barnard and Spencer 1996, s.v. "emic and etic"). Let us not forget the origin of the terms: phonemic analysis takes into account what linguistic sounds mean to native speakers, whereas phonetic analysis purports to identify sounds in a neutral way.

Because language is an important shaper of perception, and because it remains the primary means of knowing what others think, ethnomusicological emic fieldwork uses insiders' verbalizations as a starting point. Emic analysis does not, however, preclude interpreting what these insiders say. Nor does it preclude eventual etic analysis. In practice, the difference between the two approaches is a question of priority. Experimental ethnomusicologists (unlike psychologists of music) conduct research in the field, they observe music being made in its original context, they talk to musicians, and they often learn to perform themselves. In other words, their etic analyses are always complemented by a certain amount of emic fieldwork.

One way of extending the usefulness of what I have presented in this chapter is through cross-linguistic comparison, which Kenneth Pike (1967) considered to be a fundamentally etic enterprise. Elsewhere I have argued for a guarded use of comparison lest it lead to a flattening of perspectives (Benamou 2003). In particular, I suggested that the surest way of comparing respectfully is to limit oneself to only two practices at a time, taking care to see each from the

46. See, for instance, Will 1998. Others who hold similar beliefs include Simha Arom, Jean-Jacques Nattiez, and John Bailey.

perspective of the other. Here I would like to suggest that such a procedure might be extended to more than two at a time, as long as what is being compared are emic units rather than etic ones. It is perhaps too obvious to warrant mention, but characteristic features very often come to light only through contrast. Far from privileging a universalist perspective, then, this sort of comparison can, if one chooses, ensure that the distinctiveness of each practice is retained or even enhanced, and it is possible to deepen one's understanding of each tradition in question.

FOUR

HAVING *RASA*, PART I

Linguistic and Cultural Perspectives

From an examination of varieties of *rasa gendhing* (musical affect), I turn now to the degree to which music or a musician does or does not possess *rasa* in a more general sense. That is, I will no longer be looking at the particular "flavor" a piece or a performance may have, but rather at how much "taste" or feeling is in it;[1] in the case of performers, I will be looking at their ability to perceive, or to express in performance, the affective essence of a piece.

Rasa, like love, makes itself felt most conspicuously when it is missing. And since criticism tends to be more revealing than praise, as an entry into the topic of who or what has *rasa*, let us consider some of the ways in which musicians talk about its absence. The most obvious, straightforward expression for the lack of *rasa* in a musical rendition is *tidak ada rasanya* [I] (*ora ènèng rasané* [Ng]). A literal translation might be "it has no flavor," but in a musical context a closer approximation would be "it has no feeling" (these two senses, however, are often conflated, as we saw in chapter 2). A variant is *tidak ada apa-apanya* [I] (*ora ånå åpå-apané* [Ng]), which means "there's nothing there," or "nothing transpires," or "it has no effect [on the listener]." Single adjectives denoting the same thing are closely synonymous with the English word *insipid*.[2] Thus we have the following variations on a theme (the definitions are based on Poerwadarminta 1939):

1. The distinction between a *gendhing* and a performance of a *gendhing* is not always clear. In a strongly oral tradition it is even more difficult to point to "the piece" than when there is a "complete" score. Again, the recipe analogy is useful here: there exists a set of abstract materials and procedures that is identifiable as this piece and not that, and yet specific instantiations of the recipe will vary considerably. This point is taken up more explicitly in chapters 6 and 7.

2. The one exception I have found, aside from the related terms to be discussed below, is *ngglajut* (*nggelacut*?) [J], defined by Sastro Tugiyo as "absolutely smooth . . . absolutely straight" (*alus saja . . . lurus saja*) (April 29, 1992). I have no other recorded instances of this word, however, and I have not found it in any dictionary. It may belong to the local dialect of Delanggu (Sastro Tugiyo's home town). Two words that might be related are *gelacutan*, which Gericke and Roorda define as "to make haste," and *ngelajuk*, "straight ahead."

ampang [J,I]—lightweight; weak (of tobacco), insipid (of the sense of taste)

åntå [J]—not fresh-tasting (of water); insipid (of food)

cemplang [J,I]—lacking in seasoning (of vegetables, etc.); insipid (of a story or a joke)

kembå [J]—without steadfastness, without perseverance, slack, insipid (of food)

sepå [J] (*sepah* [I])—without flavor

Unlike the above expressions, the following apply primarily to performers and to their characteristic ways of playing or singing (although some may apply also to specific performances):

belum (sampai) rasa [I] (*durung råså* [Ng])—hasn't gotten to the level of *rasa* yet, doesn't yet fully understand, still lacks discernment

belum/tidak bisa merasakan/menghayati [I]—isn't (yet) able to feel/discern/understand [the true nature]

kurang greged [Ng,JI], *tidak ada greged* [JI], *greged-sautnya kurang* [JI]—lacking in energy/verve/drive/intensity, listless

kurang nges [Ng, JI]—not moving/touching

kurang menjiwai [I] (*kurang njiwani* [Ng], *kirang kasarirå* [KI])— doesn't embody/express [the *rasa*][3]

tidak mengena [I]—misses the mark, has no effect, doesn't touch [the heart]

trampil saja [I], *hanya trampil* [I]—technically proficient [and nothing more]

In addition, there is a cluster of words that have to do with surfaces or exteriority, and which also contrast with *rasa*:

luar [I]—outside

lair [J] (*lahir* [I])—exterior, apparent, physical

kulit [I,J[4]]—skin

wadhag [J] (*wadak* [I])—visible, corporeal[5]

3. A note about "expression" is in order here. In the prevailing nineteenth-century European view, which still holds sway in twenty-first-century America (and elsewhere), a musician who plays or composes "with feeling" expresses his or her personal, ineffable, inner emotion, which is almost mystically communicated to a receiver through the act of performing or composing. In the case of performers it's somewhat more complicated, because both the composer's and the performers' emotions are being conveyed simultaneously. By contrast, the notion of expression implied here is much closer to the eighteenth-century ideal of understanding—and thereby creating in the listener—a publicly agreed-upon (or, at least, publicly debatable) affect: "Every emotion . . . has its own character, one that the composer must observe and get to know as intimately as he can. Only in this way will he achieve correctness of expression" (Sulzer 1981 [1792–94]:125). See also chapter 6.

4. Significantly, there are no *kråmå* or *kråmå inggil* (high Javanese) words for *kulit* or *lair*, though there are for nearly every other visible body part, as well as for *batin* (inner self), the opposite of *lair*. Everyone's outer shell, it seems, is equally *kasar* (crude).

5. For an instance of this contrast between *wadhag* and *rasa* in the visual arts, see Boow 1988:89.

The first three of these are used to refer to the superficiality of a musician's knowledge, while the fourth refers more to the *rasa* of a specific piece.

A final category has to do with weightlessness. *Ènthèng* [J] and *ringan* [I], both meaning "lightweight," are related, through the term *ampang* (mentioned above), to the absence of *rasa*. They are thus sometimes used, with clear negative connotations, to refer to something in the music that lessens its *rasa*:

> Sometimes you're playing along, and it feels *ènthèng, ampang*. Then it turns out something was wrong—the *rebab* and *gendèr* were interpreting the melody differently. (Suhartå, May 28, 1992)

We saw, in chapter 3, how musical *rasa*s range from heavy to light. Sometimes, however, musicians use the "heavy" terms (*anteb* [J], *manteb* [J], *berbobot* [I], *berat* [I]) as synonyms for *having rasa*; they often talk as if sad or serious pieces have more *rasa* than frolicsome ones. Even though some *gendhing*s should be performed in a "light" manner (and so would have less *rasa* if performed too seriously), there remains an association between "deep" *rasa* (*rasa mendalam* [I]) and "heavy" *rasa*. That is, deeply felt emotion always has some underlying seriousness to it.

When we look at various citations in which the above expressions occur, numerous *apparent* contradictions arise. Often these involve separate statements by a single speaker. Again, in what follows, *rasa* may apply to a musician, a *gendhing*, or a performance. The contradictions can be summed up as follows:

1. Older musicians play with more *rasa* than younger ones, but sometimes their playing has no *rasa* to today's ears.
2. Analysis and technique are inimical to *rasa* (which is intuitive), and yet playing with *rasa* requires very specific, technical knowledge of the tradition.
3. People in the villages have more *rasa* than those in the cities, but court musicians, who live(d) in the cities, have (or had) more *rasa* than others.
4. Women musicians are more intuitive than men (and hence one could say that they have more *rasa*), and yet female musicians ruin the *rasa* of a performance out of ignorance.
5. Playing with notation will surely deaden one's *rasa*, and yet a knowledge of notation is necessary to perform with *rasa*.
6. Singing too fast will ruin the *rasa*, yet singing too slow will ruin the *rasa*.
7. Very ornate melodic (or rhythmic) patterns ruin the *rasa*, and yet very plain patterns are insipid.
8. There is no *rasa* if the musicians are too serious, and yet there is no *rasa* if the musicians are too playful.

In exploring the issues involved, I shall restate these eight oppositions as questions, and then present supporting quotations from both sides, taken from a variety of conversations held at different times, clumping them under three broad rubrics as I attempt to make sense of the conflicting statements. Just to clarify, the statements were not, for the most part, direct answers to the questions that head the respective groupings, but came up, rather, in disparate contexts. The first of these eight contradictions is discussed on its own, but items two through five need to be dealt with together as a group, with commentary for the whole group coming after number five, and likewise for six through eight.

AN AESTHETIC OF VENERATION

1. Do older generations have more or less *rasa* than young ones?

Younger musicians (especially at ASKI) care more about technique than *rasa*. At ASKI musicians are too restricted. They learn one pattern (*céngkok*) for a given ending note (*sèlèh*), and don't take into account the *jiwa*, or character of a particular *gendhing*—two *gendhings* that are sad will be sad in different ways (Suhartå, November 17, 1989).

If I were to play *gendhing Måråsånjå*, which is *klasik*, the *rasa* wouldn't be as good as if older people did it (even if I knew the performance practice [*garap*] better). (Sudarsono, November 22, 1991)

True despondency [in music...] is not immediately apparent; if you haven't developed a fully artistic temperament [*jiwanya belum seni betul*] you won't be able to perceive it. Take, for instance, the sadness of [*gendhing*] *Kaluntå*: the young people say, "What *is* that? That's music to put you to sleep [*kesenian ngantuk*]!" They're not yet able to comprehend it [*belum bisa merasakan*]. (Suhartå, March 26, 1992)

The old generation learned with "feeling" and played with "feeling" (as opposed to this generation, which has knowledge and analysis). (Sudarsono, July 17, 1991)

My father used to say, "*rebab* players of the current generation are often good [*baik*], but never once do they make the hair on the back of my neck stand up." (Supanggah, April 12, 1992; also in Supanggah 2009:294)

When you perform, you've got to match the character of the *gendhing*. If you know it, that is; if you don't—well, that's why the *pesindhèns* nowadays...! Whatever the *gendhing*, it's their own character that comes out. That's what's ruining our art. (Suhartå, May 2, 1992)

The old singers [*lèdhèks*], they still hung onto the principles of the "classic" *gendhings*. They didn't each do their own thing. (Sastro Tugiyo, May 6, 1992)

[*After listening to a commercially produced recording*:] His voice is still young, the level is still young [immature]. He's not able to give it a sense of repose [*semèlèh*]. [...] Actually, in a *båwå* [solo vocal introduction to a gamelan piece] that's not good. [...] It shows that he's still immature [*jiwanya masih muda*]—his inner being is not yet settled [*belum meneb*]. It's like water that's never still. Pak Marto and Pak Gun used to call that a "voice that was not yet settled." (Suhartå, April 1991)

> Your voice just got "young" again. It was better before. Normally, for Javanese people, you get more settled as you get older—your voice becomes fully mature. [...] When you get older, you deepen your [spiritual] knowledge, you settle inside, then you sing well. [Before that happens,] your voice is too frivolous [*bérag*] to be majestic [*regu*] or commanding [*berwibawa*]. (Suhartå, September 11, 1991)

> Pak Cip [Ciptosuwarso] was a great guy before. But the older he got, the crazier he acted. It's not necessarily the case that the older you get, the more settled [*meneb*] you are—it can also happen that you get more out of control instead. (Suhartå, May 9, 1992)

> Pak Cip, [during lessons, would say things like,] "that way is passé [*kunå*], it's so bland ["it has no *rasa*"; *ora ènèng rasané*]." (Suhartå, May 20, 1992)

> [The singer on that 78 rpm record,] he has a large breath capacity, but compared to current *båwå* practice his singing is unprepossessing [*tidak ada apa-apanya*]—the melody just doesn't feel right [*lagunya tidak mau*]. (Suhartå, April 8, 1991)

> If one were to judge [these old recordings,] one would have to say that the present-day *gérong* [unison male choral part] is actually nicer. (Sutarman, June 10, 1992)

Only a few of the very oldest musicians I spoke with (those over seventy years old) showed no ambivalence toward previous generations of musicians. Everyone acknowledges that the former experts knew more about the labyrinthine palace traditions, and people generally agree that they had played or sung with more *rasa* than the postwar generation. Merely invoking the name of one of the great palace musicians of yore (in arguing for a particular solution to a thorny musical question) usually settles the matter. And yet the younger musicians resent how dogmatic their elders can (or could) sometimes be.

Part of the problem for these younger musicians is that in Java age confers status, and status brings with it a certain infallibility. Traditionally, a well-brought-up Javanese person wouldn't dare contradict an older, respected musician in his presence, even if the latter were clearly wrong. To illustrate, here is an entry from my fieldnotes in which I was writing about a conversation I had had with a fairly young married couple, both of whom teach at STSI (he teaches *karawitan*, she teaches dance):

> Both said that older people don't like to be told anything by someone who's younger. For instance, dancers at RRI or at the Mangkunegaran are supposed to hold still while someone is talking [during a dance drama], according to the older dancers. The older dancers won't listen to the suggestion that the dancers move a little at those times. Similarly, if a younger musician tries to get an older singer to sing on pitch, the latter is likely to refuse because it's as if she is being taught by someone younger than she. (June 17, 1991)

An only slightly more accepting attitude to this state of affairs was evinced by Suhartå:

> Pak X, when he had written something,... he felt that it was right. And because we were Javanese, including myself, we were reluctant to correct him. I used to feel very reticent about that.... I always say to students, "rather than have me write [the notation on the board] incorrectly and then have you use it forever afterwards, [I want you to tell me if I'm wrong]." But the late Pak X was different. He didn't want to be corrected, so we all had to keep quiet. Once, when he was teaching *Pangkur Mataram* [Yogya-style *Pangkur*], he told me, "you haven't even gotten as far as Prambanan yet."[6] [...] But his own *Pangkur* was "not all the way to Yogya" yet, either. Mine was more Yogyanese than his! I had lived there before! (Suhartå, May 2, 1992)

> Even though I'm of the younger generation, I don't always trust what my elders tell me—and you shouldn't necessarily trust me, either. [...] Being Javanese, I always answered "*nggih*" [yes, sir]—but I don't always use [what they taught me] when I teach. (Suhartå, June 27, 1992)

Susilo sums up the deference one shows to one's elders by the term *nylondhoh* [J], which he defines as "aware of [one's] own ignorance and respectful of the experience of [one's] elders" (1984:123).

Where *rasa* is concerned, the main complaint younger musicians have about older musicians is that they haven't kept up with changing tastes: what once sounded good, now merely sounds old fashioned. This came out explicitly in the following reconstructed conversation with the late Waridi, an outspoken, energetic teacher (voice, *rebab*, ethnomusicology) at STSI, who was in his early thirties at the time:

> As for *båwå*s [a typically male vocal genre] that are *nyindhèni* [sung in a *pesindhèn* style], many of the older generation haven't accepted that norms have changed, and that what used to be considered good has shifted. There's nothing wrong with tastes changing, in fact, and what used to be thought of as *kurang mbawani* [not in a proper *båwå* style] might now be considered to be the way *båwås* should be sung. Pak Sastro [Sastro Tugiyo] said that he's sometimes criticized for *nyindhèni*-ing, to which he replies, "Nonsense!" (February 2, 1991)[7]

This kind of generational disagreement has probably always existed. Indeed, it is difficult to imagine major changes in musical style—which, as far as we know, have always occurred—without such conflict. The eminent choreographer Tasman Ronoatmodjo underscored this tendency as it relates to Javanese dance:

> [Dance experts] often complain and fret about how the dance situation has declined terribly and gives cause for worry.... I once heard a comment made by an expert in

6. Prambanan is a town about three quarters of the way from Solo to Yogya. The idea was probably not that he was literally singing in a Prambanan style, rather that his singing still had a lot of Solonese traits in it.

7. See Waridi 2005:378–81 for more on this point.

> *karawitan*, who had had a lifelong interest in dance. What (the late) Bapak Martopangrawit said was: "Narno kuwi ngêrti apa ora tari Klana" (Does Narno *really* understand the *Klånå* dance?)....[for Martopangrawit, Sunarno] didn't fully realize the proper character of the *Klånå* dance. But the fact of the matter is that Saudara ["Brother/Comrade"] Sunarno, oddly enough, gets lots of opportunities to dance Klånå, since lots of people—and, I would venture to say, not just the young—*like* the way he dances. What's more, the party in question had in fact become—and still is—the very model of what a Solonese-style Klånå dancer should be, for the younger generation of dancers....Such complaints are common among the leading dance figures of the older generation. (1991:2–3)

Sometimes generational differences, as perceived by the current generation, are blown out of proportion. For instance, there is a general consensus among Solonese musicians that melodic styles in all of the more complex parts used to be plainer. Several of my teachers expressed surprise upon hearing recordings of *båwå*s from the 1930s and 1940s, in which the singer put in ornamentation that was excessive even by today's standards.[8] In contrast to some of the *båwå*s, however, the *gérong* parts on these old recordings were indeed simpler and more straightforward, to the point of sounding awkward to present-day musicians.

The idea that previous generations used less ornamentation seems to be linked to the notion that past generations were better at expressing the heavier *rasa*s, since "heavy" pieces call for a plainer performance style. Past generations are always associated with older people, and so attitudes towards the past are often bound up with ideas about the wisdom that comes with age. Older musicians are felt to have the restraint and the subtle understanding necessary to bring out the deeper emotions in performance. But this understanding can only come from long experience. The massive, awe-inspiring pieces of the palace repertoire (or even shorter serious pieces) are played less and less, with the result that current generations really do lack the musical experience necessary to do the old, serious repertoire justice.[9]

Supanggah, in the closing remarks of his dissertation, evokes this ambivalence between nostalgia for a glorious, not-too-distant past, when ceremonial court culture was in its heyday, and desire for a living tradition that responds to current conditions. In several of the places where he uses the word *garap* (interpretation, working out, performance practice), we might very well substitute

8. My thanks to Philip Yampolsky for unearthing and rerecording these 78 rpm records, and to Marc Perlman for sending me a copy of the tape.

9. Ben Brinner has pointed out that the details of performing idiosyncratic pieces (*gendhing pamijèn*), of which there were many in the court repertoire, are receding from memory. He suggests that younger musicians might sometimes know that there were special patterns to be learnt, but now have almost no one left to learn them from. As a result, there may now be "an unattainable standard of competence" (1995:162).

rasa gendhing, although the two are not synonymous (see the following section for the link between the two).

> Older musicians claim that the *garap* from the period [of the Surakarta Kepatihan (c. 1870)] had reached its apogee, and that it is pointless to create a new one or to ameliorate the existing one. Does that mean, then, that current *karawitan garap* is stagnant, and that rather than developing, it is actually regressing? Indeed, shorter and shorter time limits are placed on performances.... It is not possible to keep up all of the existing *garaps*, and as a result many pieces with complicated *garaps* are rarely performed.
>
> People also say that recently the *garap* of *karawitan* has shown signs of strong renewal (for instance, in modifications of tempo, dynamics, orchestration, etc.). This is a result of [Western] influences...
>
> In view of the above observations, is it true that *garap* in Javanese music is being eroded and Westernized? We might then also ask whether the current state of *garap* is actually well suited to Javanese society, which is undergoing industrialization....
>
> ...*garap* will hopefully be able to respond to the needs of a range of circumstances... [and] help ensure the survival of gamelan music in the future. (Supanggah 1985:290–92)

AN AESTHETIC OF INTERIORITY

2. Which is more indicative of *rasa*: playing with technique or playing with feeling?

> When ASKI groups play, there's nothing wrong with the *garapan* (details of performance)—the *rebab* is fine (*bagus*), etc., but from the point of view of *rasa*, they can't compare to the village groups (*kalah sama yang ada di desa*). (Sudarsono, August 21, 1991)

> Those of the younger generation are highly skilled but nothing more [*trampil saja*]: they aren't yet able to sense the *rasa* [*belum bisa merasakan*]. (Suhartå, May 6, 1991)

> The Mangkunegaran Palace is good at attracting clever musicians [*orang pinter*] [...] but during the joint concert at TBS it was clear that in terms of *rasa* the Kraton was far superior to the Mangkunegaran, which was admittedly more polished. (Tri Hasthå Tåmå, July 5, 1991)

> What creates visual pleasure in a dance is the supple elegance—the flow, the agility; but what's *most* important is the *råså*.... A lot of people [who see us dance] say, "they're not even together—they don't flick the scarves together, they don't turn their heads together." That might be, but that's because I look at how much *råså* [the dancers] have attained. Because if you count the beats according to the book, and make the movements uniform and synchronized, it will look stiff and awkward. But sacred courtly dances [*bedhåyå* and *srimpi*] are not just commodities to be consumed with the eyes and ears. So you have to use your *råså*... And this applies to spectators,

too—not everyone is capable of appreciating *bedhåyå* and *srimpi*. (Moertiyah, June 23, 1991)

W: Nyai Béi [Mardusari] is the only *pesindhèn* who can be alternately sad [*sedhih*] and happy [*gembira*], thanks to her voice and her consummate artistry [*kepandaiannya*]. [...] She was once taught by a French person brought in by Prince Mangkunegårå VII. [...]
MLB: But did that have anything to do with *rasa gendhing*?
W: It gave her the technique—it helped. (Wignyosaputro, June 19, 1992)

The condition of the voice also affects *rasa gendhing*. [...] So does where one puts in stopping points—one's technique. Like if you take too many breaths. (Wignyosaputro, June 19, 1992)

[Some *pesindhèns*] can go either way. [They can be good for both heavy and light pieces.] It depends on them, on how skilled they are [*kepandaian dia*] at training their voices to fit the character of the piece. (Suhartå, June 11, 1992)

[During a particularly out-of-tune rehearsal:] If I listen to a *bedhåyå* or *srimpi* piece like this,[10] my sensibility [*rasa saya*] is offended [*kecewa*—"disappointed"]. The musical effect is spoiled [*rasa musikalnya kacau*]. (Darsono, June 12, 1991)

Rasa depends a lot on the *garap* [knowledgeable interpretation]. And, conversely, the performer has to understand the *rasa* of a *gendhing* so that his *garap* can bring out the *rasa*. (Harjito, May 27, 1992)

3. Who has more *rasa*: court (urban) musicians or village musicians?

The reason the dancers from the Kraton have a different *rasa* is (1) the atmosphere at the Kraton is different; (2) the colors that they wear are more subdued; (3) the incense. (Sudarsono, September 9, 1991)

Those who are trained outside the Kraton [...] are not capable of participating in the *Bedhåyå Ketawang*[11]—[they lack] the deep *rasa* necessary to perform the movements and to comprehend what the *Bedhåyå Ketawang* is all about. (Moertiyah, June 23, 1991)

The dancers from the Kraton really do have a different *rasa*. For one thing, their faces are so different. Some people say that they're technically not all that good, but when they performed *Bedhåyå Durådasih* at TBS, somehow it was really moving [*kok bisa terharu!*]. (Suraji, September 11, 1991)

10. These are pieces meant to accompany choreographed court dances for four, seven, or nine young women. The music consists of long-phrased, unison choral singing, with either full or reduced gamelan.

11. The oldest, longest, and most sacred court dance.

I only played *kenong*[12] [at the gamelan academy in the city]. I could play *gendèr* a little—badly!—it was village playing [*gendéran désa*]. (Sastro Tugiyo, April 30, 1992)

[After singing a passage from an unaccompanied song:] When you sing it that way it's *lugu* [straight, plain]. But people outside [the palace tradition] (*di luar*) consider it *berbobot* [accomplished, of high quality]. (Suhartå, December 12, 1989)

[About different versions of the *gérong* part to Ladrang *Pangkur*:] It's the village version that's more *gagah* [strong, "handsome"], more varied, more inspired; in the city it's just "simple," *lugu* [plain]. (Sudarsono, November 30, 1991)

In the Kraton they're not critical enough—"well, all right, whatever..."—It's like the Kraton Yogya. Pak Tjokro,[13] when a *klenèngan luar* [music-making session outside the palace] falls apart, he says, "Jeez! You're imitating the Kraton!" (Sutarman, June 24, 1992)

4. Who has more *rasa*: men or women?

Pesindhèns are incapable of matching the *rasa gendhing*. [...] Most *pesindhèns* are *sindhèn alam* ["natural," untrained singers]—they just imitate. [...] They can't tell the *rasa* of their own singing, and don't know what different pieces call for. (Wignyosaputro, June 19, 1992)

The performers don't always know the *unsur* [*rasa*] of the *gendhings* they sing (on many recordings the *rasa*'s all wrong); the *pesindhèns* don't study that. (Sutarman, June 10, 1992)

[*Gendhing gecul* (jocular), *prenès* (coquettish), *klasik* (classic), *kasmaran* (lovelorn):] *pesindhèns* can't tell one from another. (Sastro Tugiyo, May 6, 1992)

In musicians' lingo there's an expression for *pesindhèns*: "*swargå nunut, nerâkå katut*" [Ng] [(they) hitch along (to) heaven, (are) carried along (to) hell].[14] [...] This means that they'll follow anyone, that they don't have any independence. [...] Wherever the *niyâgâs* [instrumentalists] go, she goes too.[15] (Sașto Tugiyo, May 6, 1992)

12. A time-marking pot-gong—one of the easiest instruments to play.

13. Wasitodiningrat (alias Tjokrowasito and Wasitodipuro), an eminent musician from Yogyakarta, associated with the Pakualaman Palace (Yogya's "other" palace).

14. This expression seems to have been a common one for women in general. It is used in Kasman Singodimejo's *O, Anakku*, a letter of advice by a Javanese political prisoner to his daughter (quoted in Bonneff 1977:225). Whereas the form is only slightly different, the interpretation is quite distinct: the proverb, Singodimejo says, was intended to teach a woman her proper relationship to her husband, but he rejects it as old-fashioned. He glosses "Wong wadon iku suargané nunut, nerakané katut" as "the wife's paradise consists in following her husband; if she goes to hell, it's because she's followed him there as well."

15. The primary meaning here is metaphorical: the *pesindhèn*'s part starts and finishes later than the other parts. This allows her to hear what is coming up and sing the appropriate melodic pattern

If you want to know what music should really sound like, hire a *cokèkan* [chamber gamelan group] and don't invite a *pesindhèn*. (Sukanto, June 24, 1992)

[The *rasa*s of] *Kaluntå* and *Laler Mengeng* are different. [...] Try comparing the recordings—but the *sindhèn* will affect it. [...] Or listen to the instrumental version—it's still plain [*polos*], you can feel the true *rasa* [*bisa dirasakan betul*]. *Pesindhèn*s nowadays, [...] I can't feel the *rasa* (except if I train them to coordinate with the *rebab*). (Suhartå, March 26, 1992)

Laler Mengeng III:1

Men's vocal music is *kawengku ing lagu* [constrained or determined by—literally, "is framed by"—the (set) melody (of a piece)]. Women's vocal music is *kawengku ing råså* [determined by the *råså*]. (Wignyosaputro, June 19, 1992) [See pp. 139–40 in the following chapter for the full context of this quotation.]

When Nyai Béi ["Dame"] Mardusari sang *Pangkur* [*Paripurnå*], it was as if the people [in the audience] could cry along with her! *That* is *rasa*... art. [...] That is art, for it can deeply affect a person. (Supadmi, quoted in Walton 1996:86)

In male style there is no inner essence [*intisari*] nor are there any ornaments [*sari-sari*, another Javanese word for flower]. It is too simple. It can be notated and it is more regular and ordered [*diaturi*]. (Kestik, quoted in Weiss 1994:41)

5. Does playing with notation help or hinder *rasa*?

[*Pesindhèns*] didn't use to read *balungan* [reference melody] notation at all—they were really smart [*pandai*]. But now *pesindhèn*s read the *balungan* notation while they sing. [...] Before the [instruments] get to this or that final note, the *pesindhèn*s can see it coming. But the funny thing is that it sounded better before, when they weren't reading notation. It's kind of a mystery, really. [...] [One thing that was different was that] they didn't use many "fillers" [*abon-abon*s] [in *gendhing klasik*,[16]] even though no one told them—they just sensed it by themselves [*rasanya sendiri*]. (Sastro Tugiyo, May 6, 1992)

Most *pesindhèn*s nowadays can *nabuh* [play instruments] a little, and so use notation rather than listen to the other parts. According to Pak Mloyo, they *nyindhèni* [sing a part to] the notation rather than the *gendhing*. For instance, [the other day,] over at Pak Tentrem's, they played *gendhing Krawitan*. At one point the *balungan* plays pitch 5, but the *rebab* plays a 3. Bu [X], who was singing, went to 5 instead (which is wrong). Many younger *rebab* players (who are also overdependent on notation) go to 5 there as well. (Sukanto, April 2, 1990)

---

without knowing the piece by heart. (It is also possible to play many of the instrumental parts in this way.) The expression also alludes to the reputation of *pesindhèn*s for being somewhat promiscuous (they are literally carried to and from rehearsals on the backs of male musicians' motorcycles—an act which, in Java, often implies a sexual relationship).

16. In the calm first section of a "classic" piece, it's considered too busy-sounding if one puts in lots of optional fillers.

[If notation is too specific] it makes you stupid. [. . .] You don't have to write in all of the ornaments; there are many possible interpretations. If [it's all written down], it boxes you in [lit., "wraps around you"], it's not good. Old notation was much plainer; now they write everything out. (Suhartå, April 15, 1991)

Now you have to use a book [of notation]—for new compositions [*kréasi*], you have no choice but to read. But if all you ever do is read, in the end it's the book that's *pandai* [clever], not the person. It used to be, it was the person who was *pandai*—without a book [we] could still function—reliably and well! Now, without a book they're lost. [They say,] "I haven't memorized it yet." (Sastro Tugiyo, May 6, 1992)

When you play while reading notation, it really decreases the power of [your heart's? your *råså*'s?] vibrations. The reason is that your attention is divided between the notation and the details of playing. It's different if you've memorized the piece—then, the expression can truly come out. (Sukanto, June 4, 1990)

If you're doing work [with your various faculties], your attention is divided, and so the *rasa*'s going to be different. For example, if you're singing and reading, it's not going to reach here [your heart]. It's your eyes that are doing all the work. Your *rasa* [faculty of feeling] is not doing any work. But the *bedhåyå* singers [in the Kraton] don't read—it comes from their *rasa*. Melody, lyrics, *rasa*—you can tell the difference. Compare singing with the notation in front of you to singing from memory—[when you sing from memory] it has soaked into your very bones and marrow. The *rasa's* going to be a whole lot different. (Wignyosaputro, June 24, 1992)

So I concentrate on what I'm playing. [. . .] If my thoughts wander, it goes awry, it falls apart. So when I play, I'm in a state of meditation. That's how I'm able to attract ["pull"] those who are listening. [. . .] But if not, if you use notation, then it doesn't work. 'Cause your attention has been dragged away by the notation. (Mloyowidodo, May 2, 1992)

MLB: Do you think the old-timers would have liked present-day *gérong* if they were alive to hear it?

SUTARMAN (TARMAN): I think so. Very few of them could even read notation. [. . .] When I first taught *sindhèn* [the solo female vocal part] with notation, everyone was incredulous. [. . .]

MLB: Can a singer be good if she studies with notation?

T: Sure, she can be good. Look at Padmi, Darmi.[17]

MLB: Pak Mloyo[18] says that it's not good to use notation. [. . .]

T: That's true if you're dependent on it. It's just a tool. The goal is to be able to do without it. He's right if you *perform* with notation: then you try to perform *correctly* rather than *well* [*mencari betulnya, tidak mencari baiknya*]. After four or five years, if you've gotten past [notation], it will sound the same. People nowadays can't learn by imitation

17. Supadmi and Sudarmi, two singers who became stars, one in the group of the puppeteer Nartosabdho, the other at the national radio station in Solo, respectively.

18. Mloyowidodo (see the previous quotation).

TABLE 4.1. Gender associations (after S. Weiss 1993).

male	**female**
control as power	freedom as power
order	disorder
alus (refined)	*kasar* (crude)
rule-bound	emotional
spiritual	earthy
analytical	intuitive
garap	*rasa*
Kraton (royal palace)	*désa* (village)
use of notation	aural stimulus only

anymore, but they can do it if they're shown notation. So it's a useful tool. (June 10, 1992)

Bu [X] is prone to forget [pieces]; and she's not very sharp [*pinter*]—she learned to read and write late. [...] She often used to get the number of syllables wrong—she couldn't read, so she was a bit left behind by the others. Bu Tambang was like Bu Béi:[19] she was really good at *gendhing* notation. Bu [Y] is pretty good, but she's not as skillful [*pandai*] as Bu Tambang. (Suhartå, May 7, 1992)

One way of approaching this morass of interrelated, conflicting statements, is through Sarah Weiss's broad-ranging analysis of the social meanings of female *gendèr* players. While her overall argument is more complex, the crux of it rests on a dichotomy between male and female behaviors as they relate to Javanese ideas of power and refinement. This dichotomy is summarized in table 4.1.

The top six items in each list apply to behavior or general gender associations, whereas the bottom eight items apply to musical associations (which means that the middle five apply to both). Weiss's analysis is a useful departure point, since it weaves together all of the parameters being touched on here. Weiss herself has substantially refined this dichotomy (1998, chapters 4 and 5; 2006, chapter 4), acknowledging its limitations. I would like to offer my own emendations here, which, like those of Weiss, owe much to the work of Brenner (1995). To begin with, as we have seen in chapter 3, women are not necessarily more *kasar* (crude, coarse) than men. Not only does the most *kasar* behavior come from men, but women have their own brand of *alus*ness (refinement): "A man... might be *halus*, but he'll never be as *halus* as a prima-donnaish woman (except if he's an effeminate man)" (Suhartå, June 10, 1991). Indeed, *alus* [J] (*halus* [I]) can mean "delicate," "intricate," "graceful," "feminine," as well as

19. Tambangraras and Mardusari, both former singers at the Mangkunegaran palace.

"smooth," "unadorned," "spiritual," "masculine." A second problem is that all of the female associations on the list are also applicable to village men (with the possible exception of "freedom as power").[20] Finally, the analysis fails to take into account the contradictions brought out in the above citations.

The key to understanding the discrepancies in the many statements quoted above lies in different senses of the word *rasa*. The word, admittedly, is often best translated as "emotion" or "feelings." This is the sense in which Weiss uses it. In the citations above, the one person who consistently uses it in this sense is Sudarsono, who was one of Weiss's principal teachers. This sense of *rasa* is implied also in a series of its antonyms: *biasa* [I], *ngglajut* [J], *lugu* [I,JI], and, most notably, *alus* [J] (*halus* [I]).[21] They all express a lack of excitement, roughness, or surprise. Indeed, Sastro Tugiyo told me that a good *båwå* singer has to put in *grenjel* (bumps in the road) and *kejutan* (surprises) every now and then or the performance will be insipid. This, then, is *rasa* as emotion, as strong sensation, as transgression, as *dis*order.

But *rasa* may also have to do with understanding inner meaning, with control and refinement—that is to say, with *order*. In this second sense, male Kraton musicians—considered more spiritual, more *alus*, and more knowledgeable—have (or had) the upper hand over both female musicians and male villagers. The word *luar* [I] (outside) that is applied to non-Kraton musicians could also be taken to mean "surface." "Inside" musicians, then, are (were) more attuned to "depth"; that is, to inner meaning or deep *rasa*. (Tjahjono [1989:228ff.] has developed the analogy between the *batin* [Ng,I] or inner self and a building's center. Through juxtaposition, he has hinted at the extension of this to a geographical center such as the Kraton.)[22] Thus, Kraton musicians have less *rasa* than villagers when performing the more lighthearted, surface-oriented *gendhing*s, whereas "outside" musicians are less adept at bringing out the *rasa*s in the heavier, more serious repertoire.

"Inside" musicians at one of the modern institutions are (or were) probably the performers most widely criticized for playing without *rasa* in either sense (excepting, of course, beginners and foreigners), perhaps because of their over-reliance on notation and their relatively sterile performance environments. Another possible reason that this group was seen by some as having less *rasa* than Kraton musicians is that the younger musicians at the academies generally had more technique than the few remaining palace musicians (this is even truer of dancers). Since technique is associated with outer aspects of music, a

20. See, for instance, Perlman 1998.

21. *Biasa*: ordinary, lighthearted. *Ngglajut*: overly smooth or straight. *Lugu*: plain. As these terms (along with *alus*) appear in many of the citations under question (7), below, they are discussed in the next section.

22. See figures 4.3 and 4.4, and the discussion on pp. 112–13. Other authors, too, have pointed out the continuity between microcosm and macrocosm in Javanese thinking (Stange 1984:133; Heine-Geldern 1963 [1956]:3).

technically accomplished musician may be seen as developing technique at the expense of the inner meaning—or *rasa*—of music. This perception is certainly reinforced by the aesthetic of veneration already discussed. A similar distinction is made in the West, where child prodigies (or—in Europe—American musicians) are often said to have impressive technique but little feeling or understanding.[23]

It should be noted, however, that this last observation was very much contested when, in the summer of 2003, I presented this material to an audience of musicians and scholars at STSI (Indonesian Advanced School for the Arts) Surakarta. First, it was objected that the musical situation at the Kraton has declined considerably, so that it has actually been a long time since performances there were truly in keeping with its exalted status. Second, many of the best *seniman alam*, or "natural musicians," have been hired by STSI to enrich the ranks of its instructors. Third, an institution itself does not have musical *rasa*, only individuals do, so that such generalizations can be misleading. Fourth, the number one deciding factor of whether a musician will develop *rasa* is how *kulinå* (well acquainted) he or she is with gamelan music; that is, how much time he or she spends listening to and making music in context. It must be said, as well, that pedagogical methods at STSI have evolved considerably over time. Students now learn in a more "natural" way, with less plugging in of standard formulae. They are asked to find musical solutions themselves and are also encouraged to participate in off-campus groups. The results are encouraging indeed, and I am not alone in thinking so.

Rasa in the sense of "understanding" depends on a knowledge of what is appropriate (see below) in a given musical situation. This kind of knowledge can be summed up by the term *garap*. Whereas *garap* is often (perhaps even usually) contrasted with *rasa* (S. Weiss 1993, Brinner 1995:59), the two can also be seen as intimately linked.[24]

Garap, which Supanggah translates as "interpretation" (1985:299), and Sutton (1979, 1993) as "treatment" or "working out," is one of those crucial terms that are much easier to use than to define. As a verb, *menggarap* [I] (*nggarap* [J]) means "to work" in the senses corresponding to the past participle "wrought." One of

23. This particular platitude is even more prevalent in descriptions of prodigies who are not of European descent. Kenneth Chen has done extensive research on perceptions of Asian prodigies in Canada.

24. Although he does not use the term *rasa*, Perlman (1994) has pointed out the link between the related term *bobot* and *garap*:

> two categories used by some of the juries in the ubiquitous *gamelan* competitions [are] *leres* ('correct' playing, the avoidance of mistakes) versus *bobot* ('quality'; Suhardi [26.vii.85]). It is the latter category that is associated with the idea of *garap*; indeed, other juries use the term *garap* (rather than *bobot*) to label the category distinguished from the 'correct.' (165)

Since *bobot* (weight, maturity, quality) in this context has to do with the ineffable, individual touches that make a performance stand out, I am inclined to equate it with *rasa*.

its common uses is in connection with farming, where it means "to work the soil." It thus carries a sense of transforming something rough or vague into a fully finished product.[25] As a noun used in music talk, *garap* (or, more properly, *garapan*) refers to the specific choices musicians make collectively and individually in performing a given piece, or to the results of these choices. These include such things as instrumentation, dynamics, tempo, and melodic patterns. *Garap* is thus somewhat analogous to the term *performance practice* in Western classical music, but it extends to the notes themselves, involving far more leeway for the performers than one finds in most classical music.[26] It is also analogous to musical arrangement in jazz, although *garap* includes melodic choices made in real time that would normally come under the rubric of improvisation.

In the expression "to know *garap*," the term has the more restricted sense of "the proper way to perform pieces in the traditional repertoire." One achieves proficiency at *nggarap*-ing only by amassing a vast storehouse of experience with instrumental idioms, modal practices, and performance contexts. Experience, memory, and comparison are the factors that enable one to acquire a sense of what is appropriate. Developing a knowledge of *garap* thus goes hand in hand with developing a sensitivity to *rasa* in the sense of a deep understanding of the tradition.[27]

Knowledge of *garap* separates not only court musicians and their musical heirs from "outsiders,"[28] but also instrumentalists from singers. In the citations above, *pesindhèns* are said to ruin the *rasa* of a *gendhing* because they don't know *garap*, and not just because they are women (the same condescension is directed at male singers who never learn to play an instrument, but they have less opportunity to ruin the *rasa* of the performance, since their parts are generally more set).[29] Knowledge of *garap* is necessary to the proper realization of all difficult (i.e., serious) *gendhings*, and is nearly coterminous with a knowledge of *rasa* in these pieces. That is, a musician who *really* knows *garap* not only knows which patterns are theoretically correct, but also when they are affectively appropriate

25. Sumarsam translates the term as "way of working," "processing," or "fashioning" (1984 [1975]:303).

26. The farther back in Western music history one goes, of course, the closer one gets to oral tradition, and hence the closer, also, to interpretations that resemble Javanese *garap*. For instance, in much Renaissance music instrumentation is pretty much up to the performers. Baroque figured bass is another case in point, as are baroque and classic cadenzas. But even so, *garap* extends from minute details of rhythm to large-scale structural shaping that goes beyond performance practice in the Western written tradition.

27. For more on how musicians apply their accumulated knowledge to specific musical situations, see Supanggah 1985, Sumarsam 1984 [1975], Brinner 1995, Sutton 1979 and 1993, Perlman 1994, Vetter 1981, Forrest 1980.

28. See Perlman 1998.

29. If female *gendèr* players were accused of ruining the *rasa*, I suspect it would be because of their not knowing *garap*, and in this respect they would be no more subject to criticism than their male counterparts from the villages.

(see the next section). This is why it is misleading to contrast rules or analysis with *rasa*: many rules are made for the express purpose of bringing out the appropriate affect. (For instance, in the Kraton tradition, there is a rule against using *ciblon* drumming or *imbal* [fast, interlocking patterns], which are associated with dance accompaniment, in the most serious pieces, for this would destroy the stateliness, the *rasa regu*.)[30] It is also why notation, whose stultifying effects are generally acknowledged, is sometimes seen as aiding singers in producing the appropriate *rasa*. Instead of blindly following the lead of the instrumental parts through aural cues in real time (a process that strikes me as incomparably difficult but is sometimes considered to be indicative of a singer's stupidity),[31] *pesindhèn*s who refer to notation for the *balungan* (outline melody) as they sing can be more in control of their *garap*, and so are exercising more *rasa*. On the other hand, any performer on one of the more complex parts who reads off every note of a written-out part exercises no *rasa* at all (see chapter 5).

It is useful, here, to distinguish between explicit and implicit rules (Brinner 1995:32–39, S. Weiss 1998:152–55, Perlman 2004:21–27). If a rule is defined merely as a regularity, then all traditional musicians follow rules of some sort. But the kind of rule that is sometimes contrasted with *rasa* is an explicitly formulated rule that is then used to guide musical practice. What I am arguing here is that the two kinds of rules—implicit, intuitive versus explicit, theoretical/didactic—come together in the concept of *garap*, that *garap* is closely linked to *rasa*, and hence *rasa* is not uniquely equatable with tacit intuition.

Waridi is rather explicit in his positing *garap* as a foundation for *rasa*:

> A gamelan musician, in order to be able to produce the desired *rasa gendhing* in keeping with the specific context, must fulfill three requirements:
>
> 1. ...having a wide field of vision with regards to a varied repertoire of pieces along with their associated *garap*, and being skilled in playing instruments.
> 2. Having the capacity to choose the interpretive (*garap*) vocabulary in the form of *céngkok* (melodic or rhythmic patterns), as well as the tempo that will fit with the character of the type of piece being interpreted (*digarap*).
> 3. Understanding the particular context every time he or she is *garap*-ing a piece.
>
> The various *rasa gendhing* that are felt by Javanese listeners amount, basically, to an impression that emerges from the combined instrumental parts as they are interpreted (*digarap*) in keeping with the particular context. Such an impression can only be created if all of the parts are performed well and in a way that is right for the context. Thus *rasa gendhing* is highly determined by the musicians' ability to *garap* the piece... (2005:357–58)

30. This is widely repeated, but written confirmation can be found, for instance, in Waridi 2005:371.

31. Compare the unflattering dictum, "*swargå nunut, nerâkå katut*" (hitch along to heaven, carried along to hell), quoted and annotated on p. 100.

Additional evidence for the conceptual proximity of *garap* to *rasa* may be found in the following two excerpts from conversations with Sutarman:

> [The *rasa* of any given *mâcâpat* meter] depends on the *lelagon*.[32] [. . .] There's
> 4/1 *Dhandhanggulâ Buminatan* [*sings*].[33] But *Dhandhanggulâ Tlutur* is *nyes* [sad] [*sings*]. The
> 4/2 *rasa* is different, the *garap* is different. (Sutarman, June 6, 1992)

> T: A *båwå* singer knows: when you get to the word *jawâtâ* [godhead] [in this *båwå*], you have to make it fit. It's as if the composer is telling you where to do this or that. [. . .]
>
> MLB: Can that *sereng* [tense] line [that you just sang] be made *sem* [pleasing] with the same notes?
>
> T: [Sings.] It can, but it's *wagu* [ungainly]. It doesn't feel right. [. . .]
>
> MLB: What gives it the *sem* feeling?
>
> T: The *wiled-gregel* [ornaments].
>
> MLB: So if it's more plain . . .
>
> T: If it's more plain it feels *sereng*. It feels to me that the melody there has to be that way. You can do it otherwise, but it's awkward. The musicians of yore took that into account [when they composed these songs.]
>
> MLB: Why is it ungainly [*wagu*]?
>
> T: It doesn't fit with what you expect [*tidak rumus*]. The melodic pattern [*céngkok*] is too irregular [*tidak rumus*]. It shouldn't be that way—it feels forced. (Sutarman, June 24, 1992)

The conventions of *garap* thus help a musician be true to the nature of a piece—what I am calling *rasa gendhing*. Perlman states this same point a little differently:

> *garap* . . . has an object: it is interpretation *of* a composition. Emphasizing the "intentionality" of *garap* means evaluating *garap* according to its adequacy to its object. (1994:195)

We can further explore the relationship between *rasa* and technical knowledge or ability by examining the terms used to refer to skillful musicians. Many of these may be left-handed compliments. That is, there may be a big *but* trailing implicitly behind them (*ada tetapinya*)—"Sure, he's great technically (but he lacks *rasa*)." This is especially true of *pinter* [J,JI] (*pintar* [I]), "clever"; *prigel* [J,JI], "agile, dexterous"; and *trampil* [I,J],

32. *Mâcâpat* is a category of traditional sung verse that uses indigenous poetic meters, such as *Dhandhanggulâ* (which has ten lines per stanza, with the following pattern of numbers of syllables per line and final vowels: 10*i*, 10*a*, 8*e*, 7*u*, 9*i*, 7*a*, 6*u*, 8*a*, 12*i*, 7*a*). Each *mâcâpat* meter has a variety of tunes, called *lelagon*s, associated with it. These have been given names, many of which are associated with a locality in central Java (*Dhandhanggulâ Mangkubumèn, Dhandhanggulâ Semarangan*, etc.).

33. Sutarman probably meant this as an example of a cheerful (*sem*) version of *Dhandhanggulâ*.

"skillful."[34] Alone among these terms stands *pandai* [I] (*pandhé* [J]), which—like *pinter*—is the opposite of *bodoh* [I] (*bodho* [J]), "stupid," and can simply mean "quick to learn." But, unlike *pinter*, it is unequivocally positive. The *pandai* musician knows *garap* well enough to bring out the *rasa* of a *gendhing* in his or her performance. Someone who is *pinter* is merely quick to learn or quick to react, whereas someone who is *pandai* has internalized the essence of good taste: the *pinter* musician manipulates surfaces, whereas the *pandai* musician manipulates deeper meanings. For an example of this contrast, compare a statement by Sudarsono with one by Sastro Tugiyo:[35]

> People of my generation might be *pinter* and know a lot of *garapan*, but they can never equal the older generation in terms of *rasa*. (Sudarsono, June 6, 1991)

> MLB: What's the difference between *gérong* [unison male choral singing] nowadays and in former times?
>
> ST: [*Gérong* singers] don't fully grasp knowledge of *karawitan* and vocal music any more. They're too specialized. They've only grasped about 25 percent, 50 percent. Nowadays they often don't know how to play the *rebab*, the *gendèr*, the *kendhang*—they put singing first. You don't find too many who are *pandai*. So they can't appreciate the *rasa* of consummate *gendèr* playing, *rebab* playing that carries you away [*nganyut-anyut*], *kendhang* playing that [moves?] the listener. *Gendèr* playing that astonishes. *Rebab* playing that devastates [*mematikan*].
>
> Nowadays they haven't mastered [the other instruments enough to experience that]. (Sastro Tugiyo, April 30, 1992)

True, *wong pinter* [Ng] (a *pinter* person) in mystical circles may refer to someone who has the unusual ability to see, understand, and communicate with the spirit world: the value difference between the two terms is not absolute. But *pandhé* has as one of its oldest (and still one of its primary) meanings "metalsmith"—a revered profession that requires high-powered spiritual knowledge [J. Becker 1988]).[36] Moreover, several Javanese expressions deriving from the root *pinter* have decidedly negative connotations; *minter*, *sok pinter*, and *kuminter* all have to

34. Other terms of praise, which do not necessarily contrast with *rasa*, but which do not imply it either, are *mahir* [I,J] (accomplished), *komplit* [E,I] (*pepak* [J], complete), *lihai* [I] (skilled, clever, astute), *ngabéhi* (all-around), *mampu* (capable), *déwasa* [I] (*diwåså* [J], mature, adult), and *sudah jadi* [I] (*wis dadi* [Ng], *sampun dados* [K], fully trained). I am not sure about *wasis* [J] ("superbly competent" [Horne 1974]), which I have seen in nineteenth-century texts, but for which I have no current citations.

35. I have found at least two other citations that run along the same lines for *pandai* (Suhartå, June 25, 1992; Wignyosaputro, June 19, 1992); and four for *pinter* (Tri Hastå Tåmå, July 5, 1991; Sudarsono, December 18, 1991; Sudarsono, April 29, 1992; and Suhartå, May 14, 1992).

36. While Javanese monolingual dictionaries give only the "metal smith" meaning, several bilingual (Javanese-English, Javanese-Dutch, Javanese-Indonesian) dictionaries give "clever" or "skilled" as well. For the etymology of *pandhé* see Gonda 1973:170–71. He gives three possible derivations: Sanskrit *pandya* (learned, wise); Malay *pa-* (prefix denoting agency) + *de* (root expressing "working, making"); and Hindi and Bengali *pande* (learned man, scholar, teacher, name of a brahman caste).

do with pretending to be more clever than one is, and *minteri* means "to dupe [someone]." Such is not the case with *pandhé* or *wasis* [J] (yet another word meaning "skilled").

To sum up thus far, then, whereas technical skill is often contrasted with *rasa*, quite the contrary may be true when *rasa* refers not to feeling but to understanding. If I have emphasized the cognitive dimension of *rasa* here, it is because it sometimes gets left out when *rasa* is translated simply as "feeling."

At the same time, the notion of *rasa* as disorderly emotion clearly belongs amid the various Javanese meanings of the term, whether in a musical context or otherwise. We shall now turn to the issue of how typically Javanese this kind of *rasa* is considered to be. In other words, because Javanese culture has often been described by both cultural insiders and outsiders as emphasizing order and self control, and because *rasa* is often used (primarily by insiders) as a marker of Javanese identity, the question arises as to how *rasa* in its emotional aspect contributes to cultural self-definition.

In the most common Javanese psychological theories, one of the principal motivators of a person's behavior are the four *napsu*s (*nafs* [A]) (J. Weiss 1977:190ff., Woodward 1989:191). These are akin to drives in Western psychology. They are (1) *amarah* (*al-ammarah* [A], aggression), (2) *aluwamah* (*al-lawwamah* [A], hunger and thirst), (3) *supiyah* (*saffia* [A], acquisition, sexual desire), and (4) *mutmainah* (*mutma'innah* [A], compassion). The first three are seen as disruptive and need to be constantly held in check. The fourth is positive, but even it can lead to undesirable behavior if it is out of balance. Even though *mutmainah* is a natural drive in all humans, certain kinds of behavior associated with it are seen as typically Javanese. This desirable behavior is motivated by the learned *rasa*s: shame (*isin* [Ng]), compassion (*welas* [J], *tepå slirå* [J]), constraint or reluctance to inconvenience someone (*pekéwuh* [Ng], *rikuh* [Ng], *jiguh* [Ng], *wigih-wigih* [J]), sensitivity to others' misfortunes (*ora tégå* [Ng], *ora tegel* [Ng], *ora mentålå* [Ng]), inner peace (*tentrem* [J]), and humility (*andhap-asor* [K]). These are among the most powerful tools for maintaining harmony. In the same vein, Soerjomentaram divides *rasa* into three categories: "base" (anger, infatuation), "ordinary" (happiness, sorrow), and "exalted" (devotion to, love of, and awe of nature; awareness of life) (n.d.:9–10). Thus, while some *rasa*s are fueled by undesirable *nafsu*s, others—those having to do with an intuitive sense of appropriate behavior—help to keep these in check. Another place where this notion is echoed is in Wolff and Soepomo's study of Javanese linguistic behavior (1982:14–17). They show how the quintessentially Javanese empathetic *rasa*s regulate polite interaction.

The values that underlie these Javanese emotions are seen as being eroded by Western influence. For one thing, there is a widespread notion among middle-class Javanese that public displays of sexuality are not part of traditional culture. People often complain, for example, that young people are being led astray by U.S. movies and television. Indeed, outside influences are seen as transforming the very core of what it means to be a well-brought-up Javanese person.[37] Supanggah, when asked whether certain terms had negative or positive connotations, said that *luruh* [J] (humble) *used* to be positive, but that now it tends to be negative—children are increasingly taught to speak up. He cited traditional proverbs that all reinforce the wisdom of reticence: "kian merunduk, kian berisi" (the more [the rice stalk] stoops, the more grain it holds); "air tenang menghanyutkan" (quiet waters sweep away); "air beriak tidak dalam" (burbling water is not deep); "tong kosong berbunyi nyaring" (an empty barrel makes a loud noise). When asked whether *alus* (refined) was positive, again, he said that it used to be extremely positive, but now it is more or less neutral (Supanggah, May 17, 1992).

But this view of recent foreign influence as ruining the order and chasteness of Javanese society is at the very least an oversimplification. John Pemberton (1994) has argued that the relatively recent Javanese preoccupation with order has not always been characteristic of Javanese culture as a whole. He points out how the New Order government magnified this tendency, to the detriment of other traditional elements in which moments of chaos and anarchy play an essential role.

Overtly sexual behavior might also be more a long-standing feature of Javanese culture than is usually thought by the current middle class.[38] There are certainly aspects of present-day Javanese behavior that strike most Americans as being bawdier than the norm in the West (*wayang* humor, for instance). This discrepancy is probably due almost entirely to a difference in perspective: what is considered unacceptably overt in one culture may be perfectly ordinary in another.[39] But many Javanese also seem to have misconceptions about the Javanese past, which are fueled by what Florida calls "the cult of the *adiluhung*

37. This is also felt very strongly on a national level, but more with reference to a specifically Islamic rather than a local cultural identity (although the two are, of course, in many cases linked). Beginning in late 2005 a heated debate developed between defenders and detractors of a proposed antipornography law that would have had dire consequences for many local performing arts across Indonesia. And yet an essential component of the Islamic defenders' argument was the notion that pornography was something imposed from without, specifically from the decadent West. For several years the debate had attenuated and the law put on hold, but as of this book's going to press the project was being resuscitated.

38. See, for example, Keeler 1987:181; Florida 1996; Anderson 1990, chapter 8; Hughes-Freeland 1993; Suryakusuma 1996; and Clara van Groenendael 1985:177.

39. For instance, a man and a woman holding hands in public is still rather shocking in central Java, whereas it goes unnoticed in North America. Conversely, in Java it is not unusual for two heterosexual young men to sleep with their bodies touching, in the same bed, whereas in North America this would be considered evidence of a sexual relationship. Another example may be found in *wayang*, which can seem shockingly explicit, sexually, to a North American spectator, considering that large numbers of children are often present. And yet what may be seen, in its country of origin, as a rather tame scene from a Hollywood movie can come across as particularly titillating in Java.

(the beautiful sublime)" (1995:32ff.). That is, they see a past that was more exalted, more *alus* than the present. Yet written records seem to indicate, if anything, more openness about sexuality in an earlier era. Some of this openness was in the realm of disorderly sex governed by *supiah* (desire) (Florida 1996, Anderson 1990). But much of it was in the form of fertility rites and ritualized or symbolic sexual union. So not only was sexuality probably more a part of public life in the past, it actually contributed to social order.[40]

One thing that is clear, however, is that the deeper, more refined forms of *rasa* are culturally learned, whether we are talking about the "Javanese" emotions of restraint or the rarified realm of pure, egoless feeling (*råså sejati*). The *kasar* (coarse) emotions, on the other hand, are visceral, and hence considered precultural (it is easy, then, to see why they might be thought of as un-Javanese). In trying to understand how a *rasa* can be learned, it is important to realize that, whereas in the West emotions are generally thought of as noncognitive and instinctive,[41] in Javanese mysticism, *rasa* is at once feeling and the ultimate cognitive faculty, which is developed through culturally learned practices (Stange 1984), even if these practices are often in themselves noncognitive.[42]

The main point in all of this is that in current Javanese thought there is a prevalent notion that *certain* emotions, such as anger, sexual attraction, and greed commonly cause social and psychological disarray; while others, such as pity or reticence, help to maintain social and psychological balance.

The conceptual split between *rasa* as unrestrained emotion, on the one hand, and deep understanding and restraint on the other, suggests two different cognitive maps of who has *rasa* and who does not. Figure 4.1 shows what the map might look like when *rasa* is conceived of as overt emotion (the classes of people with the most *rasa* are in the innermost circle). The Kraton-centric map in figure 4.2, in which *rasa* is understood as knowledge of inner meaning, is essentially identical to representations of traditional Javanese kingdoms and their spheres of influence (Moertono 1981 [1968]), Laksono 1986, Behrend

40. See J. Becker 1988 and 1993 for an account of how Buddhist ideas about power and sexuality have been incorporated into Javanese conceptions of kingship and have given rise to ritualized art forms.

41. This is, of course, a gross generalization and applies most clearly to a "folk" theory of emotion. In fact, Aristotle recognized the cognitive component of emotion, as have numerous twentieth-century psychologists, philosophers, linguists, and anthropologists. (For related discussions, see Calhoun and Solomon 1984; D'Andrade 1995:218–19; Ortony et al. 1988; Lakoff 1990; Lutz and White 1986; Nuckolls 1995; Lyon 1995.) The divide between East and West is thus not so unbreachable. Aristotle, for instance, believed that "the important thing if one is to lead a fulfilled and proper life is to feel the right emotion, on the right occasion, toward the right object and in the right degree" (Scruton 1980:523)—how terribly Javanese! (For more on the "Javaneseness" of Aristotle's ethics, see Magnis-Suseno 1988:216–19.) The philosophy of Suzanne Langer (1951, 1957, 1964, 1967) also uncannily resembles, in odd ways, Javanese theories.

42. See further in this section, and S. Weiss 2003.

1989, Tjahjono 1989). It is also overlaid with degrees of *alus*ness, the most *alus* being in the center, the most *kasar* at the outer edge. (Neither conceptualization equates "most *kasar*" with "most *rasa*ful," as Weiss [1993] seems to.) Both maps are idealizations, based mostly on what a number of people were telling me (and each other) at the time of my fieldwork (c. 1990). They would certainly look different depending on whom one asked but also on the time-frame in question: some would consider them out of date, others too uncharitable towards STSI and foreigners, for instance.[43]

To underscore the analogy made earlier between the Kraton and the inner self—that is, between *dalem* [J] (inside, house, inside the palace) and *batin* [Ng,I] (inner self); and, by extension, between *njåbå* [Ng] (outside, peripheral, outside the palace) and *lair* [J] (outer self)—compare figure 4.2 with figures 4.3 and 4.4 (see also figure 2.1). Figure 4.3 is Tjahjono's redrawing of a diagram that was originally sketched for Geertz by a Javanese storekeeper (1976 [1960]:314). Figure 4.4 is Tjahjono's representation of the *kraton*-centric city of Yogyakarta (which is nearly identical in this respect to Surakarta, on which it was modeled). The similarities are noteworthy. All three maps have an *alus-kasar* orientation, the inner self (or *kraton*) being *alus*, the outer self (or rural population) being *kasar*. In all three, esoteric knowledge and spiritual power are placed at the center.

A word should be said about why I have placed foreigners at the outer edge of figures 4.1 and 4.2. Not surprisingly, *rasa* is spoken of, over and over, as being uniquely Javanese. (One indication of this is the way Javanese people frequently use *råså* [Ng] in place of *rasa* [I] when speaking Indonesian.) There are, of course, parallels in just about any music. That is, performing meaningfully, whether with feeling or deep understanding, is considered to be the province of cultural insiders (however insidership may be defined). Europeans sometimes regard American performances of classical music to be unidiomatic; Americans often consider Asian classical musicians to be mere technicians; many Afro-Americans say that Anglo-Americans lack soul; and the list could go on. Unlike most European and American claims to affective superiority, however, Javanese claims extend beyond the musical to general behavior. It is not just the ability to *express* emotion through performance that is uniquely Javanese, but the very capacity to be in tune with one's intuition and to perceive or experience certain *alus* emotional states.

This typically Javanese form of affective chauvinism was clearly formulated by the anthropologist Amrih Widodo in a conversation I once had with him. The following excerpt is reconstructed from notes:

43. These were some of the sentiments expressed to me at STSI in 2003, as previously mentioned.

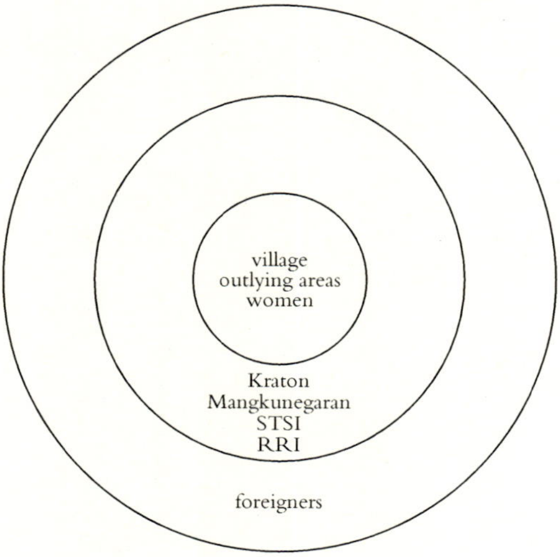

FIGURE 4.1. Degrees of *rasa* as "emotion."

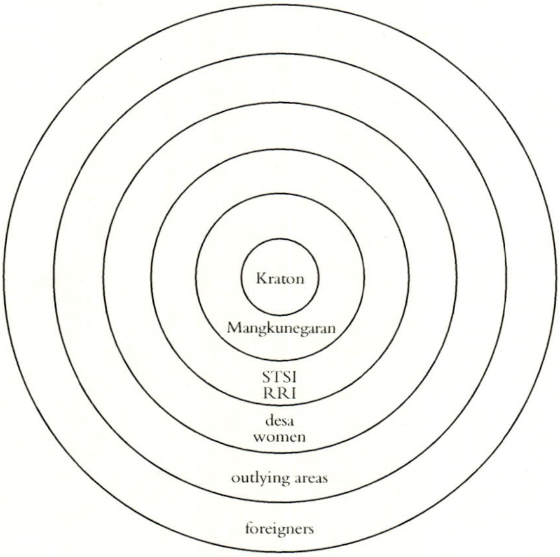

FIGURE 4.2. Degrees of *rasa* as "esoteric knowledge."

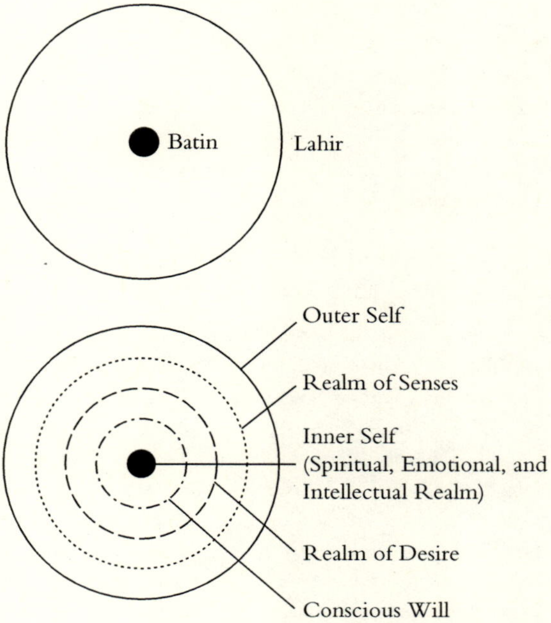

FIGURE 4.3. *Lahir* and *batin* (outer and inner self) (Tjahjono 1989:230).

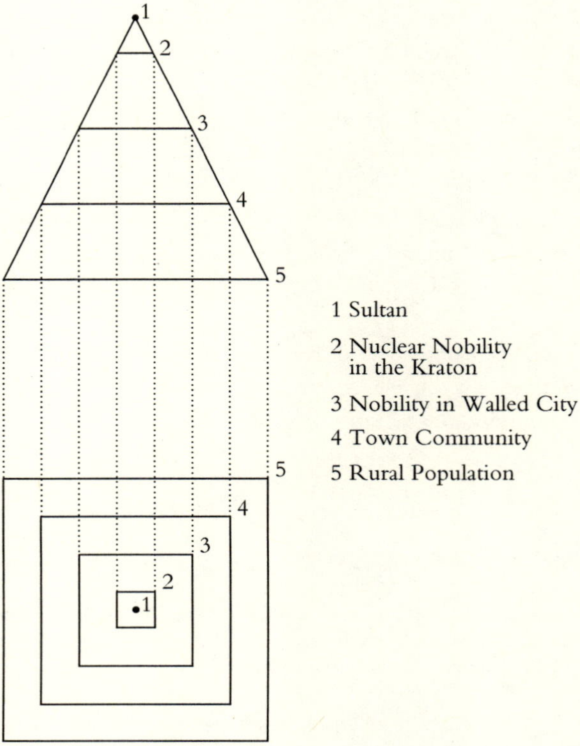

FIGURE 4.4. Conceptual layout of the town of Yogyakarta (Tjahjono 1989:203).

> *Rasa* is a kind of *tèmbok* [masonry wall] the Javanese construct around themselves. It's like when Sri Joko[44] said that Americans can study *karawitan* and become proficient at it, but they'll never understand *rasa*. *Rasa* is the last bastion the Javanese have: they might be *kalah* [outdone] economically and technologically, but they still have their culture (and *rasa*) that's unique. (Widodo, October 18, 1993)

Another instance of the same, from Waridi, in a research report summarizing an interview with Martopangrawit[45]:

> *Karawitan* hasn't evolved and flourished in Indonesia alone, but has become widespread abroad as well. . . . Foreigners, it would appear, are more enthusiastic and more serious about *karawitan* than Indonesians themselves, which leads one to worry that the place or center of gamelan teaching might shift [away from Java].
>
> When asked about this, Pak Marto [Martopangrawit] replied that there was no cause for alarm, since what's important in studying karawitan is *jiwa*[46] and *rasa*. Indonesians' *rasa* is different from that of foreigners. Both groups of people may study *karawitan*, but the process and the *rasa* are different. According to him, *rasa karawitan* is still the province of people from here [Indonesia]; foreigners only study the outward ("corporeal") aspects [of *karawitan*]. (Waridi 1986:17–18)

This last comment is particularly telling in its exclusion of foreigners. Martopangrawit was a court musician who followed Javanese mystical practice. He came from a line of *empu*s (experts) who were said to excel thanks to their *ngèlmu*, or esoteric knowledge of the tradition, achieved through spiritual discipline.[47] Much of the formerly secret knowledge of court musicians—that having to do purely with *garap*—has now been let "out" and passed on (Supanggah 1985:210–212, 232; Perlman 1994:340–350; Brinner 1995:17, 106, 160–64). The kind of spiritual knowledge alluded to here, however, has, as far as I know, been kept from foreigners and most Javanese alike.[48] I was told that before Martopangrawit died he wanted to pass on his *ngèlmu*. The only person he felt was capable of receiving it was Supanggah, who unfortunately did not make it back from Paris in time.

In an unrelated episode, a friend from the United States, who had achieved a certain competence on the *gendèr*, was told by his host mother that Americans will never perform with *rasa*, whereas for the Javanese it comes naturally. Perhaps

44. Sri Joko Raharjo is a musician and *dhalang* from Kartåsurå (near Solo) who has taught extensively in the United States.

45. The late Martopangrawit was considered by many to be the foremost expert on *karawitan* of his generation.

46. Literally, "soul." Here, it is almost synonymous with *rasa*. The verb *menjiwai* [I] (*njiwani* [J]) means to express the *rasa* of a *gendhing*—to become its soul, as it were (see chapter 2).

47. For a thorough treatment of *ngèlmu*, see J. Weiss 1977, chapter 7 and pp. 607–16. See also S. Weiss 2003.

48. For more on esoteric musical knowledge see Sastrapustaka 1984 [1953], Walton 1996:83–84, and J. Becker 1993.

she had a point: Javanese people learning gamelan for the first time *do* seem to have an intuitive sense of where the time-marking instruments enter, whereas foreigners have to intellectualize this fundamental organizing principle. But this woman was a rank beginner in an all-women's group;[49] it was highly unlikely that she had come anywhere close to being able to play with *rasa* in the sense Martopangrawit meant it (less close, one would think, than the better American gamelan musicians, who, like many British and Japanese players and singers, can function passably in a relatively advanced group, even on the hardest parts). I once asked Sudarsono (of Kentingan) if there were any such gamelan musicians who had *rasa*. He named three. To state the case in either/or terms, then, is somewhat misleading—there are too many borderline examples.

On the other hand, one cannot simply chalk up claims about the inherent Javaneseness of *rasa* simply to xenophobia. No matter what culture one grows up in, perceptual habits linked to musical affect and meaning are learned starting in infancy, and affective knowledge of music accrues through layers and layers of culturally shaped memories.[50] The question is whether, as an adult, one can accumulate enough of these memories and enough intuitive competency (wide repertoire and vocabulary of patterns, sense of syntax, sensitivity to musical and social context, adaptability and inventiveness, ability to hear and react to others), while at the same time getting rid of one's "foreign accent" (faulty intonation and pronunciation, lack of "patience" and subtle use of rubato, inappropriate timbre, unidiomatic ornamentation), to be considered, at least partially, an insider.[51] Anything less, it seems, would disqualify a foreigner as a *rasa*ful musician.

In discussing antonyms for *rasa* at the beginning of the chapter, I mentioned that terms dealing with surfaces and exteriority form a cluster. The flip side of that is a series of terms having to do with interiority, all of which are synonymous with or intimately linked to *rasa*.

We have seen how the subtle, "deep" emotions are associated with inner mental states, as well as with Kraton insidership (at one time, at least). The Indonesian word *dalam* brings together nicely these three elements, though they are lexically distinguished in Javanese by the three words *njero* [Ng] (deep, inside), *batin* [Ng] (the inner self, the seat of emotions), and *dalem* [J,KI] (the inner rooms of a house or palace, an aristocratic residence). *Rasa dalam* [I], used by several of my teachers, is very close to the English "deep feeling." *Jiwa* [I] (soul) and *isi* [I,J] (contents), both close synonyms for *rasa gendhing* (discussed in chapter 2), also play on the idea of interiority. Indeed, *isi* not only can signify

49. See chapter 1 for a description of women's groups.

50. See A. L. Becker 1995 for examples of how memory, which he calls "prior text," shapes language and patterns of thought.

51. See Brinner 1995 for a full treatment of competence as it relates to Javanese gamelan music. For an interesting problematizing of the dichotomy between insider and outsider, see Herndon 1993.

"contents," "meaning," and "spirit," but can also refer, in the expression *isi hati* [I], to one's private, innermost feelings, as in the following conversational snippet:

> Warsadiningrat, when composing *Elå-Elå Kalibeber*, poured his heart out [*mengeluarkan isi hatinya*]. All his feelings he exteriorized; at first they were deep inside . . . (Wignyosaputro, June 19, 1992)

The notion brought up here by Wignyosaputro of the inside being exteriorized, of an emotion welling up deep from within to be expressed in music, also shows up in the proverb "Lair utusané batin" [Ng] [Outer behavior is the emissary of the inner self], used by my older teachers to describe both singing and *rebab* playing. It may also refer to the compositional process, when this results not from a commission but from an inner need to pour one's feelings into music: "Some *gendhings* are composed as an *utusan batin* ("messenger from within"—out of an inner need), but some are composed on commission" (Wignyosaputro, June 24, 1992). On the receiving end of *rasa* is the expression *mengena* [I], literally "to hit the mark," which refers elliptically to touching the heart.

Finally, the Indonesian verb *mendalami* (to investigate or know deeply) may be used synonymously with *merasakan* (to feel, to understand): "I could do the
I:2 *sindhèn* part [of *Elå-Elå Kalibeber*] without the gamelan—I know it that intimately (*saya mendalami, merasakan betul*)" (Wignyosaputro, June 19, 1992).

Whether we are talking about *rasa* as unruly emotion or as deep, spiritual understanding, then, its "ex-pression" involves just that—an outward movement—and its location is deep inside, whether within the very core of a highly refined sensibility (*råså sejati*) or simply beneath the levels of sensation and rational thought.

AN AESTHETIC OF MODERATION AND SUITABILITY

6. Is it better to sing (or play) fast or slow?

> Pak Gun[52] used to say that Pak Marto's tempos sounded hurried. But Pak Gun himself was too relaxed [*kesaréhan*], too "patient" [*sabar*]. (Suhartå, November 30, 1990)

IV:5 In an *ådå-ådå*,[53] if there's too much time between words, it's never going to have a heated [*sereng*] feel. [. . .] There used to be a *dhalang*[54] at RRI, whose name was also

52. The late Gunawan Sri Hastjarjo, who had been a Kraton singer, and who had taught at ASKI.

53. *Ådå-ådå* is one of three subgenres of *suluks* (songs sung by a puppeteer in the shadow theater to set the mood).

54. This usually means a puppeteer, but in this case it meant the narrator in the "human" version of the shadow-puppet theater (*wayang wong*).

Hartå. His *ådå-ådås* were very "easeful" [*sekécå*], *laras* [i.e., he took his time]). He was incapable of indicating [through his singing] that there was about to be a battle, or that [one of the characters] was trembling with rage.[55] As a result, the *wayang wong* performance was completely bland (*tidak ada rasanya*). [. . .] My father used to say, "*Ådå-ådås* like that are just tedious." (Suhartå, December 14, 1990)

When there's a competition at RRI, and the tempo [in a *båwå*] is really slow, everyone laughs out loud. [. . .] The tempo doesn't sound like a *båwå* [*tidak mbawani*]. In *santiswaran/larasmadyå*[56] you get some singers like that, too. The better they think they are, the slower they sing. (Suhartå, April 1, 1991)

The group Ngripto Raras made quite an impression at the competitions. The young people went crazy over their fast tempos, but the older generation complained. The group never won—they were criticized for ruining Solonese *karawitan*. They often mixed in Yogyanese style—sometimes their tempos were too slow; but sometimes they were too "forced" [*fors*]. The slowest tempos of all were from the group Ngèsthi Raras. [*Sings part of* "*Gambir Sawit*":] It was really rough on the *gérong*.[57] (Suhartå, June 6, 1991)

[After listening to a commercially produced recording:] It's not good. The tempo's too relaxed [*kelarasen*]. [. . .] She takes her own sweet time. When she takes a breath she waits too long. (Suhartå, April 15, 1991)

MLB: Does the word *seseg* [cramped, tight, short of breath] have an evaluative function?
SUHARTÅ (HARTÅ): It means "fast." For instance, in a *ketawang*, if it's too *seseg* it just won't work [*tidak mau*].
MLB: So it can be a criticism?
H: Yes, it can. Often young people perform too *seseg*ly. [People say,] "Your *Puspåwarnå* doesn't feel majestic [*regu, mrabu*]. It sounds like dance drumming." [. . .] But for *Mugirahayu*, if it's too slow—not *seseg* enough—it won't work [*tidak mau*], either. *Mugirahayu* is very coquettish [*prenès*], very joyful [*énak*]. (Suhartå, May 9, 1992)

If the *båwå* singer starts right in [after the *pathetan* (unmetered, heterophonic modal prelude)], it doesn't feel right. If he waits too long, it doesn't feel right either—it's insipid [*kembå*]. (Suhartå, May 9, 1992)

Bu [Z] sings way too late [*nglèwèrs*[58]]. Whatever she sings is like that. [*Demonstrates.*] It's really insipid [*rasané kembå*]. (Suhartå, May 14, 1992)

55. These are two common functions of the *ådå-ådå*.

56. A genre of unison choral singing that is accompanied by frame drums, a pair of *kemanaks* (tubular bells), and a *ciblon* drum. Each choral piece is preceded by a *båwå*.

57. That is, they ran out of breath.

58. When used to refer to *sindhénan, nglèwèr* means to get to the final note of each phrase later than good taste requires (it is usual for the *sindhèn* to arrive somewhat later than the other parts).

Bu Gito only likes singers with large breath capacities [*napas landhung*]—because hers is large. But then they arrive at the last note of the phrase way too late [*nglèwèr*]. Bu Gito used to say of Bu Béi: "her singing doesn't sound like anything—her phrases are so short" [*sindhèn ora ånå rasané—cekak-cekak banget*]. (June 11, 1992)

7. Does melodic (or rhythmic) ornateness increase or decrease the *rasa*?

When a tone sounds for a long time, usually it is made to fluctuate, to develop, to twist and turn, to rise and fall in fixed ways until the whole of it produces a sensation of beauty. This development of a tone is called *luk* or *eluk*. *Luk* is part of *céngkok* [adaptable melodic contour]—a part that adds to the beauty of *céngkok* and thus adds to the beauty of melody. *Luk* is not just an incidental ornament of *céngkok* or melody but an organic part of melody and an essential characteristic of Indonesian *karawitan*. Melody with *céngkok* and *luk* is beautiful and whole. Melody without *luk*, without *céngkok*, is like chewed sugarcane [*sepah*]—the sweetness is gone. (Sindoesawarno, in Becker and Feinstein 1987:383)

[Commenting on Sindoesawarno:] *Sepå* [flavorless] means *terlalu lugu* [too plain]. (Suhartå, June 11, 1992)

Anteng means "totally calm"; "expressionless" [*tidak ada apa-apanya*]. It's like the way Pak [X]'s *rebab* [spike fiddle] playing used to be—too *halus* [smooth, refined, unadorned]. (Suhartå, May 2, 1992)

The beauty is in the *gregel*s [small ornaments]. [. . .] With no *gregel*s it's too bland [*ampang*]. [. . .] *Gregel* is what gives it expression [*èksprèsiné*]. (Wignyosaputro, June 24, 1992)

Bu [X]'s singing is too plain [*barès*]—it needs spicing up [*kurang bumbuné*]. (Suhartå, May 14, 1992)

After I sang *Sudiråwicitrå*, Pak Wartå[59] said, "it's still raw, it needs to be cooked, to be given a little M.S.G." [*masih mentah, masih perlu diolah,*[60] *dikasih Moto*]. After that, Pak Wakidjo[61] told me, "but you shouldn't use too many *céngkok*s [ornaments] for a *båwå* or it will sound like a *sindhèn*." (Fieldnote, December 21, 1990)

Pak [X] is a really straightforward [*lugu*] person; his *céngkok*s [melodic patterns] are also plain and straightforward. A lot of older folks like his voice: "it's nice, it's really plain [*lugu*]." But for the younger generation, whose singing is filled with melodic

59. The late Suwarto, the principal *båwå* singer at the Mangkunegaran Palace.

60. *Diolah* means "to be cooked" in Javanese, but in Indonesian (which is the language Suwarto was using) it means "to be worked on." He was clearly using the word in its Javanese meaning. See Benamou 2006 for more on food metaphors.

61. Wakidjo was until 1996 the drummer (and hence one of the lead musicians) at RRI, the national radio station in Solo. Since then he has taught part-time at STSI/ISI.

"variation" [ornamentation], it doesn't sound good [*tidak énak*]—unless he's singing an *ådå-ådå*;[62] then it's not bad. (Suhartå, September 11, 1991) IV:5

If *ladrang Sigrå Mangsah* has a plain, understated vocal part [*digarap lugu*], it won't have a happy feel to it. (Wignyosaputro, June 19, 1992)

[A musician might say to himself,] "Oh, this is *Laler Mengeng* I have to make my *gendèr*-playing simple and straightforward [*lugu*]." (Sudarsono, December 18, 1991) III:1

[The RRI *dhalang* (narrator) referred to under number six, above] ruined the *rasa* of his *ådå-ådå*s because he was putting in too many melodic embellishments [*terlalu banyak céngkok*]. (Suhartå, December 14, 1990)

Even if the voice is good, and the singer is *pinter* [clever], if he or she uses too much melodic embellishment [*variasi céngkok*], the *rasa* will be... it's like if you overdress... it's "over" [*over*—overacting]. (Sudarsono, December 18, 1991)

If the *wiledan* [choice of melodic detail] is nice, but the *embat* [intonation] and tone are not, it's not going to do anything for you as a listener [*tidak ada rasanya*]. On the other hand, the *empu*s [master musicians] tended to play with very simple *wiledan*s, and yet it was very *énak* [pleasant] to listen to. The same goes for *pesindhèn*s—they used to sing much more simply, but they had a deeper *rasa* than singers nowadays. *Pesindhèn*s nowadays go all over the place [with their voices] and sing fancy patterns. (Sukanto, April 2, 1990)

The ideal is to be able to play simply yet movingly—if you can do that you're already a mature musician [*sudah mateng*]. (Sudarsono, June 6, 1991)

8. Is seriousness or playfulness more conducive to playing with *rasa*?

Laler Mengeng is sad, [...] but if the musicians are all drunk, it's not going to sound sad. (Wignyosaputro, June 19, 1992) III:1

Even though the meaning of [*Alas Padhang*] is a prayer, if the players are drunk, it's not going to sound like anything [*tidak ada apa-apanya*]. (Wignyosaputro, June 24, 1992)

MLB: Does *bérag* [exuberant] usually have positive or negative connotations?

SUDARSONO: Actually, in terms of *rasa*, it's negative. The simplest patterns can have an effect [*bisa dirasakan*]. If it's too *bérag*, if it's too "overacting" [*overakting*], the *rasa* becomes *cekrèk*[63]—small, short, cheap... not *gagah* [manly, handsome], not good, not majestic... *jelèk* [ugly, not good]. (Sudarsono, December 18, 1991)

62. *Ådå-ådå*s are the most rapidly declaimed of the puppeteer's mood songs in the shadow theater, and are used for tense situations. They are accompanied by a rapid, almost drone-like *gendèr* part, which emphasizes important tones in the vocal melody, and which adds to the *sereng* feeling.

63. I have not found in any dictionary a definition that is even remotely related to Sudarsono's, nor have I heard anyone else use the word. The dictionaries all give something akin to "the clicking sound of a rifle being cocked or a door lock being turned." The words *cékré* (dwarfish) and *cèkrèh* (handsome) are closer in meaning (but on the recording of our conversation, Sudarsono's pronunciation is unequivocal).

> In a calm piece it doesn't feel right for the *pesindhèn* to put in all of the optional fillers. It's pleasant, but it's a forced pleasantness [*énaknya memaksa*]. It's not a joyful piece—why make it joyful [*tidak énak, kok diénak-énakké*]? (Sastro Tugiyo, May 6, 1992)

> MLB: So, musicians have to be like actors?
>
> SUHARTÅ (HARTÅ): Yes, they should be. The good ones, anyway. [*Laughs.*] The good ones are. Let's say I've just had sadness in my life, and I encounter some sad *gendhings*—well, I'm really going to appreciate that [*senang sekali*].
>
> MLB: And, for exuberant [*bérag*] *gendhings*, you also have to feel inside the . . .
>
> H: Yes! If not, you won't be in keeping with the character of the *gendhing*. You'll be lacking, in that respect. It won't be *bérag* enough. (Suhartå, May 2, 1992)

> Since Pak Turahyo died, the music at the Mangkunegaran has been too serious, *kurang greged* [without any oomph]. Every group needs someone who livens things up [*menggairahkan*], and at the Mangkunegaran that man was Pak Turahyo. (Sukanto, April 18, 1991)

Glancing through the above quotations, one cannot help but notice the prevalence of the word *too*. The problem, then, is not, say, with playfulness per se, but rather with *too much* playfulness. In every musical culture, excesses of many kinds are to be avoided. The tendency to avoid extremes, however, is particularly pronounced in Java, especially in the courtly tradition. What in central Java is considered to be boisterous music would most likely pass for subdued in neighboring Bali; what in Bali is pleasantly *ramé* [J] (*ramai* [I]; lively, bustling) in central Java is heard as *kasar* [J,I] (coarse, crude). It is a commonplace that Javanese people—especially in the *priyayi* [Ng, JI] (aristocratic) milieu—are reticent about expressing emotion overtly.[64] In fact, according to the precepts of *kebatinan* [Ng, JI] (Javanese mystical practice), one should avoid even *having* strong emotions, as this upsets one's equilibrium and prevents one from achieving inner peace.

Taking into account the difficulty in measuring such things cross-culturally, it is fair to say that, on a global scale, central Javanese musicians exercise a great deal of emotional restraint—theirs is a relatively introverted music. This can be seen, for instance, in the degree to which they avoid excess motion in

64. See, for instance, Heider 1991:20, 91; H. Geertz 1974; Mulder 1980:64–66, 1989:58–62; C. Geertz 1976 [1960]:73, 239ff.; Magnis-Suseno 1988:122ff.; J. Weiss 1977, chapter 5 and p. 527; Wolff and Soepomo 1982:64; Keeler 1975:100, 1984:123, 125, 291–92, and 1987:56, 72, 217–20. Such comments are not limited to foreign scholars by any means: non-Javanese Indonesians frequently complain about the inscrutability of the Javanese. One occasionally hears statements contradicting this stereotype. Suhartå once told me that Javanese people are quick to show their emotions ("ciri khas orang Jawa: emosinya terlalu tinggi; isi hatinya cepat sekali tercurang") (June 19, 1991). Significantly, though, this was meant as a criticism, and it might be interpreted either as polite self-deprecation or as a reflection on the sorry state of Javanese culture. For a similar complaint, see Tukiman Taruna 1987:24–25.

performance.[65] As Susan Walton has remarked, when one observes a gamelan performance with several *pesindhèns*, it is often difficult even to tell which of them is singing, so little do they move. Similarly, when a good *rebab* player performs, it is difficult to tell which finger of the left hand is being used to shorten the string length at any given time. Mloyowidodo emphasized how important it was to be controlled in one's movements:

> Deportment is part of etiquette. That includes how you hold the *tabuh* [mallet]. [. . .] When I teach at STSI, I include gamelan etiquette. [I tell them,] "If the *rebab* plays a *senggréngan*, or the *bonang* a *grambyang*,[66] you put down your cigarette, or put it out, or throw it out! [. . .] Then you listen: if it's *sléndro*, you face the *sléndro* instruments, if it's *pélog*, the *pélog* ones. After the *suwuk* [final phrase of the *gendhing*] you're not allowed to move. You're not allowed to drink[67] until the *pathet* [unmetered modal postlude] is over. When the *rebab* player puts the *rebab* down, then you can smoke again." [. . .] I tell the kids these things. (Mloyowidodo, May 2, 1992)

Kunst (1973:228) quotes a passage (which I have retranslated below) from the nineteenth-century *Serat Centhini*, which mockingly describes the excessive movement of a village *rebab* player:

> His *rebab* playing was proud as a peacock:
> His elbow marked time with the notes;
> As these got higher, his neck strained forward,
> As they got lower, it straightened back up;
> His body swayed along, back and forth.

Kunst points out the implicit contrast to a later passage from the same work, which extols the delicate finger movements and the refined, humble attitude of an accomplished court-based *rebab* player (1973:224–27).

Within central Java, then, there are degrees of restrained behavior, depending on one's proximity to the courts. But even the more exuberant among village musicians move less than, say, most European, African, or even Balinese musicians. Furthermore, as pointed out in chapter 1, court and village are more ideal types

65. What I mean by "excess" motion is anything that goes beyond what is physically necessary to produce the sound. I am positing not a logically necessary correspondence between the amount of movement and the amount of emotional outpouring, but rather a general correspondence between them. Vladimir Horowitz—one of the most aurally expressive pianists of the twentieth century—appeared as an impassive, marmoreal figure while performing. The same could be said of the violinist Jascha Heifetz. The fact that, within the realm of classical music, these artists may be considered emotional reinforces the view that classical music is relatively restrained (as compared, say, to the blues). See also Keeler 1975:100 and Pemberton 1987:17–20.

66. A *senggréngan* is a very short melodic formula that the *rebab* plays to indicate that a piece is about to begin. A *grambyang* (or *grambyangan*) is essentially the same thing, but played on the *bonang* or *gendèr*. For additional information on the entire sequence of modal formulas and sections of pieces, see the table on pp. 151–52.

67. It is normal for tea to be served at nearly all rehearsals and performances in Java.

than distinct, autonomous realities. One *dhalang* family I know, whose compound is in a large village near Solo, has ancestral ties both to the Kraton and to the villages further out. The father and mother's parting words to a friend from the United States, who had spent much time studying and performing *gendèr* in their midst, were "don't move so much when you play" (a rather un-*alus* way of expressing an *alus* notion, to be sure).[68] By and large, though, American gamelan musicians do seem to intuitively incorporate bodily restraint to some degree into their playing. During a concert at the University of Michigan, when an improvisation group not trained in Javanese music stepped in to perform an American piece on the Javanese gamelan, it was obvious to all in attendance how much more those students moved than the ones who had been playing Javanese music on the same instruments.

Related to the idea of too much bodily motion is that of overexpression, especially of a showy, theatrical sort. Sudarsono's favorite words for "hamming it up" are *show* [E] (used adjectivally to refer, for example, to an old man who has a wife and many kids but still primps like a dandy) and *over* [E] (short for "overacting"). Significantly, these are borrowed terms.[69] Conceited display runs counter to the central Javanese ideal of *alus* behavior.

Excess, then, is avoided to an unusual degree in central Javanese music. Yet if we examine the citations above, we realize that there is rarely too much of anything in an absolute way: everything is relative to a particular musical context or performance situation. This relativity is also characteristically Javanese.[70] Geertz, in another context, has made much of the notion of being *cocog* [J] (old spelling, *tjotjog*; *cocok* [I]), or suitable, and his gloss is worth quoting:

> *Tjotjog* means to fit, as a key does in a lock, as an efficacious medicine does to a disease, as a solution does to an arithmetic problem, as a man does with the woman he marries (if he does not, they will divorce). If your opinion agrees with mine we *tjotjog*; if the meaning of my name fits my character and if it brings me luck), it is said to be *tjotjog*. Tasty food, correct theories, good manners, comfortable surroundings, gratifying outcomes are all *tjotjog*. (1973:129)[71]

68. For some reason probably having to do with gender relations and perceived status, foreign female researchers in Indonesia seem to be told directly how to behave by the women in their host families, whereas foreign men tend to have to figure it out for themselves through indirect inference.

69. Only once have I heard Sudarsono use the Javanese synonym *cekrèk*. See footnote 63 and the quotation at the bottom of p. 121.

70. Nancy Cooper first got me thinking about this while we were both in Java doing fieldwork.

71. This passage first occurs in almost identical form in C. Geertz 1976 [1960]:31, in which it serves to introduce the topic of Javanese numerology. In C. Geertz 1973, the concept is used to explain the congruence "between ethos and world view, between the approved style of life and the assumed structure of reality" (p. 129). Note that Geertz translates the word primarily as a verb, but also as an adjective. This is a perfect example of Quine's indeterminacy of

The important thing, here, is the relational nature of each of the above cases: food that is *cocog* is not tasty in an absolute sense, but specifically for the speaker. Perhaps because of my French tendency to seek Cartesian order in matters of taste,[72] I was often reminded of the greater degree of relativity in Javanese judgments:

MLB: Where is the best barbershop in town?

JAVANESE FRIEND: Many foreigners find X *cocog*.

[...]

MLB: Y doesn't seem to be a very good doctor.

JAVANESE FRIEND: Well, he's *cocog* for *our* family: he doesn't charge us, and he never prescribes expensive medicine.

[...]

MLB: Where is the best tailor in the neighborhood?

JAVANESE FRIEND: I like the one over by Z, but he might not be *cocog* for Mas Marc.

These examples bring to mind a proverb quoted in chapter 3: "Idumu dudu iduku; lémbéhanmu dudu lémbéhanku" (Your saliva is not my saliva; your gait is not my gait).

There are countless other examples of relativity in Javanese practice, both musical and extramusical. If I dwell on them at length here, it is because the assessment of *rasa* in performance so depends on this notion of suitability. The very word for *I* in Javanese (*aku, kulå, kawulå, dalem, ingsun, Ibu*, etc.) varies according to who one is and whom one is addressing. Indeed, every speech act in Javanese carries with it an implicit assessment about where the speaker places him- or herself with respect to the listener and, if applicable, to the person

---

translation (1960), where two translations can function equally well, and there is no way of testing which one is "correct." In fact, Javanese and Indonesian are much less rigid when it comes to parts of speech than are European languages, and the same word frequently functions as both a verb and an adjective. Because Indonesian and Javanese do not use a copulative verb (*to be*) with adjectives, there is sometimes insurmountable ambiguity (indeed, some linguists argue that there are no adjectives in Indonesian at all, but rather stative verbs). Thus, if one translates *cocog* as "to fit," it acts as a verb, but in the very same sentence, it works equally well to translate it as "to be suitable, appropriate," in which case it is an adjective. In my mind it has always been primarily an adjective, and I confirmed this recently with several Javanese speakers. The question admittedly may have been too abstract to get a sure answer, and, unfortunately, it would be virtually impossible to construct an empirical test. For what it's worth, the *Kamus Besar Bahasa Indonesia* (the standard monolingual Indonesian dictionary) labels *cocok* as an adjective. None of my monolingual Javanese dictionaries label words according to parts of speech, identifying instead the various language registers.

72. French culture is perhaps at the absolutist end of a continuum on which North Americans are more towards the middle, and Java is quite near the relativistic end. (Of course, these assessments will vary with the subculture, the cultural domain, and individual temperament.) Even my North American friends find my (mostly French bourgeois) attitude toward food doctrinaire. The French expression for "you don't know what you're missing" is *tu as tort* (you're wrong [not to try this]). Quality, in France, is experienced almost as a palpable trait, and its assessment is an empirical exercise. When there are disagreements over taste, they are rarely resolved by a relativizing move by the parties involved.

being discussed (see the section on the Javanese language in Technical Notes). This keen awareness of relative status affects all aspects of behavior. An *alus* person would never brag to someone of equal or higher rank—it isn't even proper to speak proudly of one's own students or one's own family members! But that same person, when talking to someone of inferior rank, might freely deliver an entire litany of his or her own accomplishments.[73] Prices in the traditional market system are just as relative. A good price is one that is *cocog* to both parties concerned. Someone who has his (or, less often, her) dignity to guard (and who is likely to be of a relatively high economic status) will accept a price that is higher than someone who has no qualms about entering into the fray of open negotiation. Conversely, a seller at the market will size up a prospective buyer and adjust his or her opening and final prices accordingly.[74] In these examples, it is the *relation* between two speakers that determines appropriate behavior. But assessing relative status itself depends on one's being able to place oneself (and others) in relation to society as a whole.

Indeed, Magnis-Suseno has argued that, from the Javanese perspective, knowing one's place is the key to inner and social harmony, and social harmony is the ultimate goal of Javanese ethics (1988:93–95, 125–28, 145–64):

> Javanese people do not assign moral value according to abstract norms, but rather according to whether one acts in a manner suitable to one's placement [within society and the cosmos]. Whether an act is right or wrong is not judged by reference to principles, but rather by how it fits into the whole. The mark of an appropriate act is that it result in societal well-being and the inner sense that everything is *cocok*. (159)

Magnis-Suseno goes on to show how this ethics of appropriateness is exemplified by *wayang* stories (pp. 160–67)—an idea he borrowed from Benedict Anderson (1965). In the *Mahabharata* as it is told through *wayang*, there are no absolutes of good and evil, as there are, say, in most Hollywood Westerns.[75] Many of the knights on the "bad" side (the side of the Kuråwås) are admired for acting in accordance with their duty, while at times the knights on the "good" side (the side of the Pendhåwås) are castigated for not acting in a knightly way, no matter how just their cause.[76]

73. I am indebted to Alan Feinstein for helping me understand this apparent anomaly in polite Javanese behavior.

74. For more on Javanese bargaining practices, see Keeler 1975:99, 1984:108, 297–310, and 1987:54–55; and Brenner 1995.

75. The comparison is particularly apt. In both cases the audience (or at least part of the audience) watches shadows projected on a screen; both art forms are extremely popular and cut across class lines; both reflect and shape deep cultural values, which are presented through a standard narrative structure; both have standardized character types, of which one is the hero with whom the audience identifies; and in both the dramatic atmosphere is greatly enhanced by music.

76. According to Anderson (1965:6), the relativistic morality found in *wayang* is typically Javanese but is being overtaken by a Western conception of the forces of good and evil.

But an act does not have to be one of grave moral import in order for Magnis-Suseno's assertion to be applicable. Many practices that are suitable to one social class are not so to another. Whereas, until recently, men of middle or upper social class used to avoid being seen in public wearing shorts, there was no such proscription for working-class men. Indeed, the most statusless adults of all, the mentally ill, frequently go about naked without causing the slightest disturbance. The appropriateness of house shapes (Tjahjono 1989), batik patterns (Boow 1988), and personal names (*Kitab* 1991:77–78) depends (or depended) entirely on one's social class. Furthermore, commoners would never dare get married during the month of Surå, because it would bring misfortune to the family; but that is precisely when the royal family often has its weddings—a demonstration of the king's superior spiritual power. Relativity is also evident in the impossibility of characterizing Javanese social interaction as either formal or informal:

> [The Javanese] do not prize either formality or informality as good in itself. Instead, they praise the ability to be *luwes* [graceful, supple, smoothly flowing, adaptable], to act appropriately in any situation. Being luwes means having a sensibility to the play of oppositions and distinctions which give form to Javanese relationships. (Keeler 1975:93)

Relativity is at the heart of Javanese numerology, which is used to choose, *inter alia*, where a building is to be built, when an important event should take place, or whom one's son or daughter should marry.[77] Affordable books (*primbons*) that explain how to determine who or what is *cocog* are sold everywhere. In them one finds lists of integer values (*neptu*) of the various calendrical units that define Javanese birthdays.[78] Calculations based on how these various integers add up are used to predict not only whether a baby will have a happy life, but also whether a prospective couple is *cocog* or not. When to build a house, when to move into one, or when to get married are (or were) all determined not first by practical criteria but by particular coincidences within the calendrical system. All of these considerations have to do with the coordination between the empirical and the spirit world (Magnis-Suseno 1988:90–92). Again, one's actions must always take into account one's relations to other beings—whether corporeal or not.

Commensurate with the importance of relativity in Javanese culture, the list of synonyms for "suitable," "proper," "fitting" in Indonesian and Javanese is formidable: *cocog* [J], *cocok* [I]; *cucuk* [J]; *dilanji* [J]; *empan-papan* [J]; *gathuk* [J], *gatuk* [I];

77. See C. Geertz 1976 [1960]:30–35; Tjahjono 1989:73, 110–12, 341–49; Subalidinata 1985; *Kitab* 1991; Magnis-Suseno 1988:90–92.

78. For an explanation of the Javanese calendrical system, see A. L. Becker 1979, Becker and Becker 1981, Walton 1987, and Robson 1992:145–46. For a detailed account of *neptu* calculation and how it is put to use, as well as other forms of Javanese divination, see J. Weiss 1977, chapter 10 and pp. 616–66.

genah [J,I]; *ilok* [J]; *jodho* [J], *jodoh* [I]; *laras* [J], *salaras* [J], *selaras* [I]; *layak* [I,J]; *mathuk* [J]; *mèmper* [J]; *menurut* [I]; *merdésa* [I]; *mungguh* [Ng], *menggah* [K], *semenggah* [I]; *pantas* [I]; *pas* [I,J]; *patuk* [J]; *patut* [Ng,I], *pantes* [K]; *runtut* [J,I]; *sekadar* [I]; *senonoh* [I]; *sepadan* [I]; *serasi* [I]; *sesuai* [I]; *sreg* [J,I]; *tepat* [I]; *trep* [J]; *tumrap* [J]; *yogyå* [J], *yogia* [I].[79] Of these, I have heard *cocog, laras, mathuk, mungguh, runtut, pas, sesuai, tepat,* and *trep* all used in a musical context. *Cocog* is by far the most common, and the broadest in scope as well.[80] Relativity in music shows up in whether a performance style is deemed *cocog* to the piece, to the genre, to the performer(s), or to the performance context. Often the word used to describe this criterion is *mungguh* (appropriate). "*Mungguh* is the interpretation (penggarapan) of a piece in keeping with its character. . . . It can also mean the rightness of a chosen piece for its function and time of performance. It can also be used for the rightness of the instrumentation" (Waridi 2005:373–74). A good performer must try as much as possible to adjust his or her *garap* (interpretation) to bring out the appropriate *rasa* in any given piece or performance context. On the other hand, each performer has a *watak*[81]—an inborn personality (J. Weiss 1977:59ff.)—that cannot be entirely circumvented. Some people are just better at expressing certain *rasa*s than others. The specifics of this fit, between performer and *rasa*, is the topic of the section on *rasa* and evaluation in chapter 5. Here I investigate the adjustments performers make in order to be *cocog* with the situation or with the other performers.

Under "performance context" I include the medium, the venue (the sponsor, performance space, instruments, audience), and the geographical region. The same piece will be performed differently according to whether it is done in a "concert" setting (*klenéngan* [J,JI]), a *wayang purwå* [Ng] (shadow-puppet play), *wayang wong* [Ng] (musical drama with characters drawn from the shadow theater), *langendriyan* [J,JI] (sung, danced drama), *kethoprak* [J,JI] (folk theater), or *sendratari* [I] (dance drama). *Wayang purwå* performances are characterized by fast tempos, and the *rasa* of the music should support (*mendukung* [I]) the dramatic atmosphere. This last point is equally true of all but the concert setting (although, even there the principle can operate in vestigial form). In *wayang wong,* which tells the same stories as *wayang purwå* but in half the time, pieces are often shortened.[82] In *langendriyan,* because the dancers/singers are often out of breath, their phrases tend to be shorter and less ornate. *Kethoprak* versions tend to be lighthearted, with lots of *senggakan* (vocal interjections). Accompaniment to *sendratari* is characterized by rapid and frequent tempo changes, starkly

79. The even greater number of synonyms in Kawi (Old Javanese) shows just how entrenched this idea is in Javanese culture. Suparlan's Indonesian-Kawi dictionary [1991] lists forty-eight Kawi words under *pantas*, and forty-two under *sesuai*; there is very little overlap between the two lists.

80. Keeler (1975:108) lists *cocog* as one of the three most common Javanese words for describing both music and social interaction. The other two are *kepénak* ("comfortable," pleasing, nice) and *råså*.

81. Related terms are *pembawaan* [I], *gawan* [Ng], *bektan* [K]; *dhasar* [J], *dasar* [I].

82. For an excellent discussion of music in *wayang wong*, see Susilo 1984.

contrasting dynamics, and very short, often incomplete versions of pieces. Only a few pieces normally are performed in *all* of these artistic contexts, but there is considerable overlap of repertoire between any two of them.

As an example, two distinct venues with clear consequences for the choice of *garap* (performance practice) are palace and "outside" performances. Both of the royal palaces in Solo have distinctive styles that differ from each other as well as from the nonpalace styles. But, as many former occasions for music-making in the palaces no longer exist, and as many of the former court musicians moved out of the courts after independence, these distinctions are not as marked as they once were. Differences in venue, which entail differences in the relations between the musicians, between them and the sponsor, and between them and the audience, affect a performance mainly in the degree of formality of the proceedings, which is often inversely proportional to the amount of freedom the musicians feel they have.[83]

Since *karawitan* is highly collective, anything one musician does will affect others. This collectivity is reflected in the expressions *pådhå ngrasakké*[84] [Ng] (to feel/interpret together) and *adu råså, adu semu* [Ng] (to match *rasa* with *rasa*, hints with hints) (Sukanto, June 4, 1990).

> Each musician will adjust his interpretation based on what the others are doing. So you can't really say that a given *rebaban*,[85] for instance, will produce *rasa x*; it depends also on what else is going on. (Supanggah, June 17, 1992)

Some of the specifics of the interaction between musicians in performance have been dealt with by Sumarsam (1984), Perlman (1994, chapters 3 and 4), Walton (1996:96–98), Suyenaga (1984), Keeler (1975), Benamou and Supanggah (2006) and, most extensively, by Brinner (1985, 1995).

Experienced musicians constantly adjust their melodic (and rhythmic) patterns to what their fellow musicians are doing, with some of the parts acting more as leaders, and others more as followers. The *rebab*, for instance, if it is present, is almost always the primary melodic leader. The drum, however, acts as the rhythmic leader. But musical leadership has the decidedly Javanese trait of adjusting to the "followers." In a sung *pathetan* (puppeteer's mood-setting song), for instance, the instruments must normally follow the voice, using their respective melodic idioms.[86] But, at the same time, the singer has to be aware of and adjust

83. For a detailed comparison of performances of the same piece in two very different kinds of venues, see Vetter 1981. For the effect of patronage on gamelan performance see Santosa 2001 and 2002.

84. This expression is quoted by C. Geertz (1976 [1960]:278) in his two pages devoted to gamelan music. Despite his limited understanding of the technical aspects of *karawitan*—or perhaps because of it!—he is the first Western scholar to focus on *rasa* as the key to understanding Javanese music.

85. A *rebaban* is a melody played by the *rebab* (spike fiddle), or a particular working out of the *rebab* part to a piece.

86. According to Martopangrawit, who was as idiosyncratic as he was influential, the *voice*—contrary to popular conception—must follow the *rebab* (Sudarsono, August 28, 1991). For the more standard interpretation, see Brinner 1985:33ff.

to what the musicians are doing (Supanggah, August 29, 1991). One prominent *dhalang* is criticized by musicians for showing off his beautiful voice and copious breath supply, with no regard for the poor *rebab* player, who finds himself *kehabisan céngkok* (running out of patterns) (Supanggah, March 27, 1991).

Another example of how Javanese leadership is ideally cooperative rather than coercive, is in the way a *kendhang* (drum) player leads. If the *kendhang* player tries to assert an abrupt change of tempo when the other musicians are not ready to follow, everything falls apart. What should happen, then, is that the *kendhang* player suggests a tempo change, and everyone carries it out together. One word that is used to describe this kind of sensitivity to the group is *angon* [J] (to herd) (AL Suwardi, Jan. 1995). Drummers, like herders and teachers, must "lead from behind." This means that if the musicians are beginners, the drummer will not choose *iråmå*s ("tempo levels"—see Appendix B), *laya*s (tempos), or tempo changes that are too difficult for the musicians.

Adjusting the music to the ability of the performer is common in other ways. If a part is too hard for a musician, he or his teacher will simply change the part.[87] *Pesindhèn*s routinely choose patterns that fit their voices, and a good singing teacher will suggest that a learner use the patterns of a singer who matches her voice. The *bedhåyå* singers at the Kraton, who, according to some, are chosen more for their devotion to the king than for their extraordinary singing abilities, adjust downward the absolute pitch of the difficult choral melodies they sing to fit their low vocal ranges.[88] They are much criticized for this by "outside" musicians, especially when the singers do it in *gendhing*s with full gamelan (it is not so critical in *gendhing kemanak*) (Benamou 1994a, 1996).[89] The now-retired lead *bedhåyå* singer, Tamènggito (a name she took over from the previous lead singer), spoke of the situation thus, in an imaginary conversation with an "outside" musician who sometimes helps out at the Kraton:

> You can tell those under your direction anything you want, but this is what I'm capable of [i.e., this is the way I sing]. If my pitch slips lower, you can tell me [about it] until you're blue in the face, I don't care. I'm the one who grew up in the service of the palace. You weren't even born yet, I was already here. (June 15, 1991)

87. In Balinese music, on other hand, musicians simply practice until they can do the impossible.

88. I am distinguishing here between *laras* (how high or low all the notes of a scale are) and *embat* (how large or small the individual intervals are). The first of these corresponds to, say, an orchestra tuning to A 435 versus 445; the second corresponds more or less to temperament in European music. Both *laras* and *embat*, however, are far more variable than their Western analogues, and each gamelan set has its own characteristic tuning. This is yet another area of Javanese musical aesthetics where relativity is paramount.

89. A *kemanak* is an idiophone consisting of a pair of tubular bells, one tuned slightly higher than the other, played by two musicians. A characteristic "wooOOP" sound is achieved by partially closing off the gap between the two curled flaps of the bell with the player's thumb. A *gendhing kemanak* is a unison choral piece accompanied by a sparse time-marking ensemble that features the *kemanak* as the fastest-moving part.

Relativity toward the performer also shows up in attitudes toward vocal timbre. Certain timbres are prized above all others. The rarest and most highly valued is the onomatopoetic *kung*, followed by *arum* (literally, "fragrant"—short for *keteko langu arum*, which is also partly onomatopoetic). Both terms are taken from the vocabulary of zebra-dove song (Benamou 1998a), and are untranslatable, since they describe very specific patterns of timbre, vibrato, rhythm, and melody (broadly speaking, *kung* is lower, more resonant, and slower than *arum*, for both birds and humans). But there is reluctance to establish an absolute standard:

> Some people like a *renyah* [light, agile, "crisp"] voice, some like one that's *gandhang* [resonant]. Most, though, like a voice that's *empuk-arum* [rounded—"fragrant"]. (Sutarman, June 24, 1992)

⊛ arum voice, II:3, 00:12–114, 5:01–7:54

> MLB: Is *luruh* ["humble," calm] a good thing for a voice to be?
> H: Yes, it's good. But not everyone likes that quality. Some like a *luruh* voice, some like a *trègèl* [vivacious, impetuous, agile] or *branyak* [brash, spirited, plucky] voice. (Suhartå, April 25, 1992)

⊛ *luruh* II:2, 4:37–12:30; *trègèl* II:2, 29:47–34:19

> Bu [x] is really fanatic [*fanatik*]: she only likes voices with a fast vibrato, and Bu Béi Mardusari's *céngkoks* [melodic patterns]. But in fact all vibratos are nice. (Suhartå, June 6, 1991)

Indeed, apart from the sought-after vocal qualities, a whole host of others are tolerated, if not always appreciated.

On the other hand, negative terms are not wanting:[90]

alod [J] ("tough," "hard," labored)

atos [J] ("hard")

cédhal [J] (slurred, indistinct)

kemut [I] ("stuck in the mouth," half-swallowed)

kaku [I] (stiff)

kasar [J,I] (coarse)

kau [J] ("ungainly," rough)

kemèng [J,JI] (unpleasantly light)

kementhos [J] (hard)

ketekem [J] (held back)

kotor [I], *reged* [J] ("dirty")

manja [I] ("spoiled," hyper-feminine, showy, trying to lure)

mbindheng [J,JI] (nasal)

90. I put quotation marks around literal translations when the primary musical sense was not literal (as for *kemut, kau, manja, dhoso, sumelèt, tekak*); in a couple of cases the quotation marks are there to show a metaphorical meaning (as for *atos, kotor*).

meriet [J] (extremely high)

methit [J] (sharp)

mrèngès [J] (with corners of the mouth pulled back)

ndhoso [J,JI] ("quick to anger," heavily accented)

ngåyå [J] (forced)

ngetril [D,J,JI] (tremolo)

nggrèmèng [J] (indistinct)

pélo [J,JI] (indistinct)

serak [J,JI] (hoarse)

sugal [J] (gruff)

sumelèt [J] ("intensely hot," sharp, piercing)

tekak [J,I] ("strangled," constrained)

tipis [J,I] (thin)

Many of these refer to vocal production (i.e., correctable traits) rather than vocal types (which are innate). In describing emotion terms, Geoffrey White has predicted that there will be more negative than positive evaluative terms in a lexicon:

> Not only are emotion words always evaluative in meaning, but emotion lexicons inevitably contain a preponderance of negative terms designating undesirable or unpleasant emotions. . . . We might speculate that, because much of human effort and action is devoted to bringing social realities in line with ideal models, negative emotions are more finely conceptualized and lexicalized. (1994:226)

Significantly, there are nearly twice as many *positive* terms to describe singing voices as there are negative ones in Indonesian and Javanese (there is an almost insignificant number of neutral ones).[91] If White's reasoning is sound, the disproportion of positive terms should predict an unusually wide range of ideal models for Javanese voices. And Javanese musicians do appear to accept a great variety of vocal timbres; so much so, in fact, that I have often been perplexed by some of the voices that are tolerated within an ensemble.

Perhaps because of my Euro-American background, I am particularly sensitive to the incongruity of operatic voices in a gamelan context. This never seems to bother Javanese musicians, though they will laugh about it if you point it out. They might say, "*ya, suara seriosa*" [I] (what can you do, it's a

91. See Dea 1980:154–56 for some of the most common positive terms. I am far more liberal in my criteria for what constitutes a term, and hence have amassed a much larger list (well over two hundred terms in all) than he did. Note that White's point about negative terms being more specific and clearly defined than positive ones appears to be true for Javanese and Indonesian vocal terms.

seriosa[92] voice), and then imitate it with a wry smile and a chuckle, but I have never known a singer to be made to feel unwelcome because of his or her vocal production. Sometimes tolerance toward singers has more to do with interpersonal relations. Many groups (such as the *bedhåyå* singers at the Kraton, according to some) are formed more on the basis of mutual obligations or personal ties than of musical prowess. In this respect, they are like many amateur or church organizations in the United States.[93]

The avoidance of absolutes in Javanese music is perhaps nowhere so apparent as in regional variation. Differences between urban and country norms have been much discussed in the literature, as has the split between Yogya and Solo.[94] In talking with my principal singing teacher, Suhartå, I was astounded at the specificity of the geographical styles among which he distinguished. He lived in a suburb that was only about two miles from Solo's central market, but which he nevertheless spoke of as being musically distinct from the urban style:

> In Mojosongo, if there's a *klenèngan* [music-making session], when they do *Pådåsih*[95] each person sings it differently—their villageness really comes out. Panggung[96] to the south is different from Panti Kosala[97] to the north. (Suhartå, June 6, 1991)

Whereas the distinction he makes here is primarily one between city and country, he often would speak in terms of directions toward other stylistic centers. Hence, around Solo there was Semarang to the northwest, Sragèn to the northeast, Wonogiri to the south, Yogya (and several intervening communities) to the southeast, and Boyolali (and, further out, Banyumas) to the west. Sometimes in a lesson he would say "you're singing like you're from Kartåsurå [10 kilometers from the center of Solo, on the road to Yogya]—you haven't yet

92. *Lagu seriosa* is a twentieth-century vocal genre, consisting of songs in Indonesian, usually with keyboard accompaniment, sometimes with Christian texts, which are lingeringly belted out with a wide, slow vibrato and jaw movements that are exaggerated by Javanese standards.

93. I am thinking, for instance, of Charles Ives's father's town band, in which the horn player regularly finished a piece several bars after everyone else (Cowell and Cowell 1966 [1955]:146). George Ives also had a great tolerance for unpretty but heartfelt singing:

> Once a nice young man...said to Father, "How can you stand it to hear old John Bell...sing?"...Father said, "He is a supreme musician." The young man...was horrified—"Why, he sings off the key, the wrong notes and everything—and that horrible, raucous voice—and he bellows out and hits notes no one else does—it's awful!" Father said, "Watch him closely and reverently, look into his face and hear the music of the ages. Don't pay too much attention to the sounds—for if you do, you may miss the music." (Kirkpatrick 1991 [1972]:132)

94. For city versus country, see, for instance, S. Weiss 1993, Perlman 1998, Pigeaud 1938, Lelyveld 1931, Hughes-Freeland 1995, Clara van Groenendael 1985, and Supanggah 1985:48–55. For Yogya versus Solo, see Kunst 1973 [1934], Sutton 1991a, Lindsay 1985, Pickvance 2005.

95. *Bå wå sekar må cå pat Dhandhanggulå Pådåsih*, one of the most common *båwå*s used to precede *gendhing Gambir Sawit, sléndro sångå*.

96. An intersection on the road to Mojosongo, less than a mile from Solo's central market.

97. A hospital about one third of a mile north of Panggung.

reached Solo."[98] In former times, it seems, each *désa* (village) had its own style.[99] In fact, some would argue that differences between regions are gross enough to render any Kraton-*désa* distinctions almost meaningless. Both contrasts—between city and village, and between the villages themselves—are summed up in the saying, already quoted in chapter 1, "Désâ mâwâ cârâ, negârâ mâwâ tâtâ" [The village has its ways, the city its etiquette]. This is how Mloyowidodo explained the proverb to me:

> Negârâ refers to the Kraton: at court every bodily movement is regulated by custom [*sedâyâ kawontenan mobah-mosik ditâtâ*]. In the *désâ* [rural areas] they have *cârâ*s [ways]. Each *désâ* [village] has its own *cârâ*. So you follow the custom of wherever you are. (Mloyowidodo, May 2, 1992)

Such distinctiveness operates even on a micro level as well. Each gamelan ensemble has its own *cârâ*—its own way of doing things. One of the tests of musicians joining another group as guests is how well they can adjust to the idiosyncrasies of that group (Supanggah 1985:268–69).

It would be disingenuous of me to leave the subject of relativity in Javanese music without mentioning a clear case of subversion with regard to *cocog*ness. In general, it is true, musicians do their best to bring out the *rasa* of a piece, and their reputations as musicians depend on this ability. Increasingly, though, musicians will decide to modify the usual treatment of a *gendhing* in a way that alters its *rasa* considerably. Nartosabdho is often cited as the trailblazer in this respect, and many have followed in his footsteps. To the refined, serious Kraton repertoire he often applied more exuberant village and regional styles (faster tempos, vocal interjections, virtuosic drumming), ending up with a hybrid that was gayer and livelier than the staid ways of doing these pieces. Sometimes, though, he would do the opposite: he would add *bedhayan* singing (a court style typified by a unison chorus, either all female or mixed, singing

Compare II:1, IV:4

98. *Baru Kartâsurâ—belum Solo.* He may have been partly putting me on or speaking metaphorically: perhaps what he meant was that a little bit of Yogyanese style had crept into my voice, not that Kartâsurâ had an identifiable style.

99. Whereas, on a large scale, regionalism appeared to be holding its own—at least as of the early 1990s (Sutton 1991a)—there is no question that on a local level there has been ever increasing standardization. In former times, to be sure, there were institutions whose styles were emulated outside of their immediate environs (Supanggah 1985:205–6). The influence of prestigious groups, though, has increased tremendously because of cassette recordings. Starting with Nartosabdho, many of these much-emulated groups have been professional *wayang* troupes. Another factor is the yearly crop of graduates from the state-run schools, who seek work wherever they can get it (the best ones typically stay on at their respective alma maters, others may move to another city). The yearly competitions that used to be run regularly by the national radio stations have also exerted an influence, since the organizers distributed notation for the pieces to be performed, and imposed fairly strict guidelines on how to *nggarap* (interpret) them. (On the other hand, the competitions sometimes widened the repertoire in general circulation, since the organizing committees often sought out little-known pieces.)

melismatic, drawn-out melodies) to an otherwise playful piece, thereby at once making the piece more serious, and enlivening the otherwise stately *bedhayan* element. He is both admired and vilified for these innovations. For all of the controversy, Nartosabdho may be seen as homogenizing *rasa* into a pleasant catchiness rather than effecting a 180-degree turn (Supanggah, June 17, 1992).

Occasionally, though, out of sheer perversity, a musician will *nggarap* [J] (interpret) a piece so as to go completely against its accepted nature. Such acts are ironic exercises, in which the musician tests his ability to do something utterly outrageous and still get away with it. While it is considered relatively easy to make a serious piece happy, it is far more difficult (but perhaps more acceptable) to create a sense of grandeur or sadness in a usually frolicsome piece. Here is an account of just such an experiment:

> I once tried something on my own. Pak Marto [Martopangrawit] didn't fault me for doing it, either. I took *Rujak Jeruk*, which is usually very *bérag* [exuberant], a bit *gecul* [jocular], and made it *susah* [sad]. [...] That had never been done before: a *gendhing* that was happy—one that was used for merry-making, for *tayuban*[100]—and which was then changed into a sad piece. (Suhartå, March 26, 1992)

Of course, the success of the experiment will depend largely on the credentials of the person doing the experimenting:

> How much you can get away with straying from convention depends a lot on who you are. If I *nggarap* a *gendhing* in an unconventional way, everyone remarks on how *pinter* [clever] I am. If one of my students does exactly the same thing, everyone is outraged. (Supanggah, June 17, 1992)

It is impossible for us to know the extent to which such radical experimentation went on in past centuries. What is clear is that people talk of it as a recent development, and one that has upset the equilibrium of a rich tradition—rich both in geographical variety and in expressive range.

> What saddens me is that *gendhings*, which are/were so richly diverse in their *rasas*, in their colors [*yang begitu kaya dengan rasa yang berbeda, warna yang berbeda*], nowadays are reduced to a single color [to push things a little]. The trailblazer [*pelopor*] in the change to a monochromatic situation was Nartosabdho.... He was the first to play around with the [traditional] *rasa* of a *gendhing*. (Supanggah, June 17, 1992)

100. *Tayuban* is a form of ritualized dance in which a group of male musicians and at least one female dancer/singer are paid to perform in an informal setting. The word "ritualized" may invoke the wrong image: there is usually a lot of heavy drinking and the revelry goes on all night. The male guests take turns dancing with the hired dancer/singer. *Tayuban* appears to have originated in very old fertility rites. It is now associated with "rough" village ways, though it used to be common among city gentry as well (Hughes-Freeland 1995:199; Sumarsam 1995:121, 256–57). See Hughes-Freeland 1993 for a description of a relatively recent village *tayuban*.

To sum up, *rasa* as an attribute can be variously assigned to different groups of people depending on the *rasa* in question. Palace musicians, men, and older musicians tend to be better at the deeper *rasa*s; village musicians, women, and younger musicians tend to be better at the lighter ones. The amount of *rasa* a performance has is equally contingent. It depends above all on appropriateness to its context. This is dealt with further in the next chapter.

FIVE

HAVING *RASA*, PART 2

Musicianship

RASA AND IMPROVISATION

[Javanese] performers act as inventors, as improvisers, always and everywhere. When they play or sing, they are constantly seeking, experimenting, altering, adapting, "playing" around with the phrases according to their respective intentions, *rasa*s, and capacities for invention. It is the phrases they shape in this way that are called *céngkok*s.

One could say that a *céngkok* is more or less any sequence of pitches that allows a melodic phrase to flower [be developed]. By "flower" I mean that it must be filled in, beautified, enlivened. For it is in the nature of *céngkok* to move and to live. That is, it is grasped by the senses as something that moves, whose form is constantly changing. . . .

Céngkok is what gives the melody its character: it is the soul of melody. It can be shaped by the performer to have a certain character or spirit. When an artist wants to disclose ["unfurl"] his feelings, he can do it entirely through manipulating the *céngkok*. A melody whose *céngkok* has been refined has been given a spirit, has been fully "enculturated." That's why many melodies that are used in a joyous context may also be used for a regal affair or in a devotional setting. To achieve this flexibility, the performer need only work out his or her *céngkok*s in a suitable way. (Sindoesawarno [n.d.]:62, 64)[1]

[You are] given this much space: [you can go] here, or here, or here. So each [gamelan] group will [play] differently. This group plays *Gambirsawit* this way, with [the pattern called] *puthut gelut*; the other [group] also plays *puthut gelut*, but it's different. That's what is called *karawitan* [traditional gamelan music]. II:2

Sure, there are rules: you have to do this, you can't pass there; so it's orderly [*teratur*], but there is freedom. *That* is what is called *karawitan*.

1. This passage was reproduced (without citation) in Siswanto 1983:26. Readers interested in a different rendering into English may look in Becker and Feinstein 1987:378, 381, where they will also find Sindoesawarno's illustrative musical examples.

> So you can't say "it has to be like this"—you can't say that, because [the musician] is given latitude [*kelonggaran*]. So if two groups play *Gambirsawit* and [they play it] exactly the same, then that isn't karawitan. (Martopangrawit, February 24, 1986; translated and quoted in Perlman 1994:180 [words in square brackets provided by Perlman])

> *Garap* [working out, interpretation, arrangement, improvisation] thus relates to the domains of creation and interpretation—one might even say of inspiration and imagination. It is the spirit that makes a [gamelan] orchestra come alive, the inspiration that guides each musician's interpretation.... Thus, in the traditional Javanese arts, the performer always has a great deal of freedom of *garap*.... Actually, *gendhings* are nothing more than vehicles [for the performer], fertile ground waiting to be worked (*garaped*). The musicians, who have their own individual interpretations (*garap*), are the ones who make possible the great flexibility in performance. *Garap* is what determines the quality of a musical performance. It is also how one judges the quality of a musician: through his mastery of *garap* he demonstrates his sensibility [= *rasa*?] as well as his ability to create, to adapt to circumstances, and to collaborate with other musicians. (Supanggah 1985:110, 292)

One day in 1994, during a conversation with Nur Intan Murtadza, a Western-trained Malaysian musician interested in Javanese gamelan, she asked me an intriguing question. I had just finished summarizing (and justifying) my research topic—which ultimately developed into the subject of this book—and had told her how important *rasa* was in understanding Javanese music. If that was so, she wanted to know, why don't Javanese musicians talk about *rasa* more when teaching in the United States?

My immediate answer was that most of us foreigners never get good enough for it to come up—much of the time, our teachers are worried enough about just getting through a piece. But this is only part of the answer. Part of it must also lie in a certain Javanese chauvinism (foreigners are incapable of having *rasa*—so why try?). Related to this is the attitude, held by many older Javanese, that certain kinds of knowledge have to be earned—indeed, as we have seen, some knowledge is secret—or else sought out on one's own in a process called *golèkånå dhéwé* (seek for yourself). But I doubt that that is a major factor here, for I found musicians more than willing, when asked, to talk about *rasa gendhing*: *rasa* in the sense of "affect" is not privileged information.

Upon further reflection, it dawned on me that the main reason Javanese musicians teaching abroad neglect to talk about *rasa* is that most Americans rarely *nggarap*—we hardly ever make stylistic decisions as we perform (there are, of course, notable exceptions to this). That is, we write down or tape an instrumental or vocal part as performed by our respective teachers, and we memorize it as exactly as we can: there are few delightful surprises in the course of American gamelan rehearsals or concerts. This has the distinct advantage of preventing us from doing some very unstylistic things, but it means that the *process* we use in making music is very different from what an experienced Javanese musician uses.[2] An extreme analogy might be the sounds parrots make in imitation of human speech. For Javanese performers, as well as for Americans performing Javanese music, in order for there to be *rasa* there has to be an element of choice—of conscious manipulation in reaction to a specific situation.

In fact, Javanese musicians sometimes do talk about *rasa* with their American groups. Like Molière's Monsieur Jourdain, who spoke prose all his life unaware of his achievement, American gamelan students are probably being told about *rasa* much more than they realize. I have heard Murtadza's own gamelan teacher, Minarno, try to impart some of the *rasa* of the music he was teaching on several occasions. For instance, once, during a rehearsal for a dance accompaniment, he pointed out how the opening *Ayak-Ayak* (a *wayang* (shadow theater) piece with an undulating melody) and the one at the end of the suite should be played differently. The first one was "like a king walking" (a translation of *mrabu* [regal]? *regu* [stately]? *wibåwå* [commanding, imposing]?), whereas the one at the end was much happier. This, significantly, was with a fairly inexperienced group. Nevertheless, it is probably the case that Javanese musicians talk even more about *rasa* with their advanced students, who stand a better chance of being able to adjust their performance accordingly.

Compare IV:1 and IV:11

There is plenty of evidence in Javanese music talk—or at least in that which is prompted by a querying ethnomusicologist—that improvisation plays a vital role in giving *rasa* or meaning to a musical utterance. For one thing, the melodies of the male vocal genres used in *karawitan* are often described as being devoid of *rasa*. Of these, two genres are by far the most representative (few if any of the other male genres are specific to one gender): *båwå* (an extended vocal introduction to a gamelan piece) and *gérongan* (the unison choral singing that is an integral part of the overall gamelan texture). The following conversation is a case in point.

MARC: Do male voices also fall into two groups [with respect to *rasa gendhing*]?

WIGNYOSAPUTRO: Male singing cannot contribute to a *wibåwå* or *prenès* [coquettish] effect. In fact, male singing is "allround"—the Javanese word is *ngabéhi* [from *kabèh* (everything)]—it works for everything. That's because the *gérong* has limited melodic patterns. The *gérong* is set. Even if the *gérong* isn't sad, the *sindhénan* [*sindhèn* part] still can be—so that just goes to show!

2. See Bamberger and Zipporyn 1992 for additional reasons why rote memorization is not always the best learning device. For more on differences between Javanese and American gamelan musicians with respect to their musical competence and how they acquire it, see Brinner 1995. The passages in the book that describe Javanese competence and its acquisition are too numerous to cite, but those focusing on why Americans rarely develop all of the same skills are as follows: pp. 67–68, 100–101, 140–43, 148–50, 300, 314.

II:2, 1:43–4:35; III:4, 1:00–4:21

M: What about solo male singing, like *båwås*?

W: *Båwå* melodies have no *rasa*. There's no such thing as a sad *båwå*.

M: Really?

W: Really. What can you do, *båwå* melodies are set!

M: Is it that they can't be classified at all [according to *rasa*], or . . .

W: No, they can't. [. . .] Male singers are limited: they're not free to do different things. "If you're going to pitch 6, it's gotta be like so; if to pitch 5, it's gotta be like so." But the *sindhèn* has all sorts of ways of getting to pitch 6. Male singing is *kawengku ing lagu* [J] [constrained by the melody], but female singing is *kawengku ing råså* [J] [constrained by *rasa*].[3] (June 19, 1992)

Part of what Wignyosaputro is getting at here is that these two male genres require far less decision making on the part of the singers than does the primary female genre, *sindhénan srambahan* (general-purpose *sindhénan*), and this is what prevents them from having *rasa*.

But let us examine this distinction a little more closely. Is it true that *båwå* singers make no choices in performance? Once, during a rehearsal in the United States, I was asked to sing a *båwå* I had never sung before. When I protested, our teacher said, "Just read the notes." In fact, *båwå* singers do much more than "just read the notes":

> A good *båwå*, besides being sung with a good voice, must be sung with the complete range of *gregel-wiled* [melodic ornaments]. What we just heard on the tape is far too plain. I would have to say that it's under par. It's the way a beginner would sing:
>
> 6 1̇ 2̇ 1̇ ˇ 2̇ 3̇
> Lir sad på
>
> It's like whatever's in the notation and nothing more. If you ask me, it's *kurang garapan* [underwrought, not fully worked out]. (Suhartå, April 1, 1991)

Like most Javanese notation, *båwå* notation is a shorthand. For instance, a phrase (in *sléndro*) notated as

2 1 1 . 2 3 5 ' 2 . 3 2 1 . 6̣

(e.g., in Slamet Suparno 1980/1981:6) would never be sung "straight" by an experienced singer, who instead might sing it, inter alia, in any of the following ways:[4]

3. I have freely edited this for the sake of concision.

4. These examples were all given to me by Suhartå during a lesson on the *båwå Kenyå Kedhiri*. He characterized example A as belonging to Sutarman. B was typical of Sastro Tugiyo, while C was associated with Gunawan Sri Hastjarjo and the Kraton. D and E, he said, were Sastro Tugiyo when he was acting crazy (*dhèglèngan*), that is, under the influence of alcohol. It should perhaps be mentioned that he was rather critical of all of them except B (Suhartå, April 11, 1990).

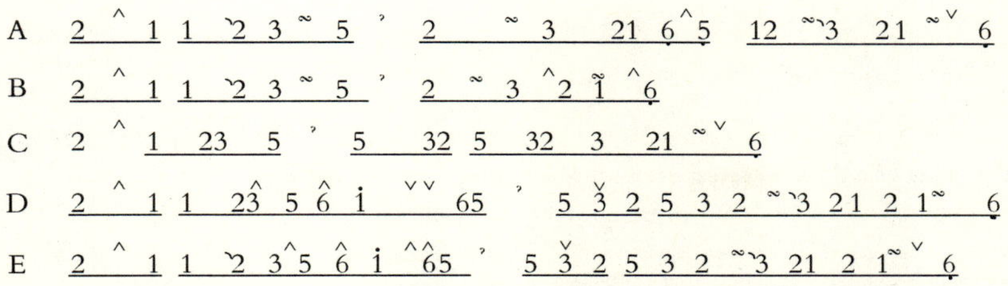

5/1

However, such additions and changes to the notation all come under the category of *gregel-wiled* (ornamentation).[5] More far-reaching choices, which affect the melodic contour and final pitch of a phrase, come under the category of *céngkok* (melodic formula).[6] *Båwå* singers rarely have to choose between *céngkoks*.[7] They deal, for the most part, only with "surface" features (Schenkerian terminology is astonishingly apt):

> MLB: Do *båwås* have the same *rasas* as *gendhings*?
> MLOYOWIDODO: For *båwås* it depends on the poetry. [...] The *båwå* is not like the *sindhèn* part. *Båwås* have their own molds they have to be cast in. [...] They can't be changed. (March 19, 1992)

> MLB: Are there *båwås* that are *prenès* and others that aren't?
> SASTRO TUGIYO: *Båwås* are limited. [I] don't really dare [mess with them]. You can only be so bold. You can only deviate so far. Just enough to give it some flavoring—like what I was saying earlier about it not being "sour" enough: "So let it be sour a little! It tastes just like water!" "That *båwå* was fine, but it was smooth as glass." [...] "Every now and then, go ahead, put in a little swerve in the road." (April 29, 1992)

Gérong singing is even more limited in the opportunities it affords for personal interpretation. Since it is by definition unison group singing, there is no room for individual choice of *céngkok*, and only a little room for *gregel-wiled*.[8]

5. These terms are very slippery, and I will not try to define them precisely here. See Dea 1980:111–42, Sindoesawarno 1984:395–96, Waluyo 1991:115, Suyoto 1992:142, Suparno 1984/1985: 10–14, Hatch 1980:159ff., 490–91, and Giles 1985:133–35 for some valiant attempts to pin them down. Other terms sometimes used to refer to ornamentation are *luk* and *variasi*.

6. See Martopangrawit 1984:14; Supanggah 1985:145–49; Forrest 1980; Sutton 1978 and 1993:192–93; Kunst 1973 [1932]:334; Walton 1987:11–15; and Perlman 1994:177–78.

7. Exceptions are when they are changing either the *laras* (tuning system) of a *båwå* (e.g., from *pélog* to *sléndro*) or its final gong tone (to adjust to the *gendhing* that follows). Another area where they have some choice is in figuring out a solo melody to substitute for the usual *jineman* (short choral passage inserted in a *båwå*), when this is left out, although this is usually fairly straightforward.

8. Like *bedhåyå* dancers, who, in the Solonese Kraton tradition, should not be absolutely uniform in their movements, *gérong* singers should use subtle individual variants when singing, as long as these do not detract from the overall impression of unity (it is not good, for instance, for one singer to sing much louder than the others). Failure to use *gregel-wiled* will result in a *kembå* (insipid) sound—like a "PKK" group (see chapter 1). It is sufficient, however, for only one member to put in ornaments. Different groups often have different versions of *gérong* parts, and sometimes *gérong* singers who do not often sing together discuss which version to use before they start singing (more often they diverge the first time through a piece, and hopefully come to an agreement by the next time around). A certain amount of divergence, then, is tolerated, except in a top-notch professional *wayang* performance, a music school performance, a professional recording or radio broadcast, or in a competition.

The same sorts of comments are made about the female vocal genres that require very little spontaneous decision making:

> MLB: What is the difference between a voice for *langgam* [sentimental popular genre] and one for *klenéngan* [classical concert repertoire]?
> SASTRO TUGIYO: Well, the difference is that [in the latter case the singers] have mastered *gregel-wiled-céngkok* [Javanese semi-improvised ornamentation and melodic formulas]. [. . .] In a *klenéngan* of *gendhings*, you need a lot of *céngkoks*. But for *langgam*, there isn't so much in the way of *céngkok-wiled*. There's just the one melody.
> MLB: Oh, so you don't have to make up—
> S: *céngkoks*?
> MLB: —*céngkoks* yourself, you just follow what's already there.
> S: That's right. In a *klenéngan*, in "classical" [music], you have to make them up yourself. And if you were to make them match the ones for *langgam* it wouldn't be very pleasant. It would be like *sindhèn* for beginners. Because [*langgam* singers] haven't mastered the use of *céngkoks*. [. . .] That's why, in all the world, there's nothing that can compare to the *céngkoks* of Javanese *gendhings*. The *gregels* and *wileds* of Javanese *gendhings*, which pierce the feelings in your heart—there's nothing outside of Java that can compare. (May 6, 1992)

palaran ● *Dhandhang-gulå* II:3, 1:20–4:52

> MLB: Is there such a thing as a *palaran*[9] that's *gobyog* [boisterous]—or isn't there?
> SUDARSONO: No, there isn't. There's just *sereng* [tense] or[. . .] *Palarans* have fixed melodies. "*Dhandhanggulå* is like this, *Asmåråndånå* is like that"—they're very rough, from the point of view of their *rasas*. Because of the rhythm [i.e., the repeated strokes of the *kenong*?]; one could call them *sereng*. . . (November 30, 1991)

Furthermore, these considerations are not limited to vocal music. Note the following comment about Panuju, a drummer who got his start during the colonial era at the Mangkunegaran and its associated radio station, SRV (the precursor to RRI):

> Pak Panuju's extraordinary ability as a drummer lay in his talent for matching the drum patterns to the *isi* ["content"] of the piece. For example, in *gendhing* [X] he would make up new patterns not used for any other piece. (Sukanto, April 2, 1990)

Imitating established musicians—a necessary pedagogical step—is often disparaged when practiced by mature musicians, who should have developed their own ways of doing things. That is, unless you are making interpretive decisions, you're not really making music. A word sometimes used for someone who merely imitates others is *ilon* [J] (mirror-like). (A related expression, *kethèk ngilon*

9. *Palaran* is a genre in which a solo vocalist is accompanied by a reduced gamelan. The instruments play repetitive patterns while the singer sings texts and unmetered melodies based on *måcåpat* (a genre of classical sung verse).

[J], "a beggar's monkey, looking at himself in a mirror," was used in the old days to refer derisively to someone who played from notation [Mloyowidodo, May 2, 1992].) Sudarsono clearly equates the ability to make distinctions in performance with having *rasa*, and, conversely, unthinking imitation with the lack of it:

> It used to be that the musical accompaniment for palace scenes in *wayang* would be different according to the personalities of the characters in the scene. But now very few people can *garap* [interpret] those *gendhing*s. At most it's just the same old *Asmåråndånå, Ayun-Ayun*, some composition or other of Nartosabdho's, and the like, and we're just *latah*[10] in going along with that. We just do it out of expediency. But if the pieces are chosen with *rasa*, the results are very different. (Sudarsono, December 11, 1991)

Another example is when, in our three-way conversation, Wignyosaputro asked Suhartå about the singers from the village of Ngadirejo (some twenty miles to the southeast of Solo), who were being taught in the extension program run by STSI. His question was whether they had reached the level of *rasa* yet (*sampai rasa, belum?* [JI]). Suhartå's answer was, "they've only gotten to the memorizing stage" (*nembé taraf ngapalaken* [K]).

There is, however, a puzzling anomaly—a case in which *rasa* does not seem to be linked with interpretive creativity. I noted at the beginning of chapter 4 how, where *rasa* is concerned, "heavy" and "deep" are correlated. And yet the "heavy" pieces tend to be more set, with *less* improvisatory freedom, *less* leeway for trying out different *céngkok*s:

> Usually *gendhing*s that are *prenès* [lighthearted] are actually harder to make *céngkok*s for. (Sudarsono, November 22, 1991)

> It's actually harder to *nyindhèni* [sing *sindhèn* to] a simple piece like *Gambir Sawit* than it is a big heavy piece with a specific *garapan* [interpretation, set of standard variants]. In the latter case it's all laid out for you—you just have to learn what the *garapan* is; whereas in the first case it calls for real invention. (Sudarsono, October 23, 1991)

II:2

> MLB: If a piece is *prenès* [coquettish] because it's easy to *garap* [work out] in different ways, does that mean that *regu* [stately] pieces are harder?
>
> SUPANGGAH: Not really. *Prenès* pieces give more leeway. *Regu* pieces *sudah minta begitu* [call for a certain way]. For example, if the *balungan* is low, the *sindhén* part does not have a lot of possibilities. (Supanggah, October 24, 1993)

gendhing prenès III:4; gendhing regu I:1

10. *Latah* is a mental disorder in which a person repeats uncontrollably, as if in a state of trance, what the people around her (or, less often, him) say. It is "a psychological disorder prevalent among adult Indonesian and Malaysians (mostly women). It can be caused by a sudden noise, shock or command. In the state of *latah*, the victim appears to lose awareness of him/herself and his/her surroundings and can only imitate, often accompanied by vulgar language, what he/she hears or sees. Anyone who attracts his [*sic*] attention can make him do any action by pretending to do that action. This condition can last for hours or until the victim drops in exhaustion; recovery to a normal state of consciousness then takes place" (Stevens and Schmidgall-Tellings 2004, s.v. "latah").

I offer the following interpretation as a possible explanation for this anomaly. The problem lies, once again, in different connotative meanings of the word *rasa*. The kind of *rasa* typical of Kraton musicians is one that aims to create, in musician and listener alike, a deep inner calm and a sense of order. One reason that the *céngkok*s (melodic patterns) are set for the "heavy" pieces, is that some great musician or musicians in the past, whose names are sometimes still remembered, came up with a superb way of bringing out the *alus* (refined, spiritual) *rasa*s of these pieces. The kind of spontaneity that results in *rasa* in the sense used in the preceding discussion of improvisation seems to be linked especially to the lighter affects—*rasa*, that is, as emotion or intuition, whose presence results in a sense of surprise and disorder for the listeners. This second sense of *rasa* is more familiar to Westerners and is almost synonymous with expressiveness.

Gambir Sawit II:2; Elå-Elå Kalibeber I:2

A parallel and related inconsistency in Solonese music talk lies in the assessment of difficulty. Sometimes a *gendhing* like *Gambir Sawit* is said to be the hardest to perform well, because it is played so often that it is difficult to make it sound fresh. At other times, a *gendhing* like *Elå-Elå Kalibeber* is proclaimed to be the hardest in the repertoire, owing to the unique nature of its associated *garap*, which the musicians must fully master for the *rasa* of the *gendhing* to emerge (Benamou and Supanggah 2006). Whereas *Gambir Sawit* requires more *rasa* in the sense of inventiveness, *Elå-Elå Kalibeber* requires more *rasa* in the sense of esoteric knowledge.

RASA AND EVALUATION

The primary situation in which *rasa* terms naturally come up is in evaluating a specific performance. Evaluative uses of *rasa* terms may at times be positive, but it is more common to use them to criticize.[11] Examples of the former are *semu banget* [Ng] (so subtle, so appropriate), *manteb banget* [Ng] (really solid), *gagah sanget* [K] (very virile sounding); examples of the latter are *gregedé kurang* [Ng] (not enough "oomph"), *kurang nges* [Ng,JI] (leaves you cold), *lugu banget* [Ng] (too plain), *terlalu bérag* [JI] (too rambunctious). Most of my relevant citations deal with vocal music, since that was my main focus, but many of the same criteria apply to instrumentalists as well. The adage, already quoted in chapter 4, "Lair utusané batin" [Outward behavior is the emissary of the inner self], applies especially to the voice and the *rebab*—the two sound producers in the gamelan that most intimately involve the human body (along with the *suling* [end-blown bamboo flute], which is musically of minor importance)—but it can be extended to other instruments as well. The idea is that the musician's basic disposition will come out in the music, no matter what he or she does. The principal

11. See White 1994:226, and the section in chapter 4 (pp. 131–32), in which this passage is discussed.

Javanese word for "disposition" is *watak*;[12] it has several components (J. Weiss 1977:59ff.). For the most part, *watak* is already determined at birth. In Javanese psychology, the basic substratum of personality—inborn traits that can never be eradicated, only controlled at best—is the *dhasar* [J] (base). *Dasar suara* [I] (*dhasar suårå* [Ng], *dhasar swanten* [K]; basic nature of the voice) is thus the voice one is born with.[13] This is the closest one comes, in Javanese, to a translation of the English term "vocal timbre" (most Javanese musicians use the Indonesian neologism, *warna suara*, "voice color," in a much broader way):

> Your vocal timbre [*dasar suara*] is something you have from childhood, from birth. It's God-given, they say. (Suhartå, August 7, 1991)

> Pak Panggah's[14] [*rebaban*]—[*sings with a fast vibrato and fast ornaments*]—it's like his voice when he sings. Unquestionably. It emanates from inside, comes out through the hands. [. . .] Whenever someone's [performance style] does not originate from within, it will return [to its original state]. Usually, if they're imitating [someone else's style], they'll eventually go back to their own personality. (Suhartå, April 25, 1992)

One's *watak* is thus primarily made up of inborn traits. But it includes learned behavior as well, in that it is partly determined by life experiences and by how one is culturally brought up. If one comes from a *priyayi* (aristocratic) background, one has an advantage in performing pieces with a calm, spiritual *rasa*. If one has a sad life, one is likely to gravitate towards, and be good at expressing, the sad *rasa*s:

> MLB: When actors have to play, say, a scene in which they have to cry, they recall a really sad event in their own lives, so that real tears will flow. Does something similar happen in the case of musicians? For instance, to prepare mentally for a sad piece, do they need to recall something sad?
>
> SUHARTÅ: I suppose one could do that. But, in fact, [musicians who perform sad pieces well], as it happens, will have had more sadness than happiness in their lives—like Pak Marto [. . .]. [But someone] like Panggiyo[15] has had more happiness than sadness. So that, when he plays *rebab* in a sad piece, he can't really feel it. He used to come to me for help with sad *rebab* playing. [Panggiyo:] "How is the hand position here?" [Suhartå:] "It's harder that way—you should do it this way. 'Steal' with this finger, like this." I knew more than he did, even though he was a better *rebab* player. And he knew that I was better at sad playing. [. . .] My hand position—my fingers found their places all by themselves: "Let's go this way, now this way." (May 2, 1992)

12. Other related terms, most of which will not be discussed further, are *kepribadian* [I], *kapribadèn* [J]; *bawaan* [I], *gawan* [Ng], *pembawaan* [I]; *lagéyan* [J]; *leléwå* [J]; *kodrat* [I,J]; *dhasar* [J], *dasar* [I]; *karakter* [D,I]; *sipat* [J], *sifat* [I]; *perangai* [I]; *kebiasaan* [I]; *tabiat* [I]; *laku* [Ng,I], *lampah* [K]; and *solah* [J].

13. *Pembawaan* ("that which is brought [from birth]") is sometimes used nearly in the same way (see Dea 1980:117).

14. Rahayu Supanggah's.

15. Panggiyo is a gamelan maker and teacher of gamelan music at STSI/ISI who is a few years younger than Suhartå.

As mentioned in the previous chapter, a good performance must be appropriate to the situation (the type of event, the other musicians)—but also to the repertoire at hand. This last requirement comprises two large categories: the *rasa* of the piece and the *rasa* of the genre it belongs to. Whereas *rasa gendhing* refers to mood or affect, an expression like *rasa mérong* (the feeling appropriate to the first, calm section of a *gendhing*) refers to the "*mérong*ness" of the performance (see chapter 2). I will deal with these two meanings of *rasa* separately.

As pointed out in chapter 3, just as *gendhing*s can be divided into the two overarching *rasa* categories of "light" and "heavy," singers' voices can be divided very generally into *luruh* and *trègèl*. And, like *regu* (stately) and *prenès* (coquettish) for *rasa gendhing*, these two terms can refer to specific voice types or can be used more generally to stand for an entire cluster. A singer who is *luruh* (humble, like the character Sumbådrå[16]) is likely to be calm, unaffected, and somewhat asexual. The *luruh* voice has a slow vibrato, executes ornaments relatively slowly, and tends to be low. A singer who is *trègèl* (impetuous, like the character Sri Kandhi[17]) is likely to be flirtatious, restless, youthful, and somewhat forceful. The *trègèl* voice has a fast vibrato, is very agile, and rather high. There are, of course, many other categories for both *gendhing*s and voices (Benamou 1998a; Waridi 2005:364–67, 370). But the minimal requirement for a satisfying vocal performance is that a more-or-less "heavy" piece be performed by a more-or-less *luruh* voice, and an essentially "light" piece by an essentially *trègèl* voice.[18]

Both pairs— *luruh/trègèl* and "light"/"heavy"—represent true continua, not discrete categories. Moreover, it would seem that most pieces are various shades of *prenès* [coquettish], that is, neither extremely light (*bérag* [J], exuberant) nor extremely "heavy" (*regu* [J], stately). Similarly, most voices are neither very *luruh* nor very *trègèl*:

MLB: So [. . .] there are two large categories?

SUHARTÅ: Uh-huh.

MLB: Are there any other large categories?

H: There are those in the middle. The ones in the middle include most of the *sindhèns* here [in Solo(?)]. They can go either way. But it depends on the singer—on her ability to develop her voice in such a way that it can match the character of the piece. [. . .] The *sindhèns* in the middle are the ones whose [vibratos] are not too [slow], and not

16. One of several wives of the hero Arjunå. Anderson describes her as follows: "Sumbådrå is very much the lady—elegant, gentle, reserved, utterly loyal and obedient to her husband. She represents the ideal type of the aristocratic woman" (Anderson 1965:21).

17. Another of Arjunå's wives. Anderson's description: "Srikandi is the exact opposite of Sumbadra. Talkative, strong-willed, warm-hearted, fond of hunting, an excellent archer, she is quite ready to debate with Ardjunå or take on a *satryå* [knight] in battle" (Anderson 1965:21–22). See figure 7.1 for an illustration of a *luruh* and a *trègèl* (or *branyak*) character.

18. Again, I focus on voices here, but there are also "heavy" and "light" personality types for instrumental musicians. An inveterate jokester will never do a good job on a "heavy" piece, and a brooder will never be right for a "light" one.

> too "*tril*" [tremolo-like]. [. . .] They're often the ones who succeed. [. . .] [Their voices] work well for *pélog limå*[19] [i.e., grand, stately pieces] but they also work for the more vivacious pieces later on in the evening. (June 25, 1992)

Within limits, then, the best performers can overcome their *wataks* (dispositions) and learn to express the *rasa* of almost any piece adequately by taking cues from those who have the appropriate *watak*. Many excellent musicians, though, are unable to do so, and really only sound good when performing pieces that fall within a fairly narrow range of *rasas*. The group Condhong Raos was the troupe that accompanied the immensely popular *dhalang* Nartosabdho (see chapter 1). The musicians were mostly from the town of Gombang (where they had been in a group called Ngripto Raras), and after Nartosabdho's death one of them, Joko Mujoko Raharjo, became a popular *dhalang* in his own right. Many of the same musicians joined his troupe until his own untimely death in 1992. These were among the most highly professional groups in recent history, often performing almost nightly (that is, *all night*, almost every night!). They were phenomenally talented and superbly polished, and yet, according to Supanggah, even *they* were limited in what they were able to express musically:

> If the group from Gombang [Pak Mujoko's group] or Nartosabdho's group played *Laler Mengeng*,[20] there was no way it would have sounded *sedhih* [sad], even though they may have *said* that it was *sedhih*, and they were all trying to make it *sound* sedhih. (Supanggah, June 17, 1992)

It is possible that *wayang* (shadow theater) musicians, who, more and more, are expected to be consummate entertainers, are a self-selected, extroverted group of people who naturally gravitate toward the lighter affects. A more likely explanation, though, is that they became incapable of playing in a serious manner (if, indeed, Supanggah is right) because of ingrained habits: *wayang* tempos are generally very fast by *klenéngan* (concert) standards, and the repertoire tends increasingly to the exuberant. Direct evidence of just such a shift in focus may be found in Walton's report (1996:330) of a *pesindhèn* in Anom Suroto's troupe: "She has so little opportunity to sing the 'classical' *gendhing*[s] that she has almost forgotten how to sing gendhing *Kutut Manggung*" (which is a nearly ubiquitous piece at *klenéngans*—and a rather lighthearted one, at that).

As a transition to the other relevant meaning of *rasa* in this context—the essential nature of a genre as opposed to that of a *gendhing*—let us consider

19. *Pélog limå* is a category of pieces and a melodic mode in the *pélog* tuning that is usually played at the beginning of a *klenèngan* and that has a low overall tessitura. The category has a preponderance of very long, serious pieces.

20. *Gendhing Laler Mengeng* is the quintessential sad piece.

evaluation of *rasa* in a self-conscious, formal setting, an officially sponsored competition. In 1989 the national television station (TVRI) in Yogyakarta held a *sindhèn* competition, open to anyone from the Special District of Yogyakarta and the Province of Central Java who was between the ages of 18 and 40. Suhartå was one of the judges, and he graciously allowed me to photocopy his notes from the "technical meeting" (the exact, untranslated designation) at which the panel of judges discussed the scoring procedures for that competition. The relevant section is reproduced and translated in figure 5.1. From the relative weights given to each category (4, 3, 2, 1), we may surmise that the list of items to be discussed is given in decreasing order of importance. Indeed, this order corresponds exactly to the priorities my teachers said they had when they judged competitions in general. Several of them told me that their first concern was with correctness (*harus betul dulu* [I]): singing should be in tune and correctly pronounced, and there should be no gross errors in timing or melodic pattern. If things are generally correct, then a judge can go beyond that and listen for subtleties of *rasa* and timbre—aspects that require the exercise of taste on the part of the one judging.

In practice, though, it is not always possible to distinguish between questions that admit of correctness in an absolute way and questions of aesthetics. For, as we have seen, questions of right and wrong are often couched in terms of whether something is appropriate or inappropriate: *garap* depends upon *rasa*, and vice versa. Nevertheless, the distinction is made in practice,[21] and not everyone asked to sit on a panel of judges feels qualified to assess *rasa* (Sudarsono, July 5, 1991). Javanese musicians often profess their reluctance to make absolute pronouncements about matters of interpretation and, especially, of *rasa*. One frequently hears, "there's no right way," or, in reference to varied interpretations, "they're all fine," or "that's just *my* opinion." These comments show that relativism is at least an ideal, even if one also hears the same musicians making what seem to be dogmatic pronouncements at other times.[22] It is significant, for instance, that under "timbre" in figure 5.1, the committee chairman wrote [*c*]*ukup jelas* (sufficiently clear): clarity, at least, is a quantifiable aspect of timbre that most people will agree on. Judges do not always practice what they preach, however, and are sometimes seduced by a beautiful voice into giving its possessor higher

21. Perlman has also noticed this split into two kinds of criteria (1994:165).

22. For examples of this other tendency—to see matters of interpretation as objective—see Perlman 1994:196–98. It should be pointed out that, in a Javanese context, such self-deprecating statements can be used to mean something quite different from their apparent meaning. According to Waridi (February 8, 2006), when a teacher says "but don't just listen to me—go ask others as well," that can mean "go ahead and ask others, but then you'll see that I was right." Nevertheless, there were many instances in my conversations with various teachers, when it was clear they meant that there were several equally good options. And, along the same lines, Waluyo, a vocal teacher at STSI, said that judging singing competitions goes contrary to his nature—he finds it nearly impossible to give a single ranking, since each singer has his or her own strengths, and the variety among the voices is to be relished (May 12, 2006).

Aspek yang dinilai: menjelaskan

I. TEKNIK: a. Benar
b. Angkatan dan seleh
c. Ucapan
d. Laras
} nilai ×4

II PENYAJIAN: a. Cengkok
b. Wiledan
c. Rasa
} nilai ×3

III DASAR SUARA: cukup jelas, nilai ×2

IV PENAMPILAN: hanya untuk babak final
a. Sikap
b. Busana.
} nilai ×1.

Aspects to be judged: explain

I. Technique:
a. Correct
b. Entrances and phrase endings
c. Pronunciation
d. Intonation
} score X4

II Performance/Interpretation:
a. Choice of pattern
b. Execution of pattern
c. *Rasa*
} score X3

III Vocal Quality:
reasonably [?] clear, score X2

IV Presentation: only for the finals
a. stage presence
b. dress
} score X1

FIGURE 5.1. "Technical Meeting" (July 9, 1989) for *sindhèn* competition at TVRI Yogkyakarta (excerpt).

marks than they otherwise should according to the principle of *harus betul dulu* (correctness comes first). This reticence in assigning points to *rasa* means that when the word shows up on a list of criteria (like the one reproduced in figure 5.1), it often refers not to *rasa gendhing*—which can be difficult to verbalize, and even more difficult to agree upon—but rather to the *rasa* of a genre:

> The *rasa* that is emphasized by juries during their meetings is the *rasa* of whether the performer can be said to *nyindhèni* [perform in a *sindhèn*-like way] or not, whether one *mbawanis* [performs in a *båwå*-like way] or not, whether *måcåpat* [singing] already *måcåpatis* [sounds like *måcåpat*] or not.[23] (Suhartå, December 14, 1990)

This, to repeat, is *rasa* in the sense of "-ness." In fact, each genre has its own conventions of interpretation.[24] If these are not followed, the characteristic "feeling" of the genre will evaporate. (I am using *genre*, here, rather loosely, and with full acknowledgment that the concept slips easily into *performance context* on one end, and into *structural unit* and *vocal or instrumental part* on the other. I will not attempt to artificially impose clear demarcations.) In place of the word *rasa* in this context, Supanggah prefers *leléwå* [J] (nature, character [Gericke and Roorde]; an attention-getting act [Poerwadarminta]), which he applies to any habitual way of performing:

> Consider that now there are so many different historical *leléwås* and *leléwås* of groups and regions, all of which can influence each other. As a result, it is sometimes difficult to differentiate a *sindhénan leléwå* from a *gérong leléwå*, a *sulukan leléwå*,[25] so that one often hears the complaint, "*Yèn gérong åjå kåyå sindhèn*" [don't sing *gérong* as if it were *sindhénan*]. (Supanggah 1988a:[viii])

As an example of how this works on a practical level, let us take two *leléwås*, those proper to the *mérong* of a *gendhing* and those proper to *båwås*. Before discussing the specifics of *mérong*ness, it will be useful to digress briefly into the divisions of *gendhing* form. The word *gendhing* can mean any gamelan composition, or, more specifically, it can refer to the category of pieces that have the longest *kenong* units (sixteen, thirty-two, or sixty-four "beats" per *kenong* stroke).[26] *Gendhings* in

23. On another occasion, however, Suhartå spoke specifically of *rasa* (or *kejiwaan*) *gendhing* as the primary criterion in judging *garap* at a competition: "The way you *garap*—that is, whether [your performance] fits the character of the piece—that's what's important" (August 7, 1991).

24. Other vocal genres that I have heard discussed in this way are the three categories of *suluk* (*ådå-ådå, pathetan,* and *sendhon*—songs sung by the *dhalang* in *wayang*), *sindhénan* for the *mérong* and for the *inggah* sections of a *gendhing* (respectively), *sindhénan* for *srepegan, rerepèn, urå-urå, gendhing sekar, langgam, andhegan, santiswaran/larasmadyå, sindhénan bedhayan, gérong, palaran,* and the now extinct *måcåpat paringgitan.* (These genres are defined in the glossary at the back of the book.)

25. *Sulukans* (or *suluks*) are mood songs sung by a puppeteer in the shadow theater and its offshoots. They include the subgenres of *ådå-ådå, sendhon,* and *pathetan.*

26. See J. Becker 1980, Appendix 1 for a complete explanation of gong cycles and their nomenclature. See also Martopangrawit 1984:17–39. A third, archaic meaning of the term *gendhing* is instrumental gamelan music in general (in contrast to *gendhèng*, or vocal music).

this second sense have two major, internally repeatable parts. The first of these is called *mérong*, which Martopangrawit describes as follows: "*Mérong* is one of the sections of a *gendhing* that provides an opportunity for a refined and calm playing style" (1984:24). The *mérong* is followed by a livelier section, called the *inggah* (also sometimes called *minggah*, or *ciblon, kosèk alus*, or *wiled*,[27] depending on the treatment). The normal sequence of tempos,[28] with all the subsidiary sections of a large *gendhing* of the type that is usually introduced by the *rebab* (*gendhing rebab*), is as follows (optional sections are enclosed in parentheses):

senggréngan (very short modal formula played on *rebab*, to indicate that the piece is about to begin)—moderately fast tempo

(*pathetan*[29] [modal prelude with small ensemble]—unmetered, leisurely pace)

bukå ("opening"; solo introduction)—medium fast, slowing slightly, and becoming more metric at the end; may be replaced by a *båwå* (extended solo vocal introduction)

mérong (first major section)—begins moderately fast in the first *irâmå* level (*tanggung*), but quickly settles to a very leisurely pace in the second *irâmå* level (*dados* [K])

umpak minggah (transition to second section)—speeding up to the first *irâmå* level, then quickly slowing, just before gong, through two *irâmå* changes, to a moderately fast tempo in the third *irâmå* level (*wiled* [J])

inggah or *wiled* (second large section)—moderately fast, but possibly slowing down, through another *irâmå* change, to a really brisk tempo in the fourth *irâmå* level

27. The *ciblon* is a medium-sized drum used to play lively patterns. *Kosèk alus* can be defined as the use of the largest drum instead of the *ciblon* in *irâmå wiled* to create a calm, settled mood. *Wiled* is short for *irâmå wiled*, which is the third, usually lively *irâmå* or tempo level (see Appendix B).

28. What I am calling "tempo," here, corresponds to the technical term *laya*, which refers to the surface pace of the music—the overall impression given by the entire ensemble of whether it has a hurried pace or a relaxed one (sometimes *irâmå* is used loosely in this sense). "*Irâmå* level," on the other hand, refers to the degree of expansion or contraction of the gong cycle. A gong cycle that takes roughly two minutes in one *irâmå* might take one, four, or eight minutes in another (the expansions or contractions are related to each other by factors of two). For each *irâmå* there are characteristic treatments—ways of working out specific parts by the various instruments and voices. The most obvious difference between these treatments is the *laya*, or surface tempo. Here are the standard Solonese *irâmå*s with their most common tempo associations and numerical designations, going from the most contracted to the most expanded level:

½	*lancar*	fast
I	*tanggung*	moderate
II	*dados* [K]	slow
III	*wiled*	fast
IV	*rangkep*	very fast

For a more detailed explanation of *irâmå*, see Appendix B.

29. See Brinner 1989/1990 for when and why musicians insert *pathetan*s into a musical sequence.

(*rangkep*), and then changing back to a moderately fast third *irâmâ* level by accelerating briskly or by slowing slightly

(segue to pieces with increasingly smaller gong cycles, which may include *palarans*)

suwuk (end)—usually slowing down for final gong (in pieces with a small gong cycle, tempo increases before slowing; sometimes, however, it gets faster and faster right up to the end [*suwuk gropak* (snapping off)])

(*pathetan*—unmetered, leisurely pace)

All of this is by way of introducing the following excerpt, in which Suhartå explains why a certain singer did not win a competition, even though her voice was clear (*bening* [I,J]) as well as even from top to bottom (*antal* [J]), and her pronunciation was well articulated (*wijang* [J]):

> I don't know why she didn't win. Well, the most obvious thing was that she "filled in" too much. Every *gåtrå* [four-beat unit] was filled in. In the odd-numbered *gåtrås*, there were *abon-abon* [optional fillers]; in the even ones there were the [obligatory] *wangsalans* [verse couplets]—every nook and cranny was filled in. And that had an impact on the distinctness [*kejiwaan*] of the *mérong*: it was too *prenès* [coquettish], too *trègèl* [vivacious], the *céngkoks* [melodic phrases] were too fancy. The old folks don't like that, see. According to Javanese philosophy, when you're born, your life doesn't yet have many twists and turns. It's still plain, still simple. But when you're approaching adulthood, you start fooling around with women, you're introduced to worldly pleasures, then your life is full of twists and turns. And in the shift from the simple movements [of youth] to the beginnings of adulthood—that is, from the *mérong* [first section] to the *wiled* [second section]—the tempo's going to get a bit faster there. Perhaps people are like that, too. Later, when one is about to die, the same thing happens: when people are about to die, they revive briefly first, then they die—it's like right before the *suwuk* [ending]. That's what the old folks used to say. That's the way it's done in a *klenéngan* ["concert"]. (Suhartå, August 7, 1991)

Such comparisons between the unfolding of *gendhings* and the unfolding of human life are common. The main point here, though, is that the *mérong* of even a lighthearted *gendhing* is calm, and so it is out of character to put in too many of the optional *abon-abons*. Suhartå often told me that one should also avoid excessive ornamentation in the *mérong*, and stick, rather, to simple melodic patterns. Ideally, if there are several *pesindhèns*, the most *luruh* ("humble," calm, refined) among them will sing the *mérong*, leaving the livelier *inggah* to a more *trègèl* singer. The slow vibrato, straightforward nature, and relatively unadorned singing style of the *luruh* singer are ideally suited for calm pieces.

The singing of *båwås* also has its own genre-specific *leléwå* (nature, performance style). A *båwå* is an extended solo vocal introduction that replaces the *bukå* (introduction) of a *gendhing*. It was originally always sung by a male vocalist, but now it is sometimes sung by a *pesindhèn*.[30] There are characteristic *céngkoks* (melodic contours), which are set; and *wiledans* (minor melodic variations), which are less so, as we have seen. My teachers' teachers, who are now deceased, felt very strongly that *båwå* singing should be "manly" (*gagah* [I,JI]) and therefore should not be too ornate, nor should it use *wiledans* that are associated with *pesindhèns*. They also complained (some more than others) that nowadays there are no singers who sing *båwås* in a proper *båwå* style.

As a result, Suhartå, even though he had never heard what a "proper" *båwå* singer should sound like, did his best to maintain some aspects of the defunct style, which he tried to imagine from the comments of his teachers.[31] He was most concerned about eliminating certain melodic turns, which were, in his mind, too feminine. Many of the well-known *båwå* singers use these, including the two most popular and influential singers of all. They know that they are sometimes criticized for sounding too much like *pesindhèns* but deny that they are doing anything contrary to tradition (Waridi 2005:378–81). Suhartå decries this tendency and blames it on the amount of time these male singers spend teaching *pesindhèns*, to the point that they are *kemasukan suara sindhèn* ("possessed," or influenced, by the *sindhèn* style of voice). Here is the *wiledan* (in *pélog*) that Suhartå complained about most often, followed by acceptable versions:

sindhénan: 2 ^^1 6̣
båwå: 2 ^^1 6̣
båwå: 2 1 ^6̣

Another example (also in *pélog*):

sindhénan: 7 6 ^5 3 2
båwå: 7 6 5 ^3 2

Both of the above have to do entirely with the placement and timing of the ornaments (the differences may seem minuscule, but to Suhartå the examples are worlds apart). There is one ornament, however, which he never finds appropriate for a *båwå* (again, in *pélog*), no matter what the timing: 5 ^^6 (as opposed to 5 ^ 6).

30. This is nearly always the case in all-female groups, but it also may happen whenever a *båwå sekar måcåpat* (a *båwå* with a text in modern literary Javanese that uses one of the *måcåpat* meters) introduces a newer composition.

31. In fact, he was sorely disappointed when I played him some pre-Independence recordings, on which the *båwå* singing was just as ornate as that heard nowadays (some of it even more so). Either the commonly held perception that singing styles have gone from simple to complex is inaccurate, or the recordings were not early enough, or else they were simply aberrant.

As a rule, these *sindhèn wiledans* give the *båwå* an attention-seeking coquettishness that Suhartå calls *manja* [I]—"spoiled" (in the sense of "pampered").[32] Since *mbawani* (to sing in a *båwå*-like manner) can also mean "to rule,"[33] he feels that anything coy or effeminate is distinctly out of place in *båwå* singing. He often said that a *båwå* singer needs to be *berwibawa* [I] (to exude masculine authority), or needs to have *wibåwå*[J] (prepotency). Someone who is *berwibawa* has the power to control people, not through threats or force, nor through coquettish allure, but through his commanding presence:

> Whenever someone sings a *båwå*, his *wibawa* usually affects all of his surroundings: everyone gets quiet and listens. He has to show that his is a male voice, he has to appear manly. That's how *båwå*s are. That's why, now that there are women *båwå* singers, it's really hard for us to teach them. That's what I think, anyway. All you can do is give them masculine-sounding *céngkok*s [melodic patterns] and hope for the best. Well, there might be the odd woman who can do it, whose voice can *berwibawa*. But they're really rare. And they're even rarer if they know how to sing *sindhèn*. [In that case,] if they are asked to sing in a *båwå*-like way, it's too late, they're going to have real trouble. Real trouble. There are bound to be at least some bits that are *sindhèn*-like. Without their realizing it, there are going to be two or three *sindhèn* ornaments that slip in. (Suhartå, December 14, 1990)

Båwå style, then, needs to be carefully distinguished from *sindhèn* style, even if there is disagreement on how completely.[34] But it must also be kept separate from the styles used for other vocal genres like *gérong, mắcåpat, suluk* (*pathetan, sendhon, ådå-ådå*), and *palaran*.[35] It uses more ornamentation than both *gérong* and *måcåpat* and hence is delivered more slowly and melismatically than both (on the other hand, *måcåpat* poetry needs to be pronounced more carefully, since the text is paramount). If a *båwå* is delivered *too* slowly, like a *pathetan*, it loses its *greged* ("oomph"), and so is also not *mbawani* (characteristic).[36] A *båwå* singer should not use as "heavy" a voice as that used by a *dhalang* for *suluk*s (of which *ådå-ådå*s require the "heaviest" voice), but his voice should not be as light

32. See chapter 7, footnotes 32 and 33 for more on the word *manja*.

33. The three meanings of *mbawani*—to be characteristic of a *båwå*," "to begin," and "to rule"—can be linked through its Sanskrit etymon, *bhava* (existence, manner, condition—Gonda 1973:468, 470, 494).

34. See Waridi 2005:379–81 for an interesting critique of the position I have just put forth.

35. *Gérong*: unison male chorus that is part of the gamelan ensemble; *måcåpat*: unaccompanied sung recitation of poetry; *suluk*: *dhalang*'s mood song; *pathetan*: a kind of *suluk* for calm moods; *sendhon*: a kind of *suluk* often used for sad moods; *ådå-ådå*: a kind of *suluk* often used for tense situations; *dhalang*: puppeteer; *palaran*: solo singing based on *måcåpat* accompanied by a reduced gamelan ensemble.

36. When a *båwå* is sung in a *santiswaran/larasmadyå* ensemble, however, it is usual for it to be very slow, especially coming up to the "gong," since the *gendhing* begins in what is considered to be *iråmå wiled* (Suhartå, April 1, 1991).

as when he is singing *gérong*.[37] *Båwå* singing, though masculine, should still be *luwes* (flowing, graceful) and *lunyu* [J] ("slippery," agile, fluent) Some singers interject an inappropriate *kau* [J] (awkward, ungainly) quality, which is perfectly acceptable, however, when singing *palaran* for a *gagah* (manly) character in *wayang wong*.

The point of this chapter has been to show how essential *rasa* is—in all its forms—to being a good musician. Ironically, even though a gamelan competition is the one place where evaluation of performance is the most pointedly discussed, it is also the one place where true musicianship, which is characterized by flexibility in performance, is unnecessary. Supanggah once lamented to me that it is entirely possible to win a competition simply by rehearsing long and hard with a good leader. That is, mediocre musicians who turn out a polished performance can score higher than excellent musicians who happen to play sloppily that one time, or who go against the court-influenced standards of the judges. Both performances might be *garap*ed (worked out), but in the one case the corresponding noun is *garap* as a finished product; in the other it is *garap* as process, of musicians adjusting to each other and to the situation. The difference between the two is one of knowledge, of sensibility, of intuition. It is a difference, that is, in the amount of *rasa*.

37. My principal source for this criterion is Darsono of STSI, with whom I studied singing in the summer of 1986. This notion of a "heavy" voice has been one of the hardest for me to grasp. It has something to do with difficulty of voice production—especially in the high range (it is thus associated with a low tessitura and, often, a lack of agility); but it also has to do with the force (*tekanan*) with which the melody is delivered. This last point is related to how deliberate (*tegas*) the pronunciation is, and whether the notes are held out at the ends of phrases. My teachers' timbres changed when they demonstrated "heavy" and "light" voices (from a "dark" voice to a "light" one), yet this was only a small part of the conceptual package. For one thing, the seriousness associated with a "heavy" piece may also enter into the picture. This observation, in a way, is circular. Perhaps a better way of putting it is that the conceptions of "heavy" voices and "heavy" pieces overlap and intertwine. "Heaviness" in singing, as I understand it, can best be summed up by the *impression of conviction* (as opposed to ease, prettiness, frivolity, insouciance, or lethargy) in a singer's delivery. To hear the difference between a *dhalang* (puppeteer) and a *gérong* singer performing the same *suluk*, or puppeteer's song, listen to *Gamelan de Solo* (CD 2, track 2; CD 4, track 10).

Compare II:2, 27:44 to IV:10

SIX

THE COMMUNICATION OF *RASA*, PART I

General Considerations of Expression and Perception

RASA AS EXPRESSION

Much has been said about the transparency of traditional musicians' egos in Java.[1] In keeping with prevalent theories of orality, composers, for instance, have often been presented as usually anonymous, not striving primarily for originality, and exerting little control over the final product. These observations may have been fairly accurate at one time, but they appear to be less and less so.[2] Attitudes towards performers seem to have remained more stable: musicians and dancers should be vehicles for the tradition rather than stars,[3] and they should bring out the emotional content of the piece or choreography rather than let their own personalities show through. Hughes-Freeland (1997b:485), summarizing Suryobrongto's aesthetic theories (1970, 1981), put it this way: "The dancer does not reach out to the audience ex-pressively but achieves 'expression' by an inward focus which might be described as in-pression. Rather than responding to the willed and communicative presence of the dancer's intentions, the audience is caught up in the mood of the event..." When watching the best Javanese dancers, then, one is scarcely aware of a person behind the body (this is what I meant by "transparency," above). And just as dancers "become" (*menjiwai*) the characters they portray, musicians "become" the pieces they play.

1. J. Becker 1980, 1994; Holt 1967:102, 164; Hughes-Freeland 1997a; Sutton 1993:167; Keeler 1987:198–201; Suryobrongto 1981.

2. See chapter 1. J. Becker 1980 is a thoughtful treatment of the beginnings of this shift. Rustopo 1991 discusses its continuation. Sutton 1993 discusses three categories of compositional process: traditional, innovative, and experimental. See also Mack 2004.

3. This phrase is merely a convenient shorthand. There is probably nothing as reified or as unified as The Tradition in the minds of Javanese musicians and dancers. What is clear is that good performers do not show off. Even showing too much self-confidence (*gendhung*) is considered unacceptable for musicians; it is necessary, though, for *dhalang*s, and to some extent for dancers. This difference reflects differences in social status as well as how exposed a single performer is to public scrutiny.

One can, of course, overdo these generalizations. As seen in chapter 5, originality and creativity of a sort are highly prized in Java, and probably have been for some time (for example, specific *wiledan*s [variants] are often identified with a single performer). Moreover, the reality is often different from the stated ideal: *pesindhèn*s, at least, are often now seen as stars (Sutton 1984 and 1989, Walton 1996). Many times over, Suhartå complained that when certain singers performed, it wasn't the piece that "came out," but their respective personalities. Even if self-expression should not be the goal of music making, a form of self-expression nevertheless may occur in practice.

Throughout the book I have spoken of "expressing" *rasa*. This is not so much a word-for-word translation from Indonesian or Javanese as it is an approximation of something conveyed through synonyms for *rasa*. Musicians do sometimes use transitive verbs, with *rasa* as a complement, that could be translated as "express": *menggambarkan* [I] (to represent), *memancarkan* [I] (to broadcast, to radiate), *menimbulkan* [I] (to give rise to, to bring to the surface), *mujudaken* [K] (to materialize, to realize), and *menafsir* [I] (to interpret). More commonly, though, this is made clear without the word *rasa*, or without a transitive verb governing it. Often the verb is linked to the word *gendhing*: *menghayati* [I] (to assimilate, comprehend), *menjiwai* (to become the spirit of), *kasarirå* (to become one with), *keluar* (come out). Or else *rasa* is used with *cocog* [J,I], *sesuai* [I], or *mungguh* [J] (suitable). In all of these cases, what is being "expressed" is *rasa gendhing*, and the way it is expressed is through a performance that brings out the true nature of the piece.

Nevertheless, the word "expressing" here may be somewhat misleading. In Western music—since the nineteenth century, at least—expression is associated with the communication of emotion, with revealing one's inner feelings, or with imprinting the music with one's personal stamp. Yet Suzanne Langer (inter alia) has argued persuasively that, even in the West, artistic expression is not *self*-expression:

> Now, I believe the expression of feeling in a work of art—the function that makes the work an expressive form—is not symptomatic at all. An artist working on a tragedy need not be in personal despair or violent upheaval; nobody, indeed, could work in such a state of mind. His mind would be occupied with the causes of his emotional upset. Self-expression does not require composition and lucidity; a screaming baby gives his feeling far more release than any musician, but we don't go into a concert hall to hear a baby scream; in fact, if that baby is brought in we are likely to go out. We don't want self-expression.
>
> A work of art presents feeling (in the broad sense I mentioned before, as everything that can be felt) for our contemplation, making it visible or audible or in some way perceivable through a symbol, not inferable from a symptom. . . . What is artistically good is whatever articulates and presents feeling to our understanding. (1957:25)

I suspect that Javanese musicians would, in the main, agree with Langer (in fact, she is the Western philosopher of art who is perhaps most often quoted by Javanese academics). But I am hesitant to propose a theory of expression in Javanese musical aesthetics, for I doubt there is a unitary theory to be had. Nevertheless, when Javanese musicians speak about musical expression, they seem to operate under certain assumptions: (1) a piece of music possesses a character (*rasa, watak, jiwa*) or characters; (2) a musical performance also possesses a character; (3) a sensitive listener will experience or feel the character of a performance; (4) the character of the performance may or may not be in keeping with the character of the piece, and so the performers may or may not succeed in exemplifying the character of the piece, or in creating the proper *rasa* in the listener.

When comparing these assumptions to European theories of musical expression, one finds a great deal of resemblance to the predominant eighteenth-century view, the so-called doctrine of the affections.[4] Dahlhaus denies that this has to do with expression (1985 [1977]:21), but I think he is too restrictive in his use of the word, since eighteenth-century authors themselves used *expression* (or *Ausdruck*) in writing about the affections.

Anglophone philosophers of music associate the "doctrine of the affections" with what they call the "arousal theory" of musical emotion. I do not want to get enmired in a discussion of whether music in Java is thought of as arousing emotions in the listener, expressing the psychological states of the composer, representing the form of emotions, conventionally signifying emotions, or somehow literally having emotional states.[5] I suspect all of these apply to some degree. But I do owe the reader at least a working definition of *expression* as I intend it to be understood in this context.

The broad definition I propose is as follows:

> To express the content of a piece means to play or sing with an understanding of that content, and in such a way as to make it audible to a knowledgeable listener.

What I mean by "content" here is none other than *rasa*. Most often, for Javanese musicians, *rasa* in the sense of "musical content" is a mood or affect. But it may

4. I am using "eighteenth century" loosely. Authors spoke of the affections in similar ways from the seventeenth century till the latter part of the eighteenth century. Dahlhaus places the shift to a more subjective theory of musical emotion in the Sturm und Drang period (around the 1770s) (1985 [1977]:21). The "doctrine of the affections" is "so-called" because it is now generally held that there was no "doctrine" as such. That is, there was considerable divergence in what authors of the time said the principal affections were and how these were expressed.

5. British and North American philosophers of music seem quite happy to debate this question endlessly. For some time, nearly every issue of the *British Journal of Aesthetics* or the *Journal of Aesthetics and Art Criticism* seemed to have at least one article on the subject. For a succinct description of these various positions, see Peter Kivy's article on aesthetics in *The New Harvard Dictionary of Music.*

be something more abstract than that (a melodic essence, for instance); or it may be more effable (such as the meaning of a *gendhing*'s title). Because the content is primarily an emotion, expressing a *rasa* involves both understanding and feeling, as does *rasa* itself (cf. the last sentence of the Langer quote, above). The kind of understanding I have in mind is mostly an intuitive sense of what the piece is "about," although in some cases this sense may be acquired more deliberately, more self-consciously (in a lesson, for instance, or through conversation). This understanding need not be detached; it is summed up well in the locutions *menjiwai* [I] (to become one with the soul of), *kecekel* [I] (fully grasped), *kasarirå* [K] (to take on the body of), *menghayati* [I] (to assimilate, integrate into oneself).

From this brief theoretical introduction I would like to move quickly to excerpts from two conversations that explore these issues (among others) in a more concrete, grounded way.

A CONVERSATION WITH SUPANGGAH

I will begin with a long discussion I had with Supanggah and Waridi, here reconstructed in its near entirety (the first part, having to do with Supanggah's biography, is omitted). In this conversation, held at Supanggah's home on June 6, 1992, near the end of my stay in Java, Supanggah covered many important points: the ontology of *rasa*, how it is perceived, and how it is expressed.

Since Supanggah is a very close friend, I could never quite bring myself to show up at his house with a tape recorder to interview him formally (alas!). The following, then, is presented just as I recopied it in my fieldnotes upon my return from his home. I have left it in its original form, with only a very few grammatical corrections for clarity's sake. At the end of the conversation you will find a note I made to myself at the time, as an afterthought. Here is the rest of that afterthought, which I present as a brief preface in the hopes that it may clarify some of the subtext in what follows:

> There was some confusion in our discussion, which I think stemmed from a difference in what we meant by a *gendhing*: for him it was a single performance of a *gendhing*, whereas for me it was a separate, abstract entity. (Even assuming that a *gendhing* only exists in performance, I don't see why it couldn't be thought of as an imagined, ideal performance—but perhaps that would be too rigid and limiting—ideal in what circumstances?)

The original conversation was in Indonesian with occasional sprinklings of Javanese, but much of what I wrote down was in English, with key terms left in the original.[6] Recent editorial additions are enclosed in curly brackets {} to distinguish from the original square brackets. All footnotes have been added to the original text. Parts of the conversation appear in other chapters, but I repeat them here to return them to their original context, and to give a better picture of the entire exchange. What is lost in concision is made up for, I hope, in integrity. (*M* stands for Marc Benamou, *P* for Supanggah, and *W* for Waridi.)

M: Is there such a thing as a *balungan*[7] that's *sedhih* {sad} in itself?

P: Interpreting a *balungan* as *sedhih* has a lot to do with what is traditionally thought of as *sedhih*, and depends a lot on the background of the person. {That is,} a *balungan* can actually have many different *rasa*s if the *pengrawit* {gamelan musician} has a lot of experience and can see beyond ordinary conventions. How much you can get away with straying from convention depends a lot on who you are. If I *nggarap* {arrange} a *gendhing* in an unconventional way, everyone remarks on how *pinter* {clever} I am. If one of my students does exactly the same thing, everyone is outraged.

So, a *gendhing* really can have many different *rasa*s [depending on how much experience and imagination the performers have].

M: But old people, like Pak Mloyo, speak of a given *gendhing* as having a definite *rasa*, and if you *nggarap* it in a different way it's just plain wrong.

6. I never made a conscious decision to take fieldnotes mostly in English rather than uniquely in the original language: it was entirely a matter of expediency. My sense is that this is a common procedure: all of the fieldnotes that have been excerpted in articles and books written by English-speaking ethnographers seem to have been taken in English. Geertz took his fieldnotes in English and included many excerpts in his first monograph, *The Religion of Java*. He has been criticized by Tedlock for including his English paraphrases and presenting them in indirect discourse, indented, in small print (1995:277–78). I have unwittingly followed Tedlock's suggestion of using direct discourse. What I have not done, however, is to recreate the dialogue as it might have occurred, based on whatever notes I had, months or years later.

7. The *balungan* can be defined as a kind of outline melody that performers refer to in deriving their parts or, to put it another way, as a notated melody in a collection of *gendhings*. For the most thorough treatment to date of just what the *balungan* is and how it relates to the other parts, see Perlman 2004, p. 38 and chapters 3 to 7 (see also Sumarsam 1984 [1975], Ishida 2008, and Supanggah 2009). There is no need to enter the debate about whether the *balungan* is actually heard or is merely thought/felt by the musicians; or whether it is an abstraction formed by reducing the many instrumental and vocal parts of the gamelan to a single melody, or rather a preexisting "cantus firmus" (to use Kunst's now antiquated term) from which all other parts can be derived. For our purposes, the *balungan* is the only instrumental melody that is normally written down, when notation is used to perform from (and nowadays it very often is). It is a middle-density part, the only one in the entire gamelan ensemble, besides the *gérongan* (male chorus part), that is performed in unison by more than one musician. The *saron*s (metallophones with trough resonator) and the *slenthem* (low-pitched metallophone with tube resonators), with some exceptions, play this melody as it is written, although they are limited to one octave, whereas the *balungan* has a total possible range of over two octaves. The *bonang* (two-octave set of pot-gongs) at times follows it quite closely, at others less so. The other melodic parts may stray fairly far from the notated *balungan* but usually match it at the midpoints and ends of phrases. Musicians on these parts very often figure out or remember what to play or sing by looking at the *balungan* and by using their knowledge both of the melodic idiom peculiar to their respective instrumental or vocal parts and of the accepted interpretations of the piece in question.

P: *Yang tua-tua tidak konsistèn* {*konsekuèn*?} {The older musicians are hypocritical}. In the Kepatihan era, the generation of Pak Mloyo's teachers—*they* were the ones who *merusak*ed {ruined} the tradition, who started doing all sorts of things with *garap* (such as using piano and forte)...

A given *balungan* can be interpreted in different (traditional) ways, depending on which *gendhing* you refer to.[8] The more {musical} references a musician has, the more choices he has of bringing out different *rasa*s. The *rasa* of a *gendhing* depends on the sum of all the simultaneous interpretations of the musicians. Usually they will refer to different *gendhing*s at the same time.

M: But what if people agree on what *gendhing* to refer to—won't a dominant *rasa* then clearly result?

P: This almost never happens in actual practice. What's more, having different interpretations at the same time is not only not bad, but it's what makes *karawitan* exciting: you never know what it's going to sound like. Also, each musician will adjust his interpretation based on what the others are doing. So you can't really say that a given *rebaban*, for instance, will produce *rasa x*—it depends also on what else is going on.

M: Can you give an example of a *balungan* that can be interpreted in different ways?

P: An example that occurs frequently, especially coming up to gong, is:

. . 1 . 1 1 2 3 6 5 3 2 . 1 2 6̣

{two possible interpretations on *rebab* (in *sléndro*?):}

rebaban A:	.	1	1	.	1 2	1 2	2 3	3
rebaban B:					2	3	5	6 .1̇
balungan:	.	.	1	.	1	1	2	1

A:	. 2	1 2	2 3 2	2	. 2	1 .6̣	2 1	6̣
B:	1̇2̇ 1̇2̇	2̇1̇6563.	2 1	123 2	. 2	1 6̣	2 1	6̣
bl:	6	5	3	2	.	1	2	6̣

The two have very different *rasa*s. They're both *sigrak* {energetic, agile}, but the second one is more *sigrak* than the first. It's difficult, however, to assign a specific *rasa* to each (it's easier to compare them).

What one person hears is not the same as what the next hears. It's just like when we were eating shrimp cooked with *tapé* {fermented glutinous rice}: what I tasted, and what Mas Alan tasted,[9] and what you tasted were all slightly different (i.e., our

8. When a musician learning a new piece falters, the group leader often yells out the name of a well-known piece that has a similar or identical passage, leaving it up to the learner to plug in a standard interpretation for that passage. Musicians make this kind of musical comparison all the time, whether there is a teacher around or not. It is at the heart of the learning process, but is retained in the conceptualizations of mature musicians—it is what allows one to interpret an unfamiliar piece. (See Perlman 1994, Brinner 1995, and Sutton 1993.) This kind of thinking is pervasive. It is evident, for instance, in the analogical organization of Mloyowidodo's now standard collection of *gendhing* notation: pieces with similar *balungan*s are generally placed in proximity to each other.

9. Alan Feinstein, Supanggah, and I had recently eaten in a Chinese restaurant together, where this dish, which none of us had ever tasted, was served.

perceptions were different). So that *rasa*, even from the perceiving end has a large subjective (i.e., individual) component.

M: But there are certain things that everyone seems to agree on. For example, that

III:1

Laler Mengeng is *sedhih* {sad}.

P: A lot of people say that a piece is *sedhih* without actually being able to realize that *rasa* {in performance}. [That is, to a certain extent they're just repeating things that they've heard.] For example, if the group from Gombang [Pak Mujoko's group] or Nartosabdho's group play *Laler Mengeng*, there's no way it will sound *sedhih*, even though they may *say* that it's *sedhih*, and they're all trying to make it sound *sedhih* (at least theoretically). But what people say doesn't always match up with reality (*kenyataan*). In a dramatic context, such as *wayang kulit* or *kethoprak* {vernacular theater with gamelan music}, it's much clearer what *rasa* a *gendhing* needs to have, and so there's a greater chance that musicians' interpretations will be similar.
One thing that's clear, though, musicians' vocabulary [of *garap*, of *gendhings*, of different *rasas*?] is not as *kaya* {rich} as in former times. Nowadays, everything is made to have the same *rasa*, everything is *diclèlèkké* {done for effect (?)}.

M: Is that the same thing as *diclumètké* {trivialized (?)}?

P: It's almost the same.

M: So is the situation like *wayang*, where nowadays a *wayang* has to be funny from beginning to end?

P: Yes. It used to be that humor in *wayang* had its place: *Limbukan* and the *Pånåkawan* scenes.[10] But now all sorts of characters are made to be funny. For example,... {?}, even Werkudårå.[11] Now everything is meant as a *hiburan* {entertainment}—there's no deeper meaning. The *kendhangan* {drum part} for *Pangkur* and for *ladrang Tlutur* are played exactly the same.

Pangkur III:4; *Tlutur* III:1, 7:52–14:49

W: If a singer like {X} sings *Laler Mengeng*, it doesn't sound *sedhih* at all.

P: *Minir, tapi minir tidak sedhih* {"minor" [i.e., *pélog* tuning mixed into a *sléndro* piece], but a "minor" that's not sad}. Yes, it's true that *gendhing punya watak* {*gendhings* have personalities}, but various *gendhings* have been given *predikats* {designations} over the years and these *tidak cocok lagi* {no longer fit} [with the way they're performed today].

Laler Mengeng III:1, 00:00–7:52

W: When asking for examples of *gendhings* that have a certain *rasa*, if someone answers with a *gendhing* whose title indicates the *rasa* (such as *ladrang Tlutur*, which, incidentally, isn't particularly sad musically {*tlutur* means "sad"}), that might be an indication that he or she is just mouthing words. That is, it's too easy just to pick a *gendhing* by its title.

P: What saddens me is that *gendhings*, *yang begitu kaya dengan rasa yang berbeda, warna yang berbeda* {which are so richly varied with respect to *rasa*, to color}, nowadays are reduced to a single color (to push things a little). The *pelopor* {pioneer} in the change to a monochromatic situation was Nartosabdho.

W: ...*gérong rinenggå* {*gérong* parts that are "decorated" or recomposed}...

10. *Limbukan* is a female clown scene that normally occurs during the first "act" of a shadow play, no matter what the story is, and features the character Limbuk and her mother. The *Pånåkawan* are a family of male clowns who also appear in every story.

11. Werkudårå, also known as Bimå, Bråtåsénå, and Bayusutå, is the second oldest of the five Pandhåwå brothers, the principal heroes of the *Mahabharata*. He is an imposing personage, brusque, straightforward; a man of few words and, when needed, of Herculean action.

P: . . . He was the first to play around with the [traditional] *rasa* of a *gendhing* (*Subakaståwå*, for instance). And his ability to change the *rasa* of *gendhings* just goes to show how much the *rasa* of a *gendhing* depends on the *garap*. Nartosabdho's *bedhayan*[12] is carefree and easy—different from the Kraton *bedhayan* songs which are . . . eerie (*énak sekali—béda dengan bedhayan Kraton yang . . . wingit*). III:2 Compare II:1 and IV:4

W: . . . *regu* {stately} . . .

P: Nartosabdho's *bedhayan* ends up being "sweet" (*jadi manis*).

W: Perhaps Nartosabdho's (and Mujoko's) efforts to develop *karawitan* the way they did stemmed from an effort to make their performances *semuwå* {[J] all decked out}.

M: *Semuwå*?

W: *Regeng* {bustling}, *besar* {[J] festive}, *semarak* {[I] glittering}. This shows up in their *iringan* {musical accompaniment}, in the *banyolan* {joking}, etc.

M: When I watched a Mujoko *wayang*, even though the musicians were really talented, I would just crave at least one piece that wasn't à la Nartosabdho, that used ordinary gérong.

P: And he {Mujoko} was extraordinarily talented [and even so . . .]! Well, so was Nartosabdho extraordinarily talented.

W: Pak Marto's *sindhénan* was full of different variants. Just for *sèlèh* {finalis} 3, say, he had many different *céngkoks* {melodic patterns, distinctive melodic contours}. Nowadays singers really only use one, basically—*paling, ditambah gregel, dilak-luk* {at best, they add small ornaments, they embellish the contour}. Pak Marto, being a real musician, and knowing about *gendhing* and *garap*, could make up different *céngkoks*. Singers now just imitate what they've heard; at most they *memperluas gregel dan luk* {broaden the scope of the ornamentation}.

P: People might *say*, for instance, that *Kombang Mårå* is . . . *wingit* {eerie, supernatural, awe-inspiring}. I:1

When I write a composition, I never know how it's going to turn out. Sometimes I'm shooting for a particular *rasa*, but then when the piece is actually played, I'm disappointed. (Therefore, even if you're trying to produce a certain *rasa*, it's not certain that that's what's coming out.)

[About the time I started asking about different *rasas* for the same *balungan*, or a *balungan* that's *sedhih* just by itself, Mas Panggah {Supanggah} started to get annoyed. At first I thought it was because he didn't like my trying to codify something that was not only subjective, but also very flexible according to the situation. This may have been partly true, but it turned out that he was upset mostly about the current state of *karawitan*, and the fact that, although everyone keeps using these terms for different *rasas*, no one seems to be able to bring them out {in performance} any more.]

A CONVERSATION WITH WIGNYOSAPUTRO

In my very first meeting with Wignyosaputro (just two days after the preceding one with Supanggah and Waridi), he went straight to the heart of the matter,

12. *Bedhayan* means "in the style of *bedhåyå* (sacred courtly choreographed dance) accompaniment": unison or octave choral music with long, flowing melodies.

laying out the parameters within which any discussion of *rasa gendhing* must lie. Many of the same themes that came up in my conversation with Supanggah and Waridi recur here: the relativity of perception, the impossibility of denoting *rasa* precisely with terms, the importance of *garap* in determining the *rasa* of a *gendhing*.

The following is transcribed from a tape. I have cleaned up the dialogue only slightly, abridging here and there, for the sake of readability. (A detailed transcription of the original Indonesian and Javanese is given in Benamou 1998b, Appendix D.) Portions have appeared in previous chapters, but I will repeat them here, recontextualized, in a slightly different translation. The third participant is Suhartå, who had led me through the old, narrow lanes to Wignyosaputro's patrician house and had introduced me to him. Suhartå was only intermittently present: part of the time he chose to sit outside, perhaps so as not to interfere (*H* = Suhartå, *M* = Marc, *W* = Wignyosaputro).

M: . . . I'm also interested in researching the categories of *gendhings* from the point of view of *rasa*. [. . .]

W: Well, if it's *rasa gendhing* you're after . . . It seems to me that *rasa* in music—in Javanese music, in *gendhing*—is relative: it depends on *who* the perceiver is (*siapa yang merasakan*). I'll give you an example: think of *rasa* in the physical sense—not as it relates to sound, right?—we're talking chilies, here. Everyone says that chilies are hot, right? But you have to take into account the kind of chili and who is doing the tasting (*siapa merasakan*). One person's *rasa* is going to be different from another's, right?

M: M-hm.

W: There's a Javanese saying, "Idumu dudu iduku" (your saliva is not my saliva). It continues, "lèmbéhanmu dudu lèmbéhanku" (your gait is not my gait). There you have it! So when it comes to *rasa gendhing*, you have to ask *how* the piece sounds, *who* the listener is (*siapa yang merasakan*), and *what* apparatus (*alat*) is doing the perceiving (for the *rasa* of food this is the tongue, right? but for *rasa gendhing* it's the vibrations here [the heart?]—from the ear to the vibrations here). Next, who the composer is, and in what circumstances the *gendhing* was created.

That's if you ask me.

Now, let's take, say, *gendhing Laler Mengeng*: it's just like chilies. Everyone says that chilies are hot; and people (at least musicians) say that *Laler Mengeng* is *trenyuh*—sad. Right?

M: Right.

III:1 W: But can the sadness—the *rasa*—of *gendhing Laler Mengeng* be felt (*dirasakan*) without a medium (*alat bantu*) through which to perceive (*merasakan*) it? What if
6/1 *Laler Mengeng* were played *bonangan*[13] style? *Laler Mengeng* without *gendèr*, without *rebab*, or—even more to the point—without vocals: there would be no sadness in that! And yet everyone says that *Laler Mengeng* is sad, touching, etc. So, it's like I was

13. *Bonangan* here means in the style of pieces, called *gendhing bonang*, in which the *bonang* (two-octave gong chime) is the main elaborating instrument.

saying: *who* is doing the perceiving (*siapa yang merasakan*), and *how* are they perceiving?

And that, in a nutshell, is *rasa gendhing*.

M: So, what you're saying is that it depends on a variety of factors.

W: Yes!

M: But aside from that, can *gendhings* be categorized according to *rasa*, [...] or can't they?

W: On the surface, yes, they can.

M: Like what you were saying about chilies being hot.

W: Yes! [...] For instance, *Laler Mengeng* is sad. *Pangkur* is *bérag* (exuberant), *prenès* (flirtatious). But there are versions of *Pangkur* that are not *prenès*. It depends on the *pathet* (melodic mode)... on the *laras* (tuning system: *sléndro* or *pélog*) and the *pathet*. And on the interpreters. [...] [And also on] the perceiver and the circumstances at the time it's being perceived. [...] Suppose I'm the one doing the perceiving, and *Laler Mengeng* is being performed with a complete ensemble—with *rebab* [and everything]—but everyone's drinking [alcohol]. We, as listeners, are going to feel, somehow, that the *rasa* isn't—the piece just isn't sad. [*Laughs*] As for categorizing pieces, [people do say things like], "this is sad (*sedhih*), this is happy (*gembira*), this is jocular (*gecul*), this is devotional (*khidmat*)," don't they. [...]

Pangkur III:4

W: The one category that's really difficult to perceive (*dirasakan*) is *anwibåwå* [imposing].

H: *Regu* (stately).

W: [...] It's like... the object of perception (*barang rasa*) is inaudible. It comes back to the same thing as before: how do you tell if it's regu? Well, it depends on the appreciator. [...]

W: Let's say I happen to be sad, and that I like to compose pieces. I create a piece. If the composer is able, at that moment, to really feel (*merasakan*) his sadness, and is able to pour it into the form of his creation... then, generally speaking, that piece's sadness is going to be felt (*dirasakan*) by the listener.[14] It's not just [for] one's inner self: it can extend outward. It's like pouring water into a glass—the water can overflow all around it.

M: So, what you're saying is that even though *gendhings* can be classified, there's no guaranteeing that on any particular occasion they will have their designated *rasas*.

W: Yes—[you have to look at] who's doing the enjoying. If it's the composer, then [it's transmitted] directly:... "This is sad." [He can say that] because he's the one doing the perceiving (*merasakan*). But can someone else feel what that person feels (*dirasakan*)? Not necessarily. [...]

M: Can all *gendhings* be given... designations [...] or are there ones that can't be categorized (ones for which there are no terms to describe their *rasa*)?

W: It *is* really hard to talk about *rasa*—but here goes. As I said, if [pieces] are put into categories—"this piece is sad, this is happy"—those categories are just pigeonholes. [??] "This one's sad, I'll put it here; this one's happy..." But when [the piece]

14. Note that this goes against the characterization of the traditional composer described at the beginning of the chapter.

is actually tasted (*dirasakan*), we have to ask who is doing the tasting. [It's like,] "Let me taste this sad one here. Oh! It's not sad! Wait, here's a happy one. Hey! How come it's not happy?" See? It depends on who the taster is! It's even more obvious if it's a non-musician—a layperson, in other words. In that case, there won't be any taste at all. [A musician might say,] "Ah, *Dhandhanggulå*—that's *regu* [solemn]"—there's no way a layperson's going to come up with that! [*Laughs*] Or: "*Megatruh* is full of pathos (*trenyuh*)." If the listener (*yang menikmati*) is a musician—but one who really understands (*merasakan*)—then it is possible [for him to taste the *rasa*]: "Let me pinch off a bit of this . . . hm, this is sad, [??], this is happy, this is stately, this is jocular . . ."

M: So, what's the process by which someone gains sensitivity to *rasa*? Is it that, when you're still a learner, you often hear people say "this is sad, this is jocular," or . . . I mean, if the layperson can't tell (*merasakan*), and yet musicians can, how do they learn?

W: Well, the way they learn is by interpreting and listening to a lot of different *gendhings*. Only then can they differentiate. Once, at RRI Surakarta,[15] they were having a *karawitan* competition—you know, like they do every year.

M: Yes.

W: Mas Hartå, here, is one of the judges. [*Laughs*] I used to be, too, but now I'm old and haven't been well, so I stopped judging in '85. Anyway, that particular time they explained that the elective piece had to be a *gendhing gecul* [humorous piece]. Well, some of the performers thought that *gecul* meant loud playing . . . with yells [from the *gérong*?] [. . .]—that's what the group thought. So, when the time came, they put it into practice . . . they were from the group Sekar Emas, from over there in Mojosongo. [. . .]

III:3 Good Lord, the way they banged away! The piece was *Gégot*.[16] And they thought that *gendhing gecul* just meant the *tabuhan*[17] [*Laughs*] . . . and not inner feeling, here! [*Points to heart?*] *Gecul* doesn't necessarily mean that the *balungan* [the notated melody—what the *sarons* play] will be *gecul*!

M: You mean . . .

W: I mean, they thought that it was the *balungan* that was *gecul*.

M: Oh.

W: But the *balungan* doesn't have any *rasa*. The *balungan* is just "oral" [*sic*?], I mean, it doesn't mean anything by itself.

M: And they had decided that it had to be played in a *gecul* way.

W: Yeah, that's right.

M: So, in the letters they [the organizers] sent out, they already said that—

W: Yeah, m-hm. Yeah, they were thinking, "Gee, there's never been a competition with *gecul* pieces before!" Let's see, there was *Cikar Bobrok* . . . *Gégot* . . . *Wahånå*—oh, it was the ones who did *Wahånå* who really blew it. That's because the *balungan* isn't *gecul*. Not in the

15. RRI stands for Radio Republik Indonesia. The Surakarta station has several gamelans and a large auditorium and used to sponsor competitions regularly.

16. The version on *Gamelan de Solo* (III:3), according to Supanggah, is not particularly *gecul*.

17. This word seems to mean, here, "way of striking the instruments." At times it refers to instruments struck with mallets; or to a playing technique; or, perhaps, to just the *balungan* instruments (or even, as here?, to the *balungan* itself).

least!—it's just a regular rhythm. But if you really know how to *nggarap* [interpret], then you can make it sound *gecul*!... But the *balungan* isn't like *Gégot*. [*Sings rapidly*:]

5 . 5 5 . 5 5 . 1 . 1 1 . 1 1 6/2
'é né né né né nå nå nå nå nå

It doesn't have anything like that. But they thought that that's what it meant to be gecul.

M: Oh... but actually, *gecul*ness really lies in the *garap*?

W: Yes. *Garapan råså*.[18] Yup. *Gendhing gecul* [is] *garapan råså*.... It's like... take *jinemans*[19]—some are *gecul*! [Like] *jineman Glathik Glindhing*: it's *gecul*—for those who can sense (*merasakan*) it, that is! So, you see, it depends on who the perceiver is (*siapa yang merasakan*). IV:8

M: M'hm. [*Chuckles*]

W: Mojosongo's rendition (*garapan*), to me, was nothing more than loud hammering! And there was no way they could win. Their crudeness really came out. [People said it was] *garapan kasar*.[20]... Take *gendhing Lambangsari*—to those who can sense it (*merasakan*), it's obviously *gecul*. Its *sindhèn* part is *gecul*. You know, *Lambangsari*. It has melodic patterns that are *gecul*.

M: So, [...] how do you know that? Because the *gendhing* has always been performed in a *gecul* way, or just by looking at the *balungan* you know that it should be made *gecul*?

W: Yes! I mean, you can tell a *gendhing* is *gecul* just by looking at the *balungan*. But you can tell from the vocal motives, too.... You can also tell happy *gendhings* just from the vocal parts. Take *ladrang Sigråmangsah*: if it's played plainly (*digarap lugu*) it's not going to sound happy!... Like, if you [sing? play?] it

2 . 3 3 2 7̣ 2 3 2 7̣ . 3 . 2 . 7̣ . 6̣ 6/3
ro né nå né né né né nå

—where's the happiness? "*Ro lu ro pi, lu ro pi nem*"[21] [2 3 2 7̣ 3 2 7 6] [There's no] happiness [in that!] But if you do it:

3 5 3 5 6 7 . . 2̇ 3̇ 2̇ 5 6 7
du- a du- a lo- lo lo- lo- o lo- o- ing[22]

18. This could be translated one of three ways. I think Wignyo meant only one of them (probably the second or third one). The first is "the exercise of sensibility." The second is "a *garapan* (interpretation) based on *råså*." The third is "the working out of the *råså*."

19. Short, light, metrical songs for solo *pesindhèn*, who is usually accompanied by a *gamelan gadhon* ("chamber" gamelan). (This is one of the few genres in which the instruments can truly be said to accompany the singer.)

20. This expression, "crude playing," is precisely the way Mloyowidodo described to me the playing of drunken musicians (March 11, 1992).

21. These are used as solfège syllables, although they are simply shortened forms of Javanese cardinal numbers (*ro* = 2, *lu* = 3, *nem* = 6, *pi* = 7). The *né* and *nå* in the preceding example are vocables with vowels that vaguely indicate pitch height (with higher vowels standing for higher pitches).

22. This text belongs to the category of *senggakan*, or lively vocal interjections, some of which carry a clear message, some of which are more obscure, and others of which border on nonsense. This one, it is said, makes fun of the way Chinese-language speakers pronounce Indonesian and Javanese: *dua* in Javanese is *ro*, which turns into *lo* as a result of *l/r* confusion.

then... You see? The balungan "*ro lu ro pi*" [2 3 2 7̣] is still there.[23] [...] If it's *balungan nibani*,[24] it gets reduced to . 7̣ . 6̣ —so the *slenthem*[25] by itself just plays 7̣ 6̣.

H: *Balungan rujak-rujakan*.[26] That can be made *gecul*, right?

[...]

W: Yeah, there's a *sindhèn* part for it:

6/4	.	.	2	2	.	.	3	3	6	2̇	6	3	2	6̣	2	7̣
			ru-	jak			nå-	ngkå,	ru-	jak-	é	på-	rå	sar-	jå-	nå[27]

You see? [Laughs] You do it like that, and the listener will think, "My! That's a happy, exuberant piece."

[...]

M: So, just looking at the *balungan*, an experienced musician can figure out—

W: Yes!

M: That it has to be this way or that.

W: That's right.... Then, as he gains experience... that musician is able to, we say, *tanggap sasmitå* [read between the lines]. The Javanese have a saying, "Jalmå limpad, seprapat tamat." [...]

M: What does *jalmå* mean?

W: *Jalmå* means "human being"; *limpad* means "outstanding";[28] and *seprapat tamat* [just one quarter, it's already finished] means "with just a little bit of information, that person already knows." [...]

W: So, that's what *rasa gendhing*'s all about. You don't have to be a musician—if a listener has this [the vocal line] to help him or her, that person will exclaim, "Wow! That piece is really exuberant! How boisterous!" That's what they say: "How boisterous!" [...]

M: What are the characteristics of a sad piece?

W: Hm. Sad pieces have a lot of "minor"[29] in them—in the vocal parts. That's what characterizes them. The *balungan*—there's no such thing as a "minor" *balungan*! [Laughs]

23. The sameness he is referring to is perhaps not immediately apparent to the uninitiated. It is common, in gamelan music, in elaborating a simple melody, to compress the phrase, placing it in the second half of the expanded version, and then to add an antecedent that will fill in nicely. This way both versions end the same way (the principal criterion for sameness), though they begin differently. Thus, the 2 3 2 7 of the plain version gets compressed into the second half (sung to "*lo-lo-o lo-o-ing*"), with an interpolated 5 and 6. The first half ("*du-a du-a lo-lo*")—which occurs in the metrically weak, less important part of the phrase—is simply a logical way of leading up to the second half.

24. A type of slow-moving *balungan* that is written . X . Y (where X and Y represent pitches). From the word *tibå*, "to fall onto": the melody "falls onto" the heavy beats only. (*Tibå* 6 means to end up on 6.)

25. The *slenthem* is a low-pitched metallophone with tube resonators that plays the *balungan* or notated melody.

26. That particular *balungan* can be used as the basis for a lively *sindhèn* part characterized by the use of a type of couplet that describes any one of many kinds of *rujak* (sweet and spicy fruit or vegetable salad).

27. "Pineapple salad, the salad of scholars." This is the first half of a twenty-four-syllable couplet, in which the message comes in the second half. A common continuation for this particular couplet is "Åjå nyengkå dimèn lestari widådå" (Don't strain too much so that you can ensure continued prosperity).

28. In particular, excelling in mystical knowledge.

29. *Minor* (also *minir*) is one of the terms used to refer to an altered *sléndro* scale, in which singers and *rebab* players insert pitches in-between the wide steps of the *sléndro* tuning. The result sounds like a *pélog* melody in the variable-pitch parts, with pure *sléndro* in the fixed-pitch parts.

M: Yeah.

W: If *Laler Mengeng* is just done with *bonangs* (as I was saying before), where's the sadness? "*Må må lu må nem* [5 5 3 5 6]"—it's not there. It's just a run-of-the-mill [*balungan*].

M: Are there sad pieces without "minor"?

W: Hmm... sad pieces without "minor," you say. Well, look at it this way: try playing a sad piece in *pélog*—the sadness isn't apparent.

M: Hmm. So, there are no sad pieces in *pélog*?

W: Well, if it's played right, it can be. But it won't feel the same as the *sléndro* version. [...] For instance, if you have the [*sléndro*] *balungan*

. . 3 5 . . 3 5 . . 3 5 . 6 . 5 6/5
lu må lu må lu må nem må

For an experienced musician, this in itself is a sad *balungan*, because in the back of his mind is

3 6̸ 5 3 6̸ 5 3 5 6 6̸ 5
rå - må[30] rå - må nå na né nå

—even a layperson can tell that that's sad. The *balungan* isn't sad, it *lends itself* to sadness.... Don't take my explanations to be God's truth. If you ask someone else, you'll get a different...

M: Yes.

W: Viewpoint. This is my personal point of view.

M: M-hm.

H: But there's a lot of agreement....[31]

M: That's why I'm asking different people—so I will have a basis for comparison. [...]

H: You happen to be asking Solonese people, so the terminology is all the same. But if you were to go to Wonogiri, or to Klatèn, maybe a lot of the words they'd use would be different. [*Laughs*] [...]

W: So, to sum up, *rasa gendhing*—sensing the *rasa* of a *gendhing* (*merasakan gendhing*) has a lot of factors that enter in. Like, what is the nature of the material? So, for example, it's like I was saying before about chilies: what sort of a chili is this? Is it green? Or red? Or a "shrieking" chili? If it's a "shrieking" chili, it can be green, it can be orange, it can be dark red—right? They all have different flavors. But on top of that, the tongues of those who are tasting [the chili] are all different. Mas Hartå may be the Spice King, and might have no reaction to it, but then when I taste it, [I exclaim,] "Hey, that's really hot!" See? Well, it's just like that. The general picture is that chilies

30. The slash through the number 6 indicates an altered pitch (in this case a lowering) used in the "minor" scale.

31. It was probably inappropriate for me to agree with Wignyå that his answers were idiosyncratic. Many of my teachers said that I should not take their answers as gospel. This is very likely one of the many self-effacing formulas in polite Javanese conversation (see note 22 in chapter 6). Suhartå's rejoinder is possibly meant not only to save an awkward social situation, but also to emphasize that Javanese people basically agree with each other. Indeed, in polite conversation a higher value is generally placed on agreement than on the exchange of information (Keeler 1975 and 1984:358). At less guarded times, Suhartå made no bones about the disagreements that often surface between musicians.

> are hot. [And when it comes to] *gendhings*, everyone says "*Laler Mengeng* is sad; *Pangkur pélog barang*[32] is exuberant, energetic, happy."

GENDHING, GARAP, RASA

Both Supanggah and Wignyosaputro claim (and they are not alone) that the *rasa* of a given piece depends almost entirely on *garap*. They are reluctant to essentialize the characteristics of a piece—to box it into a particular interpretation—and this no doubt stems from a distaste for standardization, as well as from a wariness of applying conceptions of musical essences that are borne of a notation-heavy tradition. In contrast to the nineteenth-century European notion of an autonomous musical work (Goehr 1994 [1992]), what they are saying is that a *gendhing* does not exist outside of performance, and hence depends largely on *garap* for its character.

At the very least, though, there is ambivalence in this regard. Although I have often heard musicians say that "there is no wrong way" of interpreting a passage, I have never met an experienced musician who did not at some point also criticize a performance for not following accepted convention. The same people who say that *garap* is everything will also, when speaking concretely, describe a particular *gendhing* as being *gecul* (humorous) or *sedhih* (sad), or will criticize a performer for not being true to the character of the *gendhing* in question.

Because Javanese musicians clearly have a notion of being "true to the work,"[33] one can posit an implicit theoretical separation between a *gendhing* and a performance of it (that is, musicians talk as if there is a distinction, even if they deny it explicitly). Accordingly, in my discussion of factors that affect *rasa gendhing* in the next chapter, I will make a broad division into those factors that apply to the *gendhing* itself (as conceived in an abstract, Platonic way), and those that apply to a particular performance of a *gendhing*. This division between essential and contingent traits corresponds roughly to a difference between normative and actual *rasa*—between the ideal *rasa* of a piece and the *rasa* that is experienced in performance. (This is not to deny, however, the evaluative component in statements about affect in actual performance; nearly all of these occur in critical or didactic contexts.)

The distinction I am making here is necessarily arbitrary, since it depends on how one defines the essence of a *gendhing*. This is very slippery ground indeed. It would be futile to attempt a rigid definition—one would have to find a Wittgensteinian rather than an Aristotelian solution. Seeking to avoid the problem, I have tried to follow the tendencies of my interlocutors (as

32. Once again, these two pieces may be compared on *Gamelan de Solo* (III:1 and III:4).

33. See Goehr 1989 for an account of how this notion applies to the European classical tradition.

Wittgenstein has taught us, we do not always need to define a concept in order to use it). In other words, I have tried to determine from context whether they were speaking about the *gendhing* or its performance. Because *garap* and *gendhing* overlap, however, so do their remarks, to some extent.[34]

This distinction gives rise to numerous circularities. One of these was outlined above (the *gendhing* has *rasa r* because of the *garap*; but the *garap* should be *g* because the *gendhing* has *rasa r*). Another has to do with categories of *gendhings*, such as *pathet* (melodic mode) or genre. For instance, *pathet barang*[35] has *rasa r* because it has *gendhings x, y*, and *z* in it, which all have *rasa r*; but *gendhings x, y*, and *z* have *rasa r* because they are in *pathet barang*. The situation is further complicated by performance context (such as time of day). A *gendhing* (or *gendhing* category) has *rasa r* because it is associated with context *c*; but the *garap* of the *gendhing* should be *g* so that the *rasa* will be *r* because it is intended for context *c*.

All of these paradoxes stem from a failure to separate deductive from inductive inference. I will not attempt to resolve them by establishing an unnatural order. Instead, I will simply acknowledge that such inconsistency is a part of the way musicians speak: they may at times speak normatively, at times descriptively; they may speak abstractly or concretely; and they may reason deductively or inductively.[36]

34. In particular, I have found it impossible to place *pathet*, or mode, into one or the other categories.

35. *Pathet barang* is one of three standard modes in the *pélog* tuning, characterized by a high tessitura and, for the most part, lighthearted pieces.

36. This point about inconsistency in musicians' thinking has been emphasized and explored more fully in Perlman 2004, chapter 1.

SEVEN

THE COMMUNICATION OF *RASA*, PART 2

Garap and Other Factors Contributing to Specific *Rasa*s

FIXED CHARACTERISTICS THAT AFFECT *RASA GENDHING*

At the end of the last chapter I introduced a distinction between a piece and a performance of a piece. To the degree that this distinction holds, we can regard some musical features as fixed—that is, as belonging to the piece proper rather than to a performance of it. It is important to point out, however, that these elements are not immutable but rather constitute the identifying features of a piece. They are thus spoken of as if they were fixed, even though, like everything in a living tradition, they are subject to variation.

Those characteristics of a *gendhing* that musicians speak of as if they were fixed are (1) its genre; (2) its gong cycle; (3) its *laras* and *pathet*;[1] (4) its name; and (5) its *balungan* (outline or reference melody). In addition, certain associations may be considered to be fixed, since they are generally accepted and frequently referred to as if they belonged to the *gendhing*. The first four elements of the above list are all parts of a complete *gendhing* title (not all *gendhing* titles include all four, however), and so are clearly thought to count among its identifying features. The fifth element, the *balungan* (reference melody), is somewhat less straightforward and will require a lengthier explanation.

The genre of a piece sets up certain expectations of its *rasa*. Following is a partial list of genres and some associated *rasa*s (*genre*, here, is taken rather loosely to mean any named category of pieces not covered by the other elements of a *gendhing* name; "pieces" are also conceived loosely to include songs):

1. *Laras* has many meanings; here I am using it to refer to the two tuning systems used in Javanese music, *sléndro* and *pélog*. *Pathet* is akin to the English "melodic mode."

★ *ådå-ådå*—*sereng* (heated, angry) IV:5

★ *andhegan*—*prenès* (flirtatious) III:4, 6:30

★ *ayak-ayak*—at the beginning of a *wayang* overture: *angker* (haunted), *mrabu* (regal), *tenang* (calm); at the end of a *wayang, klenèngan*, or suite: *gembira* (joyous), *legå* (relieved), *lejar* (cheered), *ayu* ("pretty"), *manis* ("sweet") IV:1, IV:11

★ *dolanan*—"playful" (literally and figuratively!) IV:6

★ *gendhing bedhayan*—*wingit* (spectral), *wibåwå* (commanding), *agung* (exalted) II:1

★ *gendhing bonang*—*wingit* (spectral), *wibåwå* (imposing), *sereng* (heated) 6/11

★ *gendhing gendèr*—*sereng* (tense)[2]

★ *gendhing sekar*—*kasmaran* (lovelorn), *gagah* (manly), *sereng* (tense) I:3

★ *inggah*—*prenès* (lighthearted), *bérag* (exuberant) II:2, 12:27–27:44

★ *jineman*—*prenès* (coquettish), *santai* (relaxed), *gecul* (humorous) IV:7, IV:8

★ *mérong*—*regu* (stately) II:2, 4:37–12:27

★ *palaran*—for *wayang*: *sereng* (heated), *gagah* (manly), *sedhih* (sad); for *klenèngan*: *énak* (easeful, pleasing), *prenès* (lighthearted), *gembira* (happy) II:2, 38:10–41:55; II:3

★ *pathetan*—*legå* (relieved), *lejar* (cheered), *regu* (potent), *santai* (relaxed) I:1, 25:25–28:00; II:2, 0:00–1:40; IV:10

★ *sampak*—*sereng* (heated)

★ *sendhon*—*tlutur* (sad), *kasmaran* (lovelorn) IV:2

★ *srepegan*—*sereng* (tense) II:3, 0:00–1:14

We have already seen that the length of the gong cycle is related to its *rasa* (chapter 3). In general, the larger the *gendhing*, the calmer the *rasa*. Small *gendhings* thus lend themselves to the opposite affects: mirth, joy, anger, lust—any *rasa* that evokes excitement.

★ **ådå-ådå**: puppeteer's mood song for tense situations; **andhegan**: vocal cadenza ("stopping"); **ayak-ayak**: piece with a four-beat gong cycle, usually used in the shadow theater to accompany spatial movement such as traveling; **dolanan**: "play song," based on, or in the style of children's songs; **bedhayan**: in the style of accompaniment to the sacred, courtly bedhåyå dance; **gendhing bonang**: a long gamelan piece using only relatively loud bronze instruments and drums, in which the *bonang* is the melodic leader; **gendhing gendèr**: a piece in which the *gendèr* plays the introduction; **gendhing sekar**: a gamelan piece based on a *måcåpat* melody; ***måcåpat***: sung poetry using literary Javanese in indigenous poetic meters; **inggah**: the second, livelier section of a *gendhing* with a medium to large gong cycle; **jineman**: a song for solo female singer and gamelan, often with an irregular structure; **mérong**: the first, calm section of a piece with a medium to large gong cycle; **palaran**: highly ornamented *måcåpat* singing with a *srepegan*-like accompaniment; **pathetan**: puppeteer's mood song for calm situations; unmetered, heterophonic, modal prelude; **sampak**: piece with one-beat-long gong cycle used for scenes involving fighting and the like; **sendhon**: puppeteer's mood song usually for sad situations; **srepegan**: piece with two-beat-long gong cycle used for traveling or preparing to fight.

2. Barry Drummond (pers. comm.) feels that this is, at the very least, an overgeneralization, and indeed there seem to be many exceptions. My principal source for this is Sukanto (June 24, 1992).

Laras and *pathet*, while among the identifying features of a *gendhing*, can, for some pieces with multiple versions, be a matter of choice for the performers, and so may enter into the realm of *garap*. For example, one can choose to do *Onang-Onang* in *laras sléndro* or *laras pélog*. As for the six *pathet*s, their associated *rasa*s have much to do with performance context—in particular, the time of the evening in which they are typically performed. Because of the complexities involved, *laras* and *pathet* are treated in a separate section.

The proper name of a piece—as opposed to those portions of the title that identify it generically—has much to do with its perceived *rasa*. In the previous chapter, Waridi was quoted as saying that titles are not necessarily good indicators of *rasa*. The implication was that someone who identified a *gendhing*'s *rasa* by its title very likely did not have a very deep knowledge of *karawitan*. This is undoubtedly often the case. However, the late Sukanto—by all accounts someone with a deep knowledge of *karawitan*—once told me that the three qualifications of an *empu* [J,I] (master) were that he (1) excel [in mystical knowledge?], (2) have beautiful *garap*, and (3) understand a *gendhing*'s *isi* (content). It is the last point that is of interest here. *Isi*, as already noted in chapter 2, can be used in musical contexts as a synonym for *rasa*. On the other hand, Sukanto often used it to mean specifically the musical content of a piece as revealed in its title (he once said that not all *gendhing*s have an *isi*[3]). The relationship between the two is often hidden—it's something a musician has to search for. An
III:1 example is the *gendhing Laler Mengeng*, the quintessential sad piece. The title, on the surface, seems to mean "The Fly Buzzes." But, according to Sukanto, the first word is really a corruption of *lar-ler* [J] (to nod off). The second word (*mengeng*) thus takes on its other meaning of "dazed, in a quandary." The picture is of someone overcome by difficult circumstances. This interpretation is much more in accordance with the *rasa* of the piece and presumably can help a performer understand how to play it properly—and a listener how to listen to it. Many other examples of such titles could be adduced. The point here is that a *gendhing*'s name, far from being an irrelevant distraction, is often part of the process of ascribing *rasa* to it.

In trying to identify the fixed elements of a gamelan piece, one must in some way or other deal with the slippery concept of the *balungan*.[4] For our purposes it does not matter whether we are talking about the notated melody or the

3. According to Wignyosaputro, titles that have real musical meaning are typical of the *aku tak yåså* (composed out of a creative urge) variety, as opposed to commissioned works (June 24, 1992). (See the section "An Aesthetic of Interiority" in chapter 4.) Mloyowidodo, on the other hand, told me that titles that have a connection to musical content are *péngetan*s (commemorations) (Mloyowidodo, May 2, 1992).

4. For fuller treatments of this elusive concept, see Sutton 1978 and 1979; Sumarsam 1984 [1975], 1994, and 1995; Supanggah 1985, 1988b, 1990, and 2009; Perlman 1994 and 2004; and Ishida 2008. See also note 7 in chapter 6.

"inner melody" (Sumarsam's term) that is sometimes said to be felt but not heard by experienced musicians (both may be called *balungan*). The notated melody, in Solonese music, tends to conform closely to the *bonang, saron*, and *slenthem* parts, whereas the "inner melody" tends to follow the *rebab*, the *gendèr*, and the *gambang* (or they follow it). The two *balungans*—the notated one and the *rebab*-like melody—usually converge at important structural points, as do all of the instrumental and vocal parts in general. In this sense, they are essentially "the same" for a Javanese musician. Occasionally, however, they diverge temporarily at these points. Some musicians like to find reasoned justifications for the exceptions (see Perlman 2004), others are happy to chalk them up to *rasa*—it just "sounds better" that way.

There is a sense, in other words, in which the notated melody is a distorted "inner melody," adjusted so as to make a nice *saron* and *bonang* part (each instrument of the gamelan is sometimes said to translate the *balungan* into its own language). Supanggah considers only the "inner melody" to be the essence of a *gendhing*[5]—that thing which allows a musician to identify a piece and to perform it concertedly yet independently along with others. It is at once a sort of abstract composite of all of the various parts, and a blueprint from which to create an independent part that will fit with the others. Nevertheless, both melodies—that is, the *balungan* in both its senses—are relatively fixed for each piece, and both may be referred to by musicians when describing the piece's character.[6] For our purposes, then, we can for the nonce disregard this otherwise important distinction.

Despite Wignyosaputro's claims to the contrary (see the previous chapter), the *balungan* can have an effect on the *rasa* of a piece.[7] In fact, he gave me just such an example. In describing *gendhing Babar Layar*, a stately *gendhing bonang*, he pointed out a passage in the beginning that was *gecul* (humorous) even though there are no vocal parts. This he attributed to the subdivided beat in the *balungan* (the Javanese term is *balungan kadhalan*—literally, a lizard-like movement in the *balungan*) (June 19, 1992):

. . 6 5 4 5 6 1 . . 6 5 4 5 6 1 . . 6 5 4 5 6 1 ◎ 7/1

In many other examples, as well, rhythm is the element that gives the *balungan* its character. Sudarsono told me that pieces which lend themselves to a *gobyog* [J] (boisterous) treatment usually have a strong rhythm in the *balungan* (November

5. See Sukanto's comment on p. 101, in which he quotes Mloyowidodo as distinguishing between the *gendhing* and the notation (he then provides an instructive example).

6. I say "relatively" because different versions of a piece may coexist in a single region, or, more commonly, across regions. Ideally, in any given performance there will be agreement as to which version to use. See Sutton 1993, Vetter 1981, Supanggah 1990, and Perlman 1994.

7. He was perhaps overstating the case in order to make a point about the importance of *garap*, and in particular, vocal *garap*.

30, 1991). Similarly, what seems to distinguish the many moods of *gendhing Elå-Elå* I:2 *Kalibeber* (see fig. 3.19) is above all the wide variety of rhythms in the *balungan*.

Pitch relations can affect the *rasa* of the *balungan* as well. Suhartå feels that the *balungan* itself can express sadness (contrast this with Wignyosaputro's statements in the previous chapter). One example he gave was closely modeled on a phrase from Martopangrawit's 1966 composition *ketawang Pamegatsih, sléndro manyurå*. For Suhartå, the *balungan* phrase 5 5 6 5 3 2 1 2 was sad in and of itself. He compared it to other hypothetical, closely related phrases in which the *balungan* was not sad:

5	5	6	5	3	2	1	2	(sad)
5	6	5	3	2	1	2	6	(not sad)
5	6	5	3	2	1	6	5	"
5	5	6	5	2	1	6	5	"
.	5	6	5	2	3	2	1	"

The first phrase, according to him, gets its sadness partly from its restricted range and from its mixing of *pathet sångå* with *pathet manyurå* (Suhartå, April 8, 1992).[8]

All *gendhings* in the repertoire have associations. These associations may be of a musical nature, or they may be more contextual.[9] When they are fixed by convention, musicians speak of these otherwise variable features as if they were part of the *gendhing* itself. An innovator can, of course, consciously go against convention by making, say, a happy piece sad—or, more usually, a sad piece happy (see the end of chapter 4). But this can be just as iconoclastic as drastically changing the *balungan*, and cuts to the very identity of the piece.

By *musical* associations I mean certain details of *garap* (performance practice) that have become standard. With the lighter repertoire, outside the palaces, these are for the most part mere expectations; whereas with the more serious repertoire in the court tradition, the associated interpretations tend to take the form of injunctions. In either case, the line between the *rasa* of the *gendhing* itself and the *rasa* of the *garap* becomes quite blurred. Examples might include the decision of whether to go into *iråmå rangkep* or not, or whether to use lively *ciblon* drumming or the more staid *kosèk alus*.[10] Part of associating a *garap* with a particular *balungan* has to do with similarities between pieces—intertextual associations (see note 8 in chapter 6, and the analysis of *Titipati*, later in this chapter). Further details are treated in the section on *garap*.

8. See the section, below, on *laras* and *pathet*, as well as the end of chapter 4.

9. This distinction between context and "the music itself," associated with nineteenth-century European thought, is also part of the way some Javanese musicians write about music. See, for instance, Supanggah 1985.

10. *Iråmå rangkep* is a stretched-out tempo level with fast, playful treatment. *Kosèk alus* is characterized by the use of the *kendhang gendhing* in *iråmå wiled* (the usual tempo level for the livelier second section of a *gendhing*). See Appendix B, as well as further on in this chapter for explanations of *iråmå*.

Because a piece is typically used in particular social and artistic contexts, these will be associated with the *gendhing*, even when it is contemplated in the abstract or listened to from a decontextualized recording. But these associations are not always tied into the very identity of a piece, and so they also belong under "Variable Characteristics," below. Examples of social contexts (which overlap somewhat with genres) are weddings, *tayuban*s (all-night, communal ritual dancing), children's games, court rituals, or informal evening concerts (*klenèngan*s). All of these carry with them allied *rasa*s. The most important of the nonmusical artistic contexts is *wayang kulit* [I,Ng], or the shadow-puppet theater. Every type of scene (court audience, preparation for battle, combat, travel, meditation) has its own piece or pieces, as do many of the several hundred characters.[11] These associations exert a powerful influence on listeners and musicians alike. Other such artistic contexts include *wayang wong* [Ng] ("human" *wayang*, a kind of dance drama), *kethoprak* (traditional theater), *langendriyan* ("opera" with singing dancer/actors), *sendra tari* (dance dramas), dance set pieces, *bedhåyå*, and *srimpi* (ritual court dances). (See "An Aesthetic of Suitability" in chapter 4.)

VARIABLE CHARACTERISTICS THAT CONTRIBUTE TO *RASA GENDHING*

As both Supanggah and Wignyosaputro emphasized in the conversations reproduced in chapter 6, the effect a *gendhing* has on the listener depends to a large extent on what actually happens in performance (rather than on the *gendhing* as an abstract entity). Indeed, because *gendhing*s are so fluid, their stable elements so sketchy, it is really up to the performers to create the appropriate *rasa* through their interpretive decisions, which go under the name of *garap* and are grouped, in what follows, largely into Western categories of musical elements. This is mostly a matter of convenience. Javanese categories were not sufficient to organize the material, since they did not cover all of the relevant remarks I have collected. I maintain, nevertheless, that what I am bringing together here (namely how *rasa*s are created musically) does have some coherence for Javanese musicians despite my departure from purely Javanese categories. For one thing, I have an excellent precedent in Supanggah 1985, chapter 4 (see as well Supanggah 2009, chapter 4), which uses a combination of Javanese and Western terms, dividing up *garap* into "*laras*" and "*pathet*" (tuning system and melodic mode, i.e., pitch), "*irama*" (i.e., rhythm), "intensity," and "choice of instrument" (i.e., timbre).

11. Kunst lists a number of these (1973:338–43). See also Probohardjono 1964 [1957] and 1984 [1966]. Note that, although I have used the present tense in this paragraph, it is becoming rarer and rarer in Java to see a "traditional" *wayang* that uses conventional music (see chapter 1, as well as Perlman 1999, Mrázek 2002 and 2005, J. Susilo 1996, and Nugroho 2003, inter alia).

Whereas *garap* covers nearly every aspect of sound production (use of electronic technology would normally be excluded), it does not include performance context. Context influences *garap* profoundly, however, and so it plays a major role in determining the *rasa* of a performance. I have divided context into two subcategories: the performers themselves and the circumstances in which they find themselves.

PITCH RELATIONS AND *RASA*

Leaving aside for the moment both *laras* and *pathet*, I first consider the effects of melodic contour, range, and instrumental tuning.

In talking to Suhartå, melodic leaps were often pointed to in explaining why a certain passage had a certain *rasa*. Usually he saw leaps as contributing to a *gagah* (virile) feeling (especially when ascending?). The contrast, for him, is between the athleticism of the leap and the smooth, feminine refinement of a winding, vinelike melody. Occasionally leaps may be felt to reinforce a feeling of sadness (Suhartå, April 9, 1992). However, the phrase 5 5 6 5 2 1 6 5 (see the paragraph on sad *balungan*s on p. 176), with a leap from the 5 to the 2, can only be made sad by the *rebab*: this is really a kind of "borrowed" sadness (i.e., the *balungan* itself is not sad) (Suhartå, April 8, 1992).

The opposite of melodic leaps, conjunctness, is literally as well as figuratively *alus* (it is both smooth and refined). Perhaps this is why, according to Hardjito (October 17, 1993), a melody that makes a smooth connection between widely separated registers characterizes *regu* (stately) pieces.

The direction of the melodic contour can also play a role. At least in the *pesindhèn* part, approaching a note from above gives it a *prenès* (flirtatious) or *bérag* (exuberant) feel (Wignyosaputro, June 19, 1992; Supanggah, October 24, 1993; Suhartå, August 7, 1991).

Before leaving the subject of melodic contour, mention should be made of a fascinating, if idiosyncratic little treatise by the great philosopher Soerjomentaram entitled *Seni Suara* (Music [literally, "The Art of Sound"]). In it he sets forth the notion that the more notes there are in a scale, the more agitated the effect; the fewer the notes in the scale, the more *sunyi* (desolate, serene) the *rasa*. As a result, *sléndro*, with its five tones, is more serene than *pélog*, with its seven; the two- and three-toned archaic gamelans *kodhok ngorèk* and *monggang* are more serene yet; and the most serene melody of all is the piece called *Gangsaran*, which consists entirely of a repeated drone (except for the punctuating gongs, of course—but these, Soerjomentaram says, distract from the true nature of the melody). Such is the serenity of *Gangsaran* that it has the power to "halt the functioning of the five senses. If one is capable of withstanding its stillness, then one will be released from the clutch of the five senses, and will be at one with the universe" (Soerjomentaram n.d.:13). This is the exact opposite of the usual interpretation: *Gangsaran* is usually thought of as the quintessential *sereng* (tense, angry) piece, presumably because of its frequent gongs, the feeling of anxious waiting in the drone, and its associations with fighting in dance contexts. But Soerjomentaram is not to be lightly dismissed just because his ideas are unusual or because he was not a musician. Experts in mystical knowledge are sometimes felt to have superior insights into music: thanks to their highly developed *råsås*,[12] they can see and feel things that ordinary people cannot.

The effects of range are straightforward: higher pitches are felt to be cheerful (★*prenès*, ★*bérag*, ★*birahi*, ★*ènthèng*, ★*gembira*, ★*sigrak*) lower pitches serious (★*regu*, ★*agung*, ★*wingit*, *alus*, ★*tenang*, *sereng*, ★*khidmat*, ★*wibåwå*, ★*sedhih*, ★*manteb*). This is true of a *balungan*, a *céngkok* (melodic formula), a singer's voice, or a gamelan tuning.

Each gamelan has its own distinct tuning. In my experience, this is even true when one gamelan's tuning has been copied from another's; there are several reasons for this. Copying a tuning, at least nowadays, usually begins by matching the *gendèr barung* of the gamelan to be tuned either to another *gendèr barung* or to a set of loose keys that are kept by a tuner as a master. There will inevitably be differences in how this tuning is then transferred to the other instruments of the gamelan. Furthermore, because the idiophone (particularly bronze) gamelan instruments are extraordinarily rich in overtones, it is impossible to match two notes with complete precision, since no two keys—even on the same type of instrument—have the same exact timbre. That is, if you are able to match the fundamental exactly, you are unlikely to match all of the overtones, and so the aural impression of the pitch will be different.[13] But not all gamelans are even copied from the same master, although standardization seems to be increasing in this regard. Considerable variation exists, for instance, in the absolute highness or lowness of an overall tuning. This difference is referred to as *laras*, the same term that is used to distinguish *sléndro* from *pélog*, and in this sense is synonymous with the French term *diapason*. To give an idea of just how much gamelans may vary in this regard—particularly in older sets—consider that out of twenty-eight *sléndro* gamelans measured by Surjodiningrat (1969, table 5), the note closest to A 440 (pitch 5) varied from 377 Hz to 466 Hz, or a difference of 367 cents (nearly four half steps).[14] Although this is not out of line with the entire range of tunings across Europe over a span of several centuries (Randel

★ **birahi**: passionate; **ènthèng**: lightweight, lighthearted; **gembira**: joyous; **sigrak**: fresh, agile; **agung**: great, impressive; **wingit**: spectral, awesome; **tenang**: calm; **khidmat**: devotional; **wibåwå**: commanding; **sedhih**: sad; **manteb**: solid, weighty

12. See p. 41 for the subtle difference between *rasa* and *råså*.

13. For a more technical explanation of why the pitches of the idiophones in the gamelan are perceptually indeterminate see Schneider and Beurmann 1993.

14. I am indebted to Gabriel Weinreich for converting Surjodiningrat's hertz to cents.

1986:639), it is vastly more of a difference than modern performers of European music are used to.

Gamelan tunings, however, have subtler differences than the mere highness or lowness of the overall tuning. They also differ from one set of instruments to another with respect to the exact intervals between any two steps of the scale (somewhat like the differences between mean-tone and equal tuning, but often more pronounced). These individual temperaments are called *embat. Sléndro* tunings are frequently discussed in the literature, but in conversation ordinary gamelan musicians rarely use the specialized terms for them. Experts in these matters generally say that there are two categories of *sléndro embat*. One is *embat Larasati*; the other is *embat Sundari*.[15] The word *larasati* happens to mean "pleases the heart," and *sundari* means "beautiful woman" in Old Javanese (Zoetmulder and Robson 1982). But these names refer more specifically to two characters from the *Mahabharata*. Larasati was raised by a shepherd, but was actually of noble birth. She was married to Arjunå (the principal hero of the *Mahabharata*), and, as a warrior, even outdid Sri Kandhi (another of Arjunå's wives, known for her bravery and her skill as an archer). Larasati was *branyak* (brash but not crude) of character, shown by her upturned[16] gaze (see figure 7.1). Dèwi Sundari (or Sitisundari), on the other hand, was married to Radèn Ångkåwijåyå. Ever the dutiful wife, when her husband was killed in battle she followed him to the grave by taking her own life. She was *luruh* (humble) of character, which is shown in her delicate features (subtle details of nose, eyes, mouth) and her downcast gaze (see figure 7.1).

There have been many attempts to define the difference between the two *embat*s, and almost as many theories about wherein the difference lies. Some posit that the intervals in *embat* Sundari get larger as you go up the scale, whereas in *embat Larasati* they get smaller (Padmosoekotjo [1960?]:48, Kunst 1973:252–53). Others point to specific intervals in each that are larger or smaller than the plain, equidistant intervals of *embat lugu*. All agree that *embat Sundari* is calm and refined (*ruruh, luruh, regu*) and *embat larasati* is coquettish or spritely (*nènès-kenès* [coquettish, hyper-feminine], *lincah* [spritely], *sigrak* [fresh, buoyant]). Kunst's authority, a certain Sulardi, called the former *sereng* (tense, vigorous, angry), and the latter *seneng* (carefree, pleasing)—a slightly eccentric interpretation, but still in keeping with the basic contrast between seriousness and playfulness (Kunst 1973:253).

15. Variant names of the two *embat*s include Rarasati, *rarasati*, and *larasati* for Larasati; and *nyundari*, Sendari, *nyendari, sundari*, and *sendari*, for Sundari (capital letters indicate a proper name, lowercase indicates an everyday word). There is, in fact, a third *embat*—an equidistant *sléndro* tuning called *embat lugu*—but this appears to be largely theoretical.

16. "Upturned" here is a symbolic rather than a purely physical category. Her gaze is physically closer to horizontal, but conceptually it contrasts with downcast.

FIGURE 7.1. Larasati and Dewi Sundari (Hardjowirogo 1982 [1949]:202, 207).

TIME AND *RASA*

As odd as Soerjomentaram's ideas might be with respect to scales, they can be generalized to a widely accepted, unstated principle with respect to rhythm and texture: the greater the density of sound events,[17] the more excited or agitated the *rasa*. Thus, at one extreme we have *bérag* (exuberant) and *sereng* (tense, angry); at the other, *regu* (stately), *khidmat* (devotional), *meneb* (settled); in the middle are *sedhih* (sad) and the refined side of *prenès* (flirtatious).

The principle of "event density as agent of excitement" applies to many aspects of gamelan music. I shall begin with tempo. As mentioned in chapter 5, there are at least two distinct concepts relating to tempo that both go under the name of *irâmâ* [J] (or *irama* [I]). To distinguish between them, Javanese academics use the term *laya*[18] to mean "surface tempo," reserving the term *irâmâ* to

17. I've borrowed the phrase "event density" from Warren Senders, a performer of jazz and Hindustani music, whom I heard interviewed on the radio.

18. *Laya* is a term borrowed from Indian music theory, in which it is used to mean many different things (tempo; sense of timing; rhythm; or ratio between the beats, groupings of beats, and rhythmic cycle—in this sense, it is somewhat akin to *irâmâ*!) (Gautam 1980:22; Rowell 1992:202–3; Holyrode 1972:199–200, 273). This is one of many words of Sanskrit derivation consciously introduced (or re-introduced) into modern Indonesian with some of the same connotations Latin or Greek words have in English. For example, substituting the Sanskrit-derived *wanita tuna susila* ("woman without morals")

refer to the various density ratios between the rhythmic strata used in gamelan music (see Appendix B, as well as Pickvance 2005:58–62). The link between surface tempo and *rasa* is summarized by Supanggah in the following excerpt (he uses the term *irama waktu* [literally, "the pace of time"] in place of *laya*):

> *Irama* plays a determining role in creating the character and affect of a *gendhing*, since it will greatly influence the choice of *wiledans* [patterns] (this is particularly true of *irama waktu*). A rapid tempo will tend to encourage the musicians to use more animated, gay, and complex *céngkoks* and *wiledans*; a slow *irama waktu*, however, invites them to use ones that are calm, solemn, simpler, etc. As a result, there is a tendency to use a slow *irama waktu* in interpreting *gendhings* that are sorrowful, solemn, dignified, serious, etc.; and to use a faster *irama waktu* for *gendhings* that are gay, comical, lively, etc. (Supanggah 1985:163–64)

Some of the Javanese and Indonesian terms used to describe the effect of a fast tempo are *rongèh* [J] (fidgety), *gobyog* [J] (boisterous), *sereng* [J] (heated), *tegang* [I] (tense), *semangat* [I] (enthusiastic), and *bérag* [J] (exuberant). Along the same lines, a tempo that is too fast can destroy a *regu* [J] (stately) or *mrabu* [J] (regal) feeling (Suhartå, May 9, 1992).

Slow *iråmå*: II:2, 38:10–41:02 and II:3, 5:01–7:55; fast *iråmå*: II:3, 8:15–9:56

A slow tempo in *palarans* has a feminine (*kemayu, kèwèk, manja*) feel, whereas a fast tempo is more appropriate for a manly (*gagah*) effect. This is because of the conventions of *langendriyan* and *wayang wong*—the two theatrical traditions that make the greatest use of the genre—in which male characters tend to sing *palarans* when they are about to fight.[19] The slow tempo gives rise to more long-winded, relaxed, ornamented melodic lines, whereas the fast tempo encourages a more direct, forceful style of singing. When a vigorous, masculine vocal line is sung too slowly, the effect is *njelèhi* (boring) or *kurang greged* (listless). In *sindhénan* (another vocal genre), on the other hand, the contrast is not so much between feminine and masculine, as between calm pieces (*kalem, tenang, klasik, pélog limå*)—in which the singer can take her time getting to the final note of a pattern, and thus needs to have excellent breath control—and lively pieces, in which she should not dally and may take more frequent breaths.[20] In *sulukans* (mood-setting songs of the *dhalang* in a shadow-puppet performance), a fast delivery is important for *ådå-ådås* (puppeteer's mood songs for tense situations), and a slower delivery is appropriate for *pathetans* (songs for a peaceful atmosphere).

---

for *pelacur* feels somewhat like using *meretrix* for *prostitute*. Using *laya* for "surface tempo" (which most musicians simply call *iråmå*) feels somewhat like using *prolatio* for *beat sub-division*.

19. *Langendriyan* is a dance drama in which the dancers sing dialogue; *wayang wong* is a dance drama based on the traditional shadow theater.

20. The noted *pesindhèn* Gitotenoyo once told Walton that, according to Pak Jarwå (a master musician of yore), her long final notes and leisurely pace (made possible by her ample breath capacity) resulted in a calm, settled *rasa* (Walton 1996:107).

All these tempos and *iråmå*s are largely controlled by the drummer, so the temporal aspect of the collective *garap* (interpretation) is under his command. Conversely, each instrumentalist should adjust his or her part to fit the desired mood suggested by the tempo and *iråmå* set by the drummer. (Recall that each *iråmå* has a usual *laya* or surface tempo—and hence a general mood—associated with it. Again, see Appendix B.) In *iråmå dados*, which tends to be slow and dignified, the performers will choose simple patterns with relatively fewer notes. In *iråmå wiled* and *iråmå rangkep*, on the other hand, in which the *laya* is relatively fast, the patterns have a lot of notes occurring in quick succession.[21] Here is an example of a *gendèr* part in *iråmå dados* (*kembang tibå* technique), and an equivalent pattern in *iråmå wiled* (*ukel pancaran* technique):[22]

r.h.: 6 5 3 5 6 . 5 6 5 6 1̇ 6 2̇ 6 1̇ 6 5 (ir. dados) 7/3
l.h.: 6̣ . 1 5̣ 2 6̣ . 1 5̣ . 6̣ 5̣ 6̣ 1 2 3 1

r.h.: 6 .5.3.5.6 .3.5.6.5 6.6.6.65 6.6.6.65 (ir. wiled) 7/4
l.h.: 6̣ .12.126̣1 2.16̣5̣.5̣. .6̣5̣6̣.5̣.6̣ .1.2.321

Another example of the effect of note density on *rasa* was given to me by the eminent musician Rasito Pangrawit of Banyumas. He felt that playing every note in the undulating *bonang* technique called *pipilan* was *kurang wibåwå*—"lacking in commanding presence." In the first example below there are too many notes; in the second example, notes on the strong beats are left out, thus creating a more satisfying effect:

bonang: 2 3 2 3 2 1 2 1 (*kurang wibåwå*) 7/5
balungan: 2 3 2 1

bonang: 2 3 2 . 2 1 2 . (standard Solonese *pipilan*) 7/6
balungan: 2 3 2 1

The principle of event densities applies to other things besides melodic patterns. I have already mentioned how, other things being equal, the more frequent the gongs are struck in a gamelan piece, the more heated the *rasa*. This is why in the *inggah* of a large *gendhing*, the *kethuk* usually plays twice as frequently as in the *mérong*. Also in the *inggah* the drummer usually switches to the *ciblon*, and the *bonang*s play *imbal*.

21. Sindoesawarno provides a characterization of each *iråmå* according to *rasa* (1987 [1955]:377). I have not included it here because it does not seem to correspond to current musical practice (or perhaps to current nomenclature?). See also Supanggah 2009:267–69.

22. These examples are based on a combination of versions taught by Hardjito (as transcribed in Forrest 1980:78) and very similar versions I learned orally from AL Suwardi. *Kembang tibå* literally means "falling flower," presumably meaning a melody ("flower") that goes directly to its goal without too many twists and turns ("falls"). *Ukel pancaran* literally means "flowing (or radiant) curlicue." According to Soetandyo (2002:33), *ukel pancaran* patterns are *kembang tibå* patterns that have been filled in, resulting in a spritely, dynamic effect (*lincah dan dinamis*).

The "vertical" density of the musical texture also affects the *rasa*. I am including it here because, in a stratified texture such as this, a thicker vertical texture also means greater linear event density. Among the most stately pieces in the repertoire are the austere *gendhing bonang*, which are open and transparent
II:1, 12: 18–15: 45 in texture. At the other extreme is a style of playing called *pinjalan*,[23] probably the thickest texture achieved in Solonese gamelan playing. In a piece treated in *pinjalan* style, no one is playing the plain *balungan*—everyone is doing some variation on it, and the resulting atmosphere can be bustling indeed. Whereas in most other treatments the *demung, saron barung*, and *slenthem* all play in unison, here the only part that is doubled is that of the *saron barungs*—even the (usually) two *demungs* divide their melody, hocket style. The nineteen distinct parts create a dense sound that, other things being equal, would make for a festive, cheerful mood. This, according to Suraji (pers. comm.) is indeed what it does in a piece such as *ladrang Wilujeng*, which is often done this way. However, other factors may intervene. Traditionally, *pinjalan* is associated with **srepegan*, **ayak-ayakan*, and accompaniment for **bedhåyå* and **srimpi* dances from the Kraton. In these contexts, also according to Suraji, it has, rather, an *agung* (exalted, noble) feeling.[24] I contend that this difference might be ascribed to associated contexts, which outweigh the natural tendency for musical busyness to sound cheerful in Javanese music more generally. The question remains, of course, why the musicians who first created *pinjalan*, and linked it to contexts that called for grandeur, chose that particular treatment. Could it have had something to do with the almost overwhelming event density of large-scale Javanese rituals, including those at the Kraton?[25] Perhaps *ramé* (bustling) and *agung* are not so far apart as they might at first seem.

It will come as no surprise, then, that the pieces played on the sacred *sekatèn*[26] gamelans also use *imbal* in the *saron* section. These pieces are generally considered to be *regu*,(stately) but, oddly, the repertoire consists of only the *inggah* of

* **srepegan**: a genre taken from the shadow theater, associated with battles or traveling; **ayak-ayakan**: similar to *srepegan*, but with a more relaxed feel; **bedhåyå**: ritual, courtly, choreographed group dancing with highly abstract, esoteric symbolism; **srimpi**: similar to *bedhåyå*, but with four dancers instead of nine

23. *Pinjalan* ("like a flea") can apply to any part that plays consistently a half-beat late. What I am referring to specifically here is a treatment in which the *demungs* play a slow *imbal* pattern, and the *slenthem* plays on their off-beat.

24. I am indebted to Barry Drummond for first pointing out to me the more serious, lofty side to *pinjalan*.

25. I'm thinking, for instance, of important rituals in which multiple gamelans are playing simultaneously within the capacious central courtyard of the palace, and how in former times there would be a string quartet added to the mix!

26. *Sekatèn* is an annual festival, held on the grounds of the Great Mosque (on the west side of the Kraton's north plaza [the same is true of the Kraton in Yogya]), celebrating the birth of the prophet Mohammed.

gendhings that also have a *mérong* when played on an ordinary gamelan. *Sekatèn* gamelans do not have any of the "front-row" parts (*rebab, gendèr, gambang, siter*, singers), and so the rhythmic density is nowhere near as high as in the full gamelan for *klenèngans*. In this sense, the music of the *sekatèn* gamelan is very similar to *gendhing bonang*, in which the *inggah* is quite active, and in which this activity makes for a *sereng* (tense, heated) rather than a *bérag* (exuberant, mirthful) feel (Suhartå, March 26, 1992). Even vibrato is not immune from our basic principle. A quick vibrato, on *rebab* or in singing, is more appropriate for a lively atmosphere, whereas a slow vibrato is said to indicate a calm personality that is better suited to the more serious repertoire.

Another aspect of singing that follows along similar lines is text-setting. The *pesindhèn* has considerable leeway in her choice of text; the main thing is to select one in the right verse form. But even within the standard twenty-four-syllable couplet (called *wangsalan*) that is used more than any other kind of text, she can decide how many syllables to use in a musical phrase. In a calm piece she will choose mostly four or eight; for a more lively effect she will sometimes use twelve in a line. But for the liveliest effect (only possible with certain *balungans*), she sings a text taken from the *rujak-rujakan* category (literary couplets beginning with a reference to fruit salad). In this case, all twenty-four syllables may be delivered in a single instrumental phrase. (OWM audio example 6/4, transcribed and discussed on p. 168, is of the *rujak-rujakan* type, but with only twelve syllables to a phrase.) Another way of increasing the event density of the *sindhèn* part is to add *isèn-isèn*: "fillers." With a few restrictions, these can be added at will between lines of the *wangsalan* text. In calm pieces they are to be largely avoided.

There is one aspect of musical time not entirely covered by the density principle, and that's irregularity. In solo singing, a little bit of irregularity is necessary to breathe life into the melodic line. Solo singing, such as *mâcâpat* or *båwå*, is said to lack *greged* (or *greged-saut* [oomph, vigor, intensity of expression]) if delivered with absolute regularity, the way a beginner does. Another term used for this kind of lifeless singing is *kembå* (insipid).

The same can be said of *rebab* playing, and in subtle ways, of nearly every other instrument in the ensemble. The *rasa*ful placement of a gong or *kempul* stroke is extremely subtle and cannot be counted out—it must be felt. Unlike the instruments of a Western orchestra, those of a gamelan ensemble should not, apart from the few doubled parts, line up too strictly with each other.

DYNAMICS AND *RASA*

Javanese musicians do pay attention to dynamics: clear norms apply to balance, phrasing, and volume level. These are not, however, a primary source of expression. As a general rule, loud playing is reserved for a boisterous musical mood.

It may, however, contribute to a feeling of grandeur (particularly in *gendhing bonang*), or to a *sereng* (tense) atmosphere. Otherwise, dynamics are usually subdued and fairly even. *Wayang* and dance accompaniment make considerably more use of dynamic change than does concert music. Particularly in dance dramas, frequent and sudden dynamic shifts are an important source of creating dramatic mood contrasts. This has now spilled over somewhat into concert playing, so that one finds techniques, like the onomatopoetic *jengglèng*,[27] used to enliven the atmosphere (Supanggah 1985:195–98).

jengglèng: III:4, 13: 18–15: 10

For those accustomed to the constant shading of dynamics in most Western concert music, Javanese music might seem rather inexpressive in this area. Indeed, there is a preference for terraced dynamics, and one of the surest ways to sound un-Javanese in singing is to put in a lot of crescendos and decrescendos within a single phrase. The instrument that is the most variable in terms of small, rapid changes in dynamics is the *rebab*. I have not heard an explanation for why this is the norm for the most vocal-sounding of all instruments, whereas singers themselves do not make much use of the same capacity they have for dynamic variation. Perhaps there is a technical reason: it is important for the relatively soft *rebab* to be heard, and so it is common to accent beginnings of notes; however, it would be impossible to sustain that level of volume on a long note, so that the usual shape of a single note on the *rebab* is >——<, which makes for nearly constant variation in loudness over the course of a phrase.

TIMBRE AND *RASA*

Certain musical timbres themselves carry affective connotations. The *siter* is generally regarded as cheerful (Supanggah called it *renyah*—"pleasantly crackly to the tooth" [May 17, 1992]). Padmosoekotjo ([1960?]:45) also places the *suling* (end-blown bamboo fipple flute) in this category, saying that it makes things *gayeng* (pleasant, lively). Here, timbre overlaps with pitch, since the high pitch range of both of these instruments undoubtedly contributes to their cheerfulness. The *rebab* is good at creating sadness, and a good *rebab* player must be *alus* (calm, smooth, refined). According to Sukanto, the *gendèr* usually plays the *bukå* (introduction) for *gendhing*s that are *sereng* (June 24, 1992). Similarly, of the three kinds of *suluk*, (puppeteer's mood songs) only *ådå-ådå*s—which are *sereng*—are accompanied by the *gendèr* alone. The *bonang* is naturally *ramé* [J] (lively): in former times, no *bonang* was used to accompany *wayang*—if the gamelan was too *ramé* it was considered unpleasant (Mloyowidodo, March 11, 1992). The gong provides a *legå* (relieved, contented) feeling (Suhartå, May 9,

27. *Jengglèng* is a humorous device characterized by a sudden accentuation in the *saron*s, signaled by the drum, and usually occurring on an off-beat or on a metrically weak beat.

1992). According to Warsadiningrat, singers in general introduce an element of cheerfulness (Soebantar [1968]:10–11). This is particularly true of members of the *gérong* (unison male chorus), who are nearly always viewed as bearers of mirth.[28] A *gendhing* that is performed with *gérong* generally loses all claims to seriousness. The *pesindhèn*, however, is capable of a wider range of *rasa*s. She will never be capable of conveying satisfactorily a *gagah* (virile) or *sereng* (tense) mood, but if she is good she can convey sadness, awe, flirtation, and happiness (Suhartå, March 26, 1992; May 2, 1992). For both men and women, different vocal timbres are appropriate for different *rasa*s (see "*Rasa* and Evaluation" in chapter 5).

ORNATENESS AND *RASA*

Ornateness is an aspect of gamelan music that combines pitch and rhythm. The way ornateness affects *rasa* follows our basic principle of event density: the more ornate a pattern, the livelier the *rasa*. Since ornate patterns tend to use more pitches than plain ones, it is now apparent that Soerjomentaram was not so eccentric after all: in his characterization of *Gangsaran*, more pitches *can* make the music more sensuous, less spiritual. Sad, stately, or commanding pieces should be performed with little ornamentation. Flirtatious or exuberant pieces need to have a certain amount of ornamentation or they will sound insipid. Vocal ornamentation is related to tempo (both *laya* and *iråmå*) in that it takes time to draw out a phrase with lots of fioriture: a slower tempo, paradoxically, can result in a fancier melodic line. This is why one should not take too much time in singing *ådå-ådå*s, for instance.

VOCAL TEXTS AND *RASA*

As a rule, vocal texts in *karawitan* are not expressed by the music. This is because they are chosen according to their verse forms rather than their content. The archaic or otherwise abstruse language of most lyrics further dissociates their meaning from the music. The result is that singers and listeners alike do not pay much attention to the meaning of what is being sung. This is the general picture.[29] However, in some genres, such as solo *måcåpat* singing, the meaning of the text is extremely important, as reflected in the clear diction and

28. There are some exceptions. In certain recent compositions the *gérong* is asked to sing using the altered "minor" notes that can add great sadness to a piece. One example that Suhartå referred to more than once is Martopangrawit's composition, *ketawang Pamegatsih, sléndro manyurå*, already cited on p. 176.

29. See Santosa 2001 for more on the role of textual meanings in gamelan performance.

"Nulådå" used in the *prenès* piece *Ketawang Sinom Wénigonjing*: I:3

straightforward delivery that is required.[30] Moreover, even in more heavily instrumental genres, the best singers take into account the meaning of the text they choose for a particular *gendhing*. For instance, Sastro Tugiyo eschewed using the most common *Sinom* text ("*Nulådå* . . .") for flirtatious pieces, because it consists of spiritual advice (he preferred, instead, the somewhat suggestive verse beginning "*Kéntir-kéntir*"). Going in the other direction, some *båwå* singers consider the meaning of the text when choosing their melodic variants (this is limited to broad categories of expression, and almost never takes the form of word painting).[31]

CONTEXT AND *RASA*: PERFORMERS

Performers have an impact on the *rasa* of performance in three broad areas: their personalities, their biographies, and their condition at the time of performance. I have already discussed performers' personalities in chapter 5, but I will briefly summarize and add to what I said before. For the most part, performers' personalities are talked about in terms of binary categories (which presumably lie along a continuum rather than being radically separated into distinct species). The *luruh/trègèl* (humble/impetuous) opposition discussed in chapter 5 can be linked up with other descriptors of a performer's character. Thus, *luruh* is related to the terms *anteng* (quiet, settled), *lugu* (plain, straightorward, naive), and *alus* (refined, controlled). *Trègèl*, on the other hand, is related to their opposites: *rongèh* (fidgety), *kenès* (coquettish, hyperfeminine), and sometimes *kasar* (crude). Several other oppositions are more loosely linked to *luruh/trègèl*: sad/happy, virile/feminine, and asexual/flirtatious (see table 3.1). Performers who fall toward one side or the other of these continua will be better or worse at bringing out the "*regu*ness" or "*prenès*ness" of a piece.

Another term for a performer's personality, which is related to the feminine-flirtatious side of the above dichotomy, is *manja* (spoiled, pampered).[32] I was told

30. Each *mâcâpat* meter lends a certain aura to the text through its associated character. Presumably this character derives at least in part from the tunes that go with that meter. (But the relationship between text and meter is circular: the meter also derives its character in part from the habit authors have of choosing certain meters to set certain kinds of subject matter.) Another way in which text and tune may be related is in the way some singers, like Sutarman, adjust the details of the melody (the *wiled*) to suit the particular meaning of the text (June 6, 1992; June 24, 1992). See Arps 1992 (particularly Appendix II) for additional information on the characters of *mâcâpat* meters.

31. Word painting is when some detail of the text is illustrated iconically in the music. Many obvious examples are to be found in sixteenth- and seventeenth-century madrigals. If a bird is mentioned in the words, the singers' parts include imitations of birdsong; if there is a reference to relative height, the pitch range of the melody reflects that. See Walton 1996:256–57 for a highly unusual instance of word painting in recently composed Javanese music.

32. The distinction between performers' personalities and their respective playing or singing styles is often obscured in Javanese music talk. The word *manja* fits this pattern, as it seems to refer to both.

that this is Suhartå's idiosyncratic term for a certain type of *pesindhèn*, and yet in the *Kamus Besar* (the standard dictionary of Indonesian) we find, under *kemanja-manjaan* (to act spoiled), the following example: *caranya bernyanyi masih kemanja-manjaan* (he or she still sings in a pampered way). Suhartå is not alone.[33] But, try as I might, I cannot get a handle on just what he means—I can describe it, but I cannot always recognize its musical manifestations. The picture I get from his many scattered comments is of a woman who tries to lure men with her charms, and who is not above sleeping her way to the top (to put it crudely). Musically, this translates into using showy, hyper-feminine melodic variants—even when singing a song from a masculine genre, like a *båwå* (cf. pp. 153–54). It has to do with calling attention to yourself, with showing off, with letting your own personality show through rather than focusing on the character of the piece, and, above all, with singing late. By "late," I mean getting to the final note of a phrase long after all the other parts have gone on to the next phrase (the *pesindhèn* is expected to arrive a little late, but not to overdo it). The Javanese term for this is *nglèwèr* (to hang down loosely).

Biographical details that enter into the *rasa* of a performance include anything that shapes the performer's personality. For instance, if a person has known a lot of suffering, that will usually be reflected in his or her music. Suhartå is a self-proclaimed expert on sad music and told me it was because his life had had more sadness in it than happiness (see pp. 145 and 147 in chapter 5).

Another type of relevant life experience, of course, is musical training. Many, if not most Javanese gamelan musicians have had some previous experience performing nongamelan music (see chapter 1). Sutarman had started out as a *kroncong* singer, Suhartå had been in a church choir, Wignyosaputro had received at least a partial education in Western music. Sometimes these other traditions are said to detract from a performer's ability. For instance, one very good *båwå* singer's voice used to be criticized for sounding too Islamic (i.e., Arabic), on account of his early *pesantrèn* (Muslim boarding school) education. But non-Javanese training may also be seen as an advantage. Oddly enough, several people told me that one reason the late Mardusari was so

33. It is difficult to say just how synonymous the dictionary's *kemanja-manjaan* is with Suhartå's *manja*. The *masih* (still) in the sentence implies that this is something children do—which presumably would rule out the temptress-like overtones. What the two usages might have in common is a certain attention-grabbing quality, reflected in a derived form of *manja*, namely *bermanja*, which Stevens and Schmidgall-Tellings define as "to coax, cajole, court." Along the same vein, they give "attached (emotionally)," and "intimate, familiar, confidential" for the root itself, providing another clue as to connotations of *manja* in Indonesian that are not present in the English word *spoiled*. Aside from the above-mentioned citation linking *manja* and singing, there is additional evidence for the term's being used by others than Suhartå: I have heard Druhendro—at the time, a young graduate of STSI, where Suhartå teaches—apply *manja* to the same singers Suhartå does. One might object that Druhendro got the term from his teacher. But at the very least, it is not restricted to the latter's idiolect.

good was that Mangkunegårå VII had hired a French voice teacher for her. But to my ears, operatic vocal training is quite inimical to Javanese singing—fortunately, whatever Mardusari learned from her teacher was not evident in her singing.[34]

The effects of notation on performance are discussed in chapter 4. Clearly, whether one learns *karawitan* primarily orally or by reading notation is going to affect the result. This is also true of whether one performs from memory or not—which is not at all the same thing. In general, performing without notation is felt to be much better from the point of view of *rasa*, although it is no guarantee of a successful rendition (see chapter 4).

The condition of the performers at the time of performance includes things as basic as how old they are. As mentioned elsewhere, older people are more settled, and so can interpret the heavier *rasa*s better. Younger musicians have more agility and energy, so they can bring off the more exuberant pieces better. Alcohol, which is quite common at Solonese musical events, has a strong effect on what transpires musically. It can lead to carelessness and crudeness, but it can also give rise to great creativity. Drunken Javanese musicians do not, in my experience, play sadly. Finally, musicians' relationships to each other will affect the way they perform. If they feel at ease they will be freer in their playing; if they respect each other they will play more carefully; but if they fear each other, they can freeze up. In some cases, though, a little nervousness is a good idea. According to Suhartå, this is particularly true of *pesindhèn*s who are *manja*: when they are overconfident, that's when they show off the most. If they feel *minder* [I,D] (cowed), either because the piece is difficult, or because they are with other singers who are better than they, they will be more careful.

Sometimes musicians try to do each other in. This can be good-natured fun, or it can arise out of jealousy or—in the case of a male instrumentalist and a *pesindhèn*—out of rancor at having been jilted. In such cases, if, say, the instrumentalist has been jilted by the *pesindhèn*, he might try to fake her out, to lead her to the wrong finalis. According to Sastro Tugiyo, when one finds oneself musically in over one's head, including when one has been duped into playing or singing wrong notes, it is called *kepangan*—"eaten up."

34. See Wignyosaputro's comment reproduced on p. 99. I am tempted to attribute this explanation about the source of Mardusari's success to a misguided trust in Western forms of knowledge. With the recent turn towards more overt showings of Islamic piety, I would guess that a similar reverence for Arabic forms of knowledge is increasingly common. (Until recently, a good many, if not most Javanese Muslims were proud of their distinctly Javanese version of Islam. But Indonesia may be going the way of Malaysia, where, I'm told, Arabic customs are strongly equated with Islam, so that to be a good Muslim is to adopt Arabic ways.)

CONTEXT AND *RASA*: CIRCUMSTANCES OF PERFORMANCE

The simplest way to approach the circumstances of performance is to ask the "wh-" questions: Where? When? Why? Who? What? One all-important feature that ties into all of these is the degree of formality of the occasion. For instance, the Kraton and ISI are probably the most formal places to perform, and a monthly neighborhood *klenèngan* (music-making session) among the least. Competitions were very formal for the performers, but very informal for the audience, who did not hesitate to whoop loudly every time there was an obvious mistake. The time of day also enters in. At an evening *klenèngan*, the later into the night it gets, the fewer important guests are present and the drunker the musicians become. The purpose of a performance is usually a ritual of some kind, but it can also be a radio broadcast, or just getting together for fun. Ritual performances are not necessarily stiff and formal. Most evening *klenèngans*, even the rowdiest of them, fulfill some ritual function: either to celebrate the sponsor's birthday (every thirty-five days[35]), the birth of a child, a circumcision, a wedding, or other event.

Some relevant facts about the performance context have little to do with formality. The region the musicians are from will have an effect on the *rasa*. For instance, Yogyanese musicians are said to be more *gagah* (virile), whereas Solonese musicians are more *alus* (refined, subtle, intricate, feminine) in their playing. The condition and quality of the instruments will also enter in, especially their tuning. Each set has its own *embat* (characteristic temperament) and *laras* (absolute pitch level). Generally speaking, a high *laras* is said to result in a "happier" sound than a low one (see the section on pitch relations, above). Suhartå once told me that international tours by Solonese groups have altered the tradition, because of the felt need to play fast, loud, and for a short time in order to sustain audience interest (these practices were instigated by the founder of ASKI, Gendhon Humardani) (May 7, 1992). Time limits on the performance can have a limiting effect in other contexts as well (radio broadcasts, wedding receptions in rented halls, competitions). According to Sudarsono, even the colors present can affect the performance. In the Kraton all the colors are tastefully subdued,[36] whereas in the Mangkunegaran they are a bit brighter. This, coupled with the general humility of the Kraton musicians and the proud professionalism at the Mangkunegaran, had a subtle but profound effect on the *rasa* of the performances at the two palaces.

35. The Javanese calendar has a seven-day Muslim week and a five-day market week. Any given combination of Muslim and market weekdays recurs every thirty-five days, and is the single most important element of a person's birth date.

36. Or they were until recently: the interior of the recently rebuilt Banquet Hall is purple.

LARAS, PATHET, AND *RASA*

Pathet, or Javanese modal practice, has been the subject of a very large proportion of the pages written about Javanese music, beginning with Jaap Kunst's classic monograph (1973 [1934]). *Laras* (tuning system), by contrast, is relatively simple: the differences between *sléndro* and *pélog* are as visible as they are audible. Why, then, is there so little agreement as to the respective *rasas* of *sléndro* and *pélog*, and relatively more agreement on the *rasas* of the six *pathets*?[37]

The answer has to do with the nature of generalization and of extensional versus intensional meanings of category terms. That is, a generalization will depend on which instances are taken as protoypical of a category. The more vast and heterogeneous the category, the more likely there are to be gross differences in focus from one speaker to another. What this means is that the more specific the musical entity being characterized with respect to *rasa*, the more agreement there is among Javanese musicians. Thus, the least agreement is on the two tuning systems; there is more consensus about the six *pathets*; then come specific *gendhings*; and, finally, the most agreement is to be found concerning single performances of a *gendhing*.[38]

An important related phenomenon is the way in which pieces and categories of pieces (such as *pathet* or *laras*) mutually influence each other with respect to *rasa*. That is, the character of a *pathet* is sometimes discussed as if it were the sum of the characters of all pieces in the *pathet*. It may also be described as the character(s) of the most typical pieces in the *pathet*. Sometimes, however, the *pathets* are spoken of as having characters in and of themselves, so that, other things being equal, the *pathet* a piece is in can have a determining effect on its character.

When assigning characters to the six *pathets*, musicians tend to agree most on the two extremes of *pélog pathet limå* (which is overwhelmingly serious) and

37. This observation is based on the oral and written statements of more than twenty Javanese musicians who have commented on the *rasas* of tunings and *pathets*. As a reminder, the *sléndro pathets*, in order from lowest to highest tessitura (and from most serious to least), are *nem, sångå*, and *manyurå*, whereas the three *pélog pathets* are *limå, nem*, and *barang*. The full designation of a *pathet* requires four words (*laras x, pathet y*), but this is often shortened to one or two words. This is the standard account. In fact, musicians make finer distinctions than these six categories, into which all *gendhings* are squeezed for the purposes of naming and classifying them. This is because some pieces are borrowed from one *laras* to another, with the result that within a single *pélog pathet* you might have pieces borrowed from different *sléndro pathets*, each with their own melodic conventions. One might speak, for example, of *pélog nem manyurå* to indicate that a piece being played in *pélog nem* was originally in *sléndro manyurå*, and so the patterns to be chosen in working it out should reflect that. But, as these are in essence recombinations of the six basic elements, and as I have no citations characterizing these subdivisions that go beyond the original categories, they need not concern us here.

38. A possible exception to this pattern is the characterization of genres versus that of pieces (see pp. 148–55 and 172–73). Genres are probably even more heterogeneous than *pathets*, yet there appears to be a fair amount of agreement as to their respective characters.

sléndro pathet manyurå (which is overwhelmingly light). In contrast, it is impossible to assign a single affect—or even a cluster of closely related affects—to the four intermediary *pathets*.

Several general observations recur with great regularity. First, within each *laras* the *pathets* proceed from "heavy" (*manteb* [J], *berat* [I]) to "light" (*ènthèng* [J], *ringan* [I]). That is, they range from calm (*tenang* [I,J], *anteng* [J,I]), supernaturally awesome (*wingit* [J], *angker* [J,I]), and majestic (*regu* [J], *mrabu* [J], *agung* [I,J], *wibåwå* [J]) to lively (*sigrak* [J], *rongèh* [J]), light (*gembira* [I], *bérag* [J]), and mirthful (*gecul* [J]), passing through sorrowful (*sedhih* [J], *susah* [J,I]), lovelorn (*kasmaran* [J]), and flirtatious (*prenès* [J]) in the middle (see fig. 3.1). This arrangement corresponds to the order of *pathets* in a *wayang* performance or an evening *klenèngan*: *nem, sångå*, and *manyurå* in *sléndro*; *limå, nem*, and *barang* in *pélog*.

Second, the tendency for the "later" *pathets* to be more lighthearted is due primarily to their higher register. This relation is felt to be iconic, in the sense of a natural correspondence between form and content.

Third, sadness is best expressed by *barang miring* (also called *minir, minor*, or just plain *miring*), in which the *rebab* and vocal parts use *pélog*-like intervals in a *sléndro* piece. (Interestingly enough, the deepest sadness is best evoked by a mixture of *sléndro* and *pélog* in these parts, rather than by pure *pélog*.) This effect, of notes that provide poignancy by conflicting with the basic tonal material of a piece, can also be achieved—say, on the *gendèr*—by including notes that are felt to be inimical to the *pathet* (sometimes called *dhing* tones).[39] In *pélog*, this is how all of the instrumental and vocal parts must create a feeling of sadness, since there is no exact equivalent of *miring* in *pélog* (that is, *sléndro* intervals are not used within a piece in *pélog*).[40] Moreover, the effect is considerably more obvious in *pélog*, since the three *pathets* within it tend to be pentatonic, whereas the *laras* as a whole has seven tones available (in each *pathet* two tones are normally left out of the scale). Thus, in *pélog barang*, pitches 1 and 4 stand out as clearly foreign to the mode. III:1

39. See also the example on p. 176, of a sad *balungan* given by Suhartå. The sadness resulting from mixing *pathets* might be one reason that *sléndro nem* is considered to be the most serious of the three *sléndro pathets*, since it is said to be a mixture of *sléndro manyurå* and *sléndro sångå*. On the other hand, mixing *pathets* can result in a jumbled, unsettled feeling (see the analysis of *Titipati* below).

40. The one exception is the piece *Kodhok Ngorèk, pélog barang*, which is commonly performed with *sléndro gendèr* and *gambang gångså*. It is possible that this is meant to express sadness. According to Warsadiningrat (1990 [1943]:52), the piece *Kodhok Ngorèk* was inspired by the sound called *rijal* (hence the name of one of the instruments in the ceremonial *kodhok ngorèk* ensemble). Gericke and Roorda define *rijal* as follows:

> a particular squeaking sound (or noise) similar to the sound of a kind of frog, which is heard in the latter part of the night (circa 3:00 A.M.) when all is deathly still, and which is considered by some to be the cry of the spirits of the dead, or, according to others, more specifically, the spirits of dead children. It is said that the nearer one approaches to the sound, the farther away it seems. (translated by Susan Walton in Warsadiningrat 1987 [1943]:70)

Fourth, the character of some *pathets* depends in part on similarities to other *pathets*. For instance, whether a piece in *pélog nem* sounds lighthearted or solemn will greatly depend on whether the melodic patterns used in it are closer to *sléndro manyurå* or *pélog limå*, respectively.

Most of the above observations have important qualifications. There are, for instance, some pieces in *pélog limå* that are *prenès* (flirtatious), and many pieces in *pélog barang* that are sad. Whereas *pathet barang* and *pathet manyurå* are lighthearted mainly because of their high range, other factors include associations with *wayang* scenes and other performance contexts, and with the progressively more jolly (often drunken) atmosphere of evening *klenèngans*; these other factors may reinforce or attenuate the natural tendency of high pitches to lighten the mood, depending on whether those factors have an enlivening or a depressing effect. Finally, not all pieces that use *miring* are sad, nor do notes outside of the *pathet* necessarily result in sadness. Use of pitch 4 in *pélog barang*, for example, can be interpreted not only as sad, but also as jocular (*ndagel* [J], *ngglécé* [J], *nggojèg* [J]), unpleasant (*langu* [J]), or weightless/unsubstantial (*ampang* [J]), depending on the musical context. Conversely, as noted in chapter 6, experienced musicians may recognize sadness, without any of the usual techniques of expressing it, by inferring these from the melodic gestures (for example, a contour in *sléndro* that is usually interpreted as *minir* by the *rebab*).

Jocular use of pitch 4 in *pélog barang*, III:4, 8:06, 9:36, 9:58, 10:08

Following are the primary characterizations of each *pathet* that I have encountered, arranged in the most usual order for an evening *klenèngan*:

pélog limå: calm, weighty, majestic, supernaturally awesome — I:1

sléndro nem: mostly calm, but sometimes lively or flirtatious — IV:3

pélog nem: flirtatious, agile; majestic, meditative; not usually sad — flirtatious I:3; majestic II:1

sléndro sångå: mostly solemn and imposing, but often cheerful (some disagreement as to which is dominant); may be sad or lovelorn — sad III:1

pélog barang (the most variable of all): mostly flirtatious, cheerful; often sad; may be surly, or aristocratic, calm, majestic — both solemn and cheerful I:2; II:2; flirtatious III:4

sléndro manyurå: light, gay, flirtatious

As can be seen by the large variety of affects in both the *sléndro* and *pélog pathets*, it is probably not worth trying to assign a character to either *laras* (for every characterization that a musician makes one can find another musician who contradicts it). On the other hand, most musicians do seem to agree that, as a rule, *sléndro* is "heavier" than *pélog*. This can be seen by the examples they have given of *gendhings* for which there is a version in each *laras*. In nearly all of them the *sléndro* version was said to be either sadder, more imposing, or less *èntheng* (lightweight).[41] This interpretation seems to have at least two sources. One, of course, is that there is no "minor" in *pélog*, as already mentioned. The other is that the combination of small and large intervals in *pélog* makes it easier, especially for the singers and *rebab* player, to execute rapid, highly ornamented melodies. There may also be a feeling that the uniformly wide intervals of *sléndro* iconically create a feeling of grandeur.[42]

GENDHING TITIPATI: ONE MUSICIAN'S ANALYSIS

One day, in October 1993, I was seeking recordings, for a talk I was giving, of "heavy" pieces that used *sindhénan* (solo female singing). To my astonishment, there were almost none in my collection of several hundred cassettes of central Javanese gamelan music. I looked first for pieces in *pélog limå* and *sléndro nem*, since these were the most likely *pathet*s to have serious pieces. One piece that I had no trouble finding recordings of was *gendhing Titipati, sléndro nem*. Before choosing it (finally, out of desperation, since it was one of the only pieces in those two *pathet*s for which I had more than one recording), I asked Supanggah to rate it for "*regu*ness." He was to use a scale of 1 to 10, with 1 being very *regu*, and 10 very *prenès*.

Suppanggah's answer turned out to be nuanced and complex, and it reveals how multiple factors operate in a single musical context. To begin with, he found it next to impossible to assign a rating for the piece as a whole. We proceeded to go through the *mérong* of *Titipati*, *gongan* by *gongan*.[43] IV:3, 00:19–10:22

Supanggah gave the first *gongan*—the A section in figure 7.2—a "3" (somewhat *regu*). This was more or less in keeping with my expectations. IV:3, 00:19–1:59

But the second *gongan*—section B—came out between a "6" and a "7" (somewhat *prenès*). The reason he gave was that the *gongan* as a whole is reminiscent of *gendhing Lambangsari* and *gendhing Widosari*, which are both *prenès*. [And both are in *sléndro manyurå*!] Moreover, the phrase 5 6 5 3 2 1 2 1 is extremely common. As a result, the *sindhèn* is free to do a variety of things IV:3, 1:59–4:20

41. This more or less coincides with Endraswara's characterization of the two tunings. He does not seem to be an expert musician, since his writing is full of apparent misunderstandings about musical practice and terminology. But what he has to say is interesting nevertheless: "*Slendro* is considered more virile, valiant, strong, and its range is lower—this is the man's domain. *Pelog*, on the other hand, is higher, full of *rasa*, sensitive—this is a symbol of woman" (Endraswara 2006:301). (Note that *sléndro* is not actually lower than *pélog*, and, in any case, when paired gamelan instruments are given a gender, the lower one is female!)

42. But then how does one explain the grandeur of *pélog limå*? Perhaps the sprightliness of the small intervals is offset by the low register, the expansive forms, and the plain *garap* associated with it?

43. A *gongan* is a section marked at the end by a stroke of the large gong (which is usually notated with a circle or double parentheses around the note where the gong occurs).

A	. 6̣ 5̣ .	5̣ 6̣ 1 2	. 3 2 1	6̣ 5̣ 3̣ 5̣⌒
	. 6̣ 5̣ .	5̣ 6̣ 1 2	. 3 2 1	6̣ 5̣ 3̣ 5̣⌒
	2̣ 3̣ 5̣ 6̣	3̣ 5̣ 3̣ 2̣	. . 2̣ 5̣	2̣ 3̣ 5̣ 6̣⌒
	1 1 . .	3 2 1 6̣	3 3 . .	6 5 3 ②
B	5 6 5 3	2 1 2 1	. . 1 2	3 5 3 2⌒
	5 6 5 3	2 1 2 1	. . 1 2	3 5 3 2⌒
	. 1 2 6	. . . .	6 6 1̇ 6	5 3 2 3⌒
	. 3 3 3	5 6 5 3	2 3 5 3	2 1 6̣ ⑤
C	3 3 . .	6 5 3 2	5 6 5 3	2 1 6̣ 5̣⌒
	3 3 . .	6 5 3 2	5 6 5 3	2 1 6̣ 5̣⌒
	2̣ 3̣ 5̣ 6̣	3̣ 5̣ 3̣ 2̣	6 6 . .	3 3 5 6⌒
	3 5 6 1̇	6 5 3 5	2 3 5 6	3 5 3 ②
D	1̇ 1̇ . .	3̇ 2̇ 1̇ 6	3 5 6 5	3 2 1 2⌒
	1̇ 1̇ . .	3̇ 2̇ 1̇ 6	3 5 6 5	3 2 1 2⌒
	. 1 2 6	. . . .	6 6 1̇ 6	5 3 2 3⌒
	. 3 3 3	5 6 5 3	2 3 5 3	2 1 6̣ ⑤

FIGURE 7.2. *Balungan* notation for the *mérong* of *gendhing Titipati, laras sléndro pathet nem* (Mloyowidodo 1976, vol. 1:50–51).

[as are other parts as well?].[44] It's like the patterns called "Ayu Kuning" and "Dua Lolo" in this regard.[45] Also, he said, many of the *céngkok*s (phrases) in this second *gongan* can be approached from above in the *sindhèn* part. This is true of

44. Later in the conversation, as already mentioned on p. 143, I asked him if *regu* pieces were harder, and *prenès* ones easier to *garap*. He said that *prenès* pieces were not necessarily easier, just that they gave more leeway. *Regu* pieces *sudah minta begitu* [call for a single interpretation]. For example, if the *balungan* is low, the *sindhénan* does not have a lot of possibilities.

45. "Ayu Kuning" and "Dua Lolo" are the names of two melodic formulas, which appear in a great many *gendhings*. Presumably because they are so common and singers are so confident about them, they feel free to vary them. The most usual *balungan* for "ayu kuning" in *sléndro* is

*gåtrå*s (four-beat units) like 5 6 5 3, 6 $\dot{1}$ 6 3, and $\dot{1}$ 6 5 3. In contrast, a *gåtrå* such as 2 1 2 3 has to be approached from below—it is not *prenès*, and should not be approached from above.

The third *gongan* he rated a "4" (somewhat *regu*). Supanggah did not state his reasoning, but the first and third *gongans*, which he felt were the most *regu*, both have a much lower tessitura than the other two. IV:3, 4:20–6:39

The fourth *gongan*, which is in a high register, is the most *prenès* (with a rating of "7"). It is similar to *Lobong* (*sléndro manyurå!*) and other *gendhing*s that use *andhegan*s (vocal cadenzas).[46] The melodic contour goes every which way, switching from *manyurå* to *nem* and back to *manyurå*. Our feelings are stirred up, unsettled. Upon closer inspection, then, it turned out that *Titipati*, although in *sléndro nem*, was not a good example of a "heavy" piece. In fact, this is probably why it is performed and recorded so often! IV:3, 6:39–9:38

TWO CAVEATS

As Supanggah's analysis of *Titipati* shows, all of the factors discussed in this chapter may interact with one another in ways that an inexperienced musician or listener would not be able to predict. This means that there are no simple syllogisms here. One can no more say that the presence of a given feature will necessarily produce a certain *rasa* than one can say that the presence of a given *rasa* entails a given feature. In other words, one must insert an "other things being equal" clause before every statement I have made concerning a factor and its associated affect.

Much more could be said about factors contributing to *rasa*. Given that *rasa*, like *garap*, involves nearly every aspect of music-making, any exploration into the specifics of both is potentially endless. And this does not even take into account the roughness of fit between the affect that is named and the affect that is felt. This is something that Wignyosaputro hinted at in the conversation quoted in chapter 6. It is made even more explicit in the following two exchanges with Suhartå and Supanggah, respectively:

---

6 $\dot{1}$ $\dot{3}$ $\dot{2}$ 6 3 2 1
and for "dua lolo" in *pélog*,
2 3 2 $\underset{\cdot}{7}$ 3 2 $\underset{\cdot}{7}$ $\underset{\cdot}{6}$

For examples of the former in other parts, see Martopangrawit 1984 [1975]:14,113 and Sumarsam 1984 [1975]:267. For examples of the latter, see p. 167.

46. Significantly, on the recording of *Titipati* made for *Gamelan de Solo*, the drummer, Moedjiono, called for two *andhegans* in this *gongan*, even though they are highly unusual in the *mérong* (they almost always come in the *inggah*). It would seem from this that Moedjiono might well agree with Supanggah's assessment of how *prenès* this *gongan* is.

H: Starting a long time ago I asked the old folks about the *jiwa* (spirit, soul, content) or *rasa* of *gendhing*s or *tembang*s (songs). They were often hesitant, as it turned out. They were hesitant. I mean, if they hadn't thought it over ("fished for it") ahead of time, they had nothing to say. And I'm the same way. I feel like I should say it's like this or that—well, sometimes I feel like I really have to own up and say "this is what the *rasa* is." Because the old folks weren't going to say anything. At most, they might venture a "*Gecul*!" or a "*Sedhih*!" Anything else, and they wouldn't commit. And yet they could feel the *rasa* (*bisa merasakan*)! But usually they didn't want to come out and say "This is what it is!"—they wouldn't do it.

MLB: In Western music, there are a lot of different *rasa*s as well, but sometimes people will say, "This cannot be expressed through words, through language—it can only be expressed through music." So, in English, or in any language—.

H: It can't—

M: —It can't be expressed. If it could, well, it wouldn't be music any more, it would then be language, it would be literature.

H: That's exactly right. A lot [of *rasa*s] are like that. In fact, most of them are like that. [. . .] So there really aren't any words that can represent [the different *rasa*s]. You're right! (Suhartå, March 26, 1992)

P: Even though *rasa* is really important, it's rarely talked about.

M: But there seems to be a pretty specific vocabulary for *rasa*s. In the West, on the other hand, it's generally thought that the feelings engendered by music are more or less specific to the medium of music, and so they can't really be talked about.

P: In Java the words that are used to describe *rasa gendhing* are fairly vague. They really apply only to broad categories. For instance, the *regu*ness (grandeur) of *Kombang*
I:1 *Mårå* and that of another piece are going to be slightly different, and musicians are at a loss to describe that subtle difference. (Supanggah, April 12, 1992)

Despite any lack of subtlety that may obtain in *rasa* descriptors, and despite the real dangers of trying to reduce *rasa* to rules, newcomers to the tradition *can* get closer to experiencing what Javanese musicians experience by knowing what they say. If this chapter succeeds ever so slightly in helping this to happen, its mission will have been fulfilled.

EIGHT

WHY *RASA* TALK MATTERS

PART I: *RASA* AS KEY TO UNDERSTANDING JAVANESE MUSIC

In these final pages I try to formulate an answer to the question "Why does all of this matter?" First of all, studying *rasa gendhing* matters because it matters to Javanese musicians. That alone, for me, is sufficient justification. But there is more. If an outsider wishes to understand Javanese music, I can think of no better portal through which to enter than *rasa gendhing.*

There are, of course, many kinds of musical understanding. When ethnomusicologists set out to understand a given musical tradition, they want to know who is making the music for whom, and why. They want to know how the music is changing, how it has interacted with other musics, how it is transmitted, and how it is made available to people. They want to know how the music is produced: what happens in performance, what the means of sound production are, what the physical and mental processes involved are, and how the music is put together. But they also want to know what the music means to the people who are closest to the tradition. "Musical meaning" can itself mean many things. It may include social or personal connotations; or it may include uses and functions (for instance, music that is meaningful because it cures).[1] What sometimes gets left out of ethnographic description—perhaps as a reaction against the extreme objectification of music in the European tradition—is how people respond to music aesthetically. To be sure, it is always problematic to look for a *purely* aesthetic domain anywhere outside of the Western art tradition (or, some might argue, even within that tradition!). But a domain can have a strongly aesthetic element without its being "purely" aesthetic in the

1. See Merriam 1980 [1964]:209–27 for a distinction between uses and functions of music, and McAllester 1954 for an example of how these may be essential to musical meaning: "When a traditional Navaho is asked how he likes a song, he does not consider the question, 'How does it sound?' but 'What is it for?'" (p. 5).

Kantian sense. Presumably there is a visual reason why people decorate their houses a certain way. Similarly, there must be a *musical* reason they make sounds the way they do: of all the sounds they could have chosen, why those?[2]

In modern-day Java, there is a very strong sense of the aesthetic in music, an appreciation of sound finely crafted to please the ear. Music is often made to be listened to, even if the audience is not silent, and even if the occasion is a ritual one.[3] It may be, as Judith Becker (1993) and Catherine Basset (2004:116–22) have argued, that there was once a far greater emphasis on the ritual significance of *karawitan* than there is now—layers of symbolic meaning that are now being covered by other layers. And there is no denying, as Florida (1995) and Hughes-Freeland (1997b) have pointed out, that current court-centered ideas of the sublime (*adiluhung*) were strongly shaped, in the later colonial period, by the Dutch presence. But as early as the first part of the nineteenth century (as can be seen from the *Serat Centhini*[4]), Javanese listeners showed a concern for the beauty of musical sound *qua* sound, a concern for music as an aesthetic object. And this concern is not limited to the upper classes, to the *priyayi*s (aristocrats), as Hughes-Freeland implies (1997b).[5] Musicians, who are mostly from the laboring classes,

2. Marxist-influenced scholars claim that a preoccupation with the aesthetic is uniquely European and uniquely bourgeois. For a general (not necessarily Marxist) discussion of aesthetics as a cross-cultural category, see Ingold 1996. Scruton (1997:219, 474ff.) refutes the notion that the aesthetic is limited to a certain class of Europeans at a particular time in history.

3. John Pemberton (1987) has suggested that, at Javanese weddings, music is played not to be listened to, but to establish a sense of order. He drew this conclusion from watching guests chat politely from the beginning to end of a reception, never once acknowledging the musicians. Without denying his perspicacity, I'd like to qualify his insight. First of all, if anyone in the audience is a musician, he or she listens very intently to the music (but, admittedly, at most events musicians are in the minority). Second, people in Java tend to be very good at dividing their attention. I once peeked in (illicitly but by accident) on the judging room of a gamelan contest: the music was piped in through speakers, and while it was playing, the judges were chatting and milling about, and some were munching on the snacks provided by their hosts. Yet they were able to hear instantly a mistake on the *gendèr*—perhaps the most subdued of the many polyphonic parts. And third, what Pemberton was describing was the formal wedding reception, which is often held nowadays in a rented hall. Javanese weddings usually take place over several days, and at some point there will normally be some form of informal evening entertainment, either a *klenèngan* or a *wayang*. At these events, audience members do frequently pay attention to the music, even though they are free to eat or talk.

4. The *Centhini* (also called the *Suluk Tambangraras*) is an immense, encyclopedic wandering-student romance in verse form, commissioned by the Solonese royal court in 1814 C.E.

5. I do not mean to dismiss offhand her very perceptive and complex article. I think her basic point is a good one, that ethnographers must be wary of imposing their aesthetic theories (such as the autonomy of art) on practices that are foreign to them, even if they feel a natural affinity to these practices. But I want to defend my approach against a general attitude among anthropologists that non-European arts, if they are to be talked about at all, are to be discussed only in social terms. (It is significant that at the sixth session of the Group for Debates in Anthropological Theory, those present who voted for the motion that "aesthetics is a cross-cultural category" were outvoted two to one by those opposing the motion [Ingold 1996:14].) What I am advocating here is not the exclusion of social and ritual meanings from the discussion of music, simply the inclusion of specifically aesthetic ones.

are as intent on aesthetic properties of music as anyone in Java. Taking pleasure in the abstract beauty of patterns of sound is a very Javanese pastime.[6]

If we are indeed justified in seeking to understand Javanese listeners' aesthetic responses to musical sound, then the question becomes what sorts of responses are relevant to our inquiry. In the European concert tradition, at least for musicologists of the past century or so, there has been a strong tendency to look for the meaning of instrumental music in abstract patterns of sonic events—that is, in the musical structure. Musical responses in this view are primarily cognitive. There has also been a growing contingent among music theorists and aestheticians that has chosen to look for meaning in affective responses or in affective qualities of the musical object.[7]

Although not openly debated in Java, as far as I know, this same contrast, between structure and affect, can be found in Javanese theoretical discussions of music. As Sumarsam has shown (1995), nineteenth-century writing on *karawitan* was not analytical. In fact, in nearly all the descriptions of musical sound quoted by Sumarsam from works of the time, it is the *rasa* of the music that is being described. Probably as a result of interaction with Europeans—and especially since the introduction of musical notation—Javanese *writing* on music has become increasingly analytical and technical over the past hundred years.[8] Javanese *conversations* about music, however, have retained more of an emphasis on *rasa*, and some musicians have assured me that *rasa* is the key to aesthetic understanding. Still, shop talk is filled mostly with details of melody and rhythm—it seems to be a safer topic. *Rasa* is subtler than mere notes: recall Wignyosaputro's rhetorical questions, "Where is the happiness?" "Where is the sadness?" in chapter 6. In the company of experts, *rasa* is seen as a risky subject. But this does not diminish its importance—rather the contrary.

An analogy might be found in the way a married couple typically spends more time talking about what to have for dinner than about what dinner means to them affectively. On some level we need not separate the two forms of talk: daily decisions are part of what makes a relationship work, and the way a couple talks about what to eat has implications for how they feel about each other. And since *garap* is a means to achieving the desired *rasa*, talking about the one also has implications for the other. When a gamelan ensemble leader tells the *bonang* players to use *pipilan* (undulating patterns) instead of *imbalan* (rapid hocketing),

6. See, for instance Soedarsono 1985 (cited in Suparno 1990).

7. The bibliography on this topic is very large. Three relatively recent anthologies devoted primarily to the tension between analysis and affective meaning are Robinson 1997, Krausz 1995, and Pople 1994. Robinson 2005 is an important monograph that explores various kinds of emotional responses to music.

8. See Perlman 1994 or 2004 for a discussion of the technical vocabulary that was introduced, and of possible reasons for this.

he is telling them, in essence, that the piece is too *regu* to be livened up with *imbalan*. If you *really* understand *garap*, you understand *rasa*, and vice versa.[9]

The answer, then, to the question about whether we should concern ourselves with affective or analytical responses, is that both are important, as long as both are part of what concerns the knowledgeable insider. I have chosen to focus primarily on affect in Javanese music because it has been less discussed in the English-language literature than structure has been (indeed, at the time of my research it had been well nigh ignored), and because Javanese musicians repeatedly assured me of its importance.

Words about Music

In exploring *rasa gendhing*, I have made certain assumptions that I wish now to state explicitly, for they have a bearing on the import of what I have done. First of all, I have operated under the assumption that words matter. That is, our best clue as to what musicians feel or experience when they listen to music is what they say they feel. There are at least three objections that could be made to this assumption. I shall discuss each in turn.

One objection is that the best way to find out about musical experience is to *experience* it—auditorily, tactilely, visually, kinesthetically. There is no question that there are other clues besides words to understanding music. I have learned volumes just by singing next to good *gérong* singers.[10] And certainly, observing facial expressions and social interaction is a superb way of guessing what listeners are experiencing. Yet I maintain that words remain the best way of verifying whether one's guesses are even remotely close.

An example will bring home my point. Towards the end of the very long *andhegan* (vocal cadenza) of *gendhing Budheng-Budheng*, the *pesindhèn* speaks the words "Kusumå, gandané arum" (The flower, its scent is fragrant) in a stylized, coquettish manner. It is customary in some groups for the male instrumentalists to let out gleeful catcalls at this point; sometimes the *gendèr* player makes a loud rattling noise by running the wooden handle of his mallet against the metal resonators of the *gendèr*—in short, the effect is of brief pandemonium. The musicians' reaction is similar to what they do when a *dhalang* (puppeteer) makes a particularly funny joke, especially if this joke involves innuendo about one of the *pesindhèns*. Influenced by this behavior, and above all by the caricature-like stylization in the *pesindhèn*'s speaking voice, I (and other foreign gamelan students whom I have spoken to) have found this passage to be very funny. When I asked Suhartå whether

9. Scruton (1997, chapter 13) argues, similarly, that "analysis makes sense . . . only as a prelude to criticism," and that analysis, in its broadest sense, encompasses aspects of meaning.

10. I have a friend, a successful mezzo-soprano, who claims she learned to do Rossinian coloratura passages not in her lessons, but simply by singing on the same stage as Marilyn Horne.

it was indeed humorous, he was puzzled by my question. "Funny?... No. Seductive (*merayu*), but using the vocal techniques of old-time pesindhèns" (June 11, 1992). Supanggah, independently, had the same reaction. "Funny? Not in the least! *Kemayu* (coquettish), perhaps, *prenès* (flirtatious), maybe; but not funny. Nor are the words [of the text] funny" (October 24, 1993). Had I not attended to my teachers' descriptions, I would have persisted in my ignorance.

A second objection is that people do not always feel what they say they feel or believe what they say they believe. This may result from laziness, inarticulateness, deception, resistance, forgetfulness,[11] or confusion on the part of the speaker. All of these do occur in conversation. But this objection applies to *any* statement about anything, and we certainly do not, as a result, give up entirely on language as a means for knowing what someone else is thinking.

The most disruptive of these barriers to communication is undoubtedly deception. I have no reason to suspect this having occurred while my teachers were discussing *rasa gendhing* with me. What would their motive have been? This was not esoteric knowledge, it was something they felt all musicians should know about. And was the mutual respect, trust, and affection that we felt for each other also an act of deception? Perhaps this is unduly naive of me, but I prefer to trust my friends and teachers rather than question their genuineness at every turn without probable cause. This is not to say, of course, that statements need not be interpreted, nor their sources considered. Evaluative claims, in particular, are always colored by personal relations (loyalty, fondness, resentment,

11. The forgetfulness I am referring to here is the inability to relive fully a musical experience at the moment of talking about it afterwards. Geertz highlights this problem as it relates to the ethnographic study of religion:

> When anthropologists... talk to people about their religion... it is almost invariably in a setting about as far removed from the properly religious as it is possible to get. We talk to them in their homes, or the morning after some ceremony, or at best while they are passively watching a ritual. Rarely, if ever, can we get at them when they are really involved in worship.
>
> ... [E]ven with the best will in the world an informant will have some difficulty in recapturing and formulating what religion amounts to for him, and indeed he is almost certain to render it in terms of common-sense stereotypes and rationalizations which are useful for understanding common sense but may be positively misleading if taken for veridical reports of what goes on in a ritual, the recital or hearing of a myth, the curing of a patient, or whatever.
>
> ... [M]uch of religion's practical effect... comes in terms of a kind of pale, remembered reflection of religious experience proper, in the midst of everyday life.... A clear distinction between religion experienced and religion remembered is thus an important analytical tool for understanding some otherwise difficult to understand phenomena. (1971:108–10)

All of these comments apply rather handily to music as well as to religion, and we would do well to heed Geertz's warning. That said, even he admits that "no matter how much sheer observation we carry out or how many theological treatises we read, we must [talk to people] if we are to understand anything at all" (108). Once again, I maintain that, although talking to people is only one avenue by which to learn about musical experience, and although what people say must always be interpreted in light of all of the other avenues at one's disposal, speech about music is central to understanding musical affect.

the consequences of rejection, etc.). Kofi Agawu, for one, would certainly accuse me of naiveté. He seems to take the reverse stance of mine, to the point that he claims deception is a necessary component of fieldwork (2003:210–14). He points out that in the area of Ghana where he did his research (and where he grew up) "systematic deception" is "a part of day-to-day living." In a sense, it is in Java, as well, if one includes the many forms of politeness that require one not to say what one truly thinks or feels. Although I am aware that my interlocutors may have been selective in what they told me, again, they were not, as far as I know, trying to lead me astray.

A much more likely source of trouble is hyperbole, often a result of haste in answering a poorly phrased question. Generalizations are difficult to make on the spur of the moment, and what might appear as true in one context might turn out not to apply in a host of others (see also note 11). This is a difficulty I can live with: in the long run, such confusions or inaccuracies have a way of working themselves out.

The third objection is that it is next to impossible to say precisely how music makes one feel, or what its character is. A strong rebuttal to the supposed ineffability of musical experience has been made by Frank Sibley:[12]

> It is sometimes said... that music is not really describable, that words cannot capture something so non-verbal and unique. Sometimes such objections seem to rest on misunderstandings about the nature of description. If the demand is for a description to provide a substitute for music, the demand is absurd; descriptions are never substitutes, or intended to be.... Again, no description, some assume,... could be *adequate*. But this flirts with a spurious notion of adequacy that no description could meet, in two respects[: exactness and completeness].... Such 'exactness' and 'completeness' are unattainable limits, and not uniquely with music. For given purposes, descriptions, being always selective, can be exact or complete enough. Skimpy descriptions are still descriptions, and often adequate; calling the opening of the 'Moonlight' Sonata serene or the sea angry is to describe, and excludes contrary descriptions. (1997:166–67)

Not only is music describable, but the words people use to describe it both shape and reflect their conceptualization of music in general. This is a Whorfian notion.[13] In the words of one of Whorf's heirs, Charles Frake,

12. See also Treitler 1997, in which he argues for a kind of literary description of music—more or less the opposite of musicological description—that gets at the heart of musical experience (his model for this is Proust).

13. The Sapir-Whorf hypothesis, that knowledge of the world is shaped by one's language, has been hotly debated. Whorfians—and even more so their intellectual adversaries—have a tendency to overstate their case. This is not the place to mount a full-fledged defense of the hypothesis; in part it must be seen as a reaction against the vice-like grip that realism has had on Western notions of language. Suffice it to say that most people who are proficient in two very distant languages have experienced the effects of the hypothesis. The fact that these people were able to learn a distant language in the first place, however, invalidates the extreme claim that distant languages are conceptually

> The analysis of a culture's terminological systems will not, of course, exhaustively reveal the cognitive world of its members, but it will certainly tap a central portion of it. Culturally significant cognitive features must be communicable between persons in one of the standard symbolic systems of the culture. A major share of these features will undoubtedly be codable in a society's most flexible and productive communicative device, its language.[14]

Words matter, then, insofar as they are excellent clues to what others are thinking or feeling. But they are equally effective in training us to think or feel in a certain way. Consider, for the moment, how we learn to feel shame because of something we've done or the way we are. We either learn indirectly that certain behaviors or attributes are socially disvalued, or we are told so directly. By learning indirectly, I mean we are given various clues, such as body language, facial expressions, social avoidance, or oblique remarks. I suggest that learning to respond to music is very much like learning to feel shame.

Some musical elements, however, may have iconic meaning. That is, a natural resemblance is felt between form and content—between "bright" sounds and cheerfulness, for instance. I say "felt," here, because there is almost certainly some cultural conditioning in iconicity (and like any nature-or-nurture problem, it is well-nigh impossible to prove one way or the other).

In nineteenth-century Europe, music was felt to communicate directly without the intervention of language. Mendelssohn, in a famous passage, once wrote that music is actually far more precise as a means of communication than is language (see Treitler 1997:26–27). The prevailing eighteenth-century European view of musical expression, with its ties to rhetoric, is much closer to current Javanese aesthetics, as well as to my second citation from Sibley (quoted on the next page). In both eighteenth-century Europe and contemporary Java there is/was considerable consensus about musical affect. Furthermore, language is/was largely responsible for this consensus in two different ways. The obvious one is that in both cultures musical affect is/was discussed as a perceivable feature of the music. The other is that at the core of both cultures is/was a theatrical form that uses/used music to enhance or create dramatic mood. In eighteenth-century Europe it was opera, in Java it is *wayang*. A nonlinguistic feature that the two music-cultures have in common is that music in both is/was very much tied to context. Before concert halls became common in Europe, music served var-

incommensurable (*something* must translate from one conceptual system to the other, or a learner would get nowhere, and there would be no basis on which to judge the accuracy of a translation). For an elegant defense of Sapir and Whorf's claim, see many of the essays in A. L. Becker 1995. For a convenient summary of some of the objections, see Nida 1975:184–91.

14. Frake 1980 [1962]:3. I first came across the passage in Kövecses 1990:41–42. Kövecses cites other authors as well—authors who may not be thought of as Whorfians, but who also look to ordinary language to uncover conceptual systems: Wittgenstein, Austin, and Ryle. Besides Kövecses's own study, other notable contributions in a similar vein are Lakoff and Johnson 1980 and Lakoff 1990.

ious purposes: accompaniment to religious ritual, to state ceremony, to theater, to the hunt, to drinking, and the like (Dahlhaus 1985 [1977]:20). In Java, also, certain pieces and genres are closely associated with various social occasions (*Wilujeng* with weddings, *Monggang* with grand ceremonial events). In both cases, these associations shape/shaped listeners' responses.

Outsiders who have not watched hundreds of *wayangs* or attended dozens of Javanese weddings lack the accumulated contextual memories—the "prior texts," in A. L. Becker's phrase—to know what they should be feeling when listening to *karawitan*. They are particularly dependent on verbal cues in learning how to respond to Javanese music. And, just as second-language learners need pointers about how to avoid interference from their native language, second-music learners need to *un*learn many of the cognitive and affective habits they have grown up with. They need, in Ortega y Gasset's words, to become aware of the "exuberances and deficiencies" between their own music and the one they are becoming initiated into.[15]

Charles Keil, in his study of Tiv music, dance, and aesthetics, makes the case for outsiders' attending to insiders' speech about music as follows:

> [One reason] for studying the musical terminology of another culture [is that] the exercise serves to remove some of the blinders, biases, and distortions inherent in our own vocabulary. Coming to terms with (or with terms to) another system of musical thought, we are forced to question the axioms of our own musicology. (1979:26–27)

As Sibley suggests, these "blinders, biases, and distortions" may be present whether we are verbalizing at the time or not:

> Much music is heard and appreciated without any verbal intervention. . . . Could there be reason to think that, even when we listen wordlessly (and non-pictorially), when no one offers or seeks descriptions, we nevertheless make sense of music by, without realizing it, bringing it under verbalizable concepts, and without thinking of the words that might verbalize them? (1997:169)

My Whorfian answer to Sibley's question, based on years of playing, singing, and listening to *karawitan*, is a resounding "yes!"

Some might claim that one can never learn to think and feel like someone from another culture. But few would contend that it is impossible to learn to speak a second language with near-native fluency. Moreover, part of learning to speak a new language is learning to think and feel like someone else: speaking a language well means knowing what to say, what to think, what to feel in a given social situation.[16] It is reasonable to assume, then, that one could at least approach native fluency in musical responses by following procedures similar to those of advanced language learning.

15. I am using "exuberance and deficiency" in the senses in which A. L. Becker has used them in his borrowing of Ortega y Gasset (see A. L. Becker 1995, passim).

16. See, for instance, Keeler 1984.

Wittgenstein, in his *Philosophical Investigations*, describes how we might come to know if "an expression or feeling is genuine or not":

> Can one learn this knowledge? Yes; some can. Not, however, by taking a course in it, but through '*experience*'.—Can someone else be a man's teacher in this? Certainly. From time to time he gives him the right *tip*.—This is what 'learning' and 'teaching' are like here.[17] (1958:227e)

In learning a language, or in learning to perceive music in a culturally appropriate way—that is, in learning what to think and feel—mere experience is not enough: insiders and outsiders alike need to be given tips along the way.[18] In this book I have attempted to pass along a number of these tips, while at the same time placing them in a larger matrix.

Listening Correctly

A second assumption I have made throughout the book is that there is a correct way—or, better, a correct range of ways—to perceive music. This, to some, is an extremely offensive notion. Robert Kraut has summarized the opposing point of view (with which he disagrees), as follows:

> We may be willing to insist that native discourse belongs to the natives—or, more broadly, to those with whom the natives would be willing to converse. But Beethoven's Fifth belongs to the world. *No* population enjoys privilege over any other in fixing the musical-perceptual facts constitutive of the 'real significance' of a musical piece.... Prevalent lore about music, in contrast to that about linguistic meaning, endorses a thoroughgoing pluralism: immerse yourself in the musical event and enjoy the resulting rhythmic and harmonic tingles. Do not worry whether the tingles are correct, appropriate to the musical event, or sufficiently similar to those of a maximally hip listener. One set of tingles is as good as another. (1995:111)

This view, which Kraut calls "pluralistic," is better termed "individualistic": in a cross-cultural context it is anything but pluralistic. Rather, it is just as arrogant and self-serving as the pedant who claims to know the one correct way of interpreting a Beethoven quartet. For it fails to take into account that there is such a thing as musical misunderstanding—that it is possible, in other words, to *mis*interpret a culturally embedded aesthetic object or event.[19] It fails to take

17. This passage was first brought to my attention in Berenson 1995 [1993].

18. Wachsmann (1982) gives several examples of how such "tips" may influence musical experience.

19. I am setting aside, for the moment, the question of ownership of cultural artifacts. This question becomes far more urgent when dealing with cultures, such as those of many native American groups, in which music is "owned" by specific people or groups of people. This idea of ownership goes far beyond notions of mere copyright. For instance, in some cultures, to be taught a song is to be entrusted with it—the owners of that song are responsible for not abusing it, and for assuring its continued existence. Seeger 2004 and Guy 2002 provide interesting cases of clashes between traditional and copyright-oriented notions of ownership. For concepts of ownership in Javanese traditional music, see Benamou 2005.

into account what ethnomusicologists have known for a long time, that "art and the equipment to grasp it are made in the same shop" (Geertz 1983:118). On one hand, the individualist claims that works of art are public but their interpretations are private; on the other, the cultural pluralist maintains that both artworks and their interpretations are public, but only relative to a *certain* public. It may be, as Kraut proposes, that there is no way of logically demonstrating the superiority of one or the other claim (outside of a particular context), and what we must look at are the purposes that each position serves.

If our goal is to understand music, there is no question that insiders' perspectives take epistemological precedence. But if our goal is simply to have a meaningful experience, the choice is a little less clear. Who is to say that, if I let the comments of Beethoven's peers guide my reactions to his music (to elaborate on one of Kraut's examples), I will have a richer aesthetic experience? Perhaps I do not share their penchant for pathos, heroism, purity, nobility, the sublime, Nature, and the like. Perhaps I will be repulsed by Beethoven's music (as, in fact, were some of his peers!). Or, to take a more obvious example, do I really want to know the political and historical subtexts of Wagner's operas? Difficult questions, indeed. Perhaps one must give up on choosing definitively between the two stances, looking rather at each case individually. Let me simply posit that the more culturally distant one is from an aesthetic artifact or event, the more one stands to benefit from considering carefully what the insiders have to say about it.

Musicians as Insiders

In the discussions above I used the word *insiders* several times. This term is by no means self-explanatory, for it is not always easy to determine who the insiders are. What's more, whoever they are, they do not always agree with each other. But this does not invalidate the idea that one ought to have, in Kraut's words, "a commitment to the explanatory importance of the musical perceptions and standards of taste upheld within the particular population which is *responsible for the musical event* in question" (Kraut 1992:20).[20] The fact that there are borderline members, or that there is variation within the group does not mean that the concept itself is invalid (think of Wittgenstein's notion of categories based on family resemblances); it is simply more difficult to apply.

Let us say, then, that as an ethnographer of Javanese music I am looking for insiders. Whom do I choose? A natural first choice, given limits on time, would be

20. While I find that Kraut's article sets out with great clarity the issues at stake, I do not entirely agree with his position. In particular, I do not believe that there is *one* correct interpretation, but rather a *number* of interpretations that "get it right." Furthermore, I believe that one can accept a wider or narrower range of interpretations depending on the context (only in certain circumstances would one want to say that an interpretation is just plain wrong).

those who are most knowledgeable about the tradition. In other words, with respect to Javanese music, we might distinguish between different levels of insidership—of expertise—within Javanese society. *Karawitan* may be communal, but it is not participatory, in that the audience does not normally enter into the music-making. To be a good gamelan musician requires many years of focused effort and experience: this is a highly specialized activity. And, like jazz, much of the complexity of *karawitan* is accessible only to musicians. For instance, the kind of humorous dialogue that can occur between musicians in performance is usually lost on ordinary listeners—when, for example, an instrumentalist parodies another musician's recognizable style; or plays wordlessly a melody associated with a *senggakan*;[21] or fakes out the other musicians by pretending to head toward a wrong note but at the last second landing on the right one instead.[22] In Java, most people cannot recognize one gamelan piece from another: they have very little detailed, explicit knowledge of the tradition. Musicians, on the other hand, carry on a rich, precise discourse about music.

In all honesty, though, my decision to talk to musical experts was more a result of happenstance than of calculation. My initial contacts were all musicians; I was learning to perform; and so, not surprisingly, I just fell into that world. In addition, my principal advisor in Java when I began my fieldwork was Supanggah, who helped in directing me to people he knew were both knowledgeable and articulate; these were all eminent musicians.

I do not regret my decision to ask the experts first. They spoke generously, passionately, eloquently. It would be interesting, though, to talk to nonmusicians about *rasa gendhing*, to see how their conceptions might be similar to those of the musicians I spoke to. The method of questioning would undoubtedly have to be more concrete, more deictic in nature ("What is the rasa of *this* recording?" "How is *this* piece different from *the last one*?"), but the results would be just as important, from an ethnographic perspective, and the comparison to musicians' conceptions would be most illuminating.[23]

PART II: *RASA* AND CROSS-CULTURAL COMPARISON

The search for universals in humankind's music has gone through many stages. For a time it was a taboo subject, since it evoked the ambitious but totalizing

21. A *senggakan* is a lighthearted, sung interjection by the *gérong*.

22. For instances of such humor, listen to *Gamelan de Solo* II:2, 16:55, 30:30, 35:00 and IV:3, 7:00, 7:55, 18:50–19:18. Further details about these passages may be found in the accompanying notes (pp. 48–49, 56).

23. I suspect that while nonmusicians have very little technical knowledge of music, they are more sensitive to *rasa* than they are made out to be (I am thinking, here, of all the disparaging remarks I heard about *orang awam*—"laypeople"). I have certainly found that students in the United States who are non-music majors are very sensitive to musical mood, yet often incapable of distinguishing one instrument from another.

projects of the early comparative musicologists. It was abandoned with good reason: the problem of perspective is nearly insurmountable. That is, what appears similar from one perspective appears very different from another. Constructing a theory of musical universals is a bit like comparing objects in a photograph: two trees may appear similar at *that* angle and at *that* distance, but when viewed from any other perspective they appear quite different. For instance, they may appear similar in outline but have differently shaped leaves. Or they might be bent in ways that are not visible in the photograph. Whereas it might be possible to compare two musical traditions each from the perspective of the other,[24] in comparing more than two traditions one inevitably adopts a single perspective, with an inevitable impoverishment of meaning, and with an inevitable arrogance. The main problem with cross-cultural comparison, then, is that it is impossible to find a neutral point of view from which to measure sameness or difference.

If one looks for cultural differences one will find them, and if one looks for cultural similarities one will also find them. Moreover, both searches can be the result of either good or bad intentions. That is, identifying differences may be a first step towards mutual understanding, or it can be a divisive tactic intended to show the inherent inferiority of the other. Pointing out similarities can also be a way of bridging a gap, or it can be a subtle way of refusing to recognize that another culture or subculture may be operating on a different set of assumptions, with the result that aspects of that other culture, which had appeared inexplicable, remain so. This point—the dual nature of both similarity and difference—gets lost in Agawu's attack (2003) on difference as exclusively a tool by Western ethnographers for making *Other.* His provocative book, *Representing African Music,* while ultimately salutary, is shot through with contradictions: over and over he makes use of essentializing moves himself. More importantly, he ignores the fundamental role difference plays in developing cross-cultural sensitivity: without a conscious search for difference an adult could never learn a foreign language nor become proficient in a foreign musical tradition. But his larger point questioning the very category "foreign"—which he approaches from the perspective of postcolonial studies—is well taken. What makes the category problematic is a long history of intense interaction between colonizer and colonized (see the section "Diffusion or Plurigenesis?" below).

Comparison, then, involves seeking both sameness and difference, and, if used sensitively, may be used as a tool for *unmaking* Other. But at the same time, it has always been at the heart of the production of etic knowledge and has thus been couched in a scientific paradigm of neutrality and

24. See Benamou 1989 and 2003 for two attempts to do just that.

generalization.[25] One may question, as does Bourdieu, the whole social phenomenon of scientism, of which one manifestation is a search for universals:

> Q. In your work you have made no room for universal norms—unlike Habermas, for instance.
>
> A. I tend to view the problem of rationality or norms in a strictly historicized way. Instead of asking myself if there are "universal interests," I would ask, "Who benefits from universals?" Or, better, "What are the social conditions that must be fulfilled so that certain agents have a stake in universals?" (1987:43, translation mine)

Here the reader can fill in the blank ("capitalism," "imperialism," "colonialism" are the most likely culprits). But, even if a search for universals may be seen as a product of imperialism, of exercising control, the lure of universals runs deep. Wouldn't it be wonderful to understand *human* nature? Wouldn't we all be better off if we could find commonalities among *all* humans?

Over the past several decades, researchers in the fields of ethnobiology, linguistics, and psychology have become increasingly sophisticated (perhaps speciously so) in their search for universals.[26] What the biologists and psychologists have found is that, at a certain middle level of generalization, categories might well be universal.[27] This relates most directly to chapter 3 of the present study, which deals with categories. I suspect that one would be hard-pressed to find universals in the area of musical affect (again, it depends on what one is looking for): the objects of musical perception—the emotional stimuli—are far too varied. But again, rather than look for "true" universals, one could look for preponderant trends—what Bruno Nettl has called "statistical universals" (2000). One way of using the present study for etic purposes would be to compare my

25. See Abu-Lughod 1991 for a thorough critique of generalizing modes of discourse. It should be pointed out, however, that even she cannot avoid generalizations in her own examples of particularist, narrative-based ethnography. Indeed, without them her narratives would make no sense to someone unfamiliar with Bedouin ways.

26. See Lakoff 1990 and Brown 1991 for overviews. Some of the principal names Lakoff mentions are Brent Berlin, Paul Kay, Roger Brown, Paul Ekman, and Eleanor Rosch. An ambitious (if troubling) recent attempt to demonstrate linguistic universals is to be found in Goddard and Wierzbicka 1994. With respect to music in particular, investigations into the biological basis of musical experience—though not necessarily with the goal of establishing universals—are to be found in J. Becker 2004 and Juslin and Sloboda 2001.

27. While on the surface this claim makes sense to me, I can think of many exceptions. I shall cite a few, taken from the realm of concrete objects, all of them at a middle level of specificity. There's no word for "nut" in French, only for specific kinds of nuts. There's no word for "wall" in Indonesian; one must distinguish between a masonry wall and a partition. There's no word for *jam* [I] in English; one must distinguish between a clock and a watch. There's no word for *kaki* [I] in English; one must distinguish between a foot and a leg. It could be claimed, with the possible exception of the last example, that the fact that a language is missing a word doesn't mean that the concept is missing (Eleanor Rosch has argued this with respect to color terms). And yet many of the claims for linguistic universals are made at the level of terminology and not concepts.

findings with other classifications of musical affect, that is, to base the comparison on emic description. The three that have been extensively written about in English are Indian *rasa* theory,[28] eighteenth-century European musical affects,[29] and the psychological experiments performed in the United States in the 1930s (including the famous Hevner adjective list).[30]

A more promising place to look for universals is in the area of iconicity. In a famous essay (1988 [1979]), the linguist Roman Jakobsen drew together some impressive cross-cultural data indicating that speech sounds are not completely arbitrary. That is, certain sounds seemed to be associated with certain meanings across many unrelated languages. My most general findings in chapter 7 would seem to apply equally well in European, Tiv, or many other music cultures. One example would be the correlation between high pitches and exuberance, between low pitches and sadness. One must proceed cautiously, though: similarity in a few instances does not mean that humans are hard-wired to think a certain way (we should probably be looking for widespread patterns rather than universals in the strictest sense). Moreover, the whole notion of similarity is suspect, since what counts as "exuberant" behavior (if, indeed, an equivalent term exists in the language of the people in question) will surely vary from culture to culture.[31] Or, to give another example, how might we be distorting a conceptualization of music that may not even have pitch as a distinct, analyzable category? Despite the problems, the possibility that there may be some natural psychological tendencies is intriguing.

In the preface I noted the informal experiments I have conducted with students in the United States. Sometimes I include some typically Western-sounding instrumental music (Beethoven, Herbie Hancock, Villa-Lobos) for comparison's sake. As a general rule, the responses were more homogeneous the more familiar the music, as might be expected: these were the ones with the most shared context, the most shared discourse. By contrast, the most heterogeneous were responses to the "trick" examples of Javanese music. These were of two kinds: the examples that I had found puzzling myself, like the *andhegan* (vocal cadenza) from *Budheng-Budheng* mentioned earlier in the chapter; and

28. There are hundreds of volumes spanning many centuries to choose from. Two studies that I have found helpful in explaining *rasa* in current musical practice are Gautam 1980 and Sharma 1985/1986. The most thorough treatment I've come across is Rao 2000. In view of the Sanskrit origin of the word *rasa*, Indian classical music would probably be the most interesting comparison to make. See J. Becker 1993 for holdovers in Javanese musical aesthetics from Indian philosophy.

29. The best source in English for the sake of comparison remains Wessel 1955.

30. For background on Hevner's circle, see Farnsworth 1954 and 1969. Benamou 2003 compares the circle to Javanese *rasa* categories as analyzed in chapter 3 of this book. In view of historic Sufi connections, other fruitful avenues are likely to be found in Arabic, Turkish, and Persian aesthetics (see During 2001 and Racy 2003). Demeuldre 2004 is an unprecedented attempt to compare emic accounts of a single basic emotion (bittersweetness) in over two dozen societies.

31. For many examples of semantic slippage in emotion terms, see Heider 1991.

those that I knew to have musical features that were likely to be misinterpreted by people accustomed to Western and not to Javanese music—for example, pieces in the *pélog barang* mode, which often sounds "minor" to Western ears but whose affective connotations are generally the opposite (spritely, flirtatious, cheerful, rambunctious). In 2006 I conducted similar experiments with my two classes in Java using musics from around the world (mainland Asia, Africa, North America, Europe). I did not use Javanese music for fear of being considered Java-centric by my majority non-Javanese Indonesian students, although it would have been most interesting to compare Javanese and non-Javanese responses. The results were similar to the experiments in the United States, in that the most familiar examples—Berlioz and Indian film music—had more homogeneous responses (the most heterogeneous of all was Alvin Lucier).

No matter how heterogeneous the responses, however, in all these experiments there was almost always at least one person who seemed to have intuited exactly what had been intended by the tradition bearers (to the extent that that can be known or defined with any precision): somehow he or she "got it right." Those who did so were responding to *something* in the music that evoked the sentiments being expressed. In some cases they were not even picking up on the signifiers that would have been the most obvious to an insider (*miring*, for instance—the use of *pélog*-like tones in *sléndro*, which, other things being equal, evokes sadness). But somewhere in that complex alchemy of sounds that is music, they sensed fellow humans speaking to them across a cultural divide. Were these listeners unusually sensitive, did they have a natural affinity for the culture in question, or were they just lucky? Whatever the reason for their apparent perspicacity, it seems plausible that there is a biological, pan-human aspect to musical expression, the way there is for laughter or tears.

DIFFUSION OR PLURIGENESIS?

Without going to the extreme of looking for universals, one can make more modest comparisons. In my discussions with Javanese musicians about aesthetic evaluation I could not help but be struck by similarities to European-based notions.[32] For example, good singers in both traditions should sing in tune,

32. Whenever one makes comparisons to European traditions one opens oneself to the charge of ethnocentrism. I hasten to add that I do not do this because I think of Europe as the standard against which all other cultures should be judged. I do it for the simple reason that the European musical tradition (especially in its American continuation) is what I know best—it is *my* music, the tradition with respect to which I am an insider. Moreover, since I am writing in English for an academic readership, presumably a considerable proportion of my readers will also be familiar with European music. Those who are not might be interested in one insider's attempt to characterize his music.

should pay attention to timing, should have a (culturally defined) pleasing tone, should have vocal agility, and should express the affect of the piece. In each of these areas, of course, there are many fascinating details that distinguish the two traditions. But evaluative criteria are much more similar than, say, between European and Diné ("Navajo") aesthetics (at least as these are presented in McAllester 1954). The researcher who is confronted with profoundly unfamiliar territory has a much harder task of understanding the lay of the land. This will lead to the researcher's being made more conscious of his or her own cultural assumptions, and, one must admit, to more dramatic ethnographic prose. But instead of feeling adrift, I felt rather at home with Javanese aesthetics as I perceived it: there seemed to be no sensational differences to report. In a word, I was crestfallen.

In the following passage from my fieldnotes, Supanggah, after denying that Javanese music was anything like European music, said that any similarities were a result of encroachment from the West:

> I mentioned that I had hoped to find an aesthetic that was very different from a "Western" musical aesthetic, and that instead I had found something that was actually quite similar in many ways. His first reaction was to bristle, and he said he didn't see how it could be the same.
>
> P: *Tujuannya lain, cara belajar juga lain* [Their aims are different, and their learning methods are also different]. Whereas in the West virtuosity is emphasized, in Javanese music it isn't at all. Instead of reaching a high level of skill through disciplined training, musicianship [in Java] is/was attained through ascetic exercises (*kebatinan*). Your research is actually a bit late—Pak Marto's gone, and so is Pak Turahjo. Perhaps only Pak Mloyo and Pak Mitro[33] are left from the old school. Pak Mloyo, for instance, used to memorize *gendhings* while walking all night to and from Boyolali. The people you've talked to have received Western educations, have learned music with notation, and those who have learned in a conservatory setting are even farther from traditional values. My father used to say that, among the current generation of *rebab* players, they're often "*baik*" [good], but never once do they make the hair on the back of his neck stand up. (April 12, 1992)

Supanggah is not the only one to claim that things used to be less Westernized, more Javanese. But perhaps things are not quite so simple. Let us not forget that the Dutch were in Java for some 300 years. In pre-Independence Java, much of the aristocracy had received Dutch educations, were truly fluent in Dutch, and a good number of them had Dutch family through marriage. In the nineteenth and early twentieth centuries, the Solonese courts had European bands and string ensembles as well as gamelans (Sumarsam 1995:65–71).

33. Martopangrawit, Turahyo Harjomartono, Mloyowidodo, and Mitropradonggo were all court musicians, and were considered the last of the *empu* (masters) at the time.

In contrast, today few Javanese become proficient in a European language, and my impression is that public education is not as strongly European as were the Dutch-language schools of colonial times.[34] Perhaps this explains why, as mentioned in chapter 3, younger musicians used *Javanese* terms for *rasa* when speaking Indonesian to me, and older musicians often used *Dutch* terms, even when speaking in Javanese. As for Western musical influences, there is no question that Javanese young people today hear more diatonic music than ever before. Even in Solo, far fewer than half of the radio stations in the early 1990s played gamelan music—most played Indonesian pop; my impression is that the proportion of guitar- or keyboard-based music has only increased since. This has led Supanggah (1991a, 2003) and others to worry whether the next generation will be able—or even want—to continue to perform *karawitan* (indeed, several faculty members at STSI in Solo remarked that Javanese children are rarely capable of singing in tune in *sléndro* or *pélog* any more). AL Suwardi, commenting on the degree of Western influence now as compared to earlier times, said:

> *Pengaruh mana dulu* [It depends on *which* influences you're talking about]. In terms of *istilah* [terms] and ways of analyzing, there might have been more of a Dutch influence before, but in terms of technology and mass media there's more now. (June 9, 1995)

However one may choose to compare "then" with "now," there is no denying that interaction with Europeans or with European culture has been commonplace, at least among some segments of Javanese society, for several centuries.[35] A single glance at the imported rococo-style chandeliers in the nineteenth-century *pendhåpå* of the Mangkunegaran Palace will confirm that. This means that plurigenesis—the unrelated development of similar phenomena in different areas of the globe—is an unlikely explanation for many of the parallels one can draw between Javanese and European musical thought. Dutch influence also makes this particular comparison inconclusive as evidence for psychological universals. That said, it is very difficult to prove directly that what appear to be Western ideas began through cultural diffusion. The evidence is usually circumstantial.[36] The question remains: What would Javanese music be like

34. For example, older people I knew who had gone to Dutch schools had a much more European relationship to written texts than did the younger people I met.

35. See Lombard 1990, Pemberton 1994, Florida 1995, Sumarsam 1994 and 1995, and J. Becker 1972. Kartomi denies that European culture had anything but minimal influence on gamelan music in colonial times (1990). She points out that the European population was very small in comparison to the Javanese population. But she seems to be unaware of the European music at the courts.

36. Sumarsam (1995) attempts to show Western influence in the development of a number of musical concepts. While his argument is generally convincing, often it boils down to saying that (1) a change occurred in Javanese writings about music; (2) we know people at the courts interacted with Europeans; and (3) therefore it is likely that the changes occurred as a result of contact.

today if Java had never been colonized by the Dutch? We will never know for sure.[37]

One ought not, then, go overboard with diffusionist theories. Why should it be so unlikely that people came up with similar ideas unbeknownst to each other? And why, as was often assumed, should the direction of influence always be from a "higher" culture to a "lower" one? Even if one rephrases the question to the somewhat less objectionable "dominant" and "subjugated," it is clearly not the case that borrowing is unidirectional. As an only slightly tongue-in-cheek warning against seeing European influence in all forms of change, I would like to repeat what Rasito, the noted musician from Banyumas, once said. I had asked him about recordings, like the one titled *Pangkur Pamijèn* (Quirky *Pangkur*), in which the gamelan ensemble drops out for several gong cycles, letting each of the front row instruments play individually.

> R: I think it started with Bu Tjondro's group at RRI Jakarta, and then got taken up by Basiyo.[38] It was just a way of letting each instrument be heard.
>
> M: Did it start as an imitation of Western music?
>
> R: First of all, those musicians knew nothing about Western music—and didn't care to know, either. Second, who's to say that it didn't go in the other direction? It's like Arjuna's magic weapon that could find its target whether it was visible or not—it existed long before all of these missiles, which are supposed to be so sophisticated just because they can find their targets. (Rasito, February 1, 1994)

It is doubtful, of course, that baroque concerti were influenced by *Pangkur Pamijèn*. However, it would be naive—and inaccurate—to think that the colonized had no influence on the colonizers, even in the metropole.[39] For instance, there is reason to believe that the seventeenth-century Dutch innovation of tuning carillon bells by grinding them on a lathe and comparing them to tuned metal bars had an Indonesian origin (Mendonça 2002:68).

One solution is not to worry too much about where current practices originated. We might well heed Lindsay's warning about being too essentialist in dividing East from West (1985:10ff.).[40] As Lombard has amply documented (1990),

37. Basset (2004) has tried to reconstruct a sort of *Ur-gamelan*, on the basis of what present-day Balinese music is like, as well as on her interpretation of older writings and other clues. Bali is interesting in this regard because its inhabitants never converted to Islam and they resisted Dutch control for far longer than their neighbors to the west.

38. Tjondrolukito is a famous singer from Yogyakarta who recorded dozens of cassettes with her name prominently displayed on the cover. RRI is the national radio station. Basiyo was a Yogyanese male singer who did comedy routines interspersed with songs.

39. The term *metropole* is used in postcolonial studies to distinguish the colonizers' homeland (i.e., Europe) from the colony.

40. Indeed, there may be connections between Javanese and European cultures other than those resulting from direct contact. We know, for instance, that both have been influenced by Arabic culture. Java was profoundly affected by Indian culture, and, as the Indo-European language family suggests, there was also some cultural continuity between India and Europe.

Java has always had waves of foreign influence. Why should we treat Dutch influences any differently from Indian or Arabic ones? And what would Javanese culture be without Sanskrit and the *Mahabharata*, without Arabic and the Koran? In a sense, whether or not current notions of the musical work, "*alus*ness," the aesthetic, or even *rasa* are now infused with European elements, they still qualify as Javanese culture if that's the way Javanese people conceive of them.

IN DEFENSE OF BEAUTY

Except for isolated attempts to revive the term, it has become hopelessly old-fashioned to speak of beauty in the arts. Aesthetics has come a long way from the days when it was the science of the beautiful. And, thankfully, ethnomusicologists will never return to a nineteenth-century Germanic conception of music as pure form, unsullied by other kinds of human activity (see Dahlhaus 1989 [1978]). I am not advocating that we look for autonomous rules of beauty—for universally applicable norms. Yet, if we lose sight of beauty as a value, we have lost much. It is my hope that the present study will not only aid in intellectual understanding, but will also enrich the reader's experience of Javanese music.

Kant taught us that to treat someone merely as a means to an end is amoral. Similarly, to study someone's music merely to prove a theoretical point is, as the saying goes, a crime, a sin, and a shame. Certainly for my teachers, *karawitan* has intrinsic value; this rich tradition means more to them than does just about anything else in their lives. Unlike many of the world's practices that English speakers call "music," *karawitan* is particularly susceptible to aesthetic contemplation. Indeed, the very word *karawitan* derives from *ngrawit* (delicate, well-formed, exquisite), and is related to *rerawitan* (something that is finely wrought) (Gericke and Roorda 1901). For some musics, intrinsic value does not lie so much in the beauty of sound. But the meaning of *karawitan* for Javanese musicians has very much to do with beauty, with what in Old Javanese was called *langö* (Zoetmulder 1974:172–73), but in modern Javanese might well be called *råså*. And so, my final reason why all of this matters may be summed up in a distant paraphrase of Martopangrawit's own oft-quoted hortatory poem, with which he concludes his two-volume treatise on *karawitan* theory (1984 [1972]:242): listen to what these musicians say, listen to their music and learn to *rasa* its many *rasas*, for you will be richly rewarded.

APPENDIX A

CLASSIFICATIONS OF *RASA GENDHING* FROM ORAL AND WRITTEN SOURCES

This appendix is meant as a supplement to chapter 3. In it I have included various partial classifications of *rasa gendhing*, sticking to the original spelling used by the author in question (that is, by and large, with fewer diacritics). Some of these were impromptu listings of representative *rasa*s; others were more premeditated and are presumably more complete. I have preceded each listing with a summary of what led up to it, whether this was in conversation or in a written document. As elsewhere in the book, I define *rasa gendhing* here as including any kind of mood or aesthetic effect a *gendhing* is said to convey. Also included are several classifications of the dramatic moods (*suasana*s [I]) in *wayang* that were listed in discussing *wayang* music. All Javanese and Indonesian words are translated in the full glossary at the end of the book, and all bibliographic references are listed in the "corpus" section of the bibliography.

1. Supanggah, May 17, 1992. Written, without advance preparation, at my request. The list included other *rasa*s and what Supanggah termed *qualitas* (qualities—i.e., *sifat*s?). But the other terms on the page were not laid out in a clear pattern, and so I have left them out. The question mark after *kasmaran* was Supanggah's (perhaps doubting whether *kasmaran* counts as an example of *rasa gendhing*? Or whether it counts as *prenès*?).

regu	*prenès*	*gecul*	*sedih*
gagah	*gobyog*	*ramé*	*tlutur*
sereng	*renyah*		*luruh*
mrabu	*kasmaran (?)*		*trenyuh*
bregas	*bérag*		*wingit*
			ngeres

2. Supanggah 1985:145–46. An explicit, but partial, classification of *gendhing*s by *watak* or *rasa* (*caractère, sentiment*). Note that this is almost a mirror image of figure 3.3.

   gobyog - gecul - prenès - tlutur - regu

3. Sudarsono, November 9, 1991. In answer to my query as to what *rasa gendhing* there were:

   1. *prenès*
   2. *regu* = *gagah, berwibawa*
   3. *tlutur* [sad]
   4. *gecul* = *prenès* + *gojèg* [joking]
   5. *sem* = *gagah* + *perasaan yang dalam* [deep feeling]
   6. *semangat* [enthusiasm]
   7. *trenyuh* = *cinta* [love] + *susah* [troubled]

4. Sukanto, April 17, 1992. *Gendhing*s have *watak*s, just like people:
   luruh, branyak, "dandy," *susah*

5. Sukanto, June 24, 1992. In answer to my general question about *rasa gendhing* (after a long discussion first about the relationship of *rasa gendhing* to *wayang* scenes):
   nges, sereng, èmeng, prenès, sedhih/tlutur, trenyuh, gelå, gelisah

   Note that these are mostly sad *rasa*s. Sukanto once told me that older people, like him, didn't like to put in too much *miring* (*pélog*-like intervals in a *sléndro* piece) in sad pieces, which would make them too sad. The implication was that their lives already had too much sadness in them, and so it was too painful to add more (or was it that people of his generation avoided strong emotions altogether?).

6. Wignyosaputro, June 19, 1992. In answer to my question about whether there were categories of *rasa gendhing* (not all given in a single sentence):
   sedih, bérag, prenès, gembira, gecul, khidmat

7. Sutarman, June 10, 1992. My questions about *klasik berat* led to a discussion of the limits of this term that ended with Sutarman saying, "So I think the categories of *gendhing* are"

   -*biasa* ["ordinary," lighthearted],
   -*klasik ringan* [light classic]
   -*klasik berat* [heavy classic]

8. Sastro Tugiyo, May 6, 1992. After my prodding about what terms there are for *rasa gendhing*:

   – *prenès, gobyog* [lively], *gecul*
   – *klasik, tenang* [calm], *meneng* [quiet], *tentrem* [tranquil]

   Later, in the same conversation, in discussing the different *rasa*s that *pesindhèn*s need to be able to sing, he listed
   gecul, prenès, klasik, kasmaran

9. Suhartå, December 14, 1990. In a discussion about judging singers in a competition, Suhartå said that they must be able to tell the difference, for example, between

   susah and *bérag, prenès*

10. Suhartå, March 26, 1992. I had asked what categories of *rasa gendhing* there were. The first distinction he mentioned was

    gagah vs. *sedih.*

    In addition, *sedih* may be subdivided, for example:

    - "*sedih ditinggal pacar*" (sad because your lover left you)
    - "*sedih tidak punya orang tua, kematian anak, sudah lolos*" (sad because you have no parents, because you lost a child—because someone has departed for good)

11. Suhartå, May 2, 1992. *Sléndro* is more difficult to feel/understand (*merasakan*) than *pélog*. There are a lot of different kinds within *sléndro*:

    ènthèng, ampang, mantab, regu

    Once a student came to Suhartå asking for two contrasting pieces, which he needed for his senior recital:

    gecul vs. *sedih*

12. Suhartå, June 25, 1992. After a question about the categories of singing voices, the following endpoints on three different continua came out:

    itu-itu vs. *sederhana*

    bérag vs. *anteng*

    gembira vs. *susah, sedih, trenyuh*

13. Soebantar [1968]:4. *Gendhing*s used in *wayang* can be

    gembira, sedih, humor, *bersemangat, lelah*, etc.

14. Soebantar [1968]:5. Each dramatic mood in *wayang* calls for a *gendhing* with a certain *sifat* (character):

    gagah, damai/tenteram, pertjintaan, perkawinan, gembira, kesedihan, kebentjian

15. Soebantar [1968]:78. *Grimingan* (improvised *gendèr* part that fills in between other pieces) must adjust to the dramatic mood:

    gembira, susah, emeng, marah, "humor," *lega/bebas*

16. Soebantar [1968]:78. One of the *kendhang*'s functions is to create a certain *rasa*:

    gembira, regu, humor, *sereng/santak*

17. Murtiyoso 1979/1980:9. *Iringan* (musical accompaniment) in *wayang* helps create the following *swasana*s (dramatic moods):

    lega, sedhih, gambira, sereng, mrabu, etc.

18. Murtiyoso 1979/1980:10. *Gendhing*s for *iringan* in *wayang* must be chosen in consideration of the *swasana*:
    trenyuh, mardhika [*sic*], *sereng, prihatos, prenes*, etc.

19. Murtiyoso 1979/1980:12. Through *sanggit* (creativity) the *dhalang's* performance can have the following *raos*es:
    sem, nges, renggep, cucut, prenes, etc.

20. Soeroso 1983:70. [In a long chapter on the "functions" of gamelan:] if you're stringing pieces together into a suite (*komposisi*), you can [should?] try to combine as many different characters of *gendhing*s as possible:
    agung, gembira, dinamis, tegang, susah, bersahaja

21. Darsono 1980:70. There are basically two different types of *gendhing sekar* (gamelan pieces based on *mâcâpat* songs):
    - *tenang*
    - *gobyog, sereng*, etc.

22. *Tembang Djawa*, published by Djawa Gunseikanbu, p. 6. Children need to know about the beauty of song... about expressing moods (*lairing raos*—the "birth," "exteriorizing" of moods) in *sekar* (classical Javanese song):
    adreng, sereng, wani, susah-melasih, gambira, etc.

23. Martopangrawit 1972:53. Every composer needs to know about melodic structure, because this is what will create different characters (*sifat*) in the music (also quoted in Waridi [1986]:15, but with *kenès* in place of *prenès*):
    regu, memelas, bérag, sereng, prenès, etc.

24. Djumadi 1982:178. A *rebab* player must know the character (*sifat*) of a *gendhing*:
    tenang, regu, prenes, susah, etc.

25. Soetarno [1978]:37–39. *Gendhing*s are classified according to their *rasa*s (*sentiments* [F]), their details of performance, and their structures:
    1. *kuna*
    2. *alus* (*calme et noble*) (calm and noble)
    3. *sedih, trenyuh* (*nostalgique et triste*) (nostalgic and sad)
    4. *prenes* (*érotique et sentiment de bonheur*) (erotic and feeling of contentment)
    5. *gecul* (*humoristiques*) (humorous)
    6. *keramat* (*sacré, magique, thérapeutique*) (sacred, magic, therapeutic)
    7. *popiler* = *kreasi baru* (*facile à comprendre*) (easy to understand)
    8. *dolanan* (*divertissement*) (amusement, play)

26. Soetarno 1991:4. *Bhawa* means "atmosphere" (of a *wayang* performance) or the communication (*pancaran*) of *rasa*:
    sedih, tenang, kelepasan, semangat

27. Padmosoekotjo [1960?]:50. *Gendhings* have the following *wataks* (characters):
    sigrak
    lanyap, alus
    anteng = *ruruh* + *alus*
    trenyuh
    gecul
    lega, gembira

28. Sastroamidjojo [1964?]:85. Each dramatic situation (*suasana*) in the *wayang* calls for its own characteristic melody and rhythm:

    peperangan... (combat between two knights)
    peperangan... (combat between a knight and an ogre)
    damai (peaceful)
    perkawinan (wedding)
    percintaan (romance)
    kegembiraan (happiness)
    kesedihan (sadness)
    kebencian (hate)

29. Warsadiningrat 1990 [1943]:71–72. Sultan Agung (reigned 1613–45) divided pieces into the following categories (followed by their respective *raoses*):

    1. *gendhing ageng—regu*
    2. *gendhing tengahan—sakéca*
    3. *gendhing alit—semu regu*, not *peprenesan*
    4. *gendhing prenès—bérag, sengsem, gambira, rena*
    5. *gendhing gecul—kasar* (*lucon badhutan*)

30. Warsadiningrat 1990 [1943]:110. Paku Buwana composed many pieces:
    gendhing alus, gendhing prenès, gendhing gecul

31. Sindoesawarno [n.d.]:37. Different tempos are appropriate for different moods (*suasanas*):

    medium: *senang, asmara*
    slow: *tidak senang, takut, sedih*
    fast: *kebranian, heran, marah*

32. Supanggah 2009:169. There is a kind of convention according to which certain *gendhings* have a *rasa* or character; [that is,] a given *gendhing* should

be performed in such a way that it results in a certain *rasa* that matches the *rasa* that the *gendhing* has been labeled with. The *rasa*s that are often mentioned by [musicians] are, inter alia:

Group 1	**Group 2**	**Group 3**	**Group 4**
tlutur >>>>	*biasa*	*prenès* >>>>	*gecul*
regu >>>>	*wantah* >>>>	*gagah* >>>>	*gobyog*
wingit >>>>	*lugu*	*sigrak* >>>>	*sereng*

The *rasa*s from Groups 1 and up do not progress in a continuum from endpoint 1 to endpoint 4; that is, [it is not the case that] Group 1 intensifies and turns into Group 2, which then intensifies and turns into Group 3, finally reaching a climax in Group 4 (nor, inversely do they progress in the other direction).

It is not easy to create categories for *rasa gendhing*: not only are their edges not clearly defined, but *rasa*s also depend a lot on subjective taste, and furthermore many *gendhing*s have multiple or mixed *rasa*s.

[*In an e-mail dated August 4, 2009, Supanggah further explained that what he meant in the third sentence, above, was that one rasa doesn't fade into the next through a process of intensification; that is, they are all equally intense.*]

APPENDIX B

HOW *IRÅMÅ* WORKS

Iråmå is undoubtedly one of the most confusing aspects of Javanese music to explain to Westerners, mainly because there is simply no equivalent in Western music, and hence no words with which to describe it succinctly. It can rather loosely be translated as "tempo" or "tempo level," but in some respects it is closer to "time signature," in that it has primarily to do with ratios between rhythmic densities. More specifically, it is the ratio between the faster- and the slower-moving parts, where the faster-moving parts maintain a relatively constant density and the slower-moving parts change their densities drastically from one *iråmå* to the next. The closest analogy in Western music to a section of a *gendhing* played in multiple *iråmå*s might be a set of variations in different time signatures but with all variations having the same number of measures and a fairly constant eighth-note value, so that the variations would take varying amounts of time to perform. The *iråmå*, in this case, would then correspond to the ratio between the density of the melodic figuration and the length of the measure (or, say, the harmonic rhythm). Imagine, for instance, a 2/2 variation with eighth-note figuration going to a 4/4 variation with sixteenth-note figuration: the "theme" would take twice as long in 4/4 as in 2/2, but the figuration would be going by at about the same speed in both.

In chapter 5 I defined *iråmå* as a process of expanding or contracting the gong cycle. It can also be thought of as expanding or contracting the beat. Imagine a balloon with regularly spaced asterisks along its equator. Now imagine placing three dots between each pair of asterisks so that each unit marked off by asterisks has been subdivided by four. If the balloon is blown up enough to make its circumference double in length, there is now room for twice as many dots between the asterisks. The opposite would be true, of course, were we to let out enough air so that the circumference were reduced by half—we would have half as many dots. The asterisks could be used to represent a theoretical beat, and the dots could be notes played by the faster-moving parts that fill in those beats. Note that the distance between the dots stays roughly the same whether the balloon is expanded and dots are added, or it is contracted and dots are removed.

Martopangrawit was one of the first Javanese theorists to come up with a precise definition of *iråmå* levels. He expressed the differences between *iråmå*s as different ratios between the *saron panerus* part and what he calls the "*balungan* pulse" (Martopangrawit 1984 [1972]:9–11). The *saron panerus* (the smallest, highest, and quickest of the trough-resonated metallophones called *sarons*) has the most consistent, unremitting pulse of any instrument in the ensemble and is indeed the only instrument that can act as a reliable indicator of *iråmå*. The *balungan* is a reference melody; its ontological status has been much debated.[1] For our purposes all that matters is that this is the part that commonly gets written down. In writing down a *balungan*, a musician is always aware of a steady reference pulse that may or may not be present in the *balungan* melody itself. (If a note lasts several pulses, dots are used to indicate the prolongation of the note. If a note is shorter than a pulse, lines like note beams are used above the ciphers.) There is rarely disagreement on what that pulse is. It is not, however, identical to a beat in Western music, which is always something in the vicinity of a walking or running speed. The *balungan* pulse varies far beyond those limits and is not always felt as the pulse that a listener would instinctively tap his or her foot to. That is, depending on the *iråmå*, the *balungan* pulse will be felt as half a beat, a whole beat, or two, four, or eight beats long. The *saron panerus*, on the other hand, always plays two notes per felt beat.

Most instruments of the gamelan play at a regular rhythmic density most of the time. And these densities, as has often been noted, are generally stratified, with higher densities corresponding to higher pitch ranges and vice versa. The more vocally oriented parts—the *rebab* (spike fiddle), *suling* (bamboo flute), and the vocal parts themselves—have irregular enough rhythms that they lie outside this system of stratification. All of the regular-density instruments can be divided into two groups, which I shall call simply faster and slower moving. The faster-moving parts are those that move at a rate that is usually faster than the *balungan* pulse. The slower-moving parts include all of the time markers and any melody that moves at least as slowly as the *balungan* (usually the *balungan* itself is the only melody fitting this description). In most cases the ratios described by Martopangrawit as being between the *saron panerus* and the *balungan* can be redefined more generally as those between the faster- and slower-moving parts.

In going from one *iråmå* level to the next, the tempo slows down, and the slower-moving parts become progressively less dense (they have more time from one note to the next). The faster-moving parts also slow down, but eventually they double their rate at the point where the *balungan* gets approximately twice as slow as it had been; they thus end up playing at approximately the same rate in all *iråmå* levels (remember the balloon analogy?). The slower-moving parts, on the other hand, will play faster or slower roughly by a factor of two when going between adjacent *iråmå* levels. I say "roughly," because there are usually differences of *laya* (surface tempo) between levels that make the correspondence inexact.

The standard Solonese *iråmå* levels are given below, with the most condensed *iråmå* at the top and the most expanded one at the bottom. In *iråmå lancar*, then, the slower-

1. For an excellent analytical summary of the various arguments put forward by Javanese musicians, see Perlman 2004.

moving parts will be relatively dense (their notes will come in quick succession), whereas in *irâmâ rangkep* they will be greatly stretched out. Characteristic *laya*s for each level are given in parentheses; endpoints (shown with asterisks) represent two successive notes of a slower part, while filled-in dots represent the notes of the fastest-moving parts such as the *bonang panerus* (small gong-chime) or the *gambang* (xylophone); the numbers are those commonly used nowadays, but others have been used in the past. The *saron panerus* plays half as many notes as the fastest-moving part. Please note that (1) in *irâmâ lancar* and *irâmâ gropak* the fastest-moving parts are mostly hypothetical (the *gambang* rarely plays and the *bonang panerus* has a simplified part); and (2) some theorists claim that *rangkep* is not a level unto itself, but simply a doubling of whatever level one was in previously;[2] *rangkep* is frequently used, however, to refer to the level below *irâmâ wiled.*

¼ *gropak* (fast)	★★
½ *lancar* (fast)	★.★
1 *tanggung* (moderate)	★...★
2 *dados* (slow)	★.......★
3 *wiled* (moderately fast)	★...............................★
4 *rangkep* (very fast)	★...★

As an illustration of two different *irâmâ* levels and of the transition between them, below are three versions of a single passage from *ladrang Dhengklung, laras pélog pathet limâ.* Figure B.1 represents a possible version of the *bonang barung* (the larger *bonang*) and *bonang panerus* (the smallest *bonang*) parts, along with the *balungan* in *irâmâ tanggung*. The second system shows what it might sound like in *irâmâ dados*, and the third system shows how one might get from *irâmâ tanggung* to *irâmâ dados*. Following the cipher notation are approximations in staff notation.

2. Similar qualms arise about *irâmâ gropak* (see Supanggah 2009:262–66).

B/1

bonang panerus: 424.424.454.454.424.424.515.515.

5 5

bonang barung: 4 2 4 . 4 5 4 . 4 2 4 . 1 . 1 .

balungan: 4 2 4 5 4 2 4 1

FIGURE B.1. *Balungan* and possible *bonang* parts to *ladrang Dhengklung* (second or third *kenongan*) in *iråmå tanggung*.

B/2

424.424.424.424.454.454.454.454.424.424.424.424.515.515.515.515.

5

4 2 4 . . 2 4 . 4 5 4 . . 5 4 . 4 2 4 . . 2 4 . 1 551 1 . 1 . .

4 2 4 5 4 2 4 1

FIGURE B.2. *Balungan* and possible *bonang* parts to *ladrang Dhengklung* (second or third *kenongan*) in *iråmå dados*.

424.424.454 . 4 5 4 .424.424.424.424.515.515.515.515. B/3

5

4 2 4 . 4 5 4 . 4 2 4 . . 2 4 . 1 551 1 . 1 . .

4 2 4 5 4 2 4 1

FIGURE B.3. *Balungan* and possible *bonang* parts for *ladrang Dhengklung* (second *kenongan*), transition from *irâmå tanggung* to *irâmå dados*. Note that on the recording the *bonang panerus* switches one beat later than the *bonang barung*, so that the two instruments are doubling each other for one beat: the place to switch is not determined in advanced, but rather depends on whenever it feels uncomfortably slow. Ideally they would feel the rhythm together and switch at the same time, as in the notation above.

COMPLETE GLOSSARY

This glossary is intended to include all of the non-English terms used throughout the text. It is to be used as a complement to the quick-reference short glossary of commonly used terms printed at the front of the book, which is of necessity abbreviated, both with respect to the number of entries and the definitions themselves. The glosses presented here should provide a fuller feel for the range of meanings a term may have (although I have attempted to keep these brief as well). Unless otherwise noted, all terms, to my knowledge, belong equally to *ngoko, kråmå,* and the Javanese dialect of Indonesian used in central Java (which includes many words of Javanese origin that may not be understood—or may have other meanings—in other parts of Indonesia).

The asterisks indicate *rasa* terms that appear in the book (including peripheral ones listed in chapter 3). They include terms for *rasa gendhing* as well as those descriptive of performances and performers. A good number of them would probably be rejected by some musicians as being something other than a *rasa* in the strictest sense.[1] Some terms, for example, might be considered more of a *sifat* (attribute, character), a *watak* (character, personality), or a *swasånå* (mood, atmosphere). But not all musicians distinguish carefully between these and *rasa*: at the very least they are all closely related. Other terms included here might not readily be applied to music (e.g., *mancing, menyanjung*), but were given to me only by way of explaining a term that is used for music.[2] The vast majority, however, would be included in a list of moods, characters, or aesthetic effects of a piece or performance. While this list is generously inclusive with respect to prototypicality, at the same time it leaves out many terms that are clear exemplars of *rasa gendhing*—I have included only those words specifically mentioned in the book.

My translations in this glossary emphasize the senses in which the words are used when applied to music, and some of these differ from ordinary usage.

References to photos are for the glossy insert section.

1. Supanggah in particular is quite careful on this point. My sense is that what he includes as a *rasa* is more specifically what in Indonesian is called *perasaan hati*, or emotion. But, as demonstrated in chapter 2, both *rasa* and *råså* mean a lot more than just emotion.

2. I would not normally place these on a list of *rasa gendhing*, but a criterion for inclusion here was whether a term was linked in conversation to one of my six basic terms.

At the end of some of the entries I have included some additional information, indicated by the sign ■. These additional comments indicate what lexical domains the words are usually applied to; this information is by no means definitive or complete. I am presenting here some of the results of an exercise I requested of Supanggah, in which he was to fill out a chart of some ninety-three terms (most of them *rasa* terms, broadly defined). He was to indicate, first, if the term had positive (+), neutral (ɵ), or negative (-) connotations. Next, he was to place a check in each column in which he felt the term would normally fit. The columns were as follows: *gendhing* (gamelan piece), *båwå* (solo vocal introduction), *palaran* (solo vocal genre with gamelan), *suluk* (type of song sung by a *dhalang* in *wayang*), *garap* (performance/interpretation), *swara tembang* (singing voice), *swara bicara* (speaking voice), *kepribadian* (personality), *rupa* ([personal] appearance), *makanan/bau* (food/smell), *emosi/perasaan hati* (emotion), *tingkah laku* (behavior), "touch," *gamelan* (the characteristic sound of any single gamelan set), *tari* (choreographed dance), *keris* (ritual dagger), batik, *wayang kulit, embat gamelan* (gamelan tuning).

Keep in mind that Supanggah's was a long and tedious task, and there are probably several items he would have marked differently if he had had more time to think about them. I have indicated several places where his answer seemed to leave something out, or to go against common usage (I have marked these with a pair of { }'s). Words in parentheses mean that the term may apply to them, but only under certain circumstances.

ådå-ådå—one of three categories of puppeteer's mood songs (*suluk*), characterized by accompaniment on the *gendèr* alone, and a usually rapid delivery (used for heated dramatic situations)

ådångiyah—an optional modal formula played as the first part of a *bukå*, but which is not specific to the piece being introduced but rather only to the tuning and melodic mode of the piece

***adreng** [J]—eager, impelled

ageng [K]—big, great (often used in conjunction with *gendhing, pathetan, gamelan, sekar*)

***agung**—exalted, great, noble, impressive

alit [K]—small

alok—a yell or a shout; a usually monosyllabic vocable interjected into a piece at specific points in the gong cycle, usually by the *gérong*, but occasionally by the *pesindhèns* or the instrumentalists

***alus** [J]—refined; smooth, spare; calm, controlled; fine, intricate

***ampang** [J,I]—insipid; [J] lightweight

andhegan—a break ("stopping") in the performance of a gamelan piece, which is filled in by the solo *pesindhèn* singing unaccompanied and for the most part in an unmetered rhythm

***anteb** (also **manteb**) [J]—weighty, calm, solid

***anteng** [J]—steady, tranquil

arang—see *awis*

ASKI—Akademi Seni Karawitan Indonesia (National Academy of Javanese Performing Arts); the one in Solo (ASKI Surakarta) was subsequently STSI and is now ISI

***asmårå** [J], **asmara** [I]—romantic love, lust, in love

awis [K], **arang** [Ng]—"infrequent"; see *kethuk awis*

ayak-ayak—the least tense-sounding of the three kinds of *gendhing lampah*, in which the gong is played every four beats

***badhutan** [J] **badhutan** [I]—comedy (from *badhut*, clown)

balungan—outline or reference melody (literally, "skeleton," "framework") used by musicians to derive their respective parts; notated melody (also used for deriving a large number of parts); medium-density melody usually played by the *sarons* and *slenthem*; a kind of composite melody meant to represent the basic melodic flow of a piece by incorporating elements from several different polyphonic parts

barang—"thing"; the *pélog* mode with the highest tessitura, usually limited to the pentatonic scale 2 3 5 6 7 and deemphasizing pitches 1 and 4 (see *pathet*)

barang miring—see *minir*

båwå—unmetered, solo vocal introduction to a gamelan piece, usually performed by a male vocalist, lightly accompanied by the *gendèr*, with occasional interjections by one of the larger gongs, and into which is sometimes inserted a *jineman*; the texts may be taken from either the *sekar måcåpat, sekar tengahan*, or *sekar ageng* categories of classical sung poetry

***bébas**—free, unhampered

bedhåyå (also **badhåyå**; adjective: **bedhayan**)—a genre of refined court dances performed by seven or nine young women and accompanied by unison (or octave), long-phrased, legato choral music sometimes with full gamelan, but in some cases only a very small percussion ensemble featuring the *kemanak*

bedhayan—in the style of *bedhåyå* accompaniment

***bérag** [J]—exuberant, joyful, merry, spirited, rambunctious, lighthearted

■ Θ; *gendhing, garap*, personality

***bérag alus** [J]—exuberant but refined

***bérag sanget** [K]—very exuberant

***berat** [I]—heavy; difficult; heavyhearted

■ *gendhing*, (*garap*), voice

***bersahaja** [I]—simple, uncomplicated

***bersemangat** [I]—see *semangat*

***berwibawa** [I]—commanding, potent, magisterial, imposing, having an aura of power, exuding masculine authority

■ +; *gendhing, garap*, singing voice, speaking voice, personality, behavior

***biasa** [I]—ordinary, common; lighthearted

bonang—gong-chime (set of 10 to 14 tuned pot gongs arranged in two rows and played with a pair of padded wooden beaters); *bonang barung* [photo 4]

bonang barung—medium-sized *bonang* (in most gamelans, the lowest one) that plays a leadership role in the gamelan ensemble

bonang imbal—see *bonang* and *imbal*

bonang panerus—small *bonang*, an octave higher than the *bonang barung*, playing quicker, less important parts

bonangan—played in the style of a *gendhing bonang*, that is, without the softer-sounding parts such as *gendèr, gambang, rebab*, and voice; the *bonang* part in a gamelan piece

***branyak** [J] (also **mbranyak**)—brash, spirited, plucky

■ Θ; speaking voice, behavior, gamelan tuning, *wayang*

***bregas** (also **bergas**) [J]—dapper, dashing, dressed to the hilt, natty

■ +; *gendhing, garap*, singing voice, personality, appearance, (food), behavior

Bu (shortened form of *Ibu*)—"mother" (used as term of address for adult women, sometimes where "Mrs." or "Ma'am" would be used in English)

bukå [J]—"opening," solo introduction; some pieces have only one possibility, others have several, distinguished by who or what performs the *bukå*—instrumental introductions simply name the instrument involved (e.g., *bukå rebab*), whereas vocal introductions are called *bukå celuk*

campursari [J, JI]—a vocal and instrumental genre, from the 1960s on, that mixes diatonic, Western instruments with either a full gamelan, or, more commonly, a few instruments taken from the traditional ensemble

celuk [J]—"to call" (see under *bukå*)

céngkok—melodic pattern or formula; melodic phrase; distinctive melodic contour; *wiled*

ciblon—a medium-sized, double-headed drum used for lively music, probably of plebeian origin and associated especially with dance accompaniment; the part played by the *ciblon* drum; *inggah* or other section of a *gendhing* that uses the *ciblon* [photo 3, foreground]

***cinta** [I]—romantic love, affection, to be in love with

cucut [J]—capable of manipulating words well to make an audience laugh (said of a *dhalang*)

dalam [I]—inside, within; deep

dalem [J]—inside, within; the innermost part of a house; [KI] house; a walled compound of an aristocratic family

***damai** [I]—peaceful, serene

demung—short for *saron demung*, the largest and lowest-pitched instrument of the *saron* family (in each *laras* there are usually one or two of them in a gamelan—half as many as the *saron barung*—but there may be as many as four) [photo 5, foreground]

dhalang [J] **dalang** [I]—puppeteer in a *wayang kulit* or *wayang golèk* performance, who traditionally manipulates the puppets, speaks all of the dialogue and narration (in all language levels and in both modern and archaic, vernacular and literary Javanese), directs the gamelan ensemble (including giving signals as to what piece to play when), makes jokes, sings mood songs, recites incantations, provides mood percussion and sound effects, shapes the pacing of the eight- or nine-hour performance, and helps maintain harmony with the natural and supernatural worlds (and if that isn't enough, he—or rarely she—often makes his or her own puppets); narrator in a performance of *wayang* that does not involve puppetry

*__dinamis__ [I] (from Dutch, *dynamisch*)—dynamic

*__dingin__ [I]—cold; calm (used to describe dramatic situations, but also musical performances that lack feeling)

dolanan—"play" song (from *dolan*, to play), formerly sung by children to the light of the full moon; a genre of lighthearted, catchy gamelan pieces with easily understood lyrics, associated, among other things, with clown scenes in the shadow theater

embat—the exact intervallic structure, at the microtonal level, of a gamelan tuning or of a musician's personal inner tuning (like a temperament in Western music)

*__èmeng__ [J,KI]—bewildered [J]; sad [KI]

■ – ; *gendhing*, emotion

*__énak__ [Ng, I]—delicious; comfortable; pleasing; at ease, leisurely

*__ènthèng__ [J] **èntèng** [I]—light; lighthearted; insignificant; not serious; easy; free in one's movements

■ Θ; *gendhing, garap*, singing voice, food

*__gagah__—manly [J], virile [J]; strong; handsome [I]; brave

■ +; *gendhing*, (*garap*), (singing voice), personality, behavior

gambang—trough-resonated xylophone with four-octave range, played with a pair of padded mallets [partially visible in photo 6, far left]

gambang gångså—an archaic instrument of the *saron* family, associated with the Kraton, with a range of several octaves (in that respect it is like a *gambang*); in the few pieces in which it is still used it plays a relatively fast melody, with the right hand trailing behind the left (with a half-beat delay)

*__gambirå__ [J]—see *gembira*

gambyong—a Solonese dance, which, like the *golèk* dance, depicts a young woman preening herself, and which is often performed by one or several dancers at weddings

gamelan [Ng, I] **gångså** [K]—any of various Javanese (or Balinese) instrumental ensembles containing at least some tuned percussion instruments (in Javanese the word refers only to the set of instruments, not to the musicians or the music, though in English it is often used in both of those extended senses)

*__gandrung__—head-over-heels in love, infatuated

■ Θ; *gendhing*, emotion, behavior

garap—treatment, working out, interpretation, musical arrangement, version, details of performance practice chosen for or associated with a particular piece, performance practice in general; *nggarap*

*__gecul__ [J]—impertinent, waggish, comical, jocular, roguish

■ Θ; *gendhing, garap*, personality, behavior

***gelå** [J]—disappointed, let down

***gelisah** [I]—restless, worried

***gembira** [I] **gambirå** [J]—happy, cheerful, glad

gendèr—metallophone with tube resonators; *gendèr barung* [photo 7, foreground]

gendèr barung—a gamelan instrument consisting of thin metal slabs suspended over tube resonators, which has a gentle, sustained sound and is struck with two padded mallets by a single player who generally plays a polyphonic part [photo 7, foreground]

gendèr panerus: a gamelan instrument similar to the *gendèr barung* but an octave higher, less polyphonic in the way it's played, and of lesser importance [photo 6, right middle ground]

gendhing—a gamelan piece in general; more specifically, a gamelan piece with a *kenong* unit of at least sixteen beats

gendhing bedhayan—a piece in the style of *bedhåyå* accompaniment, whether used for a *bedhåyå* dance or not (see *bedhåyå*)

gendhing bonang—a long, stately gamelan piece played on an ensemble consisting only of single-beater metallophones (*saron*s and *slenthem*), *bonang*s, time-markers, and drums (that is, only the louder instruments of a full gamelan); *gendhing bonangan*

gendhing bonangan—a gamelan piece played in the style of a *gendhing bonang*, but usually shorter, in which the *bonang* is the lead melodic instrument; *gendhing soran*

gendhing kemanak—gamelan piece for accompanying the *bedhåya* dance that features unison choral singing and a small ensemble of time-marking instruments, within which the *kemanak* has the fastest moving part

gendhing kréasi baru (also **gendhing kréasi** or **kréasi baru**) [I]—"newly created pieces": modern (post-Independence) pieces in a semipopular idiom that usually have shorter gong cycles, catchy melodies, and rapidly declaimed, easily understandable lyrics, and that are associated above all with the composer and puppeteer Ki Nartosabdho

gendhing lampah—"walking pieces," used in the shadow theater for traveling, fighting, or preparing to fight, and characterized by repetitive melodies and by very short gong cycles (one to four beats long) in which the *kempul* sometimes substitutes for the large gong (see *ayak-ayak, srepeg, sampak*); *gendhing lampah* are used in many contexts other than *wayang*, as well, but usually with similar connotations

gendhing sekar—a short gamelan piece, almost always in *ketawang* form, that is based on a *måcåpat* melody and uses a corresponding *måcåpat* text

gendhing soran—a "loud-style" gamelan piece that does not use any vocals or any of the softer-sounding instruments (*gendèr, rebab, siter, suling, gambang, gendèr panerus*), with the sole exception of the *slenthem* (an instrument in the *gendèr* family, whose sound carries well because of its low-pitched, sustained tones)

gérong—unison male "chorus" (typically about four men) that is a part of the gamelan ensemble; *gérongan* [photo 2, right middle ground]

gérongan—the part sung by the *gérong*

★**gobyog** [J]—lively, clangorous, loud and fast, bustling, following in quick succession
■ Θ; *gendhing, garap*

★**gojèg** [J]—joking, kidding, fooling around

golèk—a usually solo dance depicting a young girl grooming herself; associated primarily with Yogyakarta as well as with the wooden puppets called *wayang golèk*, the dance is often performed at weddings

gong [J,I]—a low-pitched, resonant, tuned, bossed gong, ideally made of forged bronze (there are anywhere from one to eight in a gamelan, but they all function to mark the end of the largest metric unit of a piece); the place in a time cycle where the gong is expected to play (the last beat of the cycle); an instrument that substitutes for the gong and functions the same way (*gong kemodhong*, a two-slab idiophone, with large resonators, that is tuned to create acoustic beats reminiscent of those made by the large circular gong; *gong bumbung*, a blown gong); a stroke of the gong; a point in a *gendhing* at which the gong should be played.

gongan—a time cycle, the longest metric unit in any given piece, which can vary greatly in length from piece to piece (anywhere from one beat up to 256 beats in *iråmå tanggung*), and which is marked at the end by a stroke of the gong (or, in very short *gongan*s, of the *kempul* substituting for the gong)

★**greged**—energy, vigor, verve, drive, "oomph"; determination, conviction; intensity (of expression)
■ Θ {+?}; *gendhing, båwå, palaran, suluk, garap*, singing voice, speaking voice, personality, emotion, behavior

gregel—(lit., "jolt," "jiggle," "bump") a type of short melodic ornament resembling an inverted mordent (sometimes generalized to any small melodic ornament)

grimingan—an improvisatory melodic accompaniment to speech in a *wayang* performance, played on the lone *gendèr barung*; it has the double function of filling in silence and keeping the pitches of the gamelan in the ear of the *dhalang*, who may need to launch into song before the gamelan comes in again

★**gundah gulana** [I]—despondent, depressed, in despair

★**halus** [I]—see *alus* [J]

★**héran** [I]—surprised, astonished

Ibu—formal or particularly respectful form of *Bu*

imbal—a playing technique that involves rapid alternation of two musicians using the same kind of instrument to create a single melodic line

inggah (also **minggah**)—the second, livelier part of a medium-to-large *gendhing*

irâmå [J] **irama** [I]—rhythm; tempo; "tempo level"; ratio between the faster- and the slower-moving parts; degree of expansion or contraction of a *gendhing* (see Appendix B)

irâmâ lancar—the most condensed *irâmâ* level (*irâmâ* ½) in which *balungan* beats go by at the same speed as the *saron panerus*

irâmâ rangkep—literally, "doubled" *irâmâ*—any expansion by a factor of two and subsequent filling in of a gong cycle; more commonly, the most expanded *irâmâ* level (*irâmâ* IV), in which there are sixteen strokes of the *saron panerus* for every *balungan* beat

irâmâ tanggung—"medium" *irâmâ* (*irâmâ* I), in which there are two strokes of the *saron panerus* to every *balungan* beat

irâmâ wiled—the second-most expanded *irâmâ* level (*irâmâ* III), in which there are eight strokes of the *saron panerus* to each *balungan* beat

iringan—musical accompaniment (e.g., to dance, to theater)

isi—contents, substance, musical content (sometimes related to a *gendhing*'s title but more generally to its *rasa*); an attendant spirit (used with respect to *pusâkâ*s or other objects with a rich history)

ISI—Institut Seni Indonesia (Indonesia Arts Institute); the one in Solo was formerly ASKI, then STSI, before being upgraded to ISI

*__itu-itu__ [I]—the same old thing, ordinary; lighthearted

jineman—genre of gamelan music that emphasizes the solo female singer's part, has short, often irregular gong cycles,and is usually performed on a chamber ensemble without *rebab*

jiwâ[J] **jiwa** [I]—soul, spirit, state of mind, essence

jugag—the shortest form of a *pathetan*

KâKâ—Kawruh Kaniyagan (Knowledge of Gamelan Playing), one of the first schools (early twentieth century) created for teaching gamelan in Solo

*__kaku__—stiff; awkward

*__kangen__—to miss; yearning, longing

karaton—the official Javanese form of the word *kraton*

karawitan—Javanese gamelan music; Javanese music using *sléndro* or *pélog* tunings (including vocal music)

*__kasar__—crude, coarse, rough, unrefined, vulgar

*__kasmaran__ [J,JI]—smitten, in love

■ Θ; *gendhing, garap*, emotion, behavior

*__kayungyun__ [J]—madly in love, attracted to

kébar [J]—"to show off"; a treatment (*garap*), often chosen in *ladrang*s to give them a *bérag* feel, in which the general dynamic level is high, the *bonang*s play *imbal*, the *ciblon* drum is used, the *gérong* uses *keplok* and puts in lots of *alok*s, and the *kempul* has extra strokes (including some that are syncopated)

kebatinan [I] **kabatinan** [Ng], **kabatosan** [K]—short for *ngèlmu kabatinan* [Ng]: "knowledge of interiority," mysticism, metaphysics, psychology, philosophy of life

*__kebencian__ [I]—hate (noun form of *benci*, to hate)

*__kebranian__ (also **keberanian**) [I] bravery, boldness (see also *wani*)

*__kegembiraan__ [I]—abstract noun form of *gembira*

***kelepasan** [I]—freedom, release

kemanak—pair of tubular bells ideally made of bronze, tuned close to each other in pitch, and struck in an alternating pattern with padded wooden beaters by two different players

***kemayu** (also **kumayu**) [J]—literally, "too pretty" (from *ayu*, pretty); coquettish, flirtatious; to consider oneself cute (of a girl or woman); hyperfeminine

kempul—a vertically suspended, medium-large gong with a medium-low, resonant sound, used in pieces with a smallish gong cycle to subdivide the *kenong* unit [photo 2, left-center background]

kempyang—a small pot-gong with a high, ringing sound, used to flank either side of the *kethuk* strokes in a gong cycle (the pattern is thus "pyang" "thuk" "pyang" rest)

kendhang—any of various double-headed barrel (or sometimes cylindrical) drums [photo 3]

kendhang ciblon—see *ciblon*

kendhang gendhing—the largest and deepest-sounding *kendhang*, used either by itself or together with the *ketipung*, in rather sparse patterns [photo 3, right middle ground]

***kenès**—coquettish, flirtatious, hyper-feminine; sparkling; talkative

kenong—a large pot-gong (or a set of these) with a medium-high, ringing sound, used to mark off important points in a rhythmic cycle [photo 5, right middle ground]

keplok [J]—handclap; a pattern of hocketed, stratified handclapping in a regular, highly rhythmic pattern that is provided by the *gérong* and is strongly correlated with *ciblon* drumming

***keramat** [I] **kramat** [J]—sacred, holy, possessing supernatural powers

kerep [J]—"often," "frequent"; see *kethuk kerep*

***kesedihan** [I]—noun form of *sedih*

ketawang—a common musical form (sixteen beats per gong, two *kenong*s per gong) that almost always is limited to *irâmâ* dados and uses a vocal treatment

kethoprak—genre of vernacular Javanese theater that includes singing and gamelan music, as well as some dance

kethuk—a small pot-gong with a medium-low pitch and a dull but clearly audible sound, used to mark off points in a rhythmic cycle (one level of subdivision below the *kenong* and *kempul*) [photo 5, left middle ground]

kethuk awis [K], **kethuk arang** [Ng]—a category of *gendhing* structure in which there is one *kethuk* stroke for every sixteen-beat unit, and in the *inggah* one for every eight-beat unit; in identifying a *gendhing* structure, the number following the words *kethuk awis* indicates how many *kethuk* strokes there are per *kenong* unit

kethuk kerep—a category of *gendhing* structure in which there is one *kethuk* stroke for every eight-beat unit in the *mérong*, and one for every four-beat unit in the *inggah*; in identifying a *gendhing* structure, the number following the words *kethuk kerep* indicates how many *kethuk* strokes there are per *kenong* unit

ketipung—the smallest of the *kendhangs*, used in conjunction with the *kendhang gendhing*

***kèwèk** [J]—flirtatious, coquettish; feminine

***khidmat** [I]—devotional, reverential; calm

***klasik** [J,I] (also **klassiek** [D])—classic; difficult; old; serious

***klasik berat** [I]—heavy (difficult, serious) classic

***klasik ènthèng** [J]—light (easy, lighthearted) classic

***klasik ringan** [I]—see *klasik ènthèng*

***klasik tengahan**—medium classic (neither very serious nor very gay)

klenèngan—(n.) a formal or informal music-making session of *karawitan* that may resemble a concert or a rehearsal; (adj.) concert repertoire, concert instrumentation, or concert style of performance (as opposed to theater or dance accompaniment, hybrid popular music, avant-garde music, or archaic ritual gamelans)

KoKar—Konservatori Karawitan, the precursor of SMKI

kosèk alus—a style of drumming used in *irâmâ wiled* during the *inggah* of a *gendhing* or the appropriate part of a *ladrang* that uses the *kendhang gendhing* in place of the more usual *ciblon*; choosing *kosèk alus* entails a number of other *garap* choices (such as not using *bonang imbal* where it would otherwise be expected)

krâmâ—high (respectful) Javanese

kraton (also **karaton** [J])—king's palace

Kraton—the king's palace in Solo (or in Yogyakarta), that is, the palace of the senior royal line (cf. Mangkunegaran)

kreasi baru—see *gendhing kreasi baru*

kroncong—a pan-Indonesian sentimental genre of vocal music with Portuguese roots that uses a small ensemble of Western chordophones and often a transverse flute as accompaniment (it has always been associated with nostalgia, but is now also considered old-fashioned)

***kumayu** [J]—see *kemayu*

kunâ [J] **kuno** [I]—old-fashioned, ancient

kurang [Ng,I] **kirang** [K]—not enough, lacking, not

ladrang—a common musical form with a smallish gong cycle (thirty-two beats per gong, four *kenongs* per gong)

lagu—melody, song; a vocally based gamelan piece that does not fit easily into one of the standard *gendhing* structures (the term is used especially to refer to *dolanans* or *kréasi baru*); in the terminology of Suhardi (of Yogyakarta), the *balungan* in the sense of a composite melody that sometimes deviates from the written *balungan*

langendriyan—Javanese theatrical genre of courtly origin in which all dialogue is sung by the dancers themselves, to the accompaniment of a gamelan (Java's answer to opera)

langgam—a vocal genre consisting of sentimental songs in Javanese; its melodies often have a diatonic feel, performed usually by a woman singer accompanied by a gamelan that imitates to an extent the plucked chordophones of the ensemble used for the related *kroncong* genre

*__lanyapan__ [J] (also **lanyap**)—erect head posture; *branyak*

■ Θ; appearance, behavior, gamelan tuning, *wayang*

laras—tuning system (of which there are two in Javanese music: *sléndro* and *pélog*); tuning (how high or low a gamelan is tuned—cf. the French word *diapason*); intonation (of a singer or *rebab* player); [J] appropriate, agreeable, relaxed

larasmadyå/santiswaran—unison (or octave) choral singing accompanied by frame drums, a pair of *kemanak*, and *ciblon*, and preceded by a *båwå* (*larasmadyå* uses standard *måcåpat* texts, whereas *santiswaran* uses Islamic texts that contain frequent references to Allah or the prophet Mohammed, as well as Sufi-inspired repetitious syllables)

laya [I]—surface tempo, pace (as opposed to *iråmå* or tempo level)

lèdhèk (also **talèdhèk, tlèdhèk**) [J]—a female singer/dancer who performs door-to-door or is hired to perform at a *tayuban*, sometimes associated, rightly or wrongly, with prostitution; sometimes used as a synonym for *pesindhèn*; in the Kraton, sometimes contrasted with the *pesindhèn*s who sang specifically to accompany *bedhåyå* and *srimpi* dances

lega [I] **legå** [J]—free, not busy; relieved; satisfied, pleased

*__lelah__ [I]—listless, weary

lelévå [J]—literally, "affectation," "attention-getting act"; characteristic way of doing something, nature, character

limå [Ng]—"five"; the *pélog* melodic mode with the lowest tessitura, which for the most part sticks to the pentatonic scale 1 2 4 5 6, thus leaving out pitches 3 and 7 (see *pathet*)

*__lincah__ [I]—agile, energetic, lively

luar [I] **njåwå** [Ng] **njawi** [K]—outside (more specifically, outside the Kraton, or outside the academy)

*__lucon__ (also **lelucon**) [J] joke, humor, joking

*__lucu__—funny

*__lugu__—simple, plain, unadorned, straightforward, unaffected

*__luruh__ (also **ruruh**) [J]—humble, with a downcast gaze; refined; calm

måcåpat—a genre of solo singing ("reading"), in which the text is paramount; a category of indigenous, familiar verse forms in modern literary Javanese (as opposed to the more abstruse *sekar ageng* category of Sanskrit origin)

måcåpat paringgitan—a now defunct subgenre of *måcåpat* singing that was once performed to pass the time by on-duty night watchmen at the north entrance to the Kraton in Solo, where there is an area called the *paringgitan*, or place where *ringgit*s (*kråmå* for *wayang*s) are held

*__mancing__—"to go fishing" (e.g., for men, for attention)

Mangkunegaran—the royal palace of the Solonese junior line (see also under Kraton) *__mangungkung__ [J]—mournful, sorrowful

manja [I]—spoiled, pampered; attention-seeking

*__manteb__ (also **mantab**)—(see *anteb*)

manyurå (also **menyurå**)—"peacock"; the *sléndro* mode with the highest tessitura; the third and final major section of a shadow play (see *pathet*)

*__marah__ [I]—angry

*__mardikå__ [J]—free, independent, liberated

Mas—"older brother" (used as term of address)

*__médoki__ [Ng] (from *wédok*, woman)—effeminate

melasih (also **melas asih**) [J]—inspiring pity (from *welas asih*; see also *memelas*)

*__memelas__ [J]—piteous, miserable; having pity, compassionate

■ Θ; *gendhing, garap*, singing voice, personality, emotion, behavior

*__menakutkan__ [I] (from *takut*, frightened)—frightening

*__mendalam__ [I] **njero** [Ng] **mlebet** [K]—deep, within, deep inside

■ Θ {+}; *gendhing, båwå, palaran, suluk*, singing voice, speaking voice

*__meneb__ [J]—settled, collected, calm

*__meneng__ [J]—to be silent, motionless

*__menggoda__ [I]—to tempt, to lure

menjiwai [I]—to become the spirit of; to be the very soul of; to exemplify the spirit of; to express the *rasa* of

*__menyanjung__ [I]—to flatter

*__menyenangkan__ [I]—pleasing

merasakan [I] **ngrasakaké** or **ngrasakké** [Ng] **ngraosaken** [K]—to feel, to sense, to intuit, to perceive, to hear, to "get" (in the sense of "to understand")

mérong—the first, calm section of a medium-to-large *gendhing*

minggah—see *inggah*

minir (also **minor, miring**)—"minor"; the use, in a *sléndro* piece, of *pélog*-like intervals in the vocal and *rebab* parts

miring—"slanted" (in reference to the slanted lines used on numerals to indicate altered pitches in cipher notation); see *minir*

*__mrabu__ [J] (from *prabu*, king)—regal

■ +; *gendhing, garap*, personality, appearance, behavior

*__nafsu__ [I] **napsu** or **nepsu** [J]—desire, impulse, urge; (also, **bernafsu** [I]) lustful, passionate

nem [J]—"six"; the *sléndro* mode with the lowest tessitura; the *pélog* mode with a medium tessitura that normally leaves out pitches 4 and 7, thus emphasizing the pentatonic scale 1 2 3 5 6; the first of three major sections of a shadow play (see *pathet*)

*__nènès__ [J]—see *kenès*

*__ngajèni__ [Ng] **nyuhun-nyuhun** [KI]—to respect, to honor

ngelik—"to go up," "piercing" (from *cilik*, "small"); a portion of a piece or song in a higher register than the previous section (for instance, the second major section—as opposed to the *umpak*—of nearly every *ketawang* and a great many *ladrangs*)

ngèlmu [J]—distinctly Javanese forms of esoteric, mystical knowledge or wisdom, sometimes having Sufi overtones, and acquired largely through ascetic exercises

***ngeres** [J,JI]—physically irritating; sad, touching

■ Θ—; *gendhing, garap*, singing voice, emotion, sense of touch

***nges** [J]—moving, touching, affecting; interesting, appealing, significant

■ +; *gendhing, båwå, palaran, suluk, garap*, singing voice, personality, food, gamelan tuning, *wayang*, batik, dance

nggarap [J]—to work out the details of, interpret, arrange

***ngglécé** [J]—jocular, flip

■ Θ; *gendhing, garap*, singing voice, personality, appearance, behavior

***nggreged** [J]—verbal/adjectival form of *greged*

***nglangut** [J] **melangut** [I]—infinitely far off; lonely; disturbed; sad, melancholy

■ Θ; *gendhing*, (*garap*), singing voice, emotion

ngoko—low Javanese

***ngondhok-ondhok** [J]—to have a lump in the throat; melancholy, depressed, hurt

***nyes** [J]—cold; lonely, sad

ora [Ng]—not

Pak—"father" (used as term of address, analogous to "Mr." or "Sir")

palaran—a vocal genre based on *måcåpat*, in which a solo singer is accompanied by a reduced gamelan ensemble playing something akin to *srepegan* (which, not coincidentally, is the usual way of getting into and out of a *palaran* in a suite of pieces)

pathet—melodic mode, of which there are officially three in *sléndro* (in order from lowest tessitura to highest, *nem, sångå*, and *manyurå*), and three in *pélog* (*limå, nem*, and *barang*), although there are finer distinctions to be made when a *gendhing* is borrowed from *pélog* into *sléndro*, and vice versa (for example, musicians often distinguish between *pélog nem "manyurå"* and *pélog nem "sångå"*; another word for *pathetan*

pathetan (also **pathet**)—one of three categories of puppeteer's mood songs (*suluk*), characterized by slow delivery and accompaniment on the *rebab, gendèr, gambang*, and *suling* (used for a calm dramatic situation, and to mark major structural units of the drama); an instrumental prelude or postlude based on the corresponding *suluk*, performed in a concertlike setting

pélog—one of two tuning systems used in *karawitan* (seven tones, intervals of varied sizes, melodies usually pentatonic)

pénak (also **kepénak**) [Ng]—comfortable, pleasing

pendhåpå [Ng] **pendhapi** [K] **pendopo** [I]—a large, elaborate, open-sided pavilion with a high-pitched roof, usually attached to the entrance of a building such as the house of a nobleman

peperangan [I]—battle, warfare, combat (cf. Javanese *paprangan*, "battlefield")

***peprenèsan** [J]—noun form of *prenès*

perasaan [I]—feeling

⋆**perempuan** [I]—woman; feminine, female

perkawinan [I]—marriage, wedding

⋆**pertjintaan**(also **percintaan**) [I]—(similar to *cinta*); courtship; sorrow, longing

pesindhèn (also **pasindhèn**, **sindhèn**)—a female vocalist who sings as part of a gamelan group, usually solo, in a somewhat improvisatory or reactive manner, but sometimes in a unison or octave chorus (or even occasionally, now, in counterpoint) [photo 2, foreground]

pinjalan—literally, "in the manner of a flea"; a performance treatment in which an instrument plays the same part as another instrument, echolike, a half-beat late; a treatment that includes *pinjalan* per se, but also entails certain other specific treatments in the other parts, such as *imbal demung*

pipilan—a playing technique used on the *bonang*, in which, in its simplest form, each successive pair of *balungan* notes is repeated at a speed that is faster than the *balungan* by a factor of two, resulting in an undulating melody

PKK—Pembinaan Kesejahteraan Keluarga (Improvement or Promotion of Family Welfare), a blanket term for neighborhood women's associations that provide instruction in domestic science (hygiene, cooking, nutrition, etc.) as well as group leisure activities, such as small-scale lotteries and gamelan rehearsals

⋆**polos**—plain, simple

⋆**populèr** [I] **populair** [D] (also **popiler, popular**)—popular, pop; easily understood by the masses

⋆**prasåjå** [J] **prasaja** [I]—plain, unaffected, guileless

⋆**prenès** [J] (also **pernès**)—coquettish; titillating; appealing, lighthearted; erotic, seductive

■ Θ; *gendhing, garap*, singing voice, personality, behavior

⋆**prenès alus** [J]—*prenès* but refined

■ Θ; *gendhing, garap*, singing voice, personality, behavior

⋆**prenès bérag** [J]—exuberantly *prenès*

⋆**prihatos** [K] **prihatin** [Ng]—concerned, anxious, prayerful

priyayi (also **prijaji**) [Ng,I]—aristocrat(ic)

pusåkå—sacred heirloom (such as a ritual dagger or a gamelan), which derives its symbolic and spiritual power from having been owned by a revered and potent patriarch of yore

⋆**ramé** [J] (**ramai** [I])—lively, bustling; loud and fast

■ Θ; *gendhing, garap*

rangkep [J]: doubled (see *iråmå rangkep*)

raos [K]—see *rasa*

rasa [I] **råså** [Ng] **raos** [K]—taste, feeling, affect, mood, inner meaning, faculty of taste, faculty of knowing intuitively, deep understanding

rasané, rasaning [Ng] **raosipun** [K] **rasanya** [I]—"the *rasa* of"; "it feels"; "it sounds"

rebab—bowed spike fiddle with two strings, considered the melodic leader of the gamelan (when present) [photo 1, foreground]

★regu [J]—stately, dignified, majestic; quiet, taciturn; serious, staid; calm

■ +; *gendhing, garap*, {personality?, behavior?}

renå [KI]—pleased, contented

★renggep [J]—a complex concept that Nugroho (2003:397) defines as "enthusiastic, never slacking, never giving up, believing in oneself, and expressive"

★renyah [J]—crisp; high, light and pleasant

■ Θ; *gendhing, garap*, singing voice, food

rerepèn—kind of solo singing with few constraints, often in a *måcåpat* meter, and of a teasing, admonitory, or flattering nature

★rindu [I]—to miss; yearning, longing; homesick

★ringan [I]—light; lighthearted; easy

★rongèh [J]—fidgety

■ – Θ; *gendhing*, singing voice, personality, behavior

RRI—Radio Republik Indonesia, the national radio broadcasting corporation, which has a station in Solo

rujak-rujakan—a category of *wangsalan* in which the first line begins with the words "*rujak* ____, *rujaké wong* ____,": the first blank is filled with some kind of fruit or vegetable, and the second blank is filled with some kind of person (*rujak* is a spicy, sweet, salad of grated fruits or vegetables; *wong* means "man" or "person"); the twelve syllables of each line are usually delivered rapidly in strict rhythm

★ruruh—see *luruh*

★sa'énaké dhéwé [Ng]—as one pleases, without regard for one's obligations; taking one's time

sakécå [K]—comfortable, pleasing (see also *énak* and *pénak*)

sampak—the *gendhing lampah* with the shortest gong cycle (one beat per "gong"), and the one capable of creating the tensest mood

sångå—"nine"; a *sléndro* mode with a medium tessitura; the second of three major sections of a shadow play (see *pathet*); see also under *saron sångå*

★santak (also **sentak**) [J]—angry, impatient

santiswaran (also **santiswårå**)—see *larasmadyå/santiswaran*

saron—metallophone with trough resonator, with a range of slightly more than an octave, struck with a single wooden mallet (usually plays something akin to the *balungan*) [photo 4, background and photo 5, foreground]

saron barung (also, **saron**)—medium-sized metallophone of the *saron* family [photo 4, background]

saron panerus—the smallest and highest-pitched of the *saron* instruments, unique among all the gamelan instruments in that it always plays at a nearly uniform density, regardless of the playing treatment (*garap*) or the *iråmå* level (except, of course, when changing *iråmå*s); it plays a key role in setting the tempo, changing *iråmå*s, and keeping the rhythm steady

saron sångå—a *saron barung* with nine keys used primarily to play a fast, semi-improvisatory melodic line that livens up the texture of *gendhing lampah*

★sederhana [I]—simple

★sedhih [J] **sedih** [I]—sad

■ Θ; *gendhing, garap*, singing voice, emotion

★seger [J] **segar** [I]—fresh, refreshing, pleasing

sekar [K] **tembang** [Ng]—classical Javanese sung poetry

sekar ageng [K]—classical sung poetry in old Javanese using the four-line stanzas inherited from Sanskrit verse (nowadays its use is limited to *båwås*)

sekar måcåpat—see *måcåpat*

sekar tengahan [K]—"intermediate" sung poetry (halfway between *sekar ageng* and *sekar måcåpat*) said to use moderately archaic language (though sometimes they are virtually indistinguishable from *måcåpat*)

sekatèn—an annual festival, commemorating the birth of the prophet Mohammed, that includes loud music alternately played on two massive gamelans that are set out in special pavilions in the courtyards of the Great Mosques of the three active royal courts of Java (Solo, Yogya, Cirebon)

sekati (also **sekatèn**, **sekaténan**)—auspicious instruments or pieces associated with *sekatèn* (used in conjunction with the words *gendhing* or *gamelan*)

★sem [J]—charming, enchanting, attractive

■ +; *gendhing, båwå, palaran, suluk, garap*, singing voice, speaking voice, *wayang*

semu [J]—tinged with

★semangat [I]—enthusiasm, enthusiastic

★senang [I]—to like; pleasing; happy, contented

★senang-senang—to have a good time, enjoyable, fun

sendhon—one of three categories of puppeteer's mood songs (*suluk*), characterized by accompaniment on the *gendèr, gambang*, and *suling* and by a slow delivery (often used for a sad dramatic situation)

★seneng [J]—see *senang*

senggréngan—a short modal formula (only a few bow-strokes long) performed on the *rebab*, which functions to announce the tuning and melodic mode of the piece that is about to begin and to make sure that the *rebab* is still in tune before launching into the piece

★sengsem [J]—see *sem*

★sentosa [J]—strong, sturdy

★sepi—lonely, desolate, quiet

★sereng [J]—tense, stern, surly, gruff, angry, intense, heated, vigorous, resolute

■ Θ; *gendhing, garap*, (singing voice), emotion, sense of touch

sifat [I] **sipat** [J]—nature, character, disposition

★sigrak [J]—fresh, buoyant appearance; agile, dexterous, quick

■ Θ; *gendhing, båwå, palaran, suluk, garap*, singing voice, speaking voice, behavior

sindhèn—*pesindhèn; sindhénan*

sindhénan—the *pesindhèn* part to a gamelan piece

sindhénan bedhayan—the unison or octave choral part to a *gendhing bedhayan*, whether performed by just women or by a mixed chorus

siter—box zither [photo 6, foreground; photo 9]

slenthem—a low-pitched metallophone with tube resonators, played with a single padded mallet; usually plays something akin to the *balungan* [photo 2, left middle ground]

sléndro (also **saléndro**)—one of two gamelan tunings (five tones, more-or-less equidistant)

SMKI—Sekolah Menengah Karawitan Indonesia (National High School of Javanese Performing Arts)

Solo—a court city in central Java (my research site); also Surakarta

Solonese—from or in some way related to the city of Solo

soran—see *gendhing soran.*

srepegan (also **srepeg**)—a genre of music used for *wayang* scenes in which there is much movement and often dramatic tension (traveling, fighting, preparing to fight); musically, it consists of an undulating, repetitive *balungan* melody, with the *kempul* substituting for the gong to prevent the frequent gongs in the two-beat gong cycles from getting too "clangy" (see also under *gendhing lampah*)

srimpi (adjective: **srimpèn**)—a genre of refined, choreographed court dance performed by four young women and accompanied by *gendhing bedhayan*

STSI—Sekolah Tinggi Seni Indonesia (Indonesian College of the Arts); formerly ASKI, now ISI

suasana [I]—see *swasånå*

***suka** [I] **sukå** [J]—joyful, happy, pleased

***suka hati** [I]—delighted

suling—end-blown bamboo fipple flute [photo 6, left middle ground]

suluk (also **sulukan**)—any of three types of unmetered mood songs sung by the puppeteer in the shadow theater or its offshoots; in a concertlike context *suluk*s may also be sung by a member of the *gérong*, or, in the case of *pathetan*, they may be performed instrumentally (see also *ådå-ådå, pathetan, sendhon*)

sunan—variant of *susuhunan*

***sungkåwå** [J]—grief

***susah**—troubled, sad

susuhunan—king of Solo (the head of the senior royal line)

swasånå [J] **suasana** [I]—atmosphere, situation, circumstances

takut [I]—afraid

tayub (also **tayuban**, **talèdhèkan**) [J]—an all-night ritual event, usually held in front of a home, in which the male guests take turns dancing to gamelan or *campursari* music with a professional singer/dancer (*lèdhèk*).

***tegang** [I]—tense

tembang [Ng]—song; classical sung poetry (see also *sekar* [K])

***tenang** [I]—calm, quiet, settled

tengahan—middle, medium, midlevel, moderate, in-between

⋆**tentrem** [J] **tenteram** [I]—tranquil

⋆**terharu** [I]—moved, touched

tidak [I]—not

⋆**tistis** [J]—chilled, quiet, lonely

⋆**tlutur** [J]—sad

■ Θ; *gendhing, garap*, emotion

⋆**trègèl** [J]—vivacious; impetuous; agile

■ Θ; *gendhing, garap*, singing voice, personality, behavior

⋆**trenyuh**—moved to pity; moving, affecting, sad

■ Θ; *gendhing, garap*, emotion

umpak—"base of a pillar"; the first part of a *ladrang* or a *ketawang*, usually only one *gongan* long

⋆**umum**—usual, ordinary; lighthearted

unsur—element; *rasa* (applies to *gendhing*s or *tembang*s)

urå-urå (also **uran-uran**)—a rather free way of singing *måcåpat*, that often goes outside of established rules, and that lies stylistically somewhere between *sindhénan, båwå*, and *måcåpat* proper (that is, it is unaccompanied like *måcåpat* and *båwå* but is highly ornamented, like *båwå* and *sindhénan*)

wangsalan—a poetic couplet, often used in *sindhénan*, consisting of two lines of twelve (or, rarely, eight) syllables each, in which the first line gives crossword puzzle–like clues that are answered in the second half of the couplet, which contains the main content of the couplet

⋆**wani** [Ng]—to dare; brave, defiant

wantah [J]—"pure," "genuine," "with nothing added"; the full, "normal" form of a *pathetan* (as opposed to *jugag, ageng, ngelik*)

watak—disposition, nature, character

wayang [Ng,I] **ringgit** [K]—any of several Indonesian narrative performances, mostly puppet or dance theatricals of various kinds; *wayang kulit*; a character or puppet in the Javanese shadow-puppet theater; a shadow play; a performance of a shadow play or a related theatrical (which often lasts all night)

wayang golèk [I, Ng]—puppet theater that uses three-dimensional wooden puppets (rare in Solo); a wooden puppet

wayang kulit [I,Ng]—the shadow-puppet theater; a shadow puppet; a shadow theater performance

wayang orang [I] **wayang wong** [Ng] **ringgit tiyang** [K]—Javanese theatrical genre with much choreographed (or semi-improvised) dancing, singing, and gamelan music; it has a courtly origin and is based, in its stories and many other aspects, on the *wayang purwå* (*wayang wong* literally means "people-puppet theater")

wayang purwå [Ng] **ringgit purwå** [K]—*wayang kulit* that uses stories from the *Mahabharata*

⋆**wibåwå** [J], **wibawa** [I]—masculine authority, commanding presence (see *berwibawa*)

wiled (also, **wiledan**)—"surface" (partly improvised) melody; melodic ornamentation; the third *irâmâ* level (also called *inggah* or *ciblon*); *inggah* (except for when the *inggah* does not go into *irâmâ wiled*)

***wingit** [J]—supernaturally awesome, haunted, possessed, spooky, spectral

■ Θ; *gendhing, garap*, singing voice, personality, appearance

wirèng—a choreographed court dance between two, four, eight, or more male dancers, all dressed alike, and engaged in a mock battle to which there are no victors

Yogya—Yogyakarta

Yogyakarta—a court city in central Java

Yogyanese—from Yogyakarta

BIBLIOGRAPHY

Dictionaries and Glossaries

Becker, Judith. 1988. "Glossary." In *Karawitan: Source Readings in Javanese Gamelan and Vocal Music*, vol. 3, edited by Judith Becker and Alan Feinstein. Michigan papers on South and Southeast Asia Numbers 23, 30, and 31. Ann Arbor: University of Michigan Center for South and Southeast Asian Studies.

Bruggencate, Ten K. 1978. *Engels woordenboek*. Vol. 2, *Nederlands-Engels*. 18th edition, revised by J. Gerritsen and N. E. Osselton. Groningen: Wolters-Noordhoff.

Echols, John M., and Hassan Shadily. 1989. Reprint. *Kamus Indonesia-Inggris*. 3d edition. Revised by John U. Wolff and James T. Collins. Jakarta: Gramedia. [Revised edition originally published by Cornell University Press, 1989.]

Gericke, J. F. C., and T. Roorda. 1901. *Javaansch-Nederlandsch handwoordenboek*. Revised by A. C. Vreede and J. G. H. Gunning. Amsterdam: Johannes Müller and Leiden: E. J. Brill. [First edition, E. J. Brill, 1847.]

Gonda, J. 1973. *Sanskrit in Indonesia*. 2d edition. New Delhi: International Academy of Indian Culture.

Horne, Eleanor Clark. 1974. *Javanese-English Dictionary*. New Haven, Ct.: Yale University Press.

Kamus Basa Jawa (Bausastra Jawa). 2001. Edited by the Tim Penyusun Balai Bahasa Yogyakarta (The Compiling Team of the Language Center of Yogyakarta) headed by Suwadji. Yogyakarta: Kanisius.

Kamus Besar Bahasa Indonesia. 1989. Edited by Anton M. Moeliono, Sri Sukesi Adiwimarta, Adi Sunaryo, et al. 2d edition. Jakarta: Balai Pustaka.

Kamus Indonesia-Jawa. 1991. Edited by Sudaryanto, Sukardi Mp, Syamsul Arifin, et al. Yogyakarta: Duta Wacana University Press.

Kridalaksana, Harimurti. 1984. *Kamus Sinonim Bahasa Indonesia*. Revised edition. Ende, Flores: Nusa Indah.

Labrousse, Pierre, Farida Soemargono, Winarsih Arifin, et al. 1984. *Dictionnaire général indonésien-français*. Paris: Association Archipel.

Mardiwarsito, L. 1990. *Kamus Jawa Kuna-Indonesia.* Revised edition. Ende, Flores: Nusa Indah.

Mardiwarsito, L., Sri Sukesi Adwimarta, and Sri Timur Suratman. 1989. *Kamus Indonesia-Jawa Kuna (Kawi).* 2d edition. Ende, Flores: Nusa Indah.

Masturah, Titin. 1990. *Pemerian Makna Istilah Pedalangan yang Ada Hubungannya dengan Kasatriyan, Persenjataan, Busana, Nama Tokoh Wayang Kulit Purwa Gaya Surakarta Jawa—Indonesia* (A Description of the Meanings of the Shadow Puppetry Terms related to Knighthood, Weaponry, Clothing, and the Names of Characters in *Wayang Kulit Purwå* in the Surakarta Style). Surakarta: Sekolah Tinggi Seni Indonesia.

Monier-Williams, Monier. 1979. *A Sanskrit-English Dictionary.* Oxford: Oxford University Press. [Reprint of 1899 edition.]

Murtana, I Nyoman. 1990. *Pemerian Makna Istilah Garap Pedalangan Gaya Surakarta: Jawa-Indonesia* (A Description of the Meaning of *Wayang* Performance Terms in the Surakarta Style: Javanese-Indonesian). Surakarta: STSI.

Ngafenan, Mohamad. 1990. *Dasanama Basa Jawa* (Javanese Synonyms). Semarang: Dahara Prize.

Padmasusastra. 1979. Reprint. *Serat Pathi Basa* (The Kernel of Language). Transliterated by Kamajaya. Jakarta: Balai Pustaka. [Written in 1883. Reprint of original edition, Balai Pustaka, 1916.]

Pigeaud, Th. 1989. Reprint. *Javaans-Nederlands Woordenboek.* Dordrecht: Foris Publications. [Original printing, Groningen-Batavia: J. B. Wolters, 1938.]

Poerwadarminta, W. J. S. 1939. *Baoesastra Djawa.* Groningen: J. B. Wolters.

———. 1985. *Kamus Umum Bahasa Indonesia.* 8th edition. Jakarta: Balai Pustaka.

Prawiroatmodjo, S. 1985. *Bausastra Jawa-Indonesia.* 2d edition. 2 vols. Jakarta: Gunung Agung.

Randel, Don Michael, ed. 1986. *The New Harvard Dictionary of Music.* Cambridge: The Belknap Press of Harvard University Press.

Robson, Stuart, and Singgih Wibisono. 2002. *Javanese English Dictionary.* Hong Kong: Periplus.

Rustopo. 1992. "Glossarium." In *Gendhon Humardani: Pemikiran dan Kritiknya,* edited by Rustopo. Surakarta: STSI Press.

Sasrasoeganda. 1922. *Baoesastra Mlajoe-Djawa.* 2d edition. Weltevreden, Dutch East Indies: Balé Poestaka [Balai Pustaka].

Soedarsono et al. 1978. *Kamus Istilah Tari dan Karawitan Jawa.* Jakarta: Proyek Penelitian Bahasa dan Sastra Indonesia dan Daerah.

Soetandyo. 2002. *Kamus Istilah Karawitan* (Dictionary of Gamelan-Related Terms). Jakarta: Wedatama Widya Sastra.

Stevens, Alan M., and A. Ed. Schmidgall-Tellings. 2004. *A Comprehensive Indonesian-English Dictionary.* Athens: Ohio University Press.

Suparlan, Y. B. 1991. *Kamus Indonesia-Kawi.* Yogyakarta: Kanisius.

Zoetmulder, P. J., and S. O. Robson. 1982. *Old Javanese-English Dictionary.* 2 vols. 'S-Gravenhage, The Netherlands: Martinus Nijhoff.

Corpus

Arintaka, B. 1981. *Sekar Macapat (kangge Cepengan Para Calon/Guru SD)* (*Måcåpat* Songs [Handbook for Student Teachers/Teachers of Elementary School]). [Yogyakarta]. [Quoted and translated in Arps, 1992.]

Arps, Bernard. 1992. *Tembang in Two Traditions: Performance and Interpretation of Javanese Literature.* London: University of London, School of Oriental and African Studies.

Boow, Justine. 1988. *Symbol and Status in Javanese Batik.* Nedlands, Western Australia: Asian Studies Centre, The University of Western Australia. Monograph Series no. 7.

Brakel-Papenhuijzen, Clara. 1993. "Character Types and Movement Styles in Traditional Theatre." In *Performance in Java and Bali*, edited by Bernard Arps. London: School of Oriental and African Studies, University of London.

———. 1995. *Classical Javanese Dance: The Surakarta Tradition and Its Terminology.* Leiden, the Netherlands: KITLV Press.

Brinner, Benjamin. 1985. "Competence and Interaction in the Performance of 'Pathetan' in Central Java." Ph.D. dissertation, University of California, Berkeley.

———. 1995. *Knowing Music, Making Music: Javanese Gamelan and the Theory of Musical Competence and Interaction.* Chicago: University of Chicago Press.

Daladi Hadisiswojo, Suroso. 1960. "Karawitan Vokal." Bachelor's thesis, Akademi Seni Karawitan Indonesia, Surakarta.

Darsono. "Gending-Gending Sekar." 1980. Senior thesis, Akademi Seni Karawitan Indonesia, Surakarta.

Dea, Alexander. 1980 [1979]. *Bawa: A Javanese Solo Vocal Music.* Ph.D. dissertation, Wesleyan University, Middletown, Ct.

Djumadi. 1982. *Tuntunan "Belajar Rebab"* (Manual for Studying the *Rebab*). Surakarta [Privately published].

Gitosaprodjo, Sulaiman. 1970. *Ichtisar Teori Karawitan dan Teknik Menabuh Gamelan* (Summary of the Theory of *Karawitan* and Technique of Playing the *Gamelan*). Malang, Indonesia. [Translated by Judith Becker in Becker and Feinstein, 1984.]

———. 1992. *Teori dan Praktek Bawa.* (Theory and Practice of *Båwå* [Singing]). Surkarta: [No publisher].

———, compiler. 1971. *Sekar* (Song). Malang: Keluarga Karawitan Indonesia. [Translated by Judith Becker in Becker and Feinstein 1987.]

Hardjowirogo. 1980 [1926]. *Pathokaning Nyekaraken* (Rules of Singing). 2 vols. Jakarta: Departemen Pendidikan dan Kebudayaan, Proyek Penerbitan Buku Bacaan dan Sastra Indonesia dan Daerah. Translated by Sulistijo.

———. 1982 [1949]. 6th edition. *Sejarah Wayang Purwa* (*Wayang* History). Jakarta: Balai Pustaka.

Hughes-Freeland, Felicia. 1995. "Performance and Gender in Javanese Palace Tradition." In *Male and Female in Developing Southeast Asia*, edited by Wazir Jahan Karim. Oxford: Berg Publishers.

———. 1997a. "Consciousness in Performance: A Javanese Theory." *Social Anthropology* 5/1:55–68.

Humardani, Gendhon. 1991. "Rasa Gerak Tari" (The *Rasa* of Dance Movements). In *Gendhon Humardani: Pemikiran dan Kritiknya*, edited by Rustopo. Surakarta: STSI Press.

Kaboela. 1929. *Pasinaon Dhalang* (*Dhalang* School). In *Serat Warna Sari Djawi*, edited by J. Kats. 2d edition. Weltevreden, Dutch East Indies: Boekhandel Visser.

Kussudiarjo, Bagong. 1984. "Dari Seni Tari Gaya Klasik Mataram hingga Seni Tari Gaya Kontemporer, Suatu Pridadi" [From Classical Yogyanese Dance Style to Contemporary Dance Style: One Individual], in *Tari* [Dance], edited by Edi Sedyawati. [Written in 1977.]

Legowo, Budi. [1974?]. *Karawitan Praktis* (Practical *Karawitan*). Surakarta: Widya Duta.

Long, Roger. 1979. "The Movement System in Javanese *Wayang Kulit* in Relation to Puppet Character Type: A Study of Ngayogyakarta Shadow Theatre." Ph.D. dissertation, University of Hawaii.

Maduwiyata, Djoko. 1982/1983. *Bonangan Karawitan Yogyakarta* (The Bonang Part in Yogyanese Gamelan Music). Yogyakarta: Akademi Seni Tari Indonesia.

Mardimin, Yohanes. 1991. *Sekitar Tembang Macapat* (Concerning *Mâcâpat* Song). Semarang: Satya Wacana.

Martopangrawit. 1972. *Tjatatan-Tjatatan Pengetahuan Karawitan* (Notes on Javanese Music Theory). Vol. 2. Surakarta: Pusat Kesenian Djawa Tengah and Dewan Mahasiswa ASKI Surakarta.

———. 1975. *Pengetahuan Karawitan* (Javanese Music Theory). Vol. 1. 2d edition. Surakarta: ASKI.

Moertiyah, Koes. 1991. "Tari Badhaya dan Srimpi" (*Bedhaya* and *Srimpi* Dance). Paper (and ensuing discussion) presented at the Sarasehan Tari Kraton (Discussion on Palace Dance) held at the Taman Budaya Surakarta, June 23.

Murdiati, and Untung Muljono. 1983. *Dasar-Dasar Belajar Tembang Gaya Yogyakarta* (The Rudiments of Yogyanese Song). Yogyakarta: Akademi Seni Tari Indonesia.

Murtiyoso, Bambang. 1979/1980. *Seni Pedalangan (Jawa): Unsur-Unsur Pokok* (Javanese Shadow Puppetry: Essential Elements). Surakarta: ASKI Surakarta, Proyek Pengembangan IKI.

———. 1982/1983. *Pengetahuan Pedalangan* (The Study of Shadow Puppetry). Surakarta: ASKI, Proyek Pengembangan IKI.

Nojowirongko, M. Ng. (alias Atmotjendono). [1954?]. *Serat Tuntunan Padhalangan* (Manual of Shadow Puppetry). Volumes 1 and 2 (published together). Yogyakarta: Djawatan Kebudajan, Kementerian P. P. lan K. (Cultural Bureau of the Ministry of Education, Teaching, and Culture).

Padmosoekotjo, S. [1960?]. *Ngèngrèngan Kasusastran Djawa* (Outline of Javanese Literature). Vol. 2. 3d edition. Yogyakarta: Hien Hoo Sing.

———. 1980. "Carane Ngarang Tembang" (How to Compose a Song). *Jaya Baya* 34/53 (August 31):2, 43. [Quoted and translated in Arps 1992, q.v.].

Poerbapangrawit, Kodrat. 1955. *Gendhing Jawa* (Javanese Gamelan Music). Jakarta: Harapan Masa. [Translated by Judith Becker in Becker and Feinstein, 1984.]

———. 1956. "Gamelan." *Sana-Budaja* (Musium Sana Budaja, Yogyakarta) 1/4:185–206. [Translated by Stanley Hoffman in Becker and Feinstein 1987.]

Prabowo, Wahyu Santoso. 1991. "Sosok Tari Tradisi Kraton: Sebuah Pengamatan" (The Form of Traditional Palace Dances: An Approach). Paper presented at the Sarasehan Tari Kraton (discussion on palace dance) held at the Taman Budaya Surakarta, June 23.

Prawiradisastra, Sadjijo. 1991. "Bahasa Jawa dalam Seni Tembang Macapat" (The Use of Javanese in the Art of *Mâcâpat* Singing). Paper presented at the Kongres Bahasa Jawa, Semarang.

Probohardjono, Ngabéhi Samsudjin. 1966. *Serat Sulukan Sléndro*. Solo: Ratna. [Translated by Susan Pratt Walton in Becker and Feinstein 1984.]

Sastrakartika. 1979 [1925]. *Serat Kridhwayangga: Pakem Beksa* (Manual of Court Dance). Jakarta: Departemen Pendidikan dan Kebudayaan, Proyek Penerbitan Buku Bacaan dan Sastra Indonesia dan Daerah. [Transliterated and Translated by T. W. K. Hadisoeprapta.]

Sastrapustaka, Benedictus Yusuf Harjamulya. 1953. *Wédha Pradangga Kawedhar* (Knowledge of Gamelan Revealed). Unpublished typescript (first version). [Translated by R. Anderson Sutton in Becker and Feinstein 1984.]

Sasrasumarta. 1958. *Wangsalan: Ngewrat Wewarah lan Kawruh Wangsalan, Gantjaran sarta Sekar* (Literary Riddles: Including Teachings and Knowledge of Couplets, Prose, as well as Classical Sung Poetry). Jakarta: Balai Pustaka.

Sastroamidjojo, Seno A. [1958?]. *Nonton Pertundjukkan Wajang-Kulit* (Watching a *Wayang Kulit* Performance). Yogyakarta: Pertjetakan Republik Indonesia.

———. [1964?]. *Renungan Tentang Pertundjukan Wajang Kulit* (Musings on the Shadow Theater). Jakarta: Kinta.

Sastrowiryono, W. [1978?]. *Sekar Macapat*. Yogyakarta: Bimbingan Kesenian Majelis Luhur Persatuan Taman Siswa. 2d printing. [Portions of 1980 edition quoted and translated in Arps 1992.]

Serat Centhini Latin (Romanized *Centhini*). 1985–91. 12 vols. Transliteration by Kamajaya. Yogyakarta: Yayasan Centhini Yogyakarta. Chicago: University of Chicago Press. [Originally published 1814. Quoted and translated in *Gamelan*, by Sumarsam.]

Serat Gulang Yarya. 1870. Ms. quoted and translated in *Gamelan*, by Sumarsam. Chicago: University of Chicago Press, 1992.

Serat Tjentini. [1814] 1912–15. Edited by Ng. Soeradipoera et al. Batavia: Ruygrok. Quoted and translated in *Music in Java*, 3d edition, by Jaap Kunst. The Hague: Martinus Nijhoff.

Sindoesawarno. [n.d.]. *Ilmu Karawitan* (Knowledge about Gamelan Music). Vol. 1. [Solo, Indonesia?]: Suhan. [Translated by Martin F. Hatch in Becker and Feinstein 1987.]

———. 1956. *Faktor Penting dalam Gamelan* (An Important Factor in Gamelan). *Sana-Budaja* 1/3:136–48. Reprinted in *Udan Mas* 1/2, 1/4 (1959):38–41, 85–88. [Translated by Stanley Hoffman in Becker and Feinstein 1984.]

Siswanto. 1983. *Pengetahuan Karawitan Daerah Yogyakarta* (Musicology of Yogyanese Gamelan). Proyek Pengadaan Buku Pendidikan Menengah Kejuruan. Jakarta: Departemen

Pendidikan dan Kebudayaan, Direktorat Jenderal Pendidikan Dasar dan Mengenah, Directorat Pendidikan Menengah Kejuruan.

Soebantar. [1968]. *Seni Karawitan di dalam Seni Pedalangan Wajang Kulit Purwa* (Gamelan Music in the Shadow Puppet Theater). Surakarta: Akademi Seni Karawitan Indonesia.

Soerjomentaram. [n.d.]. *Seni Suara* (Music). Yogyakarta: Soejadi. Reprinted in *Pelajaran Kawruh Jiwa* (The Study of Spiritual Knowledge). [Jakarta]: Departemen Pendidikan dan Kebudayaan, 1980. [First presented at a conference in 1951.]

Soeroso. 1983. *Gamelan B: Untuk SMKI* (Gamelan B: for the High School of Javanese Performing Arts). [Jakarta?]: Departemen Pendidikan dan Kebudayaan, Proyek Pengadaan Buku Pendidikan Menengah Kejuruan.

Soetarno. [1978]. "Le rôle de la musique dans les arts du spectacle à Java" (The Role of Music in Javanese Performing Arts). Ph.D. dissertation, Université de Paris VII.

———. 1988. *Unsur-Unsur Estetis dalam Pedalangan Wayang Kulit Jawa Tengah* (Aesthetic Elements in Central Javanese Shadow Puppetry). Surakarta: Akademi Seni Karawitan Indonesia and The Ford Foundation.

———. 1991. "Estetika Pedalangan" (The Aesthetics of Shadow Puppetry). Paper presented at the *Seminar Dosèn Sekolah Tinggi Seni Indonesia tentang Estetika Seni Pertunjukan Tradisional* (STSI Faculty Seminar on the Aesthetics of Traditional Performing Arts), February 27, STSI Surakarta.

Sukamso. 1992. *Garap Rebab, Kendhang, Gender, dan Vocal dalam Gendhing Bondhet* (The *Rebab, Kendhang, Gendèr*, and Vocal Parts in *Gendhing Bondhèt*). Surakarta: Sekolah Tinggi Seni Indonesia.

Sukirno. 1991. Identifikasi Wanda Topeng Panji Gaya Surakarta (Identification of the Facial Expressions of Surakartan Panji Masks). Surakarta: Sekolah Tinggi Seni Indonesia.

Sumarsam. 1995. *Gamelan: Cultural Interaction and Musical Development in Central Java*. Chicago: University of Chicago Press.

Supanggah, Rahayu. 1985. "Introduction aux styles d'interprétation dans la musique javanaise." Ph.D. thesis, Université de Paris VII.

———. 1991b. "Bahasa/Sastra Jawa sebagai Saran Ungkapan Seni dalam Seni Karawitan" (Javanese Language/Literature as a Means of Expression in the Art of *Karawitan*). Paper presented at the Kongres Bahasa Jawa, Semarang.

Supardi. 1991. *Sekaran Bonangan Gaya Mloyowidodo* (Mloyowidodo's Melodic "Flowerings" for *Bonang*). Surakarta: Sekolah Tinggi Seni Indonesia.

Suraji. 1991. *Onang-Onang, Gendhing Kethuk 2 Kerep Minggah 4: Sebuah Tinjauan tentang Garap, Fungsi serta Struktur Musikalnya* (*Onang-Onang*. . . : An Overview of Its Interpretation, Function, and Musical Structure). Surakarta: Sekolah Tinggi Seni Indonesia.

Suratman. 1985/1986. *Gending-Gending Dolanan Anak-Anak di Surakarta I* (Children's Play Songs in Surakarta). Surakarta: Proyek Pengembangan Kesenian Indonesia and ASKI.

Tembang Djawa kanggo ing "Sekolah Pertama" sarta "Sekolah Ra'jat" kang Basané Priboemi Basa Djawa (Javanese Song for Use in Primary Schools Using the Indigenous Javanese Language). [No date (c. 1942–45), no place of publication]: Djawa Gunseikanbu.

Walton, Susan. 1996. "Heavenly Nymphs and Earthly Delights: Javanese Female Singers, Their Music, Their Lives." Ph.D. dissertation, University of Michigan, Ann Arbor.

Waridi. [1986]. *Proses Kumulatif Unsur Unsur Musikal dalam Diri Empu Karawitan: Bapak RL Martopangrawit* (The Cumulative Process of the Musical Elements in the Person of the Master Musician: Mr. RL Martopangrawit). Surakarta: Akademi Seni Karawitan Indonesia (ASKI).

———. 2005. "Tiga Pilar Kehidupan Karawitan Jawa Gaya Surakarta Masa Pascakemerdekaan: Periode 1950–1970an" (Three Pillars of Gamelan Music in the Surakarta Style during the Post-Independence Period: From the 1950s through the 1970s). Ph.D. dissertation, Universitas Gajah Mada, Yogyakarta.

Warsådiningrat [Prajapangrawit]. 1990. *Serat Sujarah utawi Riwayating Gamelan: Wedhapradangga (Serat saking Gotek)* (The History or Story of Gamelan: Sacred Knowledge about Gamelan [Set Down from Oral History]). Surakarta: STSI/Ford Foundation. First printing missing some pages from original 1943 manuscript.

Wibowo, Fred, ed. 1981. *Mengenal Tari Klasik Gaya Yogyakarta* (Introducing Yogyanese Classical Dance). [Yogyakarta]: Dewan Kesenian Propinsi DIY.

General Works

Abu-Lughod, Lila. 1991. "Writing against Culture." In *Recapturing Anthropology: Working in the Present*, edited by Richard Fox. Santa Fe: School of American Research Press.

Agawu, Kofi. 2003. *Representing African Music: Postcolonial Notes, Queries, Positions*. New York: Routledge.

Anderson, Benedict R. O'G. 1965. *Mythology and the Tolerance of the Javanese*. Monograph Series, Modern Indonesia Project. Ithaca, N.Y.: Southeast Asia Program, Department of Asian Studies, Cornell University.

———. 1972. *Java in a Time of Revolution: Occupation and Resistance, 1944–1946*. Ithaca, N.Y.: Cornell University Press.

———. 1990. *Language and Power: Exploring Political Cultures in Indonesia*. Ithaca, N.Y.: Cornell University Press. (Some chapters previously published.)

Appadurai, Arjun. 1991. "Global Ethnoscapes: Notes and Queries for a Transnational Anthropology." In *Recapturing Anthropology: Working in the Present*, edited by Richard Fox. Santa Fe, N.M.: School of American Research Press.

Arps, Bernard. 1992. *Tembang in Two Traditions: Performance and Interpretation of Javanese Literature*. London: School of Oriental and African Studies, University of London.

———, ed. 1993. *Performance in Java and Bali: Studies of Narrative, Theatre, Music and Dance*. London: School of Oriental and African Studies, University of London.

Asad, Talal. 1986. "The Concept of Cultural Translation in British Social Anthropology." In *Writing Culture: The Poetics and Politics of Ethnography*, edited by James Clifford and George E. Marcus. Berkeley: University of California Press.

Ashcroft, Bill, Gareth Griffiths, and Helen Tifflin. 2000. *Post-Colonial Studies: The Key Concepts*. New York: Routledge.

Balkwill, Laura-Lee, and William Forde Thompson. 1999. "A Cross-Cultural Investigation of the Perception of Emotion in Music: Psychological and Cultural Cues." *Music Perception* 17/1:43–64.

Bamberger, Jeanne, and Evan Zipporyn. 1992. "Getting It Wrong." *The World of Music* 34/3:22–56.

Bantolo, Matheus Wasi. 2002. "Alusan pada Tari Jawa" (The Refined Type in Javanese Dance). Master's thesis, STSI Surakarta.

Barnard, Alan, and Jonathan Spencer, eds. 1996. *Encyclopedia of Social and Cultural Anthropology*. London: Routledge.

Barthes, Roland. 1975. *roland BARTHES par roland barthes*. Paris: Editions du Seuil.

Basset, Catherine. 2004. "Tabuh tawur: Retourner le son, renverser le sort: Roue sonore, cosmologie et structures de l'offrande" (*Tabuh Tawur*: Returning the Sound, Reversing Fate/the Spell: Wheel of Sound, Cosmology and Structures of the Offering). Volume 4 of doctoral thesis, Université de Paris X.

Beck, Herman L. 2003. *Les musulmans d'Indonésie*. Turnhout, Belgium: Éditions Brepols.

Becker, A. L. 1979. "Text-Building, Epistemology, and Aesthetics in Javanese Shadow Theatre." In *The Imagination of Reality*, edited by A. L. Becker and A. Yengoyan. Norwood, N.J.: Ablex.

———. 1995. *Beyond Translation: Essays toward a Modern Philology*. Ann Arbor: University of Michigan Press.

Becker, Judith. 1972. "Western Influence in Gamelan Music." *Asian Music* 3/1:3–9.

———. 1979. "Time and Tune in Java." In *The Imagination of Reality: Essays in Southeast Asian Coherence Systems*, edited by A. L. Becker and A. Yengoyan. Norwood, New Jersey: Ablex.

———. 1980. *Traditional Music in Modern Java: Gamelan in a Changing Society*. Honolulu: University of Hawaii Press.

———. 1988. "Earth, Fire, *Sakti*, and the Javanese Gamelan." *Ethnomusicology* 32/3:385–91.

———. 1993. *Gamelan Stories: Tantrism, Islam, and Aesthetics in Central Java*. Monographs in Southeast Asian Studies. Tempe: Program for Southeast Asian Studies, Arizona State University.

———. 1994. "'Aesthetics' and the 'Artist': Universalism and the Court Arts of Central Java, Fourteenth Century - Twentieth Century AD" In *Europe and the Orient*, edited by Drew Gerstle and Anthony Milner. Canberra: The Humanities Research Centre, The Australian National University.

———. 2001. "Anthropological Perspectives on Music and Emotion." In *Music and Emotion: Theory and Research*, edited by Patrik N. Juslin and John A. Sloboda. Oxford: Oxford University Press.

———. 2004. *Deep Listeners: Music, Emotion, and Trancing*. Bloomington: Indiana University Press.

Becker, Judith, and Alton Becker. 1981. "A Musical Icon: Power and Meaning in Javanese Gamelan Music." In *The Sign in Music and Literature*, edited by Wendy Steiner. Austin: University of Texas Press.

Becker, Judith, and Alan Feinstein, eds. 1984–88. *Karawitan: Source Readings in Javanese Gamelan and Vocal Music.* 3 vols. Michigan papers on South and Southeast Asia Numbers 23, 30, and 31. Ann Arbor: University of Michigan Center for South and Southeast Asian Studies.

Behrend, Timothy. 1985. "Karaton Surakarta Kobong." *Caraka: A Newsletter for Javanists* (University of Leiden) 6:11–15.

———. 1989. "Kraton and Cosmos in Traditional Java." *Archipel* 37:173–87.

Benamou, Marc. 1989. "Approaching and Hanging: Metrical and Melodic Organization in Javanese and Western Music." M.A. Thesis, University of Michigan.

———. 1994a. "Singing Is Believing: Javanese Attitudes towards the Bedhaya Singers at the Royal Court of Surakarta." Paper presented at the Center for Southeast Asian Studies, University of Wisconsin-Madison.

———. 1994b. "Affect, Otherness, and the Politics of Listening: *Rasa* in Javanese Music." Paper presented at the University of Alberta, Edmonton.

———. 1996. "When Insiders Disagree: On Evaluating the Bedhaya Singers at the Royal Palace in Surakarta." Paper presented at the Mid-Atlantic Chapter of the Society for Ethnomusicology meeting, Baltimore, Md.

———. 1998a. "Of Zebra Doves and Prawn Crackers: Javanese Metaphors for Vocal Types." In *Sharing the Voices: The Phenomenon of Singing*, edited by Brian A. Roberts. St. John's: Memorial University of Newfoundland.

———. 1998b. "Rasa in Javanese Musical Aesthetics." Ph.D. dissertation, University of Michigan, Ann Arbor.

———. 2002. "Wayang Character Types, Musical Categories, and a Reconsideration of the Alus/Kasar Dichotomy." In *Aspects of Performance: Puppet Theater in Contemporary Indonesia*, edited by Jan Mrázek. Ann Arbor: University of Michigan Center for Southeast Asian Studies.

———. 2003. "Comparing Musical Affect: Java and the West." *The World of Music* 45/3:57–76.

———. 2005. "La propriété, le vol, et l'emprunt dans la musique de gamelan à Java" (Ownership, Theft, and Borrowing in Javanese Gamelan Music). Paper read at the second congress of the Réseau Asie (Paris). Available on line at www.reseau-asie.com [select "version Française," "CONGRES," "2nd Congrès," "Résumés et articles des ateliers 2005 par thématique," "thématique: Savoirs, milieux et sociétés," "XXXI : Vers une anthropologie esthétique?" and finally, "Communication de Marc Benamou"; an English abstract is available by choosing "version Anglaise"; last accessed 26 July 2009]

———. 2006. "Tasting the Music of Solo." In *The Ethnomusicologists' Cookbook*, edited by Sean Williams. New York: Routledge.

Benamou, Marc, and Rahayu Supanggah. 2006. Liner notes for *Indonesia, Central Java: Solonese Gamelan: A Garland of Moods.* 4-CD set. Paris: Maison des Cultures du Monde (Inédit W 260125).

Berenson, F. M. 1995. "Interpreting the Emotional Content of Music." In *The Interpretation of Music: Philosophical Essays*, edited by Michael Krausz. Oxford: Oxford University Press, Clarendon Press. [First published 1993.]

Berlin, Brent. 1992. *Ethnobiological Classification: Principles of Categorization of Plants and Animals in Traditional Societies*. Princeton: Princeton University Press.

Bloomfield, L. 1939. "Linguistic Aspects of Science." In *International Encyclopedia of Unified Science*, Vol. 1.4, edited by O. Neurath, R. Carnap, and C. Morris. Chicago: University of Chicago Press.

Bonneff, Marcel. 1976. "Récentes études et points de vue sur la 'mentalité javanaise' et le problème du développement national en indonésie" (Recent Studies and Points of View on the "Javanese Mentality" and the Problem of National Development in Indonesia). *Archipel* 12:231–48.

———. 1977. "Le Regard des hommes: préceptes et conseils pour les femmes de Java" (The Gaze of Men: Precepts and Advice for the Women of Java). *Achipel* 13:211–34.

Boow, Justine. 1988. *Symbol and Status in Javanese Batik*. Monograph Series no. 7. Nedlands: Asian Studies Center, University of Western Australia.

Boster, James S. 1987. "Introduction." *American Behavioral Scientist* 31/2:150–62. [Special issue on intracultural variation.]

Bourdieu, Pierre. 1987. "Fieldwork in Philosophy." In *Choses Dites*. Paris: Editions de Minuit. [First published in German, 1986 but here in (the original?) French.]

Brakel-Papenhuijzen, Clara. 1992. *The Bedhaya Court Dances of Central Java*. Leiden: E. J. Brill.

———. 1995. *Classical Javanese Dance: The Surakarta Tradition and Its Terminology*. Leiden: KITLV Press.

Brandon, James R. 1970. *On Thrones of Gold: Three Javanese Shadow Plays*. Cambridge, Massachusetts: Harvard University Press.

Brenner, Suzanne A. 1995. "Why Women Rule the Roost: Rethinking Javanese Ideologies of Gender and Self-Control." In *Bewitching Women, Pious Men: Gender and Body Politics in Southeast Asia*, edited by Aihwa Ong and Michael G. Peletz. Berkeley: University of California Press.

Brinner, Benjamin. 1985. "Competence and Interaction in the Performance of 'Pathetan' in Central Java." Ph.D. dissertation, University of California, Berkeley.

———. 1989/1990. "At the Border of Sound and Silence: The Use and Function of Pathetan in Javanese Gamelan." *Asian Music* 21/1:1–34.

———. 1995. *Knowing Music, Making Music: Javanese* Gamelan *and the Theory of Musical Competence and Interaction*. Chicago: University of Chicago Press.

Brown, Donald E. 1991. *Human Universals*. Philadelphia: Temple University Press.

Buku Panduan. Revised edition. 2005. Surakarta: Program Pascasarjana STSI Surakarta.

Calhoun, Cheshire, and Robert C. Solomon, eds. 1984. *What Is an Emotion? Classic Readings in Philosophical Psychology*. New York: Oxford University Press.

Charles-Dominique, Luc. 2007. *Musiques savantes, musiques populaires: Les symboliques du sonore en France (1200–1750)* (Learned Musics, Folk Musics: The Symbolics of the Sounded in France [1200–1750]). Paris: Editions du CNRS.

Choy, Peggy. 1984. "Texts through Time: The Golèk Dance of Java." In *Aesthetic Tradition and Cultural Transition in Java and Bali*, edited by Stephanie Morgan and Laurie Jo Sears. Center for Southeast Asian Studies Monograph no. 2. Madison: University of Wisconsin.

Clara van Groenendael, Victoria M. 1985. *The Dalang behind the Wayang: The Role of the Surakarta and the Yogyakarta Dalang in Indonesian-Javanese Society*. Verhandelingen van het koninklijk institituut voor taal-, land- en volkenkunde no. 114. Dordrecht, Netherlands: Foris Publications.

Clifford, James. 1983. "Power and Dialogue in Ethnography: Marcel Griaule's Initiation." In *Observers Observed: Essays on Ethnographic Fieldwork*, edited by George W. Stocking, Jr. History of Anthropology, Volume 1. Madison: University of Wisconsin Press.

Clifford, James, and George E. Marcus, eds. 1986. *Writing Culture: The Poetics and Politics of Ethnography*. Berkeley: University of California Press.

Cook, Nicholas. 1999. "Words about Music, or Analysis versus Performance." In *Theory into Practice: Composition, Performance and the Listening Experience*, by Nicholas Cook et al. Leuven (Belgium): Leuven University Press.

Cooper, Nancy. 1994. "The Sirens of Java." Ph.D. diss., University of Hawaii.

Cowell, Henry, and Sidney Cowell. 1966. Reprint. *Charles Ives and His Music*. New York: Oxford University Press. [Originally published 1955.]

Crapanzano, Vincent. 1986. "Hermes' Dilemma: The Masking of Subversion in Ethnographic Description." In *Writing Culture: The Poetics and Politics of Ethnography*, edited by James Clifford and George E. Marcus. Berkeley: University of California Press.

Curtis, Richard. 2002. "The Wong Cilik Audience and the Dhalang Entrepeneur." In *Puppet Theater in Contemporary Indonesia: New Approaches to Performance Events*, edited by Jan Mrázek. Ann Arbor: University of Michigan Press.

Dahlhaus, Carl. 1985 [1977]. *Foundations of Music History*. Translated by J. B. Robinson. Cambridge: Cambridge University Press.

———. 1989 [1978]. *The Idea of Absolute Music*. Translated by Roger Lustig. Chicago: The University of Chicago Press.

D'Andrade, Roy. 1995. *The Development of Cognitive Anthropology*. Cambridge: Cambridge University Press.

Daryono. 1999. "Dampak Pariwisata terhadap Tari Tradisional di Karaton Kasunanan dan Pura Mangkunagaran Surakarta" (The Impact of Tourism on Traditional Dance at the Kasunanan and Mangkunegaran Palaces). M.A. thesis, Gadjah Mada University, Yogyakarta.

Daumal, René. 1982 [1970–1972]. *Rasa or Knowledge of the Self: Essays on Indian Aesthetics and Selected Sanskrit Studies*. Translated by Louise Landes Levi. New York: New Directions Books.

Davitz, Joel R. 1969. *The Language of Emotion*. New York: Academic Press. [Cited in Karl Heider, *Landscapes of Emotion: Mapping Three Cultures of Emotion in Indonesia* (Cambridge: Cambridge University Press and Paris: Editions de la Maison des Sciences de l'Homme, 1991).]

Dea, Alexander. 1980 [1979]. *Bawa: A Javanese Solo Vocal Music.* Ph.D. dissertation, Wesleyan University, Middletown, Ct.

Demeuldre, Michel, ed. 2004. *Sentiments doux-amers dans les musiques du monde: Délectations moroses dans les blues, fado, tango, flamenco, rebetiko, p'ansori, ghazal...* (Bittersweet Feelings in the World's Musics: Morose Delectations in the Blues, Fado, Tango, Flamenco, Rebetiko, P'ansori, Ghazal...). Paris: L'Harmattan.

DeNora, Tia. 2003. *After Adorno: Rethinking Music Sociology.* Cambridge: Cambridge University Press.

Devereaux, Kent [and Hastanto]. 1989. "Interview: 'It's Not Official till the Gong Is Hung': Dr. Sri Hastanto, S. Kar." *Balungan* 4/1:7–18.

Dewantara. 1936. *Wawaton Kawruh Gendhing Jawi* (Fundamental Knowledge about Javanese *Gendhing*). Yogyakarta: Wasita. Transliterated as *Kawruh Gending Djawa* (Knowledge about *Gendhing*). Solo: Sadu Budi, 1957. [Translated in Sumarsam 1995.]

Dirlik, Arif. 1994. "The Postcolonial Aura: Third World Criticism in the Age of Global Capitalism." *Critical Inquiry* 20:328–56.

Dorsey, James Owen. 1884. *Omaha Sociology.* Bureau of American Ethnology, Bulletin no. 3:205–370.

During, Jean. 2001. *L'âme des sons: L'art unique d'Ostad Elahi (1895–1974)* (The Soul of Sounds: The Unique Art of Ostad Elahi). Gordes, France: Le Relié.

Endraswara, Suwardi. 2006. *Rasa Sejati: Misteri Seks Dunia Kejawen* (Pure Feeling: the Mystery of Sex [in the] World of Javanese Mysticism). Yogyakarta: Narasi.

Epstein, A. L. 1992. *In the Midst of Life: Affect and Ideation in the World of the Tolai.* Berkeley: University of California Press.

Errington, J. Joseph. 1985. *Language and Social Change in Java: Linguistic Reflexes of Modernization.* Athens: Ohio University Center for International Studies (Center for Southeast Asian Studies, Southeast Asia Series Number 65).

———. 1988. *Structure and Style in Javanese: A Semiotic View of Linguistic Etiquette.* Philadelphia: University of Pennsylvania Press.

Fabian, Johannes. 1983. *Time and the Other: How Anthropology Makes its Object.* New York: Columbia University Press.

Farnsworth, Paul R. 1954. "A Study of the Hevner Adjective List." *The Journal of Aesthetics and Art Criticism* 13:97–103.

———. 1969. *The Social Psychology of Music.* 2d edition. Ames: The Iowa State University Press.

Fealy, Greg, and Virginia Hooker. 2006. *Voices of Islam in Southeast Asia: A Contemporary Sourcebook.* Singapore: Institute of Southeast Asian Studies.

Fiagbedzi, Nissio. 2005. *An Essay on the Nature of the Aesthetic in the African Musical Arts.* [Accra, Ghana?]: Lightning Source.

Florida, Nancy. 1987. "Reading the Unread in Javanese Literture." *Indonesia* 44:1–15.

———. 1992. "The Badhaya Katawang: A Translation of the Song of Kangjeng Ratu Kidul." *Indonesia* 53:20–32.

———. 1993. *Javanese Literature in Surakarta Manuscripts,* vol. 1, *Introduction and Manuscripts of the Karaton Surakarta.* Ithaca, N.Y.: Southeast Asia Program, Cornell University.

———. 1995. *Writing the Past, Inscribing the Future: History as Prophecy in Colonial Java.* Durham, N.C.: Duke University Press.

———. 1996. "Sex Wars: Writing Gender Relations in Nineteenth-Century Java." In *Fantasizing the Feminine in Indonesia,* edited by Laurie J. Sears. Durham: Duke University Press.

Forrest, Jeffrey Wayne. 1980. "Concepts of Melodic Pattern in Contemporary Solonese Gamelan Music." *Asian Music* 11/2:53–127.

Frake, Charles. 1980. "The Ethnographic Study of Cognitive Systems." In *Language and Cultural Description,* selected and introduced by Anwar S. Dil. Stanford: Stanford University Press, 1980. [This chapter reprinted from *Anthropology and Human Behavior,* edited by T. Gladwin and W. Sturtevant (Washington, D.C.: Anthropological Society of Washington, 1962).]

Fromm, Harold. 1985/86. "The Hegemonic Form of Othering; or, The Academic's Burden." In *"Race," Writing, and Difference,* edited by Henry Louis Gates, Jr. Chicago: The University of Chicago Press.

Gates, Henry Louis, Jr. 1986. "Talkin' That Talk." In *"Race," Writing, and Difference,* edited by Henry Louis Gates, Jr. Chicago: The University of Chicago Press. [Reprinted from *Critical Inquiry* 13/1 (1986).]

Gautam, M. R. 1980. *The Musical Heritage of India.* New Delhi: Abhinav Publications.

Geertz, Clifford. 1971. *Islam Observed: Religious Development in Morocco and Indonesia.* Chicago: University of Chicago Press. [Originally published by Yale University, 1968.]

———. 1973. "Ethos, World View, and the Analysis of Sacred Symbols." In *The Interpretation of Cultures.* New York: Basic Books.

———. 1976. *The Religion of Java.* Chicago: University of Chicago Press. [Original edition, Glencoe, Illinois: Free Press, 1960.]

———. 1983. "Art as a Cultural System." In *Local Knowledge.* New York: Basic Books. [First published 1976.]

———. 2000. *Available Light: Anthropological Reflections on Philosophical Topics.* Princeton, N.J.: Princeton University Press.

Geertz, Hildred. 1974. "The Vocabulary of Emotion: A Study of Javanese Socialization Processes." In *Culture and Personality: Contemporary Readings,* edited by Robert A. Le Vine. Chicago: Aldine.

George, Alexander. 1990. "Whose Language Is It Anyway? Some Notes on Idiolects." *The Philosophical Quarterly* 40/160:275–98.

Giles, James L. 1985. "Bawaswara in Javanese Karawitan: An Analysis of Melodic Structure and Ornamentation." Master's thesis, University of Hawaii.

Gitosaprodjo, Sulaiman. 1984. *Ichtisar Teori Karawitan dan Teknik Menabuh Gamelan* (Summary of the Theory of *Karawitan* and Technique of Playing the Gamelan). Translated by Judith Becker in Becker and Feinstein 1984. [First published Malang, Indonesia, 1970.]

———. 1992. *Titilaras Gendhing* (Notation for Gamelan Pieces). 2 vols. Surakarta: Percetakan Hadiwijaya.

———. 1997. *Titilaras Gendhing* (Notation for Gamelan Pieces), vol. 3. Surakarta: Percetakan Hadiwijaya.

Goddard, Cliff, and Anna Wierzbicka, eds. 1994. *Semantic and Lexical Universals: Theory and Empirical Findings*. Amsterdam: John Benjamins.

Goehr, Lydia. 1989. "Being True to the Work." *Journal of Aesthetics and Art Criticism* 47/1:55–67.

———. 1994. *The Imaginary Museum of Musical Works: An Essay in the Philoshophy of Music*. Oxford: Oxford University Press, Clarendon Press. [Original hardbound edition, 1992.]

Goethe, Johann Wolfgang von. 1980. *Wilhelm Meister's Years of Travel*. Vol. 2. Translated by H. M. Waidson. New York: Riverrun Press.

Goldstein, Kenneth S. 1991. "Notes toward a European-American Folk Aesthetic: Lessons Learned from Singers and Storytellers I Have Known." *Journal of American Folklore* 104:164–78.

Gonda, J. 1973. *Sanskrit in Indonesia*. 2d edition. New Delhi: International Academy of Indian Culture.

Groneman, J. 1890. *De Gamelan te Jogjakarta*. Introduction by J. P. N. Land. Amsterdam: Johannes Muller.

Grave, Jean-Marc de. 2001. *Initiation rituelle et arts martiaux : Trois écoles de kanuragan javanais* (Ritual Initiation and Martial Arts: Three Schools of Javanese *Kanuragan*). Paris: Association Archipel and L'Harmattan.

Guy, Nancy. 2002. "Trafficking in Taiwan Aboriginal Voices." In *Handle with Care: Ownership and Control of Ethnographic Materials*, edited by Sjoerd R. Jaarsma. Pittsburgh: University of Pittsburgh Press.

Hadiwidjojo. 1981. *Bedhaya Ketawang: Tarian Sakral di Candi-Candi*. Edited and translated by Astuti Hendrato and Amir Rochkyatmo. Jakarta: Balai Pustaka. [Original address given in 1971 at Universitas Saraswati, Surakarta.]

Hadiwijono, Harun. 1967. *Man in the Present Javanese Mysticism*. Baarn (Netherlands): Bosch en Keuning.

Hanslick, Eduard. 1966. *On the Musically Beautiful: A Contribution towards the Revision of the Aesthetics of Music*. Translated by Geoffrey Payzant. Indianapolis: Hackett. [First German edition, 1854. This translation is from the eighth edition of 1891.]

Hardjana, Suka. 2003. "Rasa, dalam Kelompok." In *Corat-Coret Musik Kontemporer Dulu dan Kini* (Scribbles about Contemporary Music Then and Now). Jakarta: MSPI.

Hardjowirogo. 1982 [1949]. *Sejarah Wayang Purwa* (*Wayang* History). 6th edition. Jakarta: Balai Pustaka.

Harré, R., ed. 1986. *The Social Construction of Emotions*. Oxford: Basil Blackwell.

Hastanto, Sri. 1985. "The Concept of Pathet in Central Javanese Gamelan Music." Ph.D. Dissertation, University of Durham.

Hastanto, Sri, and Kent Devereaux. 1989. See under Devereaux.

Hatch, Martin. 1980. "Lagu, Laras, Layang: Rethinking Melody in Javanese Music." Ph.D. dissertation, Cornell University.

Heider, Karl. 1991. *Landscapes of Emotion: Mapping Three Cultures of Emotion in Indonesia.* Cambridge: Cambridge University Press and Paris: Éditions de la Maison des Sciences de l'Homme.

Heine-Geldern, Robert. 1963 [1956]. *Conceptions of State and Kingship in Southeast Asia.* Data Paper number 18. Ithaca, N.Y.: Cornell University, Deparment of Asian Studies, Southeast Asia Program.

Herndon, Marcia. 1993. "Insiders, Outsiders: Knowing Our Limits, Lmiting Our Knowing." *The World of Music* 35/1:63–80.

Hevner, Kate. 1936. "Experimental Studies of the Elements of Expression in Music." *American Journal of Psychology* 47:103–18.

Hockett, Charles F. 1958. *A Course in Modern Linguistics.* New York: MacMillan.

Hoffman, Stanley. 1978. "Epistemology and Music: A Javanese Example." *Ethnomusicology* 22/1:29–88.

Holt, Claire. 1967. *Art in Indonesia: Continuities and Change.* Ithaca, N.Y.: Cornell University Press.

Holyrode, Peggy. 1972. *The Music of India.* Foreword by Ravi Shankar. New York: Praeger.

Hood, Mantle, and Hardja Susilo. 1967. *Music of the Venerable Dark Cloud: Introduction, Commentary, and Analysis.* Los Angeles: University of California Press.

hooks, bell. 1995. "'this is the oppressor's language/ yet I need it to talk to you': Language, a place of struggle." In *Between Languages and Cultures: Translation and Cross-Cultural Texts,* edited by Anuradha Dingwaney and Carol Maiers. Pittsburgh: University of Pittsburgh Press.

Houben, Vincent J. H. 1989. "Surakarta: Cité héroïque et florissante" (Surakarta: A Heroic and Flourishing City). Archipel 37:199–218.

———. 1994. *Kraton and Kumpeni: Surakarta and Yogyakarta, 1830–1870.* Leiden: KITLV Press.

Howe, David Gordon. 1980. "Sumarah: A Study of the Art of Living." Ph.D. dissertation, University of North Carolina at Chapel Hill.

Hughes-Freeland, Felicia. 1991. "Classification and Communication in Javanese Palace Performance." *Visual Anthropology* 4:345–66.

———. 1993. "*Golèk Ménak* and *Tayuban*: Patronage and Professionalism in Two Spheres of Central Javanese Culture." In *Performance in Java and Bali: Studies of Narrative, Theatre, Music, and Dance,* edited by Bernard Arps. London: University of London, School of Oriental and African Studies.

———. 1995. "Performance and Gender in Javanese Palace Tradition." In *Male and Female in Developing Southeast Asia,* edited by Wazir Jahan Karim. Oxford: Berg Publishers.

———. 1997a. Consciousness in Performance: A Javanese Theory." *Social Anthropology* 5/1:55-68.

———. 1997b. "Art and Politics: From Javanese Court Dance to Indonesian Art." *Journal of the Royal Anthropological Institute* 3/3:473–95.

Humardani, Gendhon. 1991. "Kreasi Tari 'Contemporary Dance School Wisnoe Wardhana' Tahun 1960." In *Gendhon Humardani: Pemikiran dan Kritiknya*, edited by Rustopo. Surakarta: STSI Press.

Hymes, Dell. 1996. "What Is Ethnography?" In *Ethnography, Linguistics, Narrative Inequality: Toward an Understanding of Voice*. London: Taylor and Francis.

Ingold, Tim. 1996. *Key Debates in Anthropology*. London: Routledge.

Ishida, Noriko. 2008. "The Textures of Central Javanese Gamelan Music: Pre-notation and Its Discontents." *Bijdragen tot de Taal-, Land- en Volkenkunde* 164/4:475–99.

Jakobsen, Roman. 1988 [1979]. "The Spell of Speech Sounds." In *Roman Jakobsen: Selected Writings VIII*, edited by Stephen Rudy. Berlin: Mouton de Gruyter. [Reprinted from *The Sound Shape of Language*.]

Juslin, Patrik N. 2001. "Communicating Emotion in Music Performance: A Review and Theoretical Framework." In *Music and Emotion*, edited by Patrik N. Juslin and John A. Sloboda. Oxford: Oxford University Press.

Juslin, Patrik N., and John A. Sloboda, eds. 2001. *Music and Emotion: Theory and Research*. Oxford: Oxford University Press.

Kant, Immanuel. 1960 [1763]. *Observations on the Feeling of the Beautiful and the Sublime*. Translated by John T. Goldthwait. Berkeley: University of California Press.

Kartomi, Margaret. 1990. "Music in Nineteenth Century Java: A Precursor to the Twentieth Century." *Journal of Southeast Asian Studies* 21/1:1–34.

Kayam, Umar. 1981. *Seni, Tradisi, Masyarakat*. Jakarta: Sinar Harapan.

Keeler, Ward. 1975. "Musical Encounter in Java and Bali." *Indonesia* 19:85–126.

———. 1984. *Javanese: A Cultural Approach*. Monographs in International Studies, Southeast Asia Series, no. 69. Athens: Ohio University Center for Southeast Asian Studies.

———. 1987. *Javanese Shadow Plays, Javanese Selves*. Princeton: Princeton University Press.

———. 1990. "Speaking of Gender in Java." In *Power and Difference: Gender in Island Southeast Asia*, edited by Jane Monnig Atkinson and Shelly Errington. Stanford, Calif.: Stanford University Press.

———. 1992. *Javanese Shadow Puppets*. Images of Asia. Singapore: Oxford University Press.

Keil, Charles. 1979. *Tiv Song*. Chicago: University of Chicago Press.

Kirkpatrick, John, ed. 1991. *Charles E. Ives: Memos*. New York: W. W. Norton. [First published 1972 by The National Institute of Arts and Letters.]

Kitab Primbon Betaljemur Adammakna. 1991. 51st edition. Jakarta: Buana Raya. [Compiled by Soemodidjojo Mahadewa from an anonymous manuscript in the possession of Prince Harja Tjakraningrat of Yogyakarta. Re-edited for the 50th edition by Wibatsu Harianto Soembogo. First published 1939.]

Kitayama, Shinobu, and Hazel Rose Markus, eds. 1994. *Emotion and Culture: Empirical Studies of Mutual Influence*. Washington, D.C.: American Psychological Association.

Kleinman, Sidney. 1995. [Introduction to the] *Projet concernant de nouveaux signes pour la musique* (Project concerning a New Musical Notation) [and the] *Dissertation sur la musique moderne* (Essay on Modern Music). In *Oeuvres complètes V: Écrits sur la musique, la langue et le théâtre* (Complete Works V: Writings on Music, Language, and Theater) by Jean-Jacques Rousseau. Paris: Gallimard (Coll. Bibliothèque de la Pléiade).

Kluckhohn, Clyde, and Henry A. Murray, eds. 1969. *Personality, Nature, Society, and Culture.* 2d revised edition. New York: Alfred A Knopf. [First edition, 1949. Second edition originally published 1953.]

Kövecses, Zoltan. 1990. *Emotion Concepts.* New York: Springer-Verlag.

Krausz, Michael, ed. 1995. *The Interpretation of Music: Philosophical Essays.* Oxford: Oxford University Press, Clarendon Press. [Paperback reprint. First published 1993.]

Kraut, Robert. 1992. "On the Possibility of a Determinate Semantics for Music." In *Cognitive Bases of Musical Communication,* edited by Mari Riess Jones and Susan Holleran. Washington, D.C.: American Psychological Association.

———. 1995. "Perceiving the Music Correctly." In *The Interpretation of Music: Philosophical Essays,* edited by Michael Kraus. Oxford: Oxford University Press, Clarendon Press.

Kunst, Jaap. 1948. *Begdja: Anak Penabuh Gamelan.* Jakarta: Moderne Boekhandel Indonesie. (English translation, "Begja the Gamelan Boy," recorded by Kunst in 1953, Philips 00165L.)

———. 1973. *Music in Java: Its History, Its Theory and Its Technique.* 3d edition, 2 vols., enlarged. The Hague: Martinus Nijhoff. [First edition published in Dutch as *De Toonkunst van Java* (The Hague: Martinus Nijhoff, 1934).]

Kusumadilaga. 1981. *Serat Sastramiruda.* Translated by Kamajaya, transliterated by Sudibjo Z. Hadisutjipto. Jakarta: Departemen Pendidikan dan Kebudayaan, Proyek Penerbitan Buku Sastra Indonesia dan Daerah. [Original manuscript written under Pakubuwana IX (reigned 1863–1893).]

Laderman, Carol. 1984. "A Welcoming Soil: Islamic Humoralism on the Malay Peninsula." In *Paths to Asian Medical Knowledge,* edited by Charles Leslie and Allan Young. Berkeley: University of California Press.

Lakoff, George. 1990. *Women, Fire, and Dangerous Things: What Categories Reveal about the Mind.* Chicago: University of Chicago Press. [Original edition, 1987.]

Lakoff, George, and Mark Johnson. 1980. *Metaphors We Live By.* Chicago: University of Chicago Press.

Laksono, P. M. 1985. *Tradisi dalam Struktur Masyarakat Jawa: Kerajaan dan Pedesaan* (see Laksono 1986). Yogyakarta: Gadjah Mada University Press.

———. 1986. *Tradition in Javanese Social Structure: Kingdom and Countryside: Changes in the Javanese Conceptual Model.* Translated by E. G. Koentjoro. Yogyakarta: Gadjah Mada University Press. [Originally published in Indonesian (see Laksono 1985).]

Lambert, Jean. 1997. La médecine de l'âme: Le chant de Sanaa dans la société yéménite (Medicine for the Soul: *Sanaa* Song in Yemeni Society). Hommes et musiques, no. 2. Nanterre (France): Société d'ethnologie.

———. 2004. "La souffrance d'amour des chanteurs du Yemen: Critère de compétence artistique et marqueur du statut social" (The Love-Suffering of Yemeni Singers: A Criterion of Artistic Competence and Marker of Social Status). In *Sentiments doux-amers dans les musiques du monde: Délectations moroses dans les blues, fado, tango, flamenco, rebetiko, p'ansori, ghazal...* (Bittersweet Feelings in the World's Musics: Morose Delectations in the Blues, Fado, Tango, Flamenco, Rebetiko, P'ansori, Ghazal...), edited by Michel Demeuldre. Paris: L'Harmattan.

Langer, Susanne K. 1951. *Philosophy in a New Key*. New York: New American Library, 1951.

———. 1957. *Problems of Art: Ten Philosophical Lectures*. New York: Charles Scribner's Sons.

———. 1964. *Philosophical Sketches*. New York: New American Library.

———. 1967. *Mind: An Essay on Human Feeling*. 2 vols. Baltimore: The Johns Hopkins Press.

Larson, George D. 1987. *Prelude to Revolution: Palaces and Politics in Surakarta, 1912–1942*. Dordrecht, Netherlands: Foris Publications.

Lehrer, Adrienne. 1983. *Wine and Conversation*. Bloomington: Indiana University Press.

Lelyveld, Th. B. van. 1931. *De Javaansche danskunst*. Amsterdam: Van Holkema en Warendorf.

Lindsay, Jennifer. 1979. *Javanese Gamelan*. Kuala Lumpur: Oxford University Press.

———. 1985. "Klasik, Kitsch, or Contemporary: A Study of the Javanese Performing Arts." Ph.D. dissertation, University of Sydney, Australia.

Lombard, Denis. 1990. *Le Carrefour javanais : Essai d'histoire globale*. 3 vols. Paris: Editions de l'Ecole des Hautes Etudes en Sciences Sociales.

Lortat-Jacob. 1998. *Chants de Passion : Au coeur d'une confrérie de Sardaigne* (Songs of Passion: At the Heart of a Sardinian Brotherhood). Paris: Éditions du Cerf.

Lucke, Joyce Joanna. 1995. "We All Agree: A Study of Cultural Consensus in a Hmong Community." Ph.D. dissertation, University of Wisconsin–Milwaukee.

Lutz, Catherine A. 1988. *Unnatural Emotions: Everyday Sentiments on a Micronesian Atoll and Their Challenge to Western Theory*. Chicago: University of Chicago Press.

Lutz, Catherine, and Geoffrey M. White. 1986. "The Anthropology of Emotions." Annual *Review of Anthropology* 15:405–36.

Lynch, Owen. 1990. "Introduction: Emotions in Theoretical Contexts." In *Divine Passions: The Social Construction of Emotion in India*, edited by Owen M. Lynch. Berkeley: University of California Press.

Lyon, Marot L. 1995. "Missing Emotion: The Limitations of Cultural Contructionism in the Study of Emotion." *Cultural Anthropology* 10/2:244–63.

Lysloff, René T. A. 1990. "Non-Puppets and Non-Gamelan: Wayang Parody in Banyumas." *Ethnomusicology* 34/1:19–35.

Macchiarella, Ignazio. [1995]. *Il falsobordone fra tradizione orale e tradizione scritta* (The Falsobordone in Oral and Written Traditions). Lucca: Libreria Musicale Italiana.

Maceda, José. 1986. "A Concept of Time in a Music of Southeast Asia (a Preliminary Account)." *Ethnomusicology* 30/1:11–53.

Mack, Dieter. 2004. *Zeitgenössische Musik in Indonesien: Zwischen lokalen Traditionen, nationalen Verpflichtungen und internationalen Einflüssen* (Contemporary Music in Indonesia: Between Local Traditions, National Commitments, and International Influences). Hildesheim (Germany): Georg Olms Verlag.

Magnis-Suseno, Franz. 1988. 3d edition. *Etika Jawa: Sebuah Analisa Falsafi tentang Kebijaksanaan Hidup Jawa* (Javanese Ethics: An Analysis of Javanese Philosophy of Life). Jakarta: Gramedia. [Original German edition, Munich: R. Oldenbourg, 1981.]

Mardusari. 1987. "Pengakuan Nyai Mardusari" (Dame Mardusari's Confession). *Tempo* 12 September.

Marianto, M. Dwi. 2003. "Berpikir dengan Rasa (Thinking through *Rasa*)." In *Kembang Setaman: Persembahan untuk Sang Mahaguru* (Flowers from the Same Garden: Offerings to Our Master Teacher), edited by A. M. Hermien Kusmayati. Yogyakarta: BP ISI Yogyakarta.

Martin, Gary J. 1995. *Ethnobotany: A Methods Manual*. London: Chapman and Hall.

Martopangrawit. 1984. *Catatan-Catatan Pengetahuan Karawitan* (Notes on Knowledge of Gamelan Music). Vols. 1 and 2. Surakarta: Pusat Kesenian Jawa Tengah and Dewan Mahasiswa, ASKI. [Translated by Martin F. Hatch in Becker and Feinstein 1984. Originally published 1972 and 1975—see entry under "Corpus."]

———. 1988. *Dibuang Sayang: Lagu dan Cakepan Gerongan Gending Gending Gaya Surakarta* (A Shame to Throw Away: Melodies and Texts for the Male Chorus Part to Gamelan Pieces in the Style of Surakarta). Published posthumously. Edited by Rahayu Supanggah [et al.]. Surakarta: Seti-Aji and Akademi Seni Karawitan Indonesia.

McAllester, David P. 1954. *Enemy Way Music: A Study of Social and Esthetic Values as Seen in Navaho Music*. Papers of the Peabody Museum of American Archaeology and Ethnology, Harvard University, Vol. XLI no. 3. Reports of the Rimrock Project, Values Series no. 3. Cambridge, Mass.: Peabody Museum.

Mendonça, Maria. 2002. "Javanese Gamelan in Britain: Communitas, Affinity and Other Stories." Ph.D. dissertation, Wesleyan University, Middletown, Ct.

Merriam, Alan P. 1980. *The Anthropology of Music*. Evanston, Ill.: Northwestern University Press. First published 1964.

Meyer, Leonard B. 1956. *Emotion and Meaning in Music*. Chicago: University of Chicago Press.

———. 1967. *Music, the Arts, and Ideas: Patterns and Predictions in Twentieth-Century Culture*. Chicago: University of Chicago Press.

Mloyowidodo, S. 1976. *Gending-Gending Jawa Gaya Surakarta* (Javanese Gamelan Pieces in the Surakarta Style). 2 volumes. Surakarta: ASKI.

Moertono, Soemarsaid. 1981. *State and Statecraft in Old Java: A Study of the Later Mataram Period, 16th to 19th Century*. Revised edition. Modern Indonesia Project, Monograph Series no. 43. Ithaca, N.Y.: Cornell University Southeast Asia Program. [First edition, 1968.]

Morgan, Stephanie, and Laurie Jo Sears, eds. 1984. *Aesthetic Tradition and Cultural Transition in Java and Bali*. Center for Southeast Asian Studies Monograph no. 2. Madison: University of Wisconsin Press.

Mrázek, Jan. 2005. *Phenomenology of a Puppet Theatre: Contemplations on the Art of Javanese Wayang Kulit*. Leiden, the Netherlands: KITLV Press.

———, ed. 2002. *Puppet Theater in Contemporary Indonesia: New Approaches to Performance Events*. Ann Arbor: University of Michigan Press.

Mulder, Niels. 1980. *Mysticism and Everyday Life in Contemporary Java: Cultural Persistence and Change*. 2d edition. Singapore: Singapore University Press.

———. 1989. *Individual and Society in Java: A Cultural Analysis*. Yogyakarta: Gadjah Mada University Press.

Murtioso, Bambang, Waridi, Suyanto, et al. 1998. *Pertumbuhan dan Perkembangan Seni Pertunjukan Wayang*. Surakarta: Sekolah Tinggi Seni Indonesia and Sekretariat Nasional Pewayangan Indonesia.

Negoro, Suryo S. 2000. *Kejawen: Javanese Traditional Spiritual Teaching*. Surkarta: CV Buana Raya.

Nettl, Bruno. 1985. *The Western Impact on World Music: Change, Adaptation, and Survival*. New York: Schirmer Books.

———. 1995. *Heartland Excursions: Ethnomusicological Reflections on Schools of Music*. Urbana: University of Illinois Press.

———. 2000. "An Ethnomusicologist Looks at Universals." In *The Origins of Music*, edited by Nils L. Wallin, Björn Merker, Steven Brown, et al. Cambridge, Mass: MIT Press.

Nida, Eugene A. 1975. *Language Structure and Translation*. Edited by S. Anwar. Stanford, Calif.: Stanford University Press.

Noll, Günther. 1960. "Untersuchungen über die Musikerzieherische Bedeutung Jean-Jacques Rousseaus und seiner Ideen—Allgemeiner Überblick und spezielle Darstellung seiner Ziffernschrift als Anfang einer modernen Musik-methodik" (Inquiries into the Musico-Pedagogical Significance of Jean-Jacques Rousseau and His Ideas—General Overview and Specific Description of a Modern Methodology). Ph.D. diss., Universität Humboldt, Berlin.

Nuckolls, Charles W. 1995. "The Misplaced Legacy of Gregory Bateson: Toward a Cultural Dialectic of Knowledge and Desire." *Cultural Anthropology* 10/3:367–94.

Nugroho, Sugeng. 2003. "Studi tentang Pertunjukan Wayang kulit Enthus Susmono" (A Study of Enthus Susmono's *Wayang Kulit* Performances). M.A. thesis, STSI Surakarta.

Ortony, Andrew, Gerald L. Clore, and Allan Collins. 1988. *The Cognitive Structure of Emotions*. Cambridge: Cambridge University Press.

Pemberton, John. 1987. "Musical Politics in Central Java (or How Not to Listen to Javanese Gamelan)." *Indonesia* 44:16–29.

———. 1994. *On the Subject of "Java."* Ithaca, N.Y.: Cornell University Press.

Perlman, Marc. 1991a. "Asal-Usul Notasi Gendhing Jawa di Surakarta: Suatu Rumusan Sejarah Nut Ranté" (The Origin of *Gendhing* Notation in Java: A Sketch of the History of Chain Notation). *Seni Pertunjukan Indonesia: Jurnal Masyarakat Seni Pertunjukan Indonesia* 2/2:36–68.

———. 1991b. "The Term *Karawitan*." *Balungan* 5/1:28.

———, ed. 1992. *Festival of Indonesia: Conference Summaries*. Translated into Indonesian by Tinuk Rosalia Yampolsky and Marc Perlman. New York: The Festival of Indonesia Foundation.

———. 1994. "Unplayed Melodies: Music Theory in Postcolonial Java." Ph.D. dissertation, Wesleyan University, Middletown, Ct.

———. 1998. "The Social Meanings of Modal Practices: Status, Gender, History and *Pathet* in Central Javanese Music." *Ethnomusicology* 42/1:45–80.

———. 1999. "The Traditional Javanese Performing Arts in the Twilight of the New Order: Two Letters from Solo." *Indonesia* 68:1–37.

———. 2004. *Unplayed Melodies: Javanese Gamelan and the Genesis of Music Theory*. Berkeley: University of California Press.

Pickvance, Richard. 2005. *A Gamelan Manual: A Player's Guide to the Central Javanese Gamelan*. London: Jaman Mas Books.

Pigeaud, Theodore G. Th. 1938. *Javaanse volksvertooningen: Bijdrage tot de beschrijving van land en volk* (Javanese Folk Performing Arts: Contribution to the Description of Land and People). Batavia, Dutch East Indies: Volkslektuur.

Pike, Kenneth. 1967. "Etic and Emic Standpoints for the Description of Behavior." In *Language in Relation to a Unified Theory of the Structure of Human Behavior*, 2d edition. The Hague: Mouton.

Poerbapangrawit, Kodrat. 1984. *Gendhing Jawa* (Javanese Gamelan Music). Translated by Judith Becker in Becker and Feinstein, 1984. [First published Jakarta: Harapan Masa, 1955.]

———. 1987. "Gamelan." Translated by Stanley Hoffman in Becker and Feinstein, 1987. [First published in *Sana-Budaja* (Musium Sana Budaja, Yogyakarta) 1/4(1956):185–206.]

Pople, Anthony, ed. 1994. *Theory, Analysis and Meaning in Music*. Cambridge: Cambridge University Press.

Posnett, David. 1990. "Reason and Feeling: An Appreciation of the Javanese *Rebab*." *Indonesia Circle* 52 (June):25–35.

Pratt, Carroll C. 1968. *The Meaning of Music: A Study in Psychological Aesthetics*. New York: Johnson Reprint. [Originally published, without the introduction, New York: McGraw-Hill, 1931.]

Probohardjono, Ng. S. 1964. *Gendhing-Gendhing ingkang kanggé Nabuhi Wajangan Purwa* (Pieces to Accompany *Wayang Kulit*). 5th edition. Yogyakarta: Sinduniti. [First edition, 1957. Reprinted under the authorship of Ki Siswoharsoyo by Yogyakarta: Toko Buku "S.G." (c. 1990).]

Purwadi et al. 2005. *Ajaran Ilmu Sejati Wali Songo*. Yogyakarta: Media Abadi.

Quine, Willard Van Orman. 1960. *Word and Object*. Cambridge, MA: M.I.T. Press.

Racy, A. J. 2003. *Making Music in the Arab World: The Culture and Artistry of Ṭarab*. Cambridge: Cambridge University Press.

Randel, D. M., ed. *The New Harvard Dictionary of Music*. 1986. Cambridge, MA: The Belknap Press of Harvard University Press.

Rao, Suvarnalata. 2000. *Acoustical Perspective on Raga-Rasa Theory*. New Delhi: Munshiram Manoharlal Publishers.

Ras, J. J. 1985. *Inleiding tot het modern Javaans* (Introduction to Modern Javanese). 2d edition. Dordrecht, the Netherlands: Foris Publications.

Reid, Cornelius L. 1983. *A Dictionary of Vocal Terminology: An Analysis*. New York: Joseph Patelson Music House.

Ricklefs, M. C. 1981. *A History of Modern Indonesia: C. 1300 to the Present*. Bloomington: Indiana University Press.

Robinson, Jenefer. 2005. *Deeper Than Reason: Emotion and Its Role in Literature, Music, and Art*. Oxford: Oxford University Press.

———, ed. 1997. *Music and Meaning*. Ithaca, N.Y.: Cornell University Press.

Robson, Stuart. 1992. *Javanese Grammar for Students*. Monash Papers on Southeast Asia no. 26. Clayton, Victoria: Monash University, Center of Southeast Asian Studies.

Rosch Heider, Eleanor. 1972. "Probabilities, Sampling, and Ethnographic Method: The Case of Dani Colour Names." *Man* 7/3:448–66.

Rousseau, Jean-Jacques. 1959 [1770]. *Les Confessions*. Paris: Gallimard (Coll. Bibliothèque de la Pléiade no. 11).

———. 1995 [1742]. "Projet concernant de nouveaux signes pour la musique" (Project concerning a New Notation for Music). In *Oeuvres complètes V: Écrits sur la musique, la langue et le théâtre* (Complete Works V: Writings on Music, Language, and Theater). Paris: Gallimard (Coll. Bibliothèque de la Pléiade no. 416).

Rowell, Lewis. 1992. *Music and Musical Thought in Early India*. Chicago: The University of Chicago Press.

Rustopo. 1991. *Gamelan Kontemporer di Surakarta: Pembentukan dan Perkembangannya (1970–1990)* (*Gamelan Kontemporer* in Surakarta: Its Formation and Development, 1970–1990). Surakarta: Sekolah Tinggi Seni Indonesia Surakarta.

Said, Edward W. 1979. *Orientalism*. New York: Vintage Books. [Originally published by Pantheon Books, 1978.]

Sajid. *Babad Sala* (Chronicle of Solo). 1984. Solo: Rekso Pustoko.

Salmen, Walter, ed. 1983. *The Social Status of the Professional Musician from the Middle Ages to the 19th Century*. Annotated and translated by Herbert Kaufman and Barbara Reisner. Sociology of Music Series no. 1. New York: Pendragon. [First published in German in 1971 (Kassel: Bärenreiter).]

Santosa. 1990. *Survai tentang Pengrawit dan Pesinden di Kecamatan Banjarsari dan Laweyan Surakarta* (Survey concerning Gamelan Instrumentalists and Singers in the Subdistricts of Banjarsari and Laweyan, Surakarta). Surakarta: Sekolah Tinggi Seni Indonesia Surakarta.

———. 2001. "Constructing Images in Javanese Gamelan Performances: Communicative Aspects among Musicians and Audiences in Village Communities." Ph.D. dissertation, University of California, Berkeley.

———. 2002. "Patronase dan Kehidupan Komunitas Gamelan." *Jurnal Pengkajian dan Penciptaan Seni* 1/2:223–36.

Santoso, Suroto Heru. 1995. "Pengamen Bus Antar Kota Delanggu-Klaten" (Buskers on the Bus between Delanggu and Klatèn). Bachelor's thesis, STSI Surakarta.

Sapir, Edward. 1938. "Why Cultural Anthropology Needs the Psychiatrist." *Psychiatry* 1:7–12.

———. 1962a. "Cultural Anthropology and Psychiatry." In *Edward Sapir: Culture, Language and Personality*, edited by David G. Mandelbaum. Berkeley: University of California Press. [Originally published in the *Journal of Abnormal and Social Psychology* 27 (1932):229–42].

———. 1962b. "The Emergence of the Concept of Personality in a Study of Cultures." In *Edward Sapir: Culture, Language and Personality*, edited by David G. Mandelbaum. Berkeley: University of California Press. [Originally published in the *Journal of Social Psychology* 5 (1934):408–15.]

Sastrapustaka, Benedictus Yusuf Harjamulya. 1984 [1953]. *Wédha Pradangga Kawedhar* (Knowledge of Gamelan Revealed). Translated by R. Anderson Sutton in Becker and Feinstein 1984.

Schneider, Albrecht, and Andreas E. Beurmann. 1993. "Notes on the Acoustics and Tuning of *Gamelan* Instruments." In *Performance in Java and Bali*, edited by Bernard Arps. London: School of Oriental and African Studies, University of London.

Scruton, Roger. 1980. "Emotion, Practical Knowledge and Common Culture." In *Explaining Emotions*, edited by Amélie Oksenberg Rorty. Berkeley: University of California Press.

———. 1997. *The Aesthetics of Music*. Oxford: Oxford University Press, Clarendon Press.

Sears, Laurie J. 1986. "Court and Village in Javanese Shadow Theatre: History, Power, and Political Control." Paper presented at the National Conference of the Association for Asian Studies, Boston.

———. 1996. *Shadows of Empire: Colonial Discourse and Javanese Tales*. Durham, N.C.: Duke University Press.

Sedyawati, Edi. 1981. *Pertumbuhan Seni Pertunjukan*. Jakarta: Sinar Harapan, Seri Esni no. 4.

———. 1984. "Gambyong: Menurut Serat Cabolang dan Serat Centini" (Gambyong: According to the *Serat Cabolang* and the *Serat Centini*). In *Tari: Tinjauan dari Berbagai Segi* (Dance: Observations from Various Points of View), edited by Edi Sedyawati. Jakarta: Pustaka Jaya.

Seeger, Anthony. 2004. "Traditional Music Ownership in a Commodified World." In *Music and Copyright*, 2d edition, edited by Simon Frith and Lee Marshall. New York: Routledge.

Serat Pesindhen Badhaya. 1983. Transliterated from Javanese script and translated into Indonesian by Moelyono Sastronaryatmo and Soekatmo. Proyek Penerbitan Buku Sastra Indonesia dan Daerah. Jakarta: Departemen Pendidikan dan Kebudayaan. [Composed in the 18th–19th centuries (Florida 1993). Original manuscript(s) from the 19th century?]

Sharma, Prem Lata. 1985/1986. "Rasa Theory and Indian Music." In *Classical Music of India*. Sangeet Research Academy (published for the Festival of India).

Sibley, Frank. 1997. "Making Music Our Own." In *The Interpretation of Music: Philosophical Essays*, edited by Michael Krausz. Oxford: Oxford University Press, Clarendon Press.

Siegel, James T. 1986. *Solo in the New Order: Language and Hierarchy in an Indonesian City*. Princeton, N.J.: Princeton University Press.

Sindoesawarno. 1984 [1956–59]. "Faktor Penting dalam Gamelan" (Important Factors in Gamelan). Translated by Stanley Hoffman in Becker and Feinstein 1984.

———. 1987 [1955]. *Ilmu Karawitan* (Knowledge about Gamelan Music). Vol. 1. Translated by Martin F. Hatch in Becker and Feinstein 1987.

Sindusastra. 1978. *Sejarahipun Para Ratu ing Surakarta* (The History of Kings in Surakarta). Translated into Indonesian and transliterated by Z. S. Hadi Soetjipto. Jakarta: Departemen Pendidikan dan Kebudayaan, Proyek Penerbitan Buku Bacaan dan Sastra Indonesia dan Daerah.

Siregar, Ashadi. [1990?]. *33 Profil Budayawan Indonesia* (33 Profiles of Indonesian Cultural Figures). [Yogyakarta?]: TVRI.

Siswanto. 1983. *Pengetahuan Karawitan Daerah Yogyakarta* (The Study of Yogyanese *Karawitan*). [Jakarta?]: Departemen Pendidikan dan Kebudayaan, Proyek Pengadaan Buku Pendidikan Menengah Kejuruan.

Smith, Rosalynd. 1998. "Professional for a Day: the Experience of Singing in an Amateur Symphony Choir." In *Sharing the Voices: The Phenomenon of Singing*, edited by Brian A. Roberts. St. John's: Memorial University of Newfoundland.

Soedarsono. 1984. *Wayang Wong: The State Ritual Dance Drama in the Court of Yogyakarta.* Yogyakarta: Gadjah Mada University Press.

———. 1985. *Peranan Seni Budaya dalam Sejarah Kehidupan Manusia: Kontinuitas dan Perubahannya* (The Role of Aesthetics in the History of Daily Life: Continuity and Change). Yogyakarta: Universitas Gadjah Mada. [Cited in Suparno 1990.]

Soepomo Poedjosoedarmo. 1968. "Javanese Speech Levels." *Indonesia* 6:54–81.

———. 1969. "Wordlist of Javanese Non-*Ngoko* Vocabularies." *Indonesia* 7:165–90.

Soepomo Poedjosoedarmo, and M. C. Ricklefs. 1967. "The Establishment of Surakarta, A Translation from the *Babad Gianti*." *Indonesia* 4:88–108.

Soeratman, Darsiti. 1989. *Kehidupan Dunia Kraton Surakarta 1830–1939.* Yogyakarta: Tamansiswa.

Soetarno. 1990. *Aspek Sosial Pertunjukan Wayang Kulit* (The Social Aspects of *Wayang Kulit* Performance). Surakarta: STSI, Proyek Operasi dan Perawatan Fasilitas. [See also under alternate spelling, Sutarno.]

Soewarsi. 1967. *Buku Olah-Olah: Olah-Olahan Djawi, Eropa tuwin Sanes-Sanesipun* (Cookbook: Javanese, European, and Other Kinds of Cooking). 6th edition. Jakarta: Balai Pustaka.

Sorrell, Neil. 1990. *A Guide to the Gamelan.* London: Faber and Faber, 1990.

Stange, Paul. 1980. "The Evolution of Sumarah." Ph.D. dissertation, University of Wisconsin- Madison.

———. 1984. "The Logic of Rasa in Java." *Indonesia* 38:113–34.

Subalidinata, R. S. 1985. "Primbon dalam Kehidupan Masyarakat Jawa (Unsur Sastra, Mithos, Takhayul, dan Sejarahnya)" (The *Primbon* in Javanese Life: Its Literary, Mythological, Superstitious, and Historical Dimensions). In *Aksara dan Ramalan Nasib dalam Kebudayaan Jawa*, edited by Soedarsono, Regno Astuti, and I. W. Pantja Sunjata. Proyek Penelitian dan Pengkajian Kebudayaan Nusantara (Javanologi) no. 13. Yogyakarta: Direktorat Jenderal Kebudayaan, Departemen Pendidikan dan Kebudayaan.

Sulastuti, Katarina Indah. 2006. "Konsepsi dan Indikasi *Rasa* dalam Tari Jawa Gaya Surakarta" (Concepts and Indications of *Rasa* in the Surakarta Style of Javanese Dance). Master's thesis, Sekolah Tinggi Seni Indonesia Surakarta.

Sulzer, Johann Georg. 1981. "Expression in Music." In *Music and Aesthetics in the Eighteenth and Nineteenth Centuries*, edited and translated by Peter le Huray and James Day. Cambridge: Cambridge University Press. [Originally published in *Allgemeine Theorie der schönen Künste, in einzelnen, nach alphabetischer Ordnung der Künstwörter aufeinanderfolgenden Artikeln abgehandelt*, 2d edition, 4 vols., Leipzig, 1792–94.]

Sumarsam. 1984 [1975]. "Inner Melody in Javanese Gamelan." M.A. Thesis, Wesleyan University, Middletown, Ct. In Becker and Feinstein 1984.

———. 1994. "Cultural Contact with the West: The Development of Theories of Javanese Gamelan by Indonesian Theorists." In *Music-Cultures in Contact: Convergences and Collisions*, edited by Margaret J. Kartomi and Stephen Blum. Sydney, Australia: Currency Press.

———. 1995. *Gamelan: Cultural Interaction and Musical Development in Central Java*. Chicago: University of Chicago Press.

Supanggah, Rahayu. 1985. "Introduction aux styles d'interprétation dans la musique javanaise" (Introduction to Styles of Interpretation in Javanese Music). Ph.D. thesis, Université de Paris VII.

———. 1988a. "Pengantar Editor" (Editor's Introduction) to *Dibuang Sayang*, by Martopangrawit. Surakarta: ASKI.

———. 1988b. "Balungan." Translated by Marc Perlman. *Balungan* 3/2:2–10.

———. 1990. "Balungan." *Seni Pertunjukan Indonesia: Jurnal Masyarakat Musikologi Indonesia* 1/1:115–36.

———. 1991a. "Karawitan Anak-anak: Gejala Perkembangan Karawitan Jawa yang Memprihatinkan" (Children's Gamelan Music: A Symptom of Worrisome Developments in Javanese *Karawitan*) *Seni Pertunjukan Indonesia* 2/2:1–10.

———. 1991b. "Bahasa/Sastra Jawa sebagai Saran Ungkapan Seni dalam Seni Karawitan" (Javanese Language/Literature as a Means of Expression in the Art of *Karawitan*). Paper presented at the Kongres Bahasa Jawa, Semarang.

———. 1994. "Gatra, Inti dari Konsep Gendhing Tradisi Jawa" (*Gåtrå*: The Heart of the Concept of the Traditional Javanese *Gendhing*). *Wiled: Jurnal Seni* (journal published by STSI Surakarta) 1:13–26.

———. 2002. *Bothèkan Karawitan I* (An Herb Cabinet [for] Gamelan Music I). Jakarta: Masyarakat Seni Pertunjukan Indonesia.

———. 2003. "Campur Sari: A Reflection." *Asian Music* 34/2:1–20.

———. 2005. "Jembatan Emas" (Bridge of Gold). In Rustopo and Bambang Murtiyoso, eds., *Mencermati Seni Pertunjukan III: Perspektif Pendidikan, Ekonomi & Manajemen, dan Media* (Examining the Performing Arts III: The Perspectives of Education, Economy and Management, and the Media), edited by Rustopo and Bambang Murtiyoso. Surakarta: Program Pendidikan Pascasarjana STSI.

———. 2009. *Bothèkan Karawitan II: Garap* (An Herb Cabinet [for] Gamelan Music II: Performance Practice). 2d edition. Surakarta: Program Pasca Sarjana [ISI] and ISI Press.

Supanggah, R., and T. Slamet Suparno. 1979/1980. *Notasi Karawitan*. Surakarta: ASKI, Proyek Pengembangan IKI.

Suparno, T. Slamet. 1980/1981. *Bawa Gawan Gendhing* (*Båwås* Specific to *Gendhings*). Surakarta: Proyek Pengembangan IKI, Sub Bagian Proyek ASKI Surakarta.

———. 1984/1985. *Sindenan Andegan Nyi Bei Mardusari* (Mardusari's Renditions of Vocal "Cadenzas"). Surakarta: Akademi Seni Karawitan Indonesia.

———. 1990. "Pemunculan dan Pengembangan Karawitan Mangkunegaran: Kronologi Peristiwa Karawitan di Mangkunegaran 1757–1881" (The Birth and Development of

Mangkunegaran-Style *Karawitan*: Chronology of *Karawitan* Activity at the Mangkunegaran 1757–1881). Master's thesis, Universitas Gadjah Mada.

———. 1998/1999. "Kehidupan Karawitan Sragenan pada Akhir Abad XX dengan Beberapa Ekses yang Menyertainya" (The Life of *Karawitan Sragènan* at the End of the Twentieth Century, along with a Few Excesses that Go along with It). Surakarta: STSI.

Suraji. 2005. "Sindhénan Gaya Surakarta." M.A. thesis, STSI Surakarta.

Suranto, Joko. 1995. "Musik Rock di Solo: Studi Kasus mengenai Musikalitas dan Kehidupan Musisi pada Grup Kaisar, Metal Force, Lebata dan Head Bang" (Rock Music in Solo: A Case Study about the Musicality and Musicians' Lives of the Groups Kaisar, Metal Force, Lebata, and Head Bang). Bachelor's thesis, STSI Surakarta.

Suratno. 2002. "Ki Slenk (Saya Lebih Enak Nonton Kamu): The Tactics of a Best-Selling Puppeteer." In *Aspects of Performance: Puppet Theater in Contemporary Indonesia*, edited by Jan Mrázek. Ann Arbor: University of Michigan Center for Southeast Asian Studies.

Surjodiningrat, Wasisto. 1969. *Penjelidikan dalam Pengukuran Nada Gamelan-Gamelan Djawa Terkemuka di Jogjakarta dan Surakarta* (Research into the Measuring of the Pitches of the Foremost Javanese Gamelans of Yogyakarta and Surakarta). Yogyakarta [Jogjakarta]: Universitas Gadjah Mada, Laboratorium Akustik, Bagian Mesin—Fakultas Tehnik.

Suryabrata, Bernard [Bernard Ikzerdraat]. 1987. *The Island of Music: An Essay in Social Musicology*. Jakarta: Balai Pustaka.

Suryakusuma, Julia I. 1996. "The State and Sexuality in New Order Indonesia." In *Fantasizing the Feminine in Indonesia*, edited by Laurie J. Sears. Durham, N.C.: Duke University Press.

Suryobrongto. 1970. "The Classical Yogyanese Dance." Translated by Moh. Harun Wijono and Mudjanattistomo. Yogyakarta: Lembaga Bahasa Nasional Tjabang 11 (Departemen P. & K.).

———. 1981. "Penjiwaan dalam Tari Klasik Gaya Yogyakarta" (Characterization in Classical Dance in the Yogyanese Style). In *Mengenal Tari Klasik Gaya Yogyakarta* (Understanding Classical Dance in the Yogyanese Style), edited by Fred Wibowo. Yogyakarta: Dewan Kesenian Propinsi DIY.

Susilo, Hardja. 1984. "Wayang Wong Panggung: Its Social Context, Technique and Music." In *Aesthetic Tradition and Cultural Transition in Java and Bali*, edited by Stephanie Morgan and Laurie Jo Sears. Center for Southeast Asian Studies Monograph 2. Madison: University of Wisconsin Press.

———. 1985. "Musik Kontemporer tidak Perlu Membosankan" ("Contemporary Music Doesn't Need to Try One's Patience"). *Kompas*, March 31.

Susilo, Joko. 1996. "The Solo Style of Javanese All-Night Shadow Puppet Performance: A Comparison of Traditional and Contemporary Forms." M.A. thesis, University of Otago, Dunedin, New Zealand.

Sutarno. [1978]. "Le rôle de la musique dans les arts du spectacle à Java" (The Role of Music in the Performing Arts in Java). Ph.D. dissertation, Université de Paris VII. [See also under alternate spelling, Soetarno.]

Sutton, R. Anderson. 1978. "Notes toward a Grammar of Variation in Javanese *Gender* Playing." *Ethnomusicology* 22/2:275–96.

———. 1979. "Concept and Treatment in Javanese Gamelan Music, with Reference to the Gambang." *Asian Music* 9/2:50–79.

———. 1984. "Who Is the Pesindhen? Notes on the Female Singing Tradition in Java." *Indonesia* 37:118–33.

———. 1985. "Commercial Cassette Recordings of Traditional Music in Java: Implications for Performers and Scholars." *The World of Music* 27/3:23–43.

———. 1989. Reprint. "Identity and Individuality in an Ensemble Tradition: The Female Vocalist in Java." In *Women and Music in Cross-Cultural Perspective*, edited by Ellen Koskoff. Urbana: University of Illinois Press. [Original edition, Westport, Ct.: Greenwood Press, 1987.]

———. 1991a. *Traditions of Gamelan Music in Java: Musical Pluralism and Regional Identity*. Cambridge: Cambridge University Press.

———. 1991b. *Music of Indonesia*. New York: The Festival of Indonesia Foundation.

———. 1993. *Variation in Central Javanese Gamelan Music: Dynamics of a Steady State*. Monograph Series on Southeast Asia, Special Report no. 28. De Kalb: Northern Illinois University, Center for Southeast Asian Studies.

Suyenaga, Joan M. 1984. "Patterns in Process: Java through Gamelan." In *Aesthetic Tradition and Cultural Transition in Java and Bali*, edited by Stephanie Morgan and Laurie Jo Sears. Center for Southeast Asian Studies Monograph 2. Madison: University of Wisconsin.

Suyoto. 1992. *Sindhenan Gendhing-Gendhing Sekar Versi Sastro Tugiyo* (Sastro Tugiyo's Version of the *Sindhèn* Parts for *Gendhing*s Based on *Sekar*). Surakarta: Sekolah Tinggi Seni Indonesia.

Tasman Ronoatmodjo, A. 1991. "Sedikit Renungan tentang Tari" (Some Musings on Dance). Paper presented at the Seminar Dosen Sekolah Tinggi Seni Indonesia tentang Estetika Seni Pertunjukan Tradisional (Indonesian School of the Arts Instructors' Seminar on the Aesthetics of Traditional Performing Arts). Surakarta: STSI.

Tedlock, Dennis. 1995. "Interpretation, Participation, and the Role of Narrative in Dialogical Anthropology." In *The Dialogic Emergence of Culture*, edited by Dennis Tedlock and Bruce Mannheim. Urbana: University of Illiniois Press.

Thompson, Robert Farris. 1973. "An Aesthetic of the Cool." *African Arts* 7:40–43, 64–67, 89–92.

Tirtaamidjaja, Nusjirwan. 1967. "A Bedaja Ketawang Dance Performance at the Court of Surakarta." *Indonesia* 3:30–61.

Tjahjono, Gunawan. 1989. "Cosmos, Center, and Duality in Javanese Architectural Tradition: The Symbolic Dimensions of House Shapes in Kota Gede and Surroundings." Ph.D. dissertation, University of California, Berkeley.

Tolbert, Elizabeth Dawn. 1988. "The Musical Means of Sorrow: The Karelian Lament Tradition." Ph.D. dissertation, University of California, Los Angeles.

Treitler, Leo. 1997. "Language and the Interpretation of Music." In *Music and Meaning*, edited by Jenefer Robinson. Ithaca, N.Y.: Cornell University Press.

Tukiman Taruna, J. C. 1987. *Ciri Budaya Manusia Jawa*. Yogyakarta: Kanisius.

Uhlenbeck, E. M. 1978. *Studies in Javanese Morphology*. The Hague: Martinus Nijhoff.

Vetter, Roger. 1981. "Flexibility in the Performance Practice of Central Javanese Music." *Ethnomusicology* 25/2:199–214.

———. 1986. "Music for the 'Lap of the World': Gamelan Performance, Performers, and Repertoire in the Kraton Yogyakarta." Ph.D. dissertation, University of Wisconsin-Madison.

Wachsmann, Klaus. 1982. "The Changeability of Musical Experience." *Ethnomusicology* 26/2:197–215.

Wahyono. 1990. *Sistem Pendidikan Priyayi Jawa di Surakarta* (The Educational System of Javanese Aristocrats in Surakarta). Surakarta: Sekolah Tinggi Seni Indonesia.

Walker, Robert. 1996. "Can We Understand the Music of Another Culture?" *Psychology of Music* 24/2:103–30.

Wallach, Jeremy. 1996. "Aural Autocracies: Music and Power in Island Southeast Asia." *The Society for Ethnomusicology: Middle Atlantic Chapter Newsletter* XV/2:3–6.

———. 2008. *Modern Noise, Fluid Genres: Popular Music in Indonesia, 1997–2001*. Madison: University of Wisconsin Press.

Walton, Susan Pratt. 1987. "Translator's Introduction" [to *Wédha Pradangga* by Warsadiningrat]. In *Karawitan: Source Readings in Javanese Gamelan and Vocal Music*, vol. 3, edited by Judith Becker and Alan Feinstein. Michigan Papers on South and Southeast Asia Numbers 23, 30, and 31. Ann Arbor: University of Michigan Center for South and Southeast Asian Studies.

———. 1996. "Heavenly Nymphs and Earthly Delights: Javanese Female Singers, Their Music, Their Lives." Ph.D. dissertation, University of Michigan, Ann Arbor.

———. 1997. "From Hustler to Heavenly Nymph to Pop Star: Sexual Image and Class of the Javanese Female Singer." Unpublished paper presented at the SEASSI conference, "Reflecting on the Old and New in Modern Indonesia," Tempe, Arizona State University, June 13–15.

Waluyo. 1991. *Dokumentasi Bawa Gawan Gendhing Bapak Sastro Tugiyo* (Documetation of Sastro Tugiyo's *Gendhing*-Specific *Båwås*). Surakarta: Sekolah Tinggi Seni Indonesia.

Warde, Ann. 2002/2003. "Contemporary Indonesian Composition: Elastic-Edged Experimentalism." *Asian Music* 34/1:111–53.

Waridi. 2005. "Tiga Pilar Kehidupan Karawitan Jawa Gaya Surakarta Masa Pascakemerdekaan: Periode 1950–1970an" (Three Pillars of Gamelan Music in the Surakarta Style during the Post-Independence Period: From the 1950s through the 1970s). Ph.D. dissertation, Universitas Gajah Mada, Yogyakarta.

Warsadiningrat (Prajapangrawit). 1987. *Wédha Pradangga* (Sacred Knowledge about Gamelan Music). Translated by Susan Pratt Walton. In *Karawitan: Source Readings in Javanese Gamelan and Vocal Music*, vol. 3, edited by Judith Becker and Alan Feinstein. Michigan papers on South and Southeast Asia Numbers 23, 30, and 31. Ann Arbor: University of Michigan Center for South and Southeast Asian Studies. [Original published work, Surakarta: Konservatori Karawitan Indonesia, 1972. Original manuscript written in 1943.]

Weiss, Jerome. 1977. "Folk Psychology of the Javanese of Ponorogo." Ph.D. dissertation, Yale University.

Weiss, Sarah. 1993. "Gender and *Gender*: Gender Ideology and the Female *Gender* Player in Central Java." In *Rediscovering the Muses: Women's Musical Traditions*, edited by Kimberly Marshall. Boston: Northeastern University Press.

———. 1998. "Paradigms and Anomalies: Female-Style *Gendéran* and the Aesthetics of Central Javanese *Wayang* Shadow Puppet." Ph.D. dissertation, New York University.

———. 2003. "*Kothong Nanging Kebak*, Empty yet Full: Some Thoughts on Embodiment and Aesthetics in Javanese Performance." *Asian Music* 34/2:21–49.

———. 2006. *Listening to an Earlier Java: Aesthetics, Gender, and the Music of Wayang in Central Java*. Leiden: KITLV Press.

Werner, Oswald. 1969. "The Basic Assumptions of Ethnoscience." *Semiotica* 1/3:329–338.

Wessel, Frederick T. 1955. "The Affektenlehre in the Eighteenth Century." Ph.D. dissertation, Indiana University.

White, Geoffrey M. 1994. "Affecting Culture: Emotion and Morality in Everyday Life." In *Emotion and Culture*, edited by Shinobu Kitayama and Hazel Rose Markus. Washington, D.C.: American Psychological Association.

Will, Udo. 1998. "Et quand ils n'en disent rien? . . ." (And When They Don't Talk about It? . . .). *Cahiers de musiques traditionnels* 11:175–85.

Williams, Walter. 1991. *Javanese Lives: Women and Men in Modern Indonesian Society*. New Brunswick, N.J.: Rutgers University Press.

Wiseman, Mary Bittner. 1993. "Beautiful Exiles." In *Aesthetics in Feminist Perspective*, edited by Hilde Hein and Carolyn Korsmeyer. Bloomington: Indiana University Press.

Wittgenstein, Ludwig. 1958. *Philosophical Investigations: The English Text of the Third Edition*. Translated by G. E. M. Anscombe. New York: Macmillan.

Wolff, John U., and Soepomo Poedjosoedarmo. 1982. *Communicative Codes in Central Java*. Data Paper no. 116, Linguistics Series VIII. Ithaca, N.Y.: Cornell University, Department of Asian Studies, Southeast Asia Program.

Woodward, Mark R. 1989. *Islam in Java: Normative Piety and Mysticism in the Sultanate of Yogyakarta*. Tucson: University of Arizona Press.

Yampolsky, Philip. 1987. *Lokananta: A Discography of the National Recording Company of Indonesia: 1957–1985*. Bibliography Series no. 10. Madison: University of Wisconsin, Center for Southeast Asian Studies.

Yoder, Lawrence McCulloh. 1987. "The Introduction and Expression of Islam and Christianity in the Cultural Context of North Central Java." Ph.D. dissertation, Fuller Theological Seminary.

Zoetmulder, P. J. 1974. *Kalangwan: A Survey of Old Javanese Literature*. The Hague: Martinus Nijhoff.

———. 1995 [1935]. *Pantheism and Monism in Javanese Suluk Literature: Islamic and Indian Mysticism in an Indonesian Setting*. Edited and translated by M. C. Ricklefs. Leiden: KITLV Press.

DISCOGRAPHY OF RECORDINGS CITED IN THE TEXT

Indonésie, Java Centre: Gamelan de Solo: Le jeu des sentiments/Indonesia, Central Java: Solonese Gamelan: A Garland of Moods. 2006. 4 CD set. Maison des Cultures du Monde, Inédit W 260125. Produced and annotated by Marc Benamou with help from Rahayu Supanggah. [Title shortened to *Gamelan de Solo* in citations.]

INDEX

Non-English words are not italicized here, but rather are identified, in the main entries, by the same abbreviations that have been used throughout the book (see p. xxx), with the addition of [F] for French and [OJ] for Old Javanese. Titles of compositions and literary works are enclosed in quotation marks.

In the page numbers, italics are used for passages *about* a person or that person's theories. Roman type is used to indicate pages where words *from* that person are being quoted, summarized, or paraphrased. In borderline cases, or those in which the person is both quoted and discussed, italics are usually used.

Rahayu Supanggah and Suhartå are special cases, in that they are quoted or paraphrased throughout the book: they are indexed only when they or their ideas are being commented upon, not when they are being quoted or paraphrased.

The following symbols apply: "n" = one or more footnotes on the page indicated; "d" = definition of a term given on that page (it may or may not include further discussion of the term); "/n" = reference to the entry in the main body of the text and in a footnote on the same page.

When *n*, *d*, or */n* follows the last page number in a continuous passage, the footnote referred to may be on any page within the passage, unless it is only on the first page, in which case */n* will follow the first page number.